The *Soledades*, Góngora's Masque of the Imagination

Marsha S. Collins

University of Missouri Press
Columbia and London

Copyright © 2002 by
The Curators of the University of Missouri
University of Missouri Press, Columbia, Missouri 65201
Printed and bound in the United States of America
All rights reserved
5 4 3 2 1   06 05 04 03 02

Library of Congress Cataloging-in-Publication Data

Collins, Marsha Suzan.
The soledades : Góngora's masque of the imagination / Marsha S. Collins.
p. cm.
Includes bibliographical references and index.
ISBN 0-8262-1363-4 (alk. paper)
1. Gângora y Argote, Luis de, 1561–1627. Soledades.
2. Gângora y Argote, Luis de, 1561–1627—Literary style. I. Title.
PQ6394.S6 C65 2002
861'.3—dc21   2001052470

∞™ This paper meets the requirements of the
American National Standard for Permanence of Paper
for Printed Library Materials, Z39.48, 1984.

Text Designer: Stephanie Foley
Jacket Designer: Jennifer Cropp
Typesetter: Bookcomp, Inc.
Printer and Binder: Thomson-Shore, Inc.
Typefaces: Adobe Caslon and Carlton

Publication of this book has been supported by a contribution from
the Program for Cultural Cooperation between Spain's Ministry of
Education and Culture and United States Universities.

The *Soledades*,
Góngora's Masque of
the Imagination

For my parents
and for
Jackie, Greg, and Cassie Collins

Contents

Preface ix
Acknowledgments xiii

1. A Journey to the Heart of a Polemic   1
2. A Passage to the Contemplative Life   52
3. A Poetics of Alchemy   112
4. The Masque of the Imagination   171

Conclusion   220

Notes   221
Bibliography   249
Index   267

Preface

Y este gran poema resume todo el sentimiento lírico y pastoril de los poetas españoles que le antecedieron.
El sueño bucólico que soñó Cervantes y no logró fijar plenamente, y la Arcadia que Lope de Vega no supo iluminar con luces permanentes, las dibuja de manera rotunda don Luis de Góngora. El campo medio jardín, campo amable de guirnaldas, airecillos y zagalas cultas pero ariscas que entrevieron todos los poetas del XVI y XVII está realizado en la 1ª y 2ᵈᵃ *Soledad* gongorina. Es ahí donde está el paisaje aristocrático y mitológico que soñaba Don Quijote en la hora de su muerte. Campo ordenado, donde la poesía mide y ajusta su delirio.

(And this great poem summarizes all of the lyrical and pastoral feeling of the Spanish poets who preceded him.
The bucolic dream that Cervantes dreamed and did not succeed in fully establishing, and the Arcadia that Lope de Vega did not know how to illuminate with permanent lights, Don Luis de Góngora depicts in orotund manner. The half-garden countryside, a gracious countryside of garlands, gentle breezes, and cultured but shy maidens that all sixteenth- and seventeenth-century poets glimpsed, is realized in Góngora's first and second *Solitude*. There is the aristocratic and mythological landscape of which Don Quixote was dreaming in the hour of his death. An ordered countryside, where poetry measures and regulates his delirium.)[1]

The words belong to one of Luis de Góngora's most astute critics, the poet-playwright Federico García Lorca. The pastoral poems in question are, of course, the *Soledades,* maddening enough in their complexity to drive most any reader into quixotic moments of fight or flight. Nonetheless, the haunting, astonishing beauty of Góngora's masterpiece has proved more than strong enough to keep this critic dreaming of gardens and idle zephyrs for well over twelve years. Only after completing *The* Soledades, *Góngora's Masque of the Imagination* did I realize that in many ways I had been exploring the rich implications of Lorca's highly suggestive observations.

It has become a commonplace to discuss *Don Quijote* as a compendium of major literary forms, a book that both summarizes what came before and breaks new ground in giving birth to the modern novel. In a similar but more limited fashion, the *Soledades* constitute a summa of poetic forms and advance a new type of poetic discourse with far less reaching influence than Cervantes's work, but with sufficient impact to generate a firestorm of controversy then, in 1612–1614, when the poems first circulated at court, and now, when Góngora seems to have garnered the title of poster child of postmodernism.

This challenging poet seems to have secured a permanent place in the Spanish literary canon in the twentieth century. Elsewhere, I have analyzed Góngora's movement in and out of the canon and shifting trends in readers' reception of his works over the passage of time. His verse may well be precise and cultured, but Marxists and deconstructionists alike have found his poetry sufficiently malleable to support their respective ideological approaches. Latin American writers such as José Lezama Lima and Severo Sarduy have envisioned Góngora as a kindred spirit, a model for the *neobarroco* (the new baroque) in Latin American literature. Góngora appears to have tapped into some aspect of the twentieth-century aesthetic consciousness, inspiring new works of art and critical reevaluation.[2]

While the battle rages on over interpretation of Góngora's poetry in general and the *Soledades* in particular, I have sought in *The* Soledades, *Góngora's Masque of the Imagination* to render the unusual beauty of the Gongorine masterpiece intelligible and accessible to modern readers through a process of cultural recontextualization. The chapters of my book are designed to offer the poet's discerning, self-selecting audience a conceptual map with which to navigate the bucolic labyrinth of the *Soledades*. A vast array of philosophical and aesthetic traditions converges in the poems, including, among others, Renaissance Platonism, meditational literature, pastoral poetry, natural philosophy, and the court masque. The resultant syncretic work of art thus synthesizes extant traditions, yet out of this textual crucible emerges a new poetic language, finely honed, to serve as an epistemological tool, an instrument of exploration and discovery that represents Góngora's bid to restore to the artist the magical, visionary power of the *vates*, the poet-prophet of classical antiquity charged with divining the mysteries of the universe. In Góngora's hands, poetry metamorphoses into a search for all-encompassing knowledge of transcendent truths.

The portrait of court culture encapsulated in the *Soledades*, however, remains as fascinating as this grand quest. Góngora thus makes available to his readers the dynamic, elitist world of Imperial Spain's court society. Members of this reading audience can vicariously sing, dance, watch fireworks, and wander the garden paths filled with surprises and boundless inducements to wonderment, even as they wrestle with cryptic language and allusions while playing the game of poetry. I have tried to extend the artist's engraved invitation to enter the court to a new circle of readers, and hope that, like myself, they will rest and refresh themselves by Góngora's pastoral spring as the marvelous entertainments of the *Soledades* unfold in the recesses of the mind.

Acknowledgments

I am deeply indebted to the many friends and colleagues who over the years have provided me with abundant support and encouragement in regards to this project. Without their kindness and generosity, this book would never have become a reality. My thanks to Julie Wescott, Howard Wescott, Erma Kelley, and Edith Kern, for fostering my love of poetry; and to Antonio Regalado, Eva Chou, Richard McCarrick, Robin Cantone, and Bob Cantone for fanning the spark of the creative fire. I am especially grateful to Nancy Durling and Bob Durling for going the distance on this project, listening to my ideas, and helping me through critical impasses.

Under the exceptional leadership of Ruel Tyson, two inspirational groups of scholars at the University of North Carolina at Chapel Hill's Institute for the Arts and Humanities have supplied crucial impetus in developing my ideas on Góngora. I have also been blessed with a UNC family of friends and colleagues who made certain that my journey was never solitary and always entertaining and who ensured that I made it to the final destination: Cesáreo Bandera, Jane Burns, Dino Cervigni, Vicky Gless, Darryl Gless, John Headley, Liz Lucas, Sara Mack, Catherine Maley, José Manuel Polo de Bernabé, Jacki Resnick, Alicia Rivero, and Mary Sheriff. I owe a huge debt of gratitude to Edward Dudley, whose careful reading of my manuscript and whose suggested improvements have made for a much better final result.

The members of my family have been my mainstay throughout this long sojourn, as they have been through all the others.

Finally, I wish to express my heartfelt admiration and appreciation to Alan Deyermond and Alban Forcione, the superb friends and scholars who introduced me to the magnificent world of the Spanish baroque, and who continue to inspire me every day. My thanks to both of you for helping me find my voice.

The *Soledades*, Góngora's Masque of the Imagination

1

A Journey to the Heart of a Polemic

> [T]he one who has the key to writing,
> with such great wit and grace,
> that he has no equal in the world;
> is Don Luis de Góngora.
>
> —Cervantes, *Journey to Parnassus*

> And from this moment on
> I consecrate my life
> to cursing your works,
> speaking out even while half asleep.
>
> —Quevedo, "To Don Luis de Góngora"

Footsteps of a Wandering Pilgrim...

In the dedication of Luis de Góngora's *Soledades* (Solitudes), a pilgrim-poet beckons the duke of Béjar, and, symbolically, all readers, to enter the poems' oneiric pastoral landscape.[1] For nearly four hundred years, generations of select readers have found the invitation of Góngora's pilgrim persona irresistibly alluring. The *Soledades*' labyrinthine language and perplexing panorama of metamorphosis and change have proved especially captivating to literary critics.

An initial encounter with these enigmatic poems inevitably leaves the most discriminating of readers baffled, appalled, or enthralled, and ultimately lost in Góngora's cunningly crafted linguistic maze. Such sentiments are by no means unique to the modern audience. When the *Soledades* were first circulated in 1612–1614 among the social and intellectual elite at the court of Philip III, the poems unleashed a storm of controversy over Góngora and his innovative verse. To this day, the *Soledades* remain a hermetic literary conundrum that bedazzles with sensual appeal, inspires engagement with intricate poetic discourse, and defies facile analysis and interpretation.

The *Soledades* culminated a lifetime of experimentation with poetry and theater. Like many of his contemporaries, Góngora displayed an almost obsessive fascination with topoi of metamorphosis and change, a preoccupation he internalized and enacted creatively by blending genres and styles into new, hybrid literary forms. In the poem "Angelica and Medoro," for instance, Góngora combines popular and learned traditions, molding an episode from Ariosto's *Orlando Furioso* (1516) (a mix itself of epic and romance conventions) into a ballad, a haunting tale of tragic, passionate love undermined by the mordantly ironic voice of the narrator. The medieval *pastourelle* provides the inspiration for the sonnet "De un caminante enfermo que se enamoró donde fue hospedado" (On an ill traveler who fell in love where he took lodging), in which a lost, sick pilgrim loses his heart and his life to a mysterious woman *(une belle dame sans merci)* he encounters in the wilderness. Góngora skillfully interweaves narrative and lyric components, producing a perplexing, balladlike sonnet that concludes with the inexplicable intrusion of a subjective "I" in the final line of the poem.[2]

The revolutionary poetic discourse known as *gongorismo, cultismo, culteranismo,* or simply *el estilo culto* (Gongorism, cultism, the learned, cultivated, refined style) emerged in Góngora's later works. In the play *Las firmezas de Isabela* (The constance of Isabela) (1610); the poem *Fábula de Polifemo y Galatea* (The fable of Polyphemus and Galatea) (1613), based on the ill-fated love story of Acis and Galatea in book 13 of Ovid's *Metamorphoses;* and the *Soledades,* the poet achieves a radical transformation of style that at first seems nothing more than a cornucopian excess of formal ornamentation. Although some critics have considered this style synonymous with ornamental excess and semantic vacuity, it is more accurate to identify Gongorism with erudition; elegance; wit; and stylish, polished artifice. The poet saturates the texts with rhetorical figures, heaps elaborate conceit upon elaborate conceit, contorts syntax with hyperbata, interrupts narrative flow with ellipses, and bombards his audience nonstop with synesthetic effects and allusions to classical myth. The resulting aesthetic impression is one of luminously vivid, but disjunct, protean images, loosely bound together and set in continuously shifting fields of reference. "Poetic pyrotechnics" sabotage the act of reading, disrupting and delaying readers' progress through the works and complicating their apprehension of the imaginative worlds presented.[3] In effect, linguistic obscurantism appropriates the text and displaces plot, characterization, and lyric sentiment as the focus of attention.

Many of the essential characteristics of *cultismo* coincide with fundamental aspects of Mannerism, a style that embraces refinement, elegance, self-conscious artfulness, and at times excessive stylization. Other qualities identified with Mannerism include artistic virtuosity, complexity, inventiveness, and theatricality. As in the case of *cultismo,* Mannerist works might be deemed *manieroso* (stylish) or *manierato* (stylized), depending on the eye of the beholder. Helmut Hatzfeld has described literary Mannerism as "a literary nominalism. Since it had lost contact with the essence of the Renaissance, it indulged in allusion and cryptic designation. These enigmatic means were easily enhanced by suspense, metaphors, metamorphoses, misleading oppositions, predicatively isolated *nomina pendentia,* and hyperbata. The result was a labyrinth of riddles and emblems." Góngora's *culto* works could be, and have been, labeled labyrinths, but they most definitely have not lost their ability to convey meaning on a twisted pathway to formal stylization. What is true, however, is that Gongorism stylistically parallels two movements that John Shearman associates with the origins of literary Mannerism in Italy, namely, the Ciceronianism of early sixteenth-century Rome, which stressed cultivated artifice and imitation of classical rhetoric, and *Bembismo,* which sought to create a refined vernacular style to rival that of classical Latin. Góngora echoed Bembo in stating that through his poetry he intended to elevate Castilian to the heights of classical Latin. Furthermore, the Spanish poet employed many of the techniques used by Bembo in achieving that goal, transferring abundant rhetorical ornamentation and rich vocabulary from Latin to the vernacular.[4]

Beneath the display of technical bravura and superb craftsmanship, however, lies an aesthetic and epistemological agenda. With *culteranismo,* Góngora transforms poetic discourse into a medium that enables perspicacious readers to see through the confusion of material existence and reach new intellectual and spiritual heights. As Dámaso Alonso pointed out in 1927, the language of the *Soledades,* the masterpiece of *el estilo culto,* comprises a wide range of conventions and clichés derived from the Greco-Roman tradition and Renaissance classics (especially the works of Garcilaso), recast as a new form of expression.[5] This metapoetic discourse holds up a distorting mirror to a world riddled with illusion and marked by mutability, serving as a corrective anamorphic device in which to gaze at the true reflection of the false appearances perceived by unreliable physical senses.

When Dámaso Alonso compared the style of the *Soledades* to the "pure pleasure of forms" of cubism, a statement he later repudiated as a limiting, inaccurate assessment that grew out of the aestheticizing taste of the historical moment, he inadvertently opened Pandora's box for all those who would subsequently analyze the poems as an autonomous, self-referential universe.[6] Many twentieth-century readers and critics were seduced by the polished language and perfect form of the *Soledades* and, with a few important exceptions, steadfastly resisted the ascription of any transcendent meaning to the texts. This insistent identification of the *Soledades* with *poésie pure*, however, is a gross misinterpretation of the pact Góngora implicitly establishes with his audience. Those readers who seize the hermeneutic gauntlet he flings down in the poems, exercise the senses of the mind, and sharpen their ratiocinative capabilities to grapple with the challenge of his complex language will find the impenetrable linguistic speculum transfigured into a portal through which they will pass, via the looking glass of language, into a higher realm of contemplative conceptualization and understanding.

In Gongorine aesthetics, poetic discourse occupies the privileged position of mediator, mitigating the Cartesian split between matter and spirit, and bridging the gap between affective and rational faculties, external experience and interior awareness. Poetry becomes both a mirror that imposes an ordered reflection on the apparent randomness of the sentient world and a window that functions as a heuristic vehicle through which readers glimpse the web of interrelations in nature, the teleology beyond the flux of everyday life. The hermeneutic imperative the poet foists on his readers holds the promise that those who struggle through the labyrinth of language will be rewarded with powers of perception that approximate the divine. Góngora's pilgrim-poet invites the audience to share an extraordinary adventure of transcendence in the *Soledades* and witness the power of poetry to elevate and liberate the human mind.

In his description of an aesthetics of reception, Hans Robert Jauss defines literary history as an effort to reconstitute the "horizon of expectations" in which humans actualize a given artifact, that is, as an attempt to communicate the experience of literature as a vital praxis that occurs within discrete social, historical, and aesthetic parameters. Michel Foucault has characterized the fundamental unifying episteme of Góngora's time with one word—resemblance: "[T]he sixteenth century superimposed hermeneutics and semiology in the form of similitude. To search for a meaning is to bring to light a resemblance. . . . And that resemblance is visible only in the network of signs that crosses the world from one end to the other." In fact, the quasi-mystical, near apotheosis of poetic discourse that occurs in the *Soledades* has its origins in a movement predicated on these very principles. Pansophy, nourished by the Platonic and hermetic writings of Renaissance Europe as well as the metascientific philosophy of Ramón Llull, swept Europe in the late sixteenth century. One can define this imprecise rubric as an attempt to reconcile and harmoniously integrate science and religion, empiricism and faith, into a single philosophical system that would provide access to and possession of universal knowledge. The pansophists made all forms of human knowledge into instruments of harmonious mediation and reconciliation, methods and means of discovering the unity within cosmic diversity. United by an ideal, utopian vision of a perfect society, those committed to poetry, painting, alchemy, natural philosophy, and the occult sciences embarked on a common epistemological quest, the search for God's universal truths that lay obscured by imperfect human perception of physical phenomena. To achieve this goal, the practitioners of the arts and sciences strove to eliminate the gap between intuitive and empirical knowledge, fusing the two into a higher, magical form of cognition ultimately directed toward social reform and knowledge of God. Part and parcel of this enterprise of intellectual synthesis and integration was the merging of artistic and scientific media, engendering such hybrid forms as *emblemata*, masques, and opera. As might be expected in this cultural context, poets, painters, and alchemists acquired elevated status in the major courts of Europe as guardians of esoteric secrets, priests and prophets possessing divine knowledge.[7]

The roots of pansophy lie in Renaissance humanism, which sought to retrieve for humankind the ancient sources of wisdom once deemed forever lost. The humanists bore the mark of an elite group of intellectual initiates, who identified the acquisition of classical learning with the reform and ennoblement of the human spirit. They tried to explicate and disseminate this wealth of knowledge to an educated contemporary audience. In humanist thought, language and literature occupied preeminent positions as the bases and conduits of truth and knowledge. It was believed that analytical scrutiny of language and literature would disclose hidden truths about the universe and solve the mysteries of the cosmos. This philosophical position raised the esteem of poets, philologists, and their scholarship to new heights. Among the *studia humanitatis*, poetry was especially valued as a source of moral improvement, a potential innate in its use of emblematic and allegorical language. The humanists grounded their valorization and defense of poetry in Platonic philosophy, a metaphysics legitimated by the works of the Christian Platonists Saint Augustine and Marsilio Ficino. As Charles Trinkaus confirms:

> From the time of Petrarch the underlying motive of the humanist movement, to achieve recognition of the *studia humanitatis* for the benefits they might be expected to confer on mankind, found expression in the defense of poetry for

its allegorical-theological content and in the praise of rhetoric for its inherently moral or civic content. Both arguments implied, and were accompanied by, criticisms of scholastic subject matter and methods. . . . Some . . . sought this reconciliation [with traditional Aristotelian Scholasticism and Christian theology] in a new but not entirely unscholastic approach to Aristotle; to many, Ficino's approach to Platonism proved more acceptable.

The pansophists' subsequent emphasis on intellection as the key to divine knowledge, their belief in a universal system of correspondences uniting matter and spirit, their transvaluation of sight above the other senses, and their fusion of contemplative knowledge and experiential and empirical cognition betray the influence of Platonic thought as part of the rich humanist legacy.[8]

R. O. Jones was the first critic to note the pervasive presence of Platonism in Góngora's masterpiece. In the 1954 article "The Poetic Unity of the *Soledades*," he argued that the poems have a serious intellectual and philosophical content manifested in the celebration of the virtues of Nature and the condemnation of artifice for moral debasement. Nine years later, in "Neoplatonism and the *Soledades*," Jones expanded his discussion of the theme of Nature, identifying the poet's emphasis on continuity, harmony, and fertile abundance with the philosophy of Plotinus.

Although I disagree with Jones on several major issues (in particular his judgment that Góngora deems artifice inherently corrupt), I share with him the conviction that Platonic philosophy provides the cohesive, informing intellectual model that endows the *Soledades* with transcendent meaning. In my opinion, Augustinian thought lies at the heart of the *Soledades*, illuminating the murkiest and most controversial areas of the ongoing debate about these poems. A central tenet of Augustine's philosophy is that the natural, sentient world is a poem, a veil of signs simultaneously hiding and symbolically revealing the presence of God and the realm of divine Truth. Saint Augustine envisioned Nature as a text laden with spiritual significance, a work of art with sensory appeal that cries out for decipherment: "There in the heavens, in your Book, we read your unchallengeable decrees, which make the simple learned." The readers he imagines, of course, are heavenly beings: "[The angels] read it without cease and what they read never passes away. . . . The book they read shall not be closed. For them the scroll shall not be furled. For you yourself are their book and you for ever are."[9]

This poignant moment of the *Confessions* delineates a dynamics of reading, the hermeneutic process of *allegoresis*. To reach God's immutable reality, humans must transform themselves into readers of the book of Nature as well as textual interpreters who penetrate transient material existence by establishing correspondences among images gathered by the senses and a higher order, Truth. This interpretive process links the mind and the senses just as it intertwines aesthetic and intellectual beauty. Yet, in the act of reading, sensory apprehension progressively yields precedence to intellection, which in turn produces epistemological and spiritual discovery. Augustinian hermeneutics attributes immense creative and controlling power to the mind as the locus of mediation between tangible and intangible worlds. Active thought is, by definition, internalized and consigned to individual consciousness; it is inscribed within a contemplative state in which degrees of inwardness measure ascending spiritual movement toward understanding. Saint Augustine renders reading as a drama of cognition that takes place in a cerebral theater, a play in which the mind assumes the dual role of passive spectator of sense impressions and active participant in analysis of sentient experience.[10]

Pedro Salinas intuited the presence of Augustine in the *Soledades* when he labeled Góngora a glorifier of reality: "Góngora es un enamorado de lo real. Pero lo exalta, lo sublima de tal modo que el mundo se convierte en una maravillosa fiesta de la imaginación y los sentidos" (Góngora is in love with what is real. But he exalts it, sublimes it in such a way that the world is transformed into a marvelous festival of the imagination and the senses). However, what Salinas referred to as Góngora's exaltation of the material world is actually the poet's enactment of the Augustinian hermeneutical model. If Augustine saw Nature as a poem infused with the divine testifying to the enduring presence of God, Góngora composed in the *Soledades* poems of Nature encoded with moral significance affirming a higher order of being.[11] In both cases, transcendence is reserved for a select group, those who embrace the dynamic role of reader of the Nature-Poem and accept the task of decoding symbolic language.

In the *Soledades,* Nature at times overtly draws attention to her literariness and virtually begs for interpretation. A meandering stream partially hidden by mist metamorphoses into a long compound sentence of abstruse meaning (Alonso, I:194–218; Wilson, I:185–207).[12] Cranes in flight engrave uncertain letters into the paper sky (Jammes, I:602–11; Wilson, I:584–93). Certain episodes of the *Soledades* readily divulge their moral contents, even to less discerning readers. In *Soledad* I (Jammes, 94–135; Wilson, 88–128), Góngora couches a celebration of the virtues of the pastoral life in the familiar vocabulary of the Horatian *beatus ille* topos. He contrasts the innocence and humility embodied in the goatherd's hut with the vice and vanity of the court. Frequent allusions to classical myth enrich the spiritual dimension of the poems as well. Góngora embeds the narratives of such figures as Icarus, Phaëthon, Actaeon, and Ascalaphus in pastoral nature, inserting into the *Soledades* subtexts resonant with didacticism that are subsequently redirected and reactivated in their new context. Like Augustine's vision of the natural world as a tissue of veiled signs, Nature in Góngora's poems appears before the eyes of the reader as a series of emblems and tableaux providing access to a realm of thought, conceptualization, and ideality.

The audience must comply with certain conditions, however, to begin this sojourn of transcendence. In the dedication-prologue, Góngora demarcates a solitary, contemplative, psychological space as the location of the unfolding drama of Nature and the place of reading, reflection, and interpretation. Góngora utilizes visual representation to cue readers to retreat into an inner world of silent meditation. Addressing his patron directly, the poet's pilgrim persona petitions the duke of Béjar to put aside the accoutrements of the noble pastime of the hunt and place himself in the capable hands of the poet:

> templa en sus ondas tu fatiga ardiente,
> y entregados tus miembros al reposo
> sobre el de grama césped no desnudo,
> déjate un rato hallar del pie acertado
> que sus errantes pasos ha votado
> a la real cadena de tu escudo.
> (Jammes, 27–32)

> (Burning fatigue shall soon sweet coolness find,
> And to repose thy limbs delivered here
>   Upon the turfy ground,
> Let thyself by the wandering feet be found,
> Sure paces offered unto thee alone
> And to the royal chains upon thy shield.
> [Wilson, 27–32])

Góngora informs the duke-reader that adopting a stance of withdrawal and interiority unlocks the door to the pastoral landscape of the *Soledades*. He identifies repose, physical passivity, with the liberation of the mind and senses from external reality and the freedom to refocus those faculties on an inner world of thought. In these lines, Góngora also establishes the central hermeneutical paradigm of the poems. He forges a dynamic partnership with his readers, asserting for himself the superior position of guide on the intellectual journey that he and his audience are about to begin.[13]

Although the poet proudly claims creative inspiration from the muse Euterpe, he humbly promises to use his talent in service to the duke and his patron's everlasting lyrical (not epic) fame:

> que, a tu piedad Euterpe agradecida
> su canoro dará dulce instrumento,
> cuando la Fama no su trompa, al viento.
> (Jammes, 35–37)
>
> (Euterpe, flattered by thy pitying grace,
> Her sweet canorous instrument shall yield
> If Fame deny her trumpet to the wind.
> [Wilson, 35–37])

There is more to these words than a subtle reworking of the authorial humility topos and the panegyric pledge of devotion to one's patron. In fact, Góngora skillfully inverts the more conventional poet-patron pose of supplicant and superior. He entreats the duke to relinquish his temporal power and concede supremacy and leadership to the poet in the space of the imagination. Note, however, that this private, internalized contract in no way threatens the patron's social position, yet ennobles the poet's persona in a more abstract, but perhaps more significant, way. What ostensibly begins as a subjective I-thou dialogue becomes a general assertion of the intrinsic merit and power of poets and of lyric poetry.[14] Góngora places lyric poetry and the inner life of the mind on equal footing with epic poetry and historical fame. He implies that contemplation and intellectual activity are noble, worthy, self-sufficient, and self-rewarding endeavors. The fame accrued from pursuing this strategy of epistemological inquiry, however, resides in the tacit bond between poet and reader. Góngora may lead the way into the *Soledades,* but readers must decide if they wish to follow him and whether a personal, private sense of intellectual accomplishment shared only with the poet is a sufficient amount of glory to justify the endeavor. Once they have made the commitment and crossed the threshold into the poetic landscape of solitude, readers find their decision replicated and validated throughout the poems. Mirror images of the reader dot the countryside: a shipwrecked pilgrim, a goatherd, a mountain dweller, and an islander. They have all elected to abandon an active life for one of relative isolation, contemplation, temperance, and self-limitation. In every case, these fictional counterparts to the reader occupy the moral high ground of spiritual equanimity, quiet contentment, and intellectual perspicacity.

The pilgrim-poet of the dedication-prologue rejects the traditional pose of supplicant to his patron for another important reason: to designate and consecrate a playground for the hallowed game of poetry. Frank Warnke has shown that the spirit of play pervades baroque poetry of all kinds: devotional, amorous, and elegiac. However, not until María Cristina Quintero's *Poetry as Play* have critics recognized the crucial significance of the ludic as an essential part of Gongorine aesthetics. In the *Soledades,* the ludic takes the form not of a frivolous game (an interpretation to which Jones strenuously objected), but rather of a cerebral contest in which the stakes are nothing less than the apprehension of universal truths revealed in surprising correspondences, the hidden teleology of Nature. Here, too, one perceives the legacy of Platonic thought in which poetry and philosophy share the common goals of testing wisdom and imparting knowledge. Pursuit of Truth, for both poet and philosopher, devolves as divine play, ritual activity that occurs in a special, bounded space and adheres to a certain order.[15]

Johan Huizinga has identified poetry as a "play function" that "proceeds within the play-ground of the mind, in a world of its own which the mind creates for it."[16] In the prologue, Góngora's pilgrim-poet signals readers to create a solitary space of meditation and repose, portrayed visually in the image of the lone figure in a pastoral landscape, a "combatant" in an internalized, intellectual amphitheater. He then assumes the spectators' willing complicity in their transformation into gamesters united with him on a quest for knowledge. The poet persona reserves for himself the Platonic role of poet as hierophant, the most skilled and experienced competitor, who dictates the terms of the contest to others. Once the games commence, the reader-player must puzzle out the riddles of Góngora's recondite poetry and morally encoded tableaux.

Representations of play abound in the *Soledades,* repeating in microcosm the struggling hermeneutic efforts of the reader. The wedding festivities of *Soledad* I feature antiphonal, hymeneal choruses and sporting events (the broad jump, foot races, and wrestling matches) performed in a specially constructed arena (Jammes, 958–1023; Wilson, 933–99). The atmosphere of competitive play extends even to the nuptial bed: "bien previno la hija de la espuma / a batallas de amor campo de pluma" (Jammes, I:1090–91) (How well the daughter of the sea-foam brings / A field of feathers for the strife of Love! [Wilson, I:1063–64]).[17] Many scenes of *Soledad* II present agonistic images, pitting humans against the resourceful creatures of Nature in games of mortal conflict. Fish, seals, and a sea monster battle men and women in violent encounters that the animals inevitably lose. A prince engages in the aristocratic pastime of hawking, in which the poet renders aerial combat between a crow and his adversaries (gyrfalcons and a saker) as a horrifying tennis match (Jammes, II:902–36; Wilson, II:887–920). Some of Góngora's characters even find themselves embroiled in internal conflict, battling painful memories of the past that threaten to overwhelm present equanimity. Spurned by his lady, the pilgrim wages a constant battle against memories of unrequited love. The goatherd's recollection of his youthful days as a warrior momentarily disrupts the aura of peace exuded by the countryside (Jammes, I:212–21; Wilson, I:208–17), and the mountaineer's retrospective recounting of the loss of his son isolates him from the merrymaking of the wedding guests (Jammes, I:366–502; Wilson, I:356–486). The interplay between past and present not only creates rifts in the pastoral illusion of an eternal here and now, but also mimics the conflicted consciousness of readers as they strive, on the one hand, to keep their distance from external reality and, on the other, to maintain their presence in the tenuous bounds of the poem-playground, a game space of solitude.

Whereas Huizinga has identified the ludic principle as an innately human characteristic, the aristocratic society of Góngora's day displayed a marked predilection for play that was indulged and self-consciously cultivated. The concept of play was woven into the very fabric of court life. Magnificent palaces, theaters, and formal gardens demarcated the outer boundaries of the aristocratic game space, but there were inner divisions as well: private and public quarters, salons and reception areas, rooms for domestics, and royal chambers. Like other gamesters, nobles adhered to a rigid and elaborate set of rules that governed the smallest details of everyday life. They paid strict attention to etiquette and forms of address, wore clothing modeled after royal attire, and adopted aesthetic tastes patterned after those of the recognized authorities. Insignificant gestures and mannerisms acquired symbolic importance, seemingly out of all proportion to outward appearances. The court codified and ritualized human behavior, casting a pall of ceremony over courtiers' actions. In addition, the aristocratic game exemplified and reinforced social hierarchies and the illusion of imperial majesty, wealth, and power. The rigid rules of the game forced the individual who wished to succeed within such a social structure to exercise self-control, strategy, and skill. Small wonder, then, that near the end of the seventeenth century, a world-weary Jean de La Bruyère would portray court life as a "serious, melancholy game," a veritable chess match:

> [I]l faut arranger ses pièces et ses batteries, avoir un dessein, le suivre, parer celui de son adversaire, hasarder quelquefois, et jouer de caprice; et après toutes ses rêveries et toutes ses mesures, on est échec, quelquefois mat; souvent, avec des pions qu'on ménage bien, on va à dame, et l'on gagne la partie: le plus habile l'emporte, ou le plus heureux.
>
> ([O]ne must arrange one's pieces and batteries, have a plan, follow it, parry that of one's adversary, sometimes take chances, and play capriciously, and after all these dreams and efforts, one is in check, sometimes in checkmate; often, maneuvering the pawns well, they become queens, and one wins the match: the most skillful carries the day or the happiest.)[18]

Courtiers wrote, produced, and directed their own dramatic presentations, playing their self-assigned roles around the clock. Over the course of the sixteenth and seventeenth centuries, the pendulum of sentiment toward masks (literal and figurative) and role-playing in general seems to have shifted from one of playfulness, freedom, and genuine self-expression to one of entrapment, self-serving calculation, and insensitive manipulation. Yet, in my opinion, twentieth-century critics, as a rule, projected too many modern preoccupations with existential angst and narcissistic social climbing onto the propensity for role-playing of previous centuries. As a result, in many cases, critics have ascribed anachronistic motivation onto sixteenth- and seventeenth-century texts. To my knowledge, the only text in which Góngora developed the notion of life as a game of manipulation and control—and in which human beings are marked as kings and pawns, predators and prey, in a sustained, systematic, and cynical way—is the unfinished play *El doctor Carlino* (1613). Significantly, Góngora does not portray court society in the play, but rather represents the urban bourgeoisie and seems to move toward a more sweeping indictment of the amorality of "modern life." Perhaps more in line with Góngora, and in contrast with La Bruyère, Castiglione's Federico Fregoso offers the point of view that assuming a disguise at a public spectacle affords the individual freedom,

> perché il fatto stesso di travestirsi è liberatorio e, tra le altre comodità che offre, consente a un uomo di indossare la maschera che meglio esprime il volto che crede di avere. Basta esasperare con la massima cura i tratti che per lui sono l'essenziale del suo costume e tralasciare con disinvoltura i particolari che non gli interessano, il che produce un effetto di grazia suprema. Faccio qualche esempio: se abbiamo un giovane che si veste da vecchio ma lascia ben aperta la camicia per esibire la potenza dei suoi muscoli, oppure un cavliere mascherato da bifolco o da povero pastore ma con un cavallo di gran razza e un costume evidentemente di alta sartoria, ecco che gli spettatori a prima occhiata credono di vedere in questa maschera la propria immagine mentale del tipo umano rappresentato; e poi, quando scoprono che il costume rivela qualcosa di diverso o di più, si divertono e se la godono.

> (because masquerading carries with it a certain licence and liberty, and this, among other things, enables the courtier to choose the role at which he feels himself best, to bring out its most important elements with diligence and elegance, while showing a certain nonchalance with regard to what is not essential. All of this greatly enhances the attractiveness of what he is doing, as when a youth dresses up as an old man yet wears loose attire so as to be able to show his agility; or when a knight dresses up as a country shepherd, but rides a beautiful horse and wears a handsome and appropriate costume. For the spectators assume they are seeing what they are meant to imagine, and then when shown far more than what is promised by the costume being worn they are highly amused and delighted.)[19]

The disguise paradoxically conceals, reveals, and enhances the true self of the courtier.

The carefully staged debut of the *Soledades* at court illustrates to what extent the spirit of the performance artist and theatrical player colored life in Imperial Spain. Before the manuscripts of the *Polifemo* and *Soledades* circulated at court, the poet selected two leading Spanish humanists as his first critical readers. He wrote Pedro de Valencia in May 1613, soliciting his advice regarding the works. A major intellectual figure of the time, Valencia is now perhaps chiefly known as the chronicler of Philip III and as a supporter of Góngora. His treatise on Plato's Academy, *Academia sive de juditio erga verum* (The Academy of the judgment of truth) (1596), may have had considerable impact on Gongorine aesthetics. At the beginning of 1614, the poet wrote to Francisco Fernández de Córdoba, abbot of Rute, seeking his opinion of the innovative poems. Like Valencia, Fernández de Córdoba was then esteemed as a man of great erudition, although he is now remembered primarily for his friendship with Góngora. Although both men directed rather pointed criticism at Góngora's new style of writing, a subject I will address in the second part of this chapter, on the whole they responded to the *Soledades* (and the *Polifemo*) with approbation and even lavish praise. In his return letter of June 1613, Valencia eulogized the lyric aspect of the poems, citing a Greek epigram honoring Pindar to laud Góngora: "[Q]ue cuanto se levanta la trompeta gritando encima de las flautas de los corzos, resuena sobre todas vuestra lira" ([A]s much as the trumpet rises up shouting over the flutes of roe deer, your lyre resounds above them all). If possible, in his reply of circa 1614, Fernández de Córdoba exceeded Valencia's accolades, volunteering in chivalric fashion to serve as Góngora's "champion" and to ride out in his defense "armado de pluma y libros" (armed with pen and books), conflating arms and letters with a rhetorical flourish.[20]

Why did Góngora choose Valencia and Fernández de Córdoba as the test audience for the *Soledades*? It is obvious from correspondence that both were personal friends of the poet, men he trusted and whose opinions he valued. In addition, I believe Góngora was aware of the revolutionary nature of his poetry and the immense intellectual challenge *el estilo culto* represented. As men of learning and scholars of the classics, Valencia and Fernández de Córdoba were superbly suited to penetrate the poems' mysteries, puzzle out their difficult language, and appreciate their artistry. Indeed, one could say that *gongorismo* was tailor-made for just such readers. In this light, these distinguished humanists provide a portrait of Góngora's ideal intended audience: cerebral, educated, and urbane. The poet's choice of readers had a practical, tactical purpose as well. Valencia and Fernández de Córdoba were well established at the court of Philip III. They commanded universal respect and enjoyed uncontested authority among literati and the intellectual elite. In short, they were perfectly positioned to promote Góngora and his poetry at court and to act as advocates for and defenders of his new lyrical style.

Judging the moment propitious to launch the *Polifemo* and the *Soledades*, Góngora initiated the second stage of his game plan. Needing a publicist, he turned to Andrés de Almansa y Mendoza, court gossipmonger and news bearer, to distribute the manuscripts among the elect. Almansa y Mendoza's apologia of the *Soledades* (ca. 1614–1615) bears witness to his zealous enthusiasm for the poet; however, his inclusion of a list of individuals he considered qualified to understand and discuss the poetry probably did more to hurt Góngora than to help him. Whereas Lope de Vega (one of Góngora's major detractors) appears among the anointed acolytes, Francisco de Quevedo (another prominent detractor) is conspicuously absent.[21]

To my knowledge, the poet never intended to subject these poems to the scrutiny of a mass audience. Like most of his contemporaries, Góngora viewed those who published or wrote for the general public with suspicion and disdain. He regarded the popularity of his antagonist Lope de Vega with contempt and regularly accused him of pandering to the masses. Neither the *Polifemo* nor the *Soledades* was published during Góngora's lifetime, though in his later years, financial hardship and poor health forced him to reconsider publication simply to survive. Góngora's plan to produce a commercial edition of his poetry ended with his death in 1627.[22]

I do not wish to misconstrue the poet's test-marketing of his *poesía culta* as cynical, calculating, or in any way sinister, distorting the effortless grace of Castiglione's courtier into the self-serving schemes of Machiavelli's prince. The poet merely followed the unwritten rules of the game of court life, shrewdly performing the role of a *magister ludi* by executing, to perfection, a winning strategy to introduce himself and his art at court. Whatever values one may wish to attach to Góngora's actions, with the passage of time the *Soledades* became synonymous with intellectual accomplishment, refined poetry destined for and designating refined readers. The virtue or stigma that the *Soledades* accrued from their reputation as elite poetry geared to an exclusive guild of astute, elegant consumers remains to this day.

The same ludic principle inscribed within the *Soledades*, which shaped their creation, presentation, and the contentious reception that greeted them at court, also contrived to appeal to the aesthetic taste of aristocrats. A passage from Castiglione's *Courtier* (1528) affords a nostalgic and revealing glimpse of the salon entertainment unique to this group:

[S]ubito dopo cena tutti i gentiluomini di casa si ritrovavano perabitudine nel salotto della duchessa, dove, oltre a fare festicciole, fare musica, fare i balletti che si facevano lì in continuazione, a volte si passava al dibattito, oppure si facevano intelligenti giochi di società, proposti da uno o dall'altro, nei quali i giocatori spesso utilizzavano l'enigmistica per lanciare dei messaggi cifrati a una certa persona di loro gradimento. Qualche volta nascevano altre discussioni su argomenti vari, o ci si rimbeccava con battute a bruciapelo; spesso si gareggiava a inventare quelli che oggi si chiamerebbero slogan;

([I]t was the custom for all the gentlemen of the house to go, immediately after supper, to the rooms of the Duchess; and there, along with pleasant recreations and enjoyments of various kinds, including constant music and dancing, sometimes intriguing questions were asked, and sometimes ingenious games played [now on the suggestion of one person and now of another] in which, using various ways of concealment, those present revealed their thoughts in allegories to this person or that. And occasionally, there would be a sharp exchange of spontaneous witticisms; and often "emblems," as we call them nowadays were devised for the occasion.)[23]

Castiglione's encapsulated representation of such evening diversions illustrates and anticipates, in germ, two important facets of the aesthetic horizon of expectations shared by Góngora's select public: an aesthetics of enigma and a taste for spectacle. These courtly parlor games reveal a level of participatory complexity and sophistication quite foreign to the current mass-market engagement with electronic amusements. The description foregrounds verbal games that involve witty repartee, the use of symbolic and allegorical language, and the implementation of formal rhetoric to pose questions and to persuade or lead by indirection or misdirection. The author places considerable emphasis on strategies of concealment, tactics of obfuscation employed by interlocutors to tease or goad other game players into ferreting out the underlying significance of the deceptive images and tropes. *Emblemata* provide visual stimuli that demand a similar response of active engagement from viewers. The attraction of the aesthetics of enigma, then, lies in the irresistible appeal of mental challenge to a sophisticated audience that is confident and proud of its intellectual prowess and its mastery of literature, artistic conventions and traditions, and classical and popular forms of learning. Immersion in the play of enigma engenders an unusual form of social interaction, blurring the distinction between competitors and partners, as all players are enmeshed in a collaborative game of one-upmanship, each striving to outdo or stump the other. In the manner of a round-robin, each member of the gathering of nobles successively assumes the role of inventor and solver of a linguistic or pictorial puzzle.

On a much smaller scale and in a more intimate fashion, the interplay between backgrounded continuous music and dancing and foregrounded cerebral games anticipates the dynamics of the spectacles of Góngora's time, which were lavish productions patronized by imperial courts. Guests move back and forth between the unbounded play space of music and language, alternately switching their momentary allegiance from one artistic medium to the other. While dancing, they passively observe the verbal contests before them. While engaged in rhetorical fencing matches, they watch the dancers from a distance. All of the guests are simultaneously actors and spectators, shifting constantly from one position to the other. This structural dynamics of flux and changing perspectives implicit in Castiglione's account would emerge later as a hallmark of the court masque. Added to this matrix of movement is an intense hunger for the sights and sounds of spectacle. Castiglione sets before the reader a feast for the senses, a catalyst for imaginative re-creation of a world of sumptuous attire; flickering candlelight; graceful motion; mellifluous tunes; and clever, esoteric conversation. Music, dancing, art, and symbolic language all meld into a harmonious whole, unity and diversity comfortably occupying the same ludic space. The cerebral and the sensory swirl together, forever intertwined in the writer's idealizing memory.

Góngora was well acquainted with court culture, its customs and conventions, and its aesthetic norms and taste. Although the poet did not join the court in an official capacity until 1621, when he was appointed chaplain to Philip IV, he made frequent visits to the court of Philip III at the behest of the Cathedral of Córdoba and finally moved to court in 1617. Góngora enjoyed the reputation of a privileged member of the clergy, a man of learning and letters (he attended the prestigious University of Salamanca), and an accomplished poet. His powerful patrons and contacts, such as Philip III's *privado*, the duke of Lerma, and a supportive coterie of Andalusian nobles, gained him access to the innermost circles of the Crown.

The aesthetics of enigma forms an integral part of Gongorine poetics. As one might surmise from Castiglione's nostalgic remembrance, the privileging of enigma originated at court, specifically, at the Florentine court of the Medici. The aristocratic humanist and philosopher Pico della Mirandola was the first to articulate the aesthetics of enigma. To reconcile three different types of sacred revelation (pagan mysteries, cabalistic writings, and mystical Neoplatonic documents), Pico posited that the traditions shared a rhetoric of complex symbolism built on cryptic, obscure language that simultaneously masks and reveals secrets. He used the term *poetic theology* to identify the unifying element. According to Pico, the more arcane the language and imagery employed in this system of hieroglyphics, the more profound the spiritual and philosophical secrets lurking beneath the symbolic, poetic veil. Occult language enables the poet, priest, or philosopher, or all three, to function as a guardian of sacred truths. Linguistic obscurantism keeps the masses ignorant and reserves transcendent knowledge for the intellectual elite.[24]

Understandably, with its inherent selectivity, the aesthetics of enigma flourished in the courts of sixteenth- and seventeenth-century Europe and inspired a wide range of intellectual and cultural interests, in *emblemata* and apothegms, in the cabala and the mystics, in comets and the philosophers' stone, in allegorical representations and visual illusions. The enthusiasm for emblem books, the symbolic details and design of the royal palaces and gardens, and the abundance of allegorical paintings and tapestries in Hapsburg Spain provide ample evidence of the pervasive presence of the aesthetics of enigma in the world of Góngora. In time, poetic theology's fundamental conceptual paradox of silent language that speaks and concealing words that disclose gave rise to what Rosalie Colie has described as an "epidemic of paradox" that quickly spread throughout the European intellectual community.[25] Góngora's *estilo culto* continues and develops the tradition of poetic theology and actively caters to the court's taste for enigmas and puzzles.

Góngora could not have escaped the influence of the panoply and pageantry of Hapsburg Spain. During the reign of Philip III, elaborate forms of entertainment prevailed at court: fireworks displays, masques, ballets, dramatized tournaments, and triumphal processions. In such an atmosphere, the *comedia* readily evolved into a grand spectacle of intricate stagecraft and scenery, cloud machines and mechanical cars, dramatized *emblemata* and allegorical figures, and music and dancing. The king and his favorite, the duke of Lerma, both patronized these extravaganzas and participated in them. At a masque held in 1605 to honor the birth of Prince Philip (the future Philip IV), a cloud machine bore the king and queen from their curtained upper gallery down to the floor of the performance hall where they gave thanks for God's blessings at Virtue's temple and then joined in a celebratory dance. In 1614, young Prince Philip, seemingly destined for a life tinged with dramatic flair, became ill from rocking his triumphal car to excess while playing the role of Cupid. After a pause for the ensuing mayhem and mop-up, the performance continued. And in the same year, members of the royal family and of the household of the duke of Lerma took part in Lope de Vega's *El premio de la hermosura* (The prize of beauty), a theatrical piece featuring a cave, a movable temple of Diana, a castle, a palace, mountains, and a river. The plot involved the shipwreck of an actual vessel in the stream and the survival of one character by clinging to a plank that carried him across the water.[26]

Inevitably, the enthusiasm for spectacle at court spilled over into the streets in grandiose acts of devotion and national pride that linked the Crown and the Church in the hearts and minds of the people. Royal births, marriages, and deaths; major military victories; and religious holidays offered occasions for staged representations of the majesty, might, and Catholic fervor of the Hapsburgs. Rich or ascetic (or both) penitential processions, triumphal entries, floats, fireworks, and public pardons or executions of criminals appealed to the emotions of the masses and reinforced their faith in the monarchy and the Church.[27]

As a clergyman and prominent author, Góngora was privy to the planning of such events, which were often organized and implemented by religious orders in collaboration with the Crown. In fact, he frequently entered the poetry contests associated with such celebrations. One occasion of particular importance in the life of Góngora was the 1616 festival honoring the transfer of the icon Nuestra Señora del Sagrario to a new chapel in the Cathedral of Toledo, an event for which he composed two commemorative poems. Designed and mounted by Bernardo Cardinal Sandoval y Rojas, the duke of Lerma's uncle, the spectacle illustrates the masterful use of pomp and circumstance as a symbol of temporal and divine power, a schema that typified Imperial Spain. The requisite masses, masques, and illumination ceremonies culminated with an auto-da-fé in which all the sinners were forgiven their transgressions, giving the populace an impressive example of the infinite mercy, generosity, and beneficence of king and clergy. Although we do not know if Góngora actually attended the festival, we do know that his poetic contribution and his possible presence helped consolidate his position with the Sandoval family and apparently precipitated his relocation to court the following year.[28]

In our smug, modern rush to condemn the Hapsburgs for their extravagance and indifference to the plight of the common man, we have grown insensitive to the peculiar poignancy of the court's glorification of the enigmatic and the obscure and its addiction to opulence and theatricality.[29] It is almost as if, through the force of will and the imagination, aristocrats sought to endow fragile illusionism with sufficient strength to support the weight of a far-flung empire. Exercise of the mind and senses would perhaps exorcise the demons of crumbling imperial power. At the least, cultivation of the inner realm of the imagination offered a welcome respite from socioeconomic problems and other affairs of state.

Beleaguered monarchs and courtiers alike found a place of meditation, recreation, and refuge from worldly preoccupations in the great pastime of the age: private collections. J. H. Elliott notes that enthusiasm for scientific and geographical exploration fueled the growth of this new passion:

The discovery of new worlds overseas and the increasingly close observation of nature, had brought home to European man the incredible variety and multiplicity of objects in the world he inhabited. Rich men who prided themselves on their taste and learning began to collect everything they could lay their hands on—gems, antique marbles and cameos, books and manuscripts, medals and bronzes, plants and animals, and every kind of outlandish artifact. Monarchs and private citizens created menageries and botanical gardens for their instruction and delight. Kings, cardinals, great statesmen, and public servants, like Cardinal de Granvelle, the minister of Charles V and then of Philip II, competed ferociously for masterpieces with which to furnish their private galleries.

Collectors housed their assembled natural and artificial oddities and enigmas in specially constructed cabinets, chambers, and galleries. These *Kunst*- and *Wunderkammern* were neither simple monuments of conspicuous consumption nor mere showcases of material objects and exotic flora and fauna. They served a philosophical and spiritual purpose, providing a physical and imaginative space in which the rational and affective powers of the mind and senses could meet and ascend to a higher plane. From this newly attained transcendent vantage point, spectators could contemplate in awe and wonder the pansophic ideal: the harmonious, all-encompassing teleological web of the cosmos.[30]

The collections gave viewers access to a hidden universe ordinarily beyond their reach in the course of everyday life. One could enter this space to observe the marvels of the world in solitude or in the company of friends. Both the monstrous and deformed, such as Góngora's Cyclops Polyphemus, and the beautiful and perfect, such as the poet's nymph Galatea, had a place in the collections. Situated at an unexpected crossroads of the homogeneous and heterogeneous, the sensory and the imaginative, the displays of wonders and enigmas both natural and artificial pay tribute to a burgeoning aesthetic and intellectual taste embracing synthesis and syncretism, empiricism and natural magic—the province of pansophy. John Shearman, writing of the "set piece" exemplifying the artist's virtuosity as a type of artifact characteristic of Mannerist art, provides insight into aesthetic objects that made their way into such collections:

> [T]here were many instances in North and South Europe in the Mannerist period of paintings, drawings or bronzes displayed in "cabinets of curiosities" alongside "marvels" of nature: astounding geological specimens, incredible biological freaks, thunderbolts or zoological rariora (for example, in the *Kunstkammer* of Rudolph II at Prague). The work of art, whether or not it was designed primarily to do so, was valued for its capacity to excite wonder; the point is equally true in literature.[31]

The *Soledades* could certainly be described both as a new kind of "set piece" illustrating Góngora's virtuosity and as a poetic performance designed to inspire wonderment in the readers who deign to explore the marvels of the *culto* verses.

To analyze or understand the *Soledades* in a meaningful way, modern readers must restore the poems to this cultural context. The *Soledades* are the poetic analogue of the collections of Nature's enigmas, created, gathered together, and artfully arranged and exhibited by Góngora. These personal, portable, imaginary chambers of spectacles and enigmas are available to readers at any time of day or night. The audience of readers and spectators can choose to mull over the poems' secrets and admire their craftsmanship in silent isolation, as their title suggests, or they can elect to make the *Soledades* the subject of virtually endless hours of group discussions and arguments. If readers pause to think about it, they will detect in the *Soledades* an idyllic reflection of the dazzling ceremonies and processions, the pageantry and elaborate stagecraft at court characteristic of the waning years of the Hapsburg empire. Just as the spectres of hunger, war, poverty, and disease form a tragic backdrop for the masques, parties, and spectacles of the reigns of Philip III and Philip IV, so do memories of conflict, greed, death, and disillusionment haunt the bucolic scenes of joyful singing and dancing, fireworks and banquets, hunting processions, and Nature's beauty and abundance in the poems. Like the court spectacles, Góngora's *Soledades* seem to possess a talismanic power to keep the forces of decay and destruction in abeyance and project a glowing vision of pastoral peace, harmony, and virtuous prosperity. However, we, the members of the poet's enchanted audience of readers and spectators, must never lose sight of the fact that this magical universe occupies the most potent yet most ephemeral and tenuous of confines: the human imagination.

Reshaping the Canon

Could Góngora possibly have anticipated the feeding frenzy of criticism the *Polifemo* and the *Soledades* would occasion at court? Once the poems were released into the rarefied atmosphere of the literary elite, reaction to the works rapidly disintegrated into the scholarly equivalent of a barroom brawl. The poems that had garnered praise and polite, measured criticism from Góngora's friends and mentors Valencia and Fernández de Córdoba soon became the subject of vituperative verses and prose written by a host of new enemies. As is frequently the case in academic quarrels, the target of criticism was more often than not deflected away from the poems and onto their creator. In a short time, Góngora bashing developed into a recreational growth industry. At its best, as exemplified by the endeavors of Quevedo and Lope, this fashionable sport inspired witty, satirical artifacts. At its worst, however, Góngora bashing was a puerile game of name-calling, an act of self-promotion committed at the expense of the poet's reputation.

Lope de Vega fired the opening volley in the great Góngora war. In a sarcastic, anonymous letter dated September 1615, he denounces the *estilo culto* as Babelic and warns Góngora of the potentially lethal effects of these complicated poems on readers of limited intelligence. Lope seems to have had the poet's court spokesman Almansa y Mendoza in mind. Under the guise of friendship, he urges Góngora to remove the offensive manuscripts from circulation before irreparable damage is done to his good name. The missive implies that the poems are of such inferior quality that they cannot possibly withstand the scrutiny of wise and discerning eyes.[32] A steady barrage of anti-Góngora insults, parodies, and aggressive essays followed Lope's lead. The authors of these pieces sought to save the poetic canon from the corrupting influence of *gongorismo*. The battle escalated as Góngora's supporters counterattacked with equal zeal.

Less than six years later, in an essay published in his 1621 collection, *La Filomena,* Lope subtly but significantly alters his opinion of Góngora and his innovative style. He now professes admiration and respect for his arch rival without the irony that customarily accompanies such statements. However, Lope qualifies his praise of Góngora with contempt for the poet's disciples, whom he accuses of slavishly imitating the formal elements of *culteranismo* without appropriating the master's wit, genius, or seriousness of purpose.[33] The words Lope indirectly addresses to Góngora have the confessional, conciliatory ring of a guilty conscience. Yet, even though he extends an olive branch to the inventor of the new style, Lope rails at rampant Gongorism as a threat to the clear, precise *estilo llano,* the privileged, canonical form of poetic expression. In a backhanded manner, he acknowledges the inroads that Gongorine language has already made into the canon.

Lope's fear of a shift in the preferential poetic style proved prophetic as poets embraced the cause of *gongorismo* at a rapid pace. Even one of Góngora's most vociferous opponents, the recalcitrant Juan de Jáuregui, author of *Antídoto contra la pestilente poesía de las «Soledades»* (Antidote to the pestilent poetry of the *Soledades*) (1614), eventually began to compose poetry in the cultured style. By 1634, desertions to the enemy camp had risen so high that a Góngora supporter, Francisco del Villar, snidely commented: "[L]o que me admira es, que después de haberlo satirizado, le imitan todos" ([W]hat amazes me is that after having made him an object of satire, everybody imitates him).[34]

There were other signs besides individual conversions that Gongorism had achieved canonical status. As early as 1627, Pedro Díaz de Rivas prepared annotations for the *Polifemo* and the *Soledades*, giving readers a guidebook to the newly published editions of Góngora's masterpieces and providing details designed to enhance the public's understanding of the poems and increase appreciation for their artistry. García Salcedo Coronel's annotated editions of the *Polifemo* and the *Soledades* appeared shortly thereafter, in 1629 and 1636, respectively, followed by a competing commentary, José de Pellicer's *Lecciones solemnes* (Solemn interpretations), in 1630.[35] All three commentators offer invaluable information on difficult passages and images in the poems, suggest possible sources for the texts, and inundate readers with learned references and allusions. In many ways, their rivalry and eagerness to impress the potential reading public with their own cleverness and erudition set the stage for the competitive academic playground that Góngora's poetry would become in the twentieth century. Nevertheless, the most important consequence of their efforts was the elevation and lionization of Góngora and his works, placing the poet on a par with other *auctores*, the authoritative, canonical writers who merited imitation and formal commentary in the humanist tradition: Aristotle, Virgil, Ovid, Saint Augustine, and so on.

As Lope had also predicted, the derivative progeny of *gongorismo* ultimately destroyed the prestigious reputation of the master. In the hands of inferior poets, the *estilo culto* degenerated into stilted, vacuous, frivolously ornamental poetry. Eighteenth-century rationalism and the precepts of Spanish neoclassicists eclipsed the preeminent Gongorine model. The nineteenth-century romantics virtually ignored Góngora's existence as a pivotal figure in Spanish literary history. It fell to the poets of the Generation of 1927 to resurrect creative and critical interest in Góngora.[36]

The circuslike hoopla that characterized the Góngora debate and the colorful rhetoric of its combative parties make it all too easy to forget what was at stake in the conflict. At the heart of the polemic, pro- and anti-Góngora forces battled for supremacy, that is, they fought over who and which style would dominate the poetic canon. The pastoral poems had the dubious honor of principal battlefield in this literary war, as the *Polifemo*'s Ovidian source lent authority to the text and to a degree mitigated adverse reaction to the poem's experimental discourse. As a result, the *Soledades* received the brunt of the blame for having a pernicious impact on Spanish letters.

Beneath the entertaining spectacle of allegations and accusations leveled at the *Soledades* and their creator lay three overlapping points of contention concerning the nature of poetic language, the concept of decorum, and the hierarchy of poetic genres. Pedro de Valencia and Francisco Fernández de Córdoba were the first to raise these issues. In the letters solicited by Góngora, they present their arguments in Erasmian style, peppering prose with popular aphorisms, classical sententiae, and illustrative poetry samples drawn from the established canon.

Valencia and Fernández de Córdoba object most strongly to Góngora's enigmatic poetic language. They target several facets of the *Soledades*' linguistic obscurantism for criticism: the deliberate distortion of plain language into difficult discourse, the excessive use of tropes and additional forms of rhetorical ornamentation, and the surfeit of arcane and foreign vocabulary. The scholars ground their judgments in normative precepts derived from the classical canon: the stylistic ideal of perspicuity, that is, of clarity, brevity, and precision in expression *(el estilo llano)*; the concept of beauty as natural, unaffected, balanced, and harmonious; and the purpose of poetry, the Horatian mandate to entertain and instruct. The works of authors such as Aristotle, Quintilian, Virgil, Seneca, and Horace are invoked to convince Góngora of the error of his ways. The poet's friends hold up an impressive list of artists and thinkers worthy of study and emulation—Scaliger, Minturno, Sannazaro, Petrarch, Bernardo Tasso, and Garcilaso—all models and teachers to help Góngora "correct" his poetry and return to the fold of esteemed writers.

Both scholars consistently conflate ethical and aesthetic ideals in their comments. Assuming the moral high ground, they adopt a tone of paternal disappointment and gentle chastisement toward Góngora and his new poems. Valencia in particular regards his friend's work as an act of rebellious pride, the flouting of poetic conventions for self-aggrandizement:

> [M]ás me desatentan otras [culpas] de demasiado cuidado, que son las que proceden de afectación de hincharse y decir extrañezas y grandezas, o por buscar gracias y agudezas y otros afeites ambiciosos y pueriles, o juveniles a lo menos, que aflojan y enfrían y afean.
>
> ([O]ther [faults] of excessive care [in writing] perturb me more, those that arise from the impression of prideful bloating and from saying strange and great things, or from searching for graceful turns and witty conceits and other ambitious and puerile affectations, or at the very least juvenile ones, that weaken, stultify, and disfigure.)

At the end of this rather thorough reproof, Valencia has worked up such a froth of righteous indignation that he exclaims: "[A]penas yo le alcanzo a entender en muchas partes" (I can scarcely manage to understand you in many places), a sentiment Fernández de Córdoba echoes while asking his friend to keep in mind the three Horatian virtues in poetic composition, namely, *perspicuitas, brebitas, probabilitas* (perspicuity, brevity, and plausibility).[37]

Many critics capitalized on the identification of ethics with aesthetics to denounce Góngora as a "nonbeliever." In his *Cartas filológicas* (Philological letters) (1634), Francisco Cascales asserts that Góngora has engendered a heretical poetic sect, "esta nueva secta de poesía ciega, enigmática, y confusa" (this new sect of confusing, enigmatic, and blind poetry), an act he roundly condemns on moral grounds, citing the now familiar comparison between the *estilo culto* and the Tower of Babel in support of his observation. He then baptizes the poet with the negative epithet "príncipe de las tinieblas" (the prince of darkness).[38] A cursory glance at anti-Góngora documents reveals that Cascales's hyperbolic, inflammatory rhetoric is the rule rather than the exception in the debate. The word *vicio* (vice) appears in conjunction with poetic obscurantism with startling regularity, converting what purport to be learned commentaries into diatribes resonant with moral outrage.

Fernández de Córdoba expresses greater distress than Valencia over Góngora's violation of the classical norm of beauty. He reminds the poet of the value of proportion, control, and "natural" artifice, virtues missing from the *Soledades* in his estimation. The abbot of Rute takes Góngora to task for indulgence, disproportion, and lack of moderation in employing tropes; introducing Latinate words; repeating phrases; twisting meaning with hyperbole; and distorting sentences with hyperbata. The flaws are grouped together under the rubric *cacocelia*, defined as "vicio por afectación de ornato demasiado" (vice by affectation from too much ornamentation). It is probably not a coincidence that the statement reads like a courtroom pronouncement of guilt. Far more telling, however, is his comparison of Gongorine language with a woman who obfuscates and eventually obliterates her beauty by covering her body from head to toe with mountains of jewelry. Natural beauty is made ludicrous, if not hideous, by excessive artifice. This analogy became a rhetorical commonplace in the writings of anti-*gongoristas* and took on a life of its own as each critic embellished the image with idiosyncratic alterations. Lope, for example, likens Góngora's plethora of tropes to a woman so enamored of makeup that she applies rouge not only to her cheeks, but also to her nose, forehead, and ears. The inimitable Cascales, not to be outdone in the game of Go-Get-Góngora, opts for an entirely different metaphor to capture the full horror of opaque poetry: he compares the composer of obscure verses to an artist who paints the night.[39]

One of the most hotly disputed aspects of Góngora's cultivation of erudite language concerned the relationship between poet and audience. In this discussion, issues of creative responsibility, national pride, and the inherent genius of the Castilian language come to the fore. Valencia censures Góngora for imitating the flowery Italianate style that he associates with clever conceits and wordplay. He accuses the poet of assuming a foreign, inauthentic, and insincere voice. Valencia labels the misappropriations "travesuras y apetitos de lo ajeno" (fanciful acts and appetite for the foreign), words that yet again bear the weight of paternalistic castigation and moral condemnation. What Valencia regards as a lack of proper seriousness and respect for one's own language, however, receives high praise from Fernández de Córdoba. The abbot of Rute lauds Góngora for edifying the public and enriching the Castilian lexicon by introducing foreign words in the *Soledades*. Nonetheless, he criticizes the poet for repeating the words ad nauseam, thus making the poetry irritatingly pedantic. Fernández de Córdoba reminds Góngora of the principle of moderation and warns him of the dangers of losing readers through excessive insistence on erudition:

> [N]o debe Vm. procurar escrebir para solos los doctos, porque desta suerte le entenderán y gustarán de sus obras muy pocos; . . . no querrán gastar el tiempo, y sus juicios en adivinar, qué quiso decir Vm.: . . . reduciendo a trabajo lo que había de ser meramente gusto, y matándose por entenderlo o no entenderlo.
>
> ([Y]ou should not try to write for the learned alone, because in this way very few will understand and like your works; . . . they will not want to consume time and their wisdom figuring out what you tried to say: . . . converting into work what ought to have been simple pleasure, and killing oneself for understanding or not understanding it.)[40]

Góngora has forgotten that good poets should amuse as well as instruct. In fact, his desire to instruct is so great and the language he employs is so esoteric that he risks wearying and losing his most enthusiastic readers.

Lope de Vega articulates a similar argument, but in rather blunt discourse. Waving the flag of nationalism, he proclaims the sovereign independence of the Castilian language from foreign intervention. In his opinion, the poet has a national duty to exercise restraint in adding exotic words to the mother tongue. Furthermore, the poet should not burden the reader with work: "[L]a poesía había de costar grande trabajo al que la escribiese, y poco al que la leyese" ([P]oetry should exact great toil from the one who would write it, and little from the one who would read it). Short on tact, finesse, and control, the ever explosive Cascales resorts to more hyperbolic phrases to communicate his displeasure at Góngora's grafting of Latinate words and syntax (in the form of hyperbaton) onto the national language. He believes Spanish poetry should reflect the unique genius of the Castilian tongue, which he equates with clarity, sobriety, and simplicity—classical stylistic ideals. Góngora is twice a criminal; he betrays the intrinsic qualities of his native language, and he perverts the laws of Nature herself: "Siendo pues cierto, que la lengua latina y castellana corren por diferentes caminos, quererlas don Luis llevar por una misma madre, es violentar a la naturaleza, y engendrar monstruosidades" (Since it is true that the Latin and Castilian languages flow along different courses, for Don Luis to want the same mother to bear them is to violate nature and engender monstrosities).[41] Cascales's bombastic blast portrays Góngora as a traitor who would return Castilian to a position of subservience to classical Latin.

The image of the monster haunts virtually every anti-Góngora document prompted by the *Polifemo* and the *Soledades*. According to numerous critics, Góngora willfully violated the principle of decorum in creating the poems, that is, he deliberately mismatched style and subject matter in rendering humble people and lowly topics in a lofty, elegant manner. Once again, the *Polifemo*'s mythological plot and classical source protected the poem from such criticism. The *Soledades*, however, with their idealized scenes of rustic life and seemingly idolized pastoral values, were deemed deviant, aberrant poems, in short, travesties of classical norms. In words reminiscent of Cervantes's canine critic Berganza, the abbot of Rute invokes the Aristotelian precept of verisimilitude, reminding Góngora of art's mimetic prerogative. As an example of a breach of decorum, he cites the ladylike whiteness and delicacy of the mountain women, shepherdesses, and fisherman's daughters in the *Soledades*—an impossibility for women constantly involved in hard work and exposed to harsh weather. A note of exasperation creeps into the prose as Fernández de Córdoba wonders why Góngora has chosen to ignore the model of Virgil, who reserved such pristine beauty for the immortal Galatea alone.[42]

Jáuregui raises the same issue, but in a petulant voice laced with sarcasm and condescension. He cannot fathom the link between ornamental language and ordinary people, ideas, and things. As a result, he judges Gongorine discourse "muy de reír" (very laughable) and acerbically states: "Parece a veces que va Vm. a decir cosas de gran peso, y sale con una bagatela o malpare un ratón" (It seems at times that you are going to say things of great moment and out you come with a trifle or you abort a rat). Jáuregui can scarcely contain the venom of anti-*gongorismo* that spews forth in his so-called *Antidote*. He finds Góngora guilty not only of fathering literary vermin, but also of lacking the average schoolboy's familiarity with classical models. To remedy this sad state of affairs, Jáuregui lectures the ignorant poet on the differences between the heroic style, which captures all that is great, noble, and serious in language that is consistently elevated, harmonious, and direct, and the low style, which conveys unimportant matters with mockery and merriment.[43] Depending on the critic, Góngora is either a rebel who refuses to conform to canonical expectations in regards to decorum or a dim-witted clod who by dint of stupidity or ineptitude cannot achieve decorum in composition.

The *Soledades* pose a similar challenge to traditional notions of genre. The poems defy categorization according to the classical canon, forcing critics either to disregard the elements that do not fit in a specific generic class or to rethink the entire system of classification. The *Soledades* are a generic hybrid of lyric and narrative poetry that features epic, pastoral, and romance components. Góngora has thoroughly confounded his judgmental audience by embedding subgenres—epithalamia, amoeban love songs, and dramatic soliloquies—into the text. Fernández de Córdoba resolves the quandary by relegating the poems to the lower rungs of the hierarchy of genres among bucolic, lyric verses of negligible worth. In the abbot of Rute's opinion, Góngora wastes his talent on this inferior poetic genre when he should [be composing heroic or tragic verses in the sublime style: "[S]iendo de su naturaleza ilustres piden estilo, y modo de decir fuera del vulgar, como lo hiciera Vm. si aplicara su ingenio, y genio, a lo épico, de que diera mejor que otro ninguno" ([S]ince they are illustrious by nature they require style, and an uncommon manner of speech, like you could do if you were to apply your wit, and genius, to the epic, of which you could produce one better than any other).[44] From a rigid classicist's point of view, the *Soledades* were neither fish nor fowl in the established literary hierarchy. Their lack of an identifiable classical model and their generic uncertainty made the poems indefensible on classical grounds.

Criticism of the *Polifemo* and the *Soledades* did not go unanswered. Góngora found a most eloquent champion in Pedro Díaz de Rivas, who in the *Discursos apologéticos por el estilo del "Polifemo" y "Soledades"* (Apologetic discourses for the style of the *Polifemo* and *Soledades*) (1624) responded point by point to Jáuregui's hostile attacks in the *Antídoto*.[45] In contrast to the meandering discourse and highly charged emotional tone effected by the opposition to the *estilo culto*, Díaz de Rivas approaches the issue in a logical, rational manner. He refuses to adopt a defensive stance, choosing instead to persuade readers with lucid, subtle rhetoric to prove themselves worthy of Góngora by engaging with the *Polifemo* and the *Soledades*. Díaz de Rivas's arguments are predicated on wit, organization, a dazzling array of quotations drawn from classical and contemporary *auctores*, and, above all, unshakable faith that his readers share his taste and erudition—which are mirrored in Góngora's poems.

The *Discursos* are of special interest to modern readers because they contain some of the earliest examples of analytical reading and close textual analysis of the *Polifemo* and the *Soledades,* an implicit assertion that regardless of classical precepts and categories, Góngora's poems possess innate aesthetic and intellectual value. In fact, much of Díaz de Rivas's essay advances a thesis that might well be termed *the theory of the self-selecting audience,* the policy that superior, intelligent readers will recognize the *Polifemo* and the *Soledades* as masterpieces and will readily invest the time and energy necessary to understand them. This position is remarkably similar to that advanced by Pedro Salinas, who stated that avant-garde artists eventually garner their own public.[46] Indeed, Díaz de Rivas's predilection for an active audience provides an important precedent for the twentieth-century addiction to a dynamic author-reader pact in which the audience must decipher difficult texts and assemble meaning. In both cases, readers play an indispensable role in the hermeneutic process.

In the *Discursos,* the critic successfully shifts the burden of interpretive responsibility away from the artist and onto the audience. This sleight of hand forms the single most powerful weapon in the arsenal that Díaz de Rivas trains on anti-*culto* commentary. His stratagem passes on the onus of linguistic unintelligibility to dull, lazy readers and, at the same time, frees him to build up Góngora's image in the eyes of an elite public. For example, like Fernández de Córdoba, he praises Góngora for enriching Castilian with Latinate and foreign words and for beautifying their native tongue with decorative tropes. He goes one step further, however, in describing Góngora as a careful composer who selectively mines the treasures of antiquity and contemporary foreign cultures to elevate Castilian to new heights of elegance.[47]

To the complaint that Góngora saturates poetry with unnecessary, cumbersome tropes, Díaz de Rivas replies that such embellishments seem clumsy to readers because they are accustomed to the works of only inferior poets:

> [U]só de muchos y varios tropos que parecerán demasiados a las orejas acostumbradas a oír Poemas llanos e humildes de versificadores, no de los valientes Griegos y Latinos, como Homero, Píndaro, Virgilio y Horacio, cuyas obras están llenas de galas y atrevimientos, de tropos y figuras frecuentísimas.
>
> ([H]e used many, varied tropes that probably seem too many to ears accustomed to hearing the plain and humble Poems of versifiers, not of the valiant Greeks and Latins, like Homer, Pindar, Virgil and Horace, whose works are full of ornaments and daring, of frequent tropes and [rhetorical] figures.)

Díaz de Rivas legitimates Góngora's use of tropes by reminding readers that the poet is continuing a noble, classical tradition that exalts poetry with rich, rhetorical ornamentation. He insists that Góngora has earned the right to join the ranks of venerable authors such as Pindar and Virgil. Mere "versifiers" are responsible for the current low poetic standards, and wise readers will retrain their minds and sensibilities to appreciate Góngora's cultivated style. One could compare the audience's gradual rapprochement with *culteranismo* to the slow, faltering paces of the troglodyte in Plato's analogy of the cave as the cave dweller moves toward the brilliant light of the sun: "[C]oncluyo que lo que llaman obscuridad en nuestro Poeta no es falta suya, . . . como no es falta de el Sol que yo no le pueda mirar de hito, sino de mi vista débil y flaca" (I conclude that what they call obscurity in our Poet is not his fault, . . . just as it is not the Sun's fault that I cannot look at it fixedly, but rather of my feeble, weak sight).[48]

In mounting his skillful, pro-Góngora counteroffensive, Díaz de Rivas frequently invokes the aesthetics of enigma. The critic's statements in regard to the poet's observation of decorum provide a case in point. Díaz de Rivas believes that Góngora upholds and celebrates the principle of decorum because in classical antiquity, obscure language signified profound meaning. He argues that the *Polifemo* and the *Soledades* are replete with topoi, images, and mythical and classical allusions of high-minded seriousness that require expression in the sublime style. Thus, Góngora's linguistic obscurantism is neither gratuitous nor incorrect. It indicates the superiority of the poet and his public:

> Los escritos de los Poetas suelen estar llenos de mucha filosofía, de fábulas ocultas y de historias, las cuales no podrá entender sino el que estuviere muy culto en toda lección. . . . no entenderá el no versado en los escritores tantas fábulas, historias y alusiones o imitaciones de dichos de Poetas como están engarzadas con mucha gala por todo el contexto de las *Soledades*. Y que no se entiendan por la erudición que contienen, no es falta suya, sino del que no sabe.
>
> (The writings of Poets are customarily full of much philosophy, of secret tales and stories, unintelligible except for one who is very learned in every lesson. . . . [O]ne not versed in writers will not understand as many tales, stories and allusions or imitations of Poets' sayings as are set [like gemstones] with much elegance throughout the text of the *Soledades*. And that they might not be understood on account of the erudition they contain is not their fault, but rather of the one who has no knowledge.)[49]

Adopting Pico's poetic theology to the situation at hand, Góngora plays the role of high priest in the cult of knowledge. He guards transcendent secrets from the ignorant and unworthy masses. Readers who wish to enter the poet's inner sanctum of esoterica must endure a self-inflicted rite of initiation. However, in contrast to the ceremonial rituals of the ancient mystery cults, the novices of Góngora's exclusive society must submit to an interiorized process of purification in which they ascend to the poet's intellectual pinnacle by exercising the powers of the mind. Readers gain access to Góngora's visionary universe through mental activity.

At times Díaz de Rivas seems like a minister preaching a sermon on the merits of modern aesthetics to a congregation of new converts whose faith is wavering. This proselytizing attitude appears most prominently in his rejection of the *Soledades'* classification as pastoral poetry. Díaz de Rivas contends that the *Soledades'* elevated subject matter locates the poems at the top of the hierarchy of genres:

> [S]u principal asunto no es tratar cosas pastoriles, sino la peregrinación de un Príncipe, persona grande, su ausencia y afectos dolientes en el destierro, todo lo cual es materia grave y debe tratarse afectuosamente, con el estilo grave y magnífico. Lo cual confirma Torquato Tasso, lib. *Del poema heroico*, pues dice que de materia amorosa aun se puede componer Epico Poema.
>
> ([T]heir principal plot does not deal with pastoral things, but rather with the pilgrimage of a Prince, a great person, his absence and sorrowful feelings in exile, all of which is serious material and should be treated with feeling, with a serious and magnificent style. Which Torquato Tasso confirms, in his book *On the Heroic Poem*, for he says that one can compose an Epic Poem even from amorous material.)[50]

Nothing in the *Soledades* identifies the protagonist as a prince, although as an exile from court, he could accurately be labeled an aristocrat. Díaz de Rivas is certainly right, however, that even though the poems have a pastoral setting, reminders of another world of princes and palaces, wars and voyages of discovery—material perhaps best conveyed in a heroic style—persistently invade the bucolic space.

The most revealing aspect of the passage is Díaz de Rivas's recourse to Tasso to support generic reclassification of the *Soledades*. Two elements of Tasso's modern theory of the epic aid the critic in promoting an image of Góngora as a composer of heroic verse: the notion of variety within unity and the idea that the epic and the romance are essentially the same genre. In this new critical context, agreement with Díaz de Rivas and enthusiasm for the *Polifemo* and the *Soledades* become largely a matter of personal taste, an issue of whether one clings rigidly to classical precepts or willingly embraces the recent reshaping of canonical genres:

> [E]n estas *Soledades*, si miramos al modo de decir, se ha de reducir al sublime; si a la materia, a aquel género de Poema de que constaría la *Historia ethiópica* de Heliodoro si se redujera a versos. Y siendo el estilo sublime, con todo eso, con decoro se acomoda el Poeta a las materias que trata con suma variedad.
>
> ([I]n these *Soledades*, if we examine the manner of speaking, it is equivalent to the sublime; if [we examine] the subject matter, [it is equivalent] to that [of the]

genre of Poem of which Heliodorus's *Ethiopica* would be composed if it were converted into verse. And even though [the poems] are in the sublime style, with all that that implies, the Poet properly accommodates the materials with the greatest variety.)

According to Díaz de Rivas, the unifying plot of the shipwrecked pilgrim's experiences subsumes the seemingly digressive episodes and scenes in the poems as well as the diverse characters the protagonist encounters. Moreover, he compares the *Soledades* to the *Ethiopica*, the prototypical romance (an epic in prose), thereby ennobling Góngora's masterpiece. The critic dispels the poet's reputation as a frivolous dilettante by portraying him as a poetic virtuoso who can skillfully adapt the style of his verse to each and every one of the *Soledades'* ever changing subjects. He also praises the master craftsman for his ability to inspire the audience with wonder: "siempre va causando nueva admiración" (he is always causing new amazement).[51]

Although the conflict's scale as well as its remarkable documentary record are perhaps unique, the great Góngora war embodies and perpetuates the humanist tradition of *serio ludere*. The serious games of the humanists were intellectual exercises intended both to entertain and to astonish. Diversions involving the decipherment of allegorical emblems and devices, and metaphor-laden poetry such as Góngora's, distracted and liberated game players from the mutable minutiae of the workaday world. By focusing their cerebral powers on the mental puzzle at hand, players ascended to the realm of immutable truths. Practitioners of *serio ludere* held that jokes and ludicrous tales often conceal divine secrets. Those who wished to reach those hidden gems of wisdom transformed themselves into comic competitors who engaged in reasoned, rhetorical debate over the material or issue in question. Combatants believed that playful argumentation would eventually unearth the treasure buried in the ludic jungle.[52]

Perhaps nowhere were the spirit and substance of *serio ludere* so zealously enacted as in the literary academies of sixteenth- and seventeenth-century Europe. The prototype of these organizations was the Florentine Academy established in 1442 by Cosimo de' Medici, and inspired by a classical model, Plato's Academy. Early Renaissance academies sought to revitalize the Greco-Roman tradition by engaging in an ongoing intellectual dialogue with the writers of classical antiquity, a colloquy that bridged a temporal gap of at least two thousand years. The central figure of the Florentine scholars, Marsilio Ficino, undertook the task of reconciling Neoplatonic thought with Christian ideology. The emphasis on synthesis, part of the Platonic rhetorical heritage, was characteristic of the Florentine group. For instance, Ficino's fellow academician Pico della Mirandola sought to meld all knowledge into one unified and unifying system of thought—the pansophic ideal. Such vast syncretic projects have subsequently become synonymous with the concept of humanism. Academicians also cultivated a distinctive rhetorical style of disputational dialectics, a method that grew out of the belief that rational dialogue and debate would lead the individual to a higher realm of understanding and closer proximity to Truth. The academy stressed knowledge and use of classical languages and study of obscure discourse, a medium valued for its suggestive, symbolic nature. The esteem with which cryptic, enigmatic language and symbols were held enabled academicians to merge what might otherwise have seemed totally incompatible systems of thought. Whereas Ficino assigned to Christianity the supreme position and claim to Truth of all the world's religions, he maintained as well that every religion contained Truth concealed in hermetic language. The genuine philosopher and believer exercised a divine game of *serio ludere* to uncover the essential Truth simultaneously masked and revealed by apparently undecipherable linguistic media linked and made one by the slippery and difficult tenor common to their widely divergent signifiers. From the beginning, the academy recognized that religion and poetry shared the same form of expression and the same power to emanate Truth. In accordance with Platonic tradition tying poetry with philosophy and religion, the Florentine scholars reserved for the emblematic art form the most exalted place among the arts that arose from contemplation and the spiritual touch of a divine muse. Poetry enjoyed favored status among academicians as a subject of inquiry, commentary, and debate.[53]

Academies patterned after the Florentine prototype appeared in courts throughout Italy in succeeding years. By the middle of the sixteenth century, however, a discernible shift had occurred in the organization and interests of these groups. Early academies consisted of informal, loosely structured gatherings of scholars bound together by a common vision fusing classical and Christian knowledge. With the passage of time, however, academician experts on mythology and symbolism grew ever more preoccupied with vernacular languages and literatures, with philological studies and rhetorical style, and with the planning of court entertainment. Meetings assumed a clublike air of formality, and discussions that had formerly focused on Platonic poetic theology acquired a normative bent.[54]

The Courtier provides a vivid portrait of the court academies' transition toward a more nationalistic, judgmental gathering of the elite. On four successive nights, the best and the brightest meet at the Court of Urbino in an informal salon academy to formulate a paradigm of courtly behavior and of the perfect courtier. Ensconced at the ducal palace, the participants in this apparently impromptu academy engage in witty conversation that epitomizes the praxis of *serio ludere*. The duchess of Urbino, Elisabetta Gonzaga, ostensibly presides over the evening festivities and designates a leader for the discussions. On the first evening, she wears an impresa, the letter *S,* that arouses curiosity, inspires commentary, and sets the stage for the intellectual games to come. Aretino recognizes the ludic potential of the emblem:

> "[D]ato che per sapere la verità io non sono autorizzato a usare tenaglie incandescenti e catene etratti di fune e tutte quelle belle torture che vorrei, desidero scoprirla con un gioco, e il gioco è questo: ognuno dovrà dire che cosa significa secondo lui quella 'S' che la duchessa porta scritta sul pendente che le adorna la fronte."
>
> ("[S]ince I am not allowed, as I would wish, to make use of chains, rope or fire to learn the truth about a certain thing, I would like to find it out through a game which is as follows: namely, that each one of us should say what he believes is the meaning of the letter 'S' that the Duchess is wearing on her forehead.")

He views the quest for the truth about the mysterious symbol as a competition among worthy players. Pursuing the ludic objective, Aretino then recites a sonnet he has spontaneously composed in which he interprets the perplexing device. He employs poetry as a heuristic instrument in search of truth, revealing his faith in the power of poetry to unravel enigmas and encapsulate essential truths. Although Aretino's audience receives the sonnet enthusiastically, admiration for his artistry displaces interest in his interpretation of the emblem. Such a pattern of deflection away from content and onto style would characterize the reception of Góngora's work for centuries. Nevertheless, the other members of Castiglione's salon academy display faith in language and reasoned debate similar to that of Aretino as the ludic activities proceed. At one point, Count Lodovico da Canossa states: "'Con tutto ciò, credo che in ogni cosa una perfezione ci dev'essere, anche se è così ben nascosta che non si vede; e chi conosce bene la materia deve poterla tirar fuori a forza di logica'" ("I do think there is a perfection for everything, even though it may be concealed, and I also think that this perfection can be determined through informed and reasoned argument").[55] Rational discourse and debate, the disputational dynamics of *serio ludere,* enable participants to separate the wheat from the chaff, surface appearance from the essence and the Idea.

In the course of their four-day sojourn in pursuit of a definition of the perfect courtier, the momentary academicians traverse varied rhetorical terrain. The tone of the interlocutors ranges from mirth to nostalgia, anger to idealism, and it is impossible to tell which speakers assume a sincere posture and which adopt a dramatic pose simply for the sake of argument and style. The lofty search for the ideal aristocrat often translates into the creation of a normative code of conduct and a checklist of the prerequisites and perquisites of privilege. The courtier must be of noble birth and exhibit grace in every action. He must exercise care in the choice of friends, show courage in adversity, and express love in a circumspect manner. The prescriptives extend to matters of linguistic style, and here emerge some of the same rules with which critics would later assail Góngora. All the interlocutors show signs of nascent "nationalism" in their praise of the unique genius of the Tuscan tongue and in their admiration for the contributions of Petrarch, Boccaccio, and Dante to its perfection. They urge writers and orators to imitate these *auctores* and continue the cultivation of Tuscan as a medium of expression. Count Lodovico admonishes the courtier not to add archaic words to the lexicon. He permits the introduction of foreign words and neologisms in discourse, but only sparingly and judiciously. The writer and orator should strive for elegance and lucidity in style, and although clarity does not preclude ornamentation, confusion and ambiguity should be avoided. According to the count, linguistic obscurity reveals moral weakness, the vanity and affection of the speaker and writer, just as a mask of makeup robs a woman of her natural beauty and indicates shallow character.[56]

The epoch of Spanish salon academies founded in imitation of Italian models roughly coincides with the period of Golden Age literature. Spanish academies reached their apogee as an integral part of court culture at the end of the sixteenth century and the beginning of the seventeenth, the high point of Góngora's artistic career. The numerous and heterogeneous Iberian groups inherited and continued the tradition of *serio ludere* and of normative, nationalistic discourse organized in formal or informal debate and realized in an atmosphere of quasi-playful combativeness typical of their Italian counterparts. Some coteries gathered on a regular basis at the same place under the tutelage of a noble patron who might abdicate creative responsibility for the session to a stellar literary figure. Members of these academies often received assignments to compose an original work or to prepare a subject concerning genre, style, or other topical aesthetic matters for discussion at a meeting. At times, the academicians capped off the evening's entertainment with the more-or-less spontaneous performance of a play in which the members assumed a role and produced their own extemporaneous dialogue. Not all Spanish academies adhered to this design, however, as some met only once for a special occasion and then disbanded. The academies' inherently dramatic flair extended to the point that members habitually adopted pseudonyms for their meetings, like actors who don a mask before going onstage. In certain cases, the nominal disguise is transparent, but in others, the roll book remains undecipherable, an intriguing quandary that leaves modern critics bewildered. Theatrical contentiousness pervaded the sessions of the literati. The concentration of talent and egos at assemblies contrived to generate bitter rivalries that frequently destroyed the organizations and expanded into even greater public displays of animosity. In addition to the debates and quarrels, the *vejamen,* a satirical poem or composition directed at one's adversary, was a staple of the academies, and provided ample opportunities for participants to sharpen their vituperative skills. The hothouse environment of invective doubtlessly fostered, if it did not spawn, a number of the most famous literary battles of the day, such as the war between Góngora and Lope.[57]

Many academicians, Góngora among them, participated in the *certámenes,* poetic jousts customarily sponsored by the Church or municipalities or both to celebrate a religious festival, to honor a historical occasion, or to commemorate a significant moment in the life of the royal family. The *certámenes* shared with the academies the spirit of *serio ludere,* but the festive competitions were public spectacles geared to a wider audience that encompassed the uneducated, unrefined masses. María Cristina Quintero characterizes the *certamen* as a lavish event designed to appeal to the spectators' senses:

> There was great emphasis on adornment, with even the clothes worn by the participants meriting detailed descriptions in the *relaciones* or accounts of these events that have survived. Interestingly, the visual dimension of the jousts increasingly acquired importance through pictorial representations in emblems, *jeroglíficos,* paintings, and tapestries. Such visual elements were complemented through the use of music, further underscoring the theatricality of the event. At the center of this activity was the competition among poets, who would publicly recite verses composed specifically for the occasion. Poets would then be judged and awarded prizes. Poetry became, therefore, an important verbal complement to the visual feast.

The honor, prestige, and authority bestowed on prizewinners offered strong incentive for men of letters to enter the games, but the prospect of gaining admiration from a new public held powerful appeal as well. In describing the academies and *certámenes,* Quintero has emphasized the inherent theatricality of their transformation of poetry into a subject of dramatic representation. As she points out in *Poetry as Play,* reading poetry in these ludic contexts became a theatrical performance with aural and visual dimensions that paved the way for the incorporation of various types of verse into the *comedia.* Recognizing the dramatic potential of the academies, writers made fictional replicas of the organizations part of their own creative efforts. One can experience the fruits of their artistic engagement with the academies in works such as Tirso de Molina's *La fingida Arcadia* (1621), Lope's *La Dorotea* (1632), and Gracián's *Criticón* (1657).[58]

Góngora participated actively in the most prominent literary organizations of Madrid. His name appears along with Lope, Quevedo, Cervantes, and others on the list of illustrious men of letters who frequented the salon of the count of Saldaña, the second son of the duke of Lerma. The Saldaña Academy, which enjoyed a reputation for brilliance and volatility, underwent two incarnations; the first began circa 1605 and the second and more short-lived circa 1611. The following excerpt from a letter written by Lope, dated March 2, 1612, gives some indication of the explosive, quarrelsome, yet amusing ambiance of the Saldaña gatherings: "Las academias están furiosas; en la pasada se tiraron los bonetes dos licenciados; yo ley unos versos con unos antojos de Zervantes que pareçian guevos estrellados mal echos" (The academy meetings are in a furor; in the last one, two university graduates threw their hats at each other; I read some verses with Cervantes's spectacles that looked like misshapen, smashed eggs). Góngora also belonged to the most famous of the salons, the Academy of Madrid, a group that originated in 1607 and lasted until the mid-1600s with several changes in patronage and gathering places during that period of time. The organization maintained a high profile in the cultural life of the capital for at least a quarter of a century. Lope de Vega, the star of the Academy of Madrid, reportedly presented his *Arte nuevo de hacer comedias* (The new art of writing plays) prior to the treatise's publication in 1609 at a meeting held in late 1607 or early 1608. The academy sponsored *certámenes*, and played a major role in planning and executing the city's artistic and religious festivals, such as the 1620 gala celebration of San Isidro. King Philip IV, an avid patron of the arts, honored the academy with a visit in 1622, an act that raised the group's prestige to new heights. A roster of the academy under the leadership of Sebastián Francisco de Medrano between 1617 and 1622 resembles a "Who's Who" in Spanish letters of the Golden Age. Góngora shared membership in the Medrano circle with Quevedo, Lope, Guillén de Castro, Vélez de Guevara, Tirso de Molina, Pérez de Montalbán, Calderón de la Barca, and José Pellicer (Góngora's defender and commentator), among other literati. The poet has been associated with yet another literary group in Madrid, the Academia Selvaje (also known as El Parnaso), first convoked in 1612 by Francisco de Silva, the duke of Pastrana's brother. The academy disbanded in 1614, when don Francisco left to fight in the wars of Lombardy, where he died in 1615. Pedro Soto de Rojas's discourse on poetry, delivered at the inaugural assembly of the salon, and verses composed later in praise of the gatherings, attests to the existence of the academy, but the absence of a roll book makes it impossible to identify positively as a member anyone other than Soto de Rojas and the patron himself. Nevertheless, Luis Fernández-Guerra asserted in his 1871 biography of the Golden Age playwright Juan Ruiz de Alarcón y Mendoza that the *Polifemo* and the *Soledades* debuted before an audience in readings by Góngora at the Academia Selvaje.[59] Lacking sufficient evidence to corroborate this assertion, I can neither confirm nor deny its validity, but I can safely say that Góngora, with his marked proclivity for wordplay, would have appreciated the wit in presenting the *Soledades*, written in the verse form of the *silva*, to Francisco de *Silva* at the Academia *Selvaje*.

Golden Age Spain's academania and the tradition of *serio ludere* that the academies and *certámenes* illustrated and fomented account to a large degree for the furor over the *Polifemo* and the *Soledades*, and the form and substance of the great Góngora debate. In the critical forum of the salons, Góngora and his contemporaries discussed the latest artistic issues, defined and refined their own aesthetic positions, and developed their rhetorical skills. Members expressed viewpoints, addressed opponents directly, and responded to attacks on their ideas, style, and work. They exercised sarcastic, satiric language in the *vejamen*, and, at the other end of the spectrum, employed pedantic discourse punctuated with classical references in rational argument. The assemblies were an arena in which competitive literati worked and played at reshaping the canon and aesthetic taste. The contentious, confrontational, and dramatic nature of the meetings lent the academies the ludic, theatrical quality that in turn provided the impetus for the Góngora dispute. Just as academicians' experience with polemics cast discussion over the *Polifemo* and the *Soledades* in the shape of acrimonious verbal combat characterized by extreme polarization of ideas, so too their exposure to cutting-edge aesthetic matters supplied the thematic bases for rhetorical argument about the poems.

The academies served a creative as well as a critical purpose. In these sophisticated artist workshops, members unveiled new projects to an audience of peers, who in turn offered advice, support, or condemnation. In this way, the assemblies spurred experimentation and creative interaction within the coterie of writers. One can assume that the circulated manuscripts of the *Polifemo* and the *Soledades*, as Góngora's principal achievements in the *estilo culto*, were also his principal weapons in advancing the cause of *gongorismo*, and created debate within the venue of the salons, which subsequently disseminated the new style and fanned the flames of controversy over the future of the canon.

The issues of poetic morality, language, and genres raised by the Góngora debate and the rhetoric employed by the poet's supporters and detractors alike typified the polemics and critical skirmishes that had emerged in Italy during the sixteenth century, an epoch identified as the age of criticism. Bernard Weinberg, in summarizing literary theory in sixteenth-century Italy, emphasizes the enormous range and variety of styles that critical issues and opinions assume in documents of the era:

> One finds, in this multiplicity of documents, every shade of critical thought, from the extreme literary left (the militant "moderns") to the extreme literary right (the reactionary "ancients" and the Tridentine Catholics). The highly philosophical argument is tempered by the highly personal quip, the pleasant dialogue is found in juxtaposition with the fulsome academic discourse. One finds as well the full scale of critical problems, starting with the most fundamental inquiries concerning the nature of poetry, progressing through the detailed examination of all the genres, ending with debates on diction and orthography.

These critical discussions have had lasting, widespread influence, as Baxter Hathaway notes:

> The literary theorizing done during the great burst of aesthetic speculation in sixteenth-century Italy, and to a far lesser extent in sixteenth-century France and England, bears a parental relation of both father and mother to all theorizing done since then. Either sixteenth-century theorizing contained oppositions often unresolved until later centuries, or the precarious mating of ideas which occurred then contained genes that did not become evident until later generations.[60]

The battle over the *Polifemo* and the *Soledades* was symptomatic of a period of immense unrest and upheaval in literary history, and it was one manifestation of the critical wars raging throughout Europe at the time. In Spain, just as Cervantes and Lope precipitated major shifts in prose and drama, respectively, so too did Góngora act as a catalyst in refashioning the poetic canon.

In keeping with the major disputes of the age, the Góngora war played out as yet another quarrel between the ancients and the moderns. Valencia accused the poet of copying the modern, Italianate style: "[L]o intrincado y trastocado y extraño es supositicio y ajeno, imitado con mala afectación de los italianos y de ingenios a lo moderno" ([T]he intricate and transposed and strange is spurious and foreign, imitated with bad affectation from the Italians and the minds in the modern style). Góngora had unwisely elected the wrong models to imitate, and, for Valencia, the wrong models were synonymous with modern poets. He urged his friend to shut himself off from their pernicious influence, "no ver ni oír a los modernos y afectados [poetas]" (not to see or hear the modern and affected [poets]), encouraging him instead to turn to masters of classical antiquity such as Sophocles, Pindar, Homer, Virgil, and Horace as the ideal models for imitation and to prophets such as David, Isaiah, and Jeremiah for spiritual inspiration.

Góngora's enemies found him guilty of cultivating novelty for novelty's sake, a crime consonant with vanity and with intellectual and aesthetic vacuity. Lope deemed the new *culto* embellishments distracting and superfluous: "[Y]o hallo esta novedad como la liga que se echa al oro que le dilata, y aumenta, pero con menos valor, pues quita de la sentencia lo que añade de dificultad" (I find this novelty like an alloy added to gold that enlarges and increases it, but with less value, since it removes from the sententia what it adds in difficulty). Jáuregui reminded Góngora that stylistic innovation could be considered a virtue under only certain circumstances: "Es menester advertir que la novedad en tanto es loable, en cuanto es grata y apacible al gusto de muchos o a los mejores" (It is necessary to note that novelty is laudable insofar as it is pleasant and pleasing to the taste of many or of the best). Jáuregui, of course, counted himself among "the best," and he did not by any means find the *estilo culto* "pleasing." He targeted the new and unique *(novedad)* for attack in response to Díaz de Rivas's defense of Góngora, which turned upon the axis of modernity. According to the poet's champion, the impression of stylistic "newness" created by the *Polifemo* and the *Soledades* engendered "new" controversy over poetic practices:

> Suele la novedad causar nuevos pareceres y contradiciones. El estilo del señor Don Luis de Góngora en estas últimas obras (aunque es conforme al ejemplo de los Poetas antiguos y a sus reglas) ha parecido nuevo en nuestra edad, no usada a la magnificencia y heroicidad que pide la poesía.
>
> (It is customary for novelty to cause new opinions and disagreements. The style of Mr. Luis de Góngora in these latest works [although it conforms with the example of the Poets of antiquity and their rules] seemed new in our age, not used to the magnificence and heroic style that poetry requires.)

This initial, general statement on novelty does not advocate for the superiority of the new over the traditional and canonical, nor does it identify the *Polifemo* or the *Soledades* as innovation incarnate. Díaz de Rivas explains that although Góngora's poems are not "new" in the sense of unique and unprecedented, they seem "new" in the context of current norms, taste, and expectations. He subverts the tentative, qualified association of the poet's works with modernity and identifies the judgmental criterion of novelty with the readers' lack of familiarity with classical heroic style. In other words, the illusion of Góngora's novelty and breaking of the canon arises from the ignorance of his critics and their acts of poetic misprision:

> [P]or no estar versados en la lección de los Poetas antiguos ni entender sus frasis tan llenas de tropos y tan remotas de el lenguaje vulgar, . . . condenan a ojos cerrados la obra de el *Polifemo* y *Soledades*.

([S]ince they are not versed in reading the Poets of antiquity nor in understanding their styles of expression so full of tropes and so remote from common language, . . . they condemn the works the *Polifemo* and *Soledades* with their eyes closed.)

Díaz de Rivas finds the critics of modernity and their standards of evaluation no match for Góngora, who merits a place among the classical *auctores*. Yet, in modern fashion, he admits that taste is a matter not of consensus and norms, but rather of individual preference: "[C]ada uno, según su ingenio, gusta de diferente estilo" ([E]ach person, according to his genius, enjoys a different style). Such subversion and backtracking blur the distinction between old and new, poets of antiquity and poets in the modern style, and the notion of quarrels between the ancients and the moderns.[61]

Analysis of the preceding passages by Díaz de Rivas and others reveals a strong sense of history in their need to assign Góngora a fixed historical locus in or out of the canon. Yet, whereas they all begin their arguments from polarized positions in which the ancients and moderns stand on opposite sides of the fence, in the development of their opinions the barricade collapses, and old and new, antiquity and modernity, become hopelessly muddled. As a literary concept, "newness" enjoys an impressively long history as an inherent component of the creative consciousness. José Antonio Maravall observes: "Aproximadamente, desde la época de Ovidio, el gusto por la novedad puede decirse que se hace común a la mayor parte de los escritores" (Approximately, since the epoch of Ovid, one can say that the taste for novelty becomes common for the majority of writers). Golden Age Spain shared a marked preference for *novedad* with much of sixteenth-century Europe, but for Góngora and his contemporaries, stylistic novelty signified the imitation and integration of varied models drawn from the ancient and modern worlds. In fact, an eclectic mix of continuity and change in literary texts was commonplace in Renaissance aesthetics. Like most writers of his time, Góngora maintained an active and imaginative dialogue with the great authors of antiquity, modifying styles and models from the classical canon to forge new masterpieces that effectively bridged the gap between the old and the new. The poet's transformation of the love story of Acis and Galatea as related by Ovid offers a case in point. Elaborate conceits, an ironic narrative voice, and extensive development of the Acis-Galatea-Polyphemus love triangle alter the tale dramatically and poetically in Góngora's *Polifemo,* renewing the classical model.[62]

At the beginning of the twenty-first century, we readers of Góngora should remember that the poet speaks through his verses with a double voice: that of the innovator and that of the atavist. Some critics, in their haste to appropriate *gongorismo* as a radical break with conventional forms of poetic language that anticipates the current preference for self-referential, autonomous, nonmimetic literary discourse of perpetually deferred meaning, have overlooked or seriously downplayed Góngora's deliberate imitation of the great authors and works of classical antiquity, his critical engagement with his social and intellectual milieu, and his profoundly ambivalent attitude toward *novedad* and modernity. In turning a deaf ear to the more conservative aspects of Gongorine style and perversely attempting to mold the poet into a protopostmodernist, they have missed the fact that the rebel who wanted to refashion the Castilian tongue chose classical Latin as the model for his revolution and viewed himself as a preserver and continuer of classical tradition. Conversely, Dámaso Alonso pays tribute to the conservative component in Góngora's artistry when he describes nature in the *Soledades* as the "último resultado de la evolución que arranca del bucolismo grecolatino y resurge y se completa en el Renacimiento italiano" (final result of the evolution that goes back to Greco-Roman pastoralism and springs up again and is completed in the Italian Renaissance). He also describes Góngora as "el último término de una poética: resume y acaba; no principia" (the final conclusion of a poetics: he summarizes and ends; he does not begin).[63] To fully appreciate Góngora's reshaping of the canon, we must listen to the voices of both imitator and innovator, experimenter and recidivist.

A Tantalizing Clue

A shift in the canon had clearly begun prior to the advent of the *Polifemo* and the *Soledades* at court. Although the posthumous laudation of Garcilaso established a precedent for poetic canonization, and the appearance of the aesthetics of enigma and of *culto* tendencies in Góngora's early poetry anticipated the emergence of the *culto* style, Herrera's 1580 *Anotaciones* and his own verse helped set the stage for *gongorismo*. The *Anotaciones* laid a doctrinal, normative foundation for many of Góngora's innovations by representing Garcilaso's oeuvre as learned poetry and by celebrating the ornamental rhetoric of the poet laureate's style. Herrera praised Garcilaso's use of neologisms, his imitation and integration of a variety of literary models, and his exploitation of hyperbata—the dreaded *transposiciones* or *trasapasamientos* of Góngora's critics—for aesthetic effect. Herrera's literary preferences bear witness to a shift in aesthetic taste marked by heightened interest in complexity and theatricality that occurred in the second half of the sixteenth century in Spain.[64]

Performative codes embedded in the *romanceros* (collections of ballads) and the dramatic emotional quotient of Petrarchan conventions in the lyric created a desire for highly self-conscious, theatrical poetry that would incorporate movement, speaker-audience dynamics, and strong sensory appeal into the text. So widespread were these changes in the horizon of expectations that they cut across the limits of social classes and the boundaries of discursive types. Even the rhetoric of pulpit oratory registered their impact, leading some clergymen to protest the flowery phrases and exaggerated, thespian gestures employed by certain preachers to maintain the congregation's interest in the sermon. In a 1589 treatise on oratory eloquence, Juan Bonifacio, a disgruntled Jesuit priest, expressed exasperation with such tactics:

> Es vergonzoso que ande un predicador en busca de florecillas y ponga en eso todo su cuidado, y no como los antiguos, que medían el valor de un discurso por el peso y magnitud de las cosas y de las sentencias, y no por el sonsonete de unas cuantas fracesillas sin sustancia. Todo el mundo debe mirar con el más profundo desprecio esa falsa elocuencia que se presenta, como ramera, con la cara pintada para disimular la falta de pudor y de vergüenza y tal vez de sangre y de salud. La verdadera elocuencia no necesita postizos ni coloretes; le bastan sus colores naturales y la hermosura que le da su propia robustez y la riqueza y la pureza de su sangre.

> (It is shameful for a preacher to go around looking for pretty trifles and to put all his effort into that, unlike the ancients, who measured the worth of a speech by the weight and magnitude of the topics and thoughts, and not by the singsong of some little phrases without substance. Everyone should look with the most profound scorn at that false eloquence that presents itself, like a harlot, with a painted face to hide a lack of modesty and shame and perhaps [good] blood and health. True eloquence does not need false accoutrements or colored make-up; its natural colors and the beauty given it by its own robustness and the richness and purity of its blood are sufficient.)[65]

More than twenty years before the *Polifemo* and the *Soledades*, Bonifacio voices the standard arguments advanced by Góngora's detractors. Like later defenders of the *estilo llano*, he strives to assume the moral high ground in stemming the burgeoning tide of taste for dramatic, ornamental discourse. His words ring with the same harsh tones of moral outrage and condemnation that prevail in the Góngora debate. As in Jáuregui's *Antídoto*, this critic uses disparaging remarks to convey disdain for his adversaries. He aligns himself with the plainspeaking ancients, who valued decorum and linguistic precision, a posture adopted by Góngora's opponents. Like the anti-*cultistas*, Bonifacio conjures the image of the painted harlot to convey his belief that the new emphasis on obscure words and unusual turns of phrase caters to the frivolous, vain aspects of human nature. He fears displacement of the audience's attention from the themes addressed to the artistic frills of ornamentation, a concern eventually justified by the *culto* metamorphosis of language into a bravura performer in its own right that neatly stole the show from underlying thoughts and ideas.

Although Góngora left the questions that swirl around his masterpieces unanswered, he did leave one tantalizing clue that over the years has proved as hard to unravel as any of his puzzling poems. In September 1615, Góngora wrote the now famous *Carta en respuesta* (Letter in response) to the anonymous barbed missive presumably penned by Lope de Vega earlier that month. The letter remains perhaps the most frequently cited document in the quest for a critical consensus on the meaning of *culteranismo*, but so far the poet's words have resisted analysis and denied readers a firm basis for understanding Gongorine poetics.[66]

The letter begins with a sarcastic counterattack on the numerous accusations Lope hurled in the poet's direction. Góngora disingenuously laments having to address an anonymous correspondent, indirectly chastising Lope for his cowardice and unjust conduct: "[A]sí me es fuerza el responder sin saber a quién; mas esta mi respuesta, como antes mis versos, hecho sin rebeldía" ([S]o I must respond without knowing to whom; but this response of mine, like my verses beforehand, [is] done without rebelliousness). Góngora rejects the identity foisted on him of a vain, adolescent rebel battling authority to achieve notoriety, the reputation of a puerile seeker of fame. At the same time, he defends his verse from the label of heresy and denies anyone the right to banish him and his art from the mainstream of aristocratic culture. With these controlled preliminaries completed, he then takes off his gloves and starts swinging:

> Y agradezca que, por venir su carta con la capa de aviso y amistad, no corto la pluma en estilo satírico, que yo le escarmentara semejantes osadías, y creo que en él fuera tan claro como le he parecido obscuro en el lírico.
>
> (And be happy that, since your letter came cloaked in warning and friendship, I do not cut my quill in a satirical style, so that I might teach you a lesson for such audacities, and I believe I would be as clear in that as I have seemed obscure to you in the lyrical [style].)

With the phrase *con la capa* (cloaked), Góngora informs Lope that he knows that the apparent avowal of friendship actually reveals poorly disguised animosity. Furthermore, the tongue-lashing Lope is about to receive pales by comparison with the punishment the poet could mete out if he set himself to the task. Yet, for all of Góngora's bravado, his reference to the charge of obscurantism shows that Lope has wounded his ego and his sense of aesthetic accomplishment. He quickly recovers his pride and superiority by reducing his adversary to the level of a mediocre schoolboy whose disjunct, disorganized, nonsensical sentences; missing articles; and omitted copulative conjunctions betray a dull wit and poor education. Góngora can conclude only that this badly written note is worse than a "carta de vizcaíno" (letter of a Biscayan), that is, worse than the prose of a boorish, illiterate lout. The poet states with a sneer: *"Nemo dat plus quam habet"* (No one gives more than what he has). The injured author then moves on to the proffered advice that he abandon the *culto* style before he infects younger poets with this linguistic disease, a clear allusion to Plato's exile of the poets from the Republic for their potential threat as corruptors of youth. Góngora angrily responds that it is an honor to have imitators: "[M]e holgara de haber dado principio a algo; pues es mayor gloria empezar una acción que consumarla" (I would be glad to have originated something; since it is a greater glory to begin an action than to complete it).[67] The poet may repudiate the title of rebel, but he relishes the role of innovator and originator. As he subsequently explains, however, the new style does not preclude the influence of the ancient *auctores* and can trace its foundation back to the classical world. The linking of "glory" and "action" with composition lends the poet and his work an epic, golden aura and illustrates that Góngora considers himself and other artists heroes. After achieving this lofty height in tone, he plummets to earth with a blunt warning that he will greet other letters of the same ilk with less restraint and a sharper pen.

At this point, Góngora seems to shake off the gremlin within who delivers angry retorts and seeks vengeance for suffered insults. He exchanges a tone of hostility for one of cerebral meditation, as if he has exorcised or momentarily dismissed his personal furor. The tonal shift accompanies a thematic movement in which the poet addresses what he perceives as the central, and perhaps only, substantive issues presented in the anonymous letter. The missive in question ends with a reminder of the qualities that constitute a good, moral work of art: "[L]as invenciones en tanto son buenas en cuanto tienen de útil, honroso y delectable lo necesario para quedar constituídas en razón del bien" ([C]reations are good to the degree in which they have the necessary amount of usefulness, honor, and pleasure so as to be based on the principle of goodness). Góngora focuses on this statement for the remainder of his letter and, in clever, reasoned argument, contests the assertion that he lacks the qualities of goodness listed by his rival. He formulates a rhetorical question in regards to the issue of utility: "¿Han sido útiles al mundo las poesías y aún las profecías (que *vates* se llama el profeta como el poeta)?" (Have poems and prophecies been useful to the world [the prophet is called *vates* as well as the poet]?). Invoking the *vates*, the poet-prophet of classical antiquity, Góngora identifies himself with the ancient soothsayers blessed with demiurgic visionary and creative powers. He reclaims for poets in general and himself in particular a special niche reserved for an intellectual, spiritual, and aesthetic aristocracy who, as Ficino (echoing Plato) would have it, creates when possessed by a divine frenzy. Góngora finds self-evident and universal the usefulness of poems and prophecies.[68]

Although he displays nationalism later in the letter, he clearly believes that the import and legacy of his poetry extend far beyond the boundaries of Imperial Spain and the historical moment. He defends his deliberate cultivation of obscurantism on instructional grounds, specifying education as the primary fruit of poetry. Góngora does want to fortify his position as the continuer of the philosophies and practices of Greek and Roman *auctores*, a desire that underscores the complexity of his chosen reputation as innovator. He cites Ovid's use of arcane, difficult language and style in the *Metamorphoses* as an authoritative, legitimating precedent for the *estilo culto* of his poetry:

> [Y] si la obscuridad y estilo intrincado de Ovidio . . . , da causa a que, vacilando el entendimiento en fuerza de discurso, trabajándole (pues crece con cualquier acto de valor), alcance lo que así en la lectura superficial de sus versos no pudo entender; luego hase de confesar que tiene utilidad avivar el ingenio, y eso nació de la obscuridad del poeta. Eso mismo hallará Vm. en mis *Soledades*, si tiene capacidad para quitar la corteza y descubrir lo misterioso que encubren.
>
> ([A]nd if the obscurity and intricate style of Ovid . . . causes thought to hesitate by virtue of the discourse, so that by working it [since it grows with any act of valor whatsoever] it attains what it failed to understand in a superficial reading of his verses; then one must confess that enlivening the mind has usefulness, and that was born of the poet's obscurity. You will find that same [experience] in my *Soledades*, if you have the ability to remove the shell and discover the mysteriousness that they conceal.)[69]

Góngora deftly turns the tables on his detractors by portraying his abstruse discourse as a virtue, because it forces readers to do multiple readings of the texts and sharpens their mental agility while they plumb the tangled linguistic surface for underlying meaning. The poet places enormous emphasis on reading and understanding as dynamic intellectual processes of inherent value. He congratulates Ovid and himself on exercising the audience's gray matter and performing a pedagogical service, but simultaneously he pays tribute to the ideal reader who will take on the hermeneutic challenge willingly. The poet depicts this cerebral paragon as an intellectual epic hero eager to commit "acts of valor" by "working" his powers of thought and understanding. Góngora envisions the ideal reader as an introspective Hercules, who gained immortality through superhuman labor. The image of brave, hesitant readers carefully concentrating as they pick their way through recondite verses and confusing conceits accurately captures the dynamics of reading the *Soledades*. Although the poet's insistence on the importance of the interpretive process seems to relegate the topics and ideas disclosed by such activity to secondary status, he does reassure the audience that his poetry is neither vacuous nor inconsequential. Góngora promises to reward his Herculean readers not with immortality but rather with the mysteries that lurk beneath the perplexing language of the poems.

Much of the critical commentary on this passage has focused on the final sentence. The "remove the shell" topos traditionally signifies the presence of allegory, which would make "mysteriousness" the kernel of meaning beneath the outward appearance of the verses.[70] However, I view this sentence as an indicator of how to approach and read the *Soledades*, and as an invitation-challenge to enter their bucolic landscape. The shell-kernel topos does not pertain solely to allegory, but embraces the hermeneutics of enigma and of *serio ludere* as well. Góngora indicates that the audience should regard his masterpiece as a gigantic puzzle composed of a series of riddles ready to be answered and emblems ripe for decipherment. The readers' desire to play the game and ability to adopt the strategy of reading-decoding provide the key to the poems' portal and the passport for crossing over into an imaginary land of beauty and mystery. When Góngora promises the audience that *lo misterioso* awaits at the end of the intellectual road to discovery, I do not believe he has something specific in mind. He simply offers admission to a pastoral *Wunderkammer*, a chamber of wonders situated in the readers' fancy, and assures them that the marvels on display merit time and effort. He baits a poetic hook to draw select readers into a magical space where they can stretch, entertain, and refresh their minds.

Góngora's defense of the honorable nature of the *Soledades* reveals both personal pride and nationalism: "[E]sta poesía; si entendida para los doctos, causarme ha autoridad, siendo lance forzoso venerar que nuestra lengua a costa de mi trabajo haya llegado a la perfección y alteza de la latina" ([T]his poetry[,] if understood to be for the erudite, must create authority for me, [it] being an occurrence to venerate perforce that our language has attained the perfection and sublimity of Latin at the cost of my work). The poet argues that he has honored himself and his native tongue by artfully fashioning Castilian into a language on a par with classical Latin. In a typically Gongorine example of back-to-the-future thinking, he states that he elevates and improves Castilian by drawing the language closer to its source through imitation. Góngora freely admits his own wish for fame, asserting that the latinization of Castilian will make him an "authority" among "the erudite," his intended audience and the only people who count. While he pats himself on the back, the poet cannot hide his disdain for those ignoramuses who cannot face the *Soledades*' linguistic morass: "[H]onra me ha causado hacerme oscuro a los ignorantes, que esa es la distinción de los hombres doctos, hablar de manera que a ellos les parezca griego; pues no se han de dar las piedras preciosas a animales de cerda" ([I]t has caused me honor to make myself obscure to the ignorant, since that is the distinction of learned men, to speak in such a way that it seems like Greek to them; since one should not cast pearls before swine).[71] Góngora takes pride in the exclusivity of his verses and the elimination match they occasion. He takes a retaliatory jab at his critics, whom he labels "swine," even as he places himself at the opposite, aristocratic end of the aesthetic spectrum. The mention of "Greek" reminds him of the Greek root of *poesía, poesis* (composition), which he cites with feigned artlessness shortly after the passage quoted above. The reference is not a gratuitous flaunting of personal knowledge, but rather it reinforces Góngora's identification of himself as a godlike creator, a maker and artificer who continues the tradition of the poet-prophet.

To defend the *Soledades* as a source of pleasure, the poet offers a riddle and reassurance in the form of a conundrum designed to test the reader's acuity:

> [S]i deleitar el entendimiento es darle razones que le concluyan y midan con su concepto, descubriendo lo que está debajo de esos tropos, por fuerza el entendimiento ha de quedar convencido, y convencido, satisfecho: demás que, como el fin de el entendimiento es hacer presa en verdades, que por eso no le satisface nada, si no es la primera verdad, conforme a aquella sentencia de San Agustín: *Inquietum est cor nostrum, donec requiescat in te,* en tanto quedará más deleitado cuanto, obligándole a la especulación por la obscuridad de la obra, fuera hallando debajo de las sombras de la obscuridad asimilaciones a su concepto.
>
> ([I]f entertaining the mind is to give it ideas that complete and measure it with their inventiveness, discovering what there is beneath those tropes by necessity the mind must be convinced, and convinced, satisfied: besides which, since the purpose of the mind is to seize truths, for that nothing satisfies it, if it is not the primary truth, in accordance with that sententia of Saint Augustine: *Restless is our heart, until it rests in thee,* in as much as it will be the more entertained, [if] by obliging it [the mind] to contemplate the obscurity of the work, it were to find beneath the shadows of obscurity resemblances to its inventiveness.)

A cursory examination of this passage reveals a tit-for-tat element in tone and style. Góngora literally rubs critics' noses in a signature sentence of cryptic, prolix discourse encumbered with dependent clauses, uncertain antecedents, and ambiguous meaning. Yet, even as he indulges in pointed, ironic self-parody, the poet skillfully articulates and propounds *serio ludere* in phrases that embody that very principle. He presents readers with a brainteaser that simultaneously illustrates and conceals, arouses curiosity and withholds satisfaction, communicates and remains silent—a paradoxical rule of Platonic pedagogy. Góngora's ideal audience must accept the roles of Tantalus as well as of Hercules. As he indicated earlier in the letter, the primary benefit and source of pleasure in the *Soledades* reside in the dynamic processes of reading and interpretation. Intellectual activity exercises and elevates the mind, or more accurately *entendimiento*, the rational faculty that serves humankind as the seat of thought, understanding, and creativity. Once again, Góngora stresses the dichotomy between surface appearance and underlying meaning, assuring the players of the game of poetry that something of significance can be found beneath the forest of tropes. To help readers puzzle out the enigma at hand and approach the *Soledades* informed and prepared, he offers up an unsubtle clue in the form of Saint Augustine's maxim. The saying functions on several levels as an analogue of the hermeneutic process. Augustine presents an image of man as a restless wanderer, exiled from God in life, who returns to his maker after death. However, in that same tradition, as man journeys through life, his mind perceives a lush field of imagery around him in Nature, discerns the presence of God, and in rare instances experiences moments of illumination in which he discovers unsuspected correspondences between the sentient world and the cosmos of Ideas.[72]

Like God, Góngora has created a universe of sensory experience, only the poet's is encoded in poetic discourse. Ideal readers will project themselves into the masterpiece through the exiled pilgrim protagonist, who represents both poet and audience. As they meander through the imaginary landscape, readers will suddenly experience moments of recognition and discovery when they grasp heretofore hidden truths. The intended audience of the *Soledades* metamorphoses into a group of restless wanderers, cerebral seekers of knowledge who voluntarily engage in active contemplation. Góngora indicates that in his masterpiece he has utilized language's power to symbolize a transcendent reality to its fullest potential, and the readers who struggle to unravel the enigmas, "the obscurity of the work," will elevate their minds to the highest possible degree. According to Ficino, even the restlessness of the mind has a positive value because it inspires man to search for a higher end, that is, it moves man toward God. As Ficino also stated, the mind needs images to stimulate the production of concepts, which leads to knowledge. In the *Soledades*, Góngora provides abundant stimuli in the form of conceits, intellectual catalysts that drive the mind inward and upward on an epistemological and spiritual quest. The system of correspondences to which the poet alludes when he writes of completing the mind and of finding resemblances outside to what lies inside the mind arises from the Christianization of Platonic anamnesis. As Socrates readies himself for death in the *Phaedo,* he explains to his friends that the essence of the soul is immutable and inseparable from the realm of Ideas. When the soul acquires a body in life, it retains Ideas but grows distracted and confused by the impressions of the mutable world, losing sight of its origins and forgetting that which it once knew. Yet, in times of reflection and meditation, the soul recollects its knowledge and immortality. Saint Augustine reconstitutes anamnesis as a philosophy of dynamic thought, "the movement by which the soul gathers, assembles and collects all the hidden knowledge it possesses and has not yet discovered, in order to be able to fix its gaze upon it."[73]

Closer to Góngora's epoch and following the model of Augustine, Ficino describes truth as a correspondence between the thing and the mind. Forms of things exist in the mind ab ovo, but are actualized when they meet their concrete counterparts in the world. What the poet wishes to achieve with *culto* discourse in the *Soledades* is to activate and facilitate the disclosure of inner-outer correspondences and to set in motion the transformative processes by which Ideas change from latent potentialities into essential, real truths. Góngora's verse mediates between the abstract and the concrete, and provides an intellectual corridor by means of which readers can tap into the innermost recesses of the mind, the part of the self closest to God. The text permits readers to complete themselves by integrating essential being with material substance. This integration in turn generates balance and harmony, which consequently increases pleasure. As Edgar Wind has phrased it: "'[T]ranscendence' is a source of 'balance' because it reveals the coincidence of opposites in the supreme One."[74]

Góngora has added greater depth and complexity to the riddle with oblique references to the Neoplatonic cycle of love. Often represented visually in the Renaissance by the figures of the three Graces, the Christianized version of the Platonic cycle originates with the writings of Saint Augustine, who outlined the pursuit of divine Truth as a tripartite progression from God to the mind and soul of man and back again to the celestial source. In the Augustinian model, observation of the corporeal world through the external senses leads the mind-soul to awareness of God's presence everywhere. The mind then redirects itself inwardly where the internal senses judge and read the gathered impressions. Finally, this contemplative state ends with illumination, in which the mind-soul witnesses Truth-God. In the works of Ficino, the model evolves into a trinitarian sequence of events: *emanatio*—procession or the overflowing of divine gifts; *raptio, conversio,* or *vivificatio*—rapture, conversion, or apprehension of the Supreme Being or Truth; and *remeatio*—return, movement back to God. The triadic circle translates human existence into a work of art shaped from on high. First, God showers humankind with blessings. Humans then utilize the eyes and ears of the mind to apprehend God in the world. In the end, death liberates the soul from the body and the soul returns to God. Poets and poetry, however, occupy a special place in Ficino's epistemological schema, for they enable man to experience spiritual transcendence, God, and Truth without moving from this world to the next, except within the confines of fantasy. The poet is a superhuman individual of immense knowledge and power who has exceptional ability to retire within, free the soul from the body, approach the domain of Truth, and return to share the discoveries made in contemplation with the rest of humankind. Inspired by God, he concretizes in poetry what he has seen and heard in an elevated state of rapture. His compositions speak directly to the mind of the reader-listener, who through the vehicle of poetry can transcend the limits of his own material existence to draw closer to the realm of God.[75] Góngora has taken this role of the poet as creative deity very much to heart in the *Soledades*. He provides the audience with Nature's bounty, artfully improved through linguistic magic *(emanatio)*, but it is up to the readers, stimulated by the verse's visual and auditory riches, to seize the truths made flesh, *hacer presa en verdades (raptio)*. As always, the Gongorine audience must accept full responsibility for completion of the hermeneutic circle *(remeatio)* in reconnecting with God by actualizing the potential Ideas hidden in the imagination, *"hallando . . . asimilaciones a su concepto."*

Having shown how the *Soledades* satisfy all of Lope's requirements for poetry with a solid moral foundation, Góngora concludes the game of *serio ludere* and once more dons the mask of a sorely abused victim. He testily reacts to those who have accused him of birthing Babelic verse: "[N]o van en más que una lengua las *Soledades*, aunque pudiera . . . hacer una miscelánea de griego, latín y toscano con mi lengua natural, y creo no fuera condenable" ([T]he *Soledades* are not in more than one language, although I could . . . make a medley of Greek, Latin and Tuscan with my native language, and I believe it would not be worthy of censure).[76] The poet leaves behind all rhetorical subtlety to remind his attackers of his superior intellect, education, and linguistic and aesthetic talent. He stresses the independence and near omnipotence of the artist, who ignores arbitrary, man-made rules and manipulates his medium as he sees fit. Góngora refuses any and all constraints imposed by self-proclaimed arbiters of morality and good taste. He informs his adversaries that if he had wanted to make a linguistic hodgepodge of the *Soledades*, he would have done so and in exemplary fashion with results beyond reproach. He does not exclude the possibility of undertaking such a task in the future.

Góngora carries the defiant stance apparent here to the end of the letter, where he takes a parting shot at his critics, "los émulos que tengo, granjeados más de entender yo sus obras y corregirlas que no de entender ellos las mías" (the emulators I have, [who have] gained more from my understanding their works and correcting them than their not understanding mine).[77] In a final gesture of self-aggrandizement, the poet applauds his own generosity in helping his numerous inferiors while chastising them for repaying him with undeserved cruelty. With a bold stroke, he dismisses his enemies as jealous rivals who have tried and failed to imitate him successfully, have sought and learned from his expert advice, and have proved too lazy or too stupid to appreciate his genius.

A discerning ear detects the assertive voice of the virtuoso in Góngora's petulant final rejection of his adversaries and their attacks on the *Soledades*. Condemnation follows closely on the heels of an eloquent, spirited, and highly conceptualized defense of the *estilo culto*—in essence, of his personal poetics. A discerning eye would also recognize in the poet who portrays himself and his art in the *Carta en respuesta* a kindred soul of the Italian Mannerists, who considered artists godlike entities and their works timeless, virtuoso performances.[78] As Góngora stated, the beauty and significance of his pastoral poems can be appreciated only by those who share his aesthetic ideals of stylized, sophisticated elegance and cultivated cerebralism. The reader who embraces these same values cannot possibly resist Góngora's invitation-challenge to enter the *Soledades*' green world of artifice and intellect.

2

A Passage to the Contemplative Life

> Meanwhile the mind, from pleasure less,
> Withdraws into its happiness;
> The Mind, that ocean where each kind
> Does straight its own resemblance find;
> Yet it creates, transcending these,
> Far other worlds and other seas,
> Annihilating all that's made
> To a green thought in a green shade.
>
> —Marvell, "The Garden"

Góngora's "Pastoral of Solitude"

With a supporting cast large enough for a Cecil B. DeMille extravaganza and elaborate stagecraft worthy of a Busby Berkeley musical, the *Soledades* seem an unlikely candidate for the label "pastoral of solitude." Yet, so Renato Poggioli rightly christened Góngora's masterpiece in *The Oaten Flute* (1975), noting that the poems represent the culmination of a trend in Renaissance pastoral identifiable in large part with Petrarchan influence. He characterized this generic shift as a progression toward melancholic, contemplative, subjective, and lyrical tonalities marked by Stoic and Epicurean elements that celebrate solitude as a source of freedom from destructive passions and as a space of wisdom, as well as of spiritual refreshment and recreation. Poggioli opined that in the *Soledades*, "pastoral solitude ceases to be a retreat from and becomes a triumph over the world."¹ In essence, Góngora displaces the sixteenth-century pastoral's central amatory focus and transforms the green landscape into an idealized fictional world that in an unsettling, paradoxical fashion contrasts with the urban, aristocratic milieu of the poet yet merges with contemporary city and court society in unexpected ways. Even as the *Soledades* spotlight the role and experience of the solitary reader, they also stress the disclosure of "[f]ar other worlds and other seas," the wonders of Nature shaped and mediated by the artistry of a network of Gongorine conceits.

How should readers approach this garden maze? How can they derive pleasure and meaning from a visit to Góngora's pastoral otherworld? Umberto Eco has defined fictional worlds as finite microcosms inhabited by entities with distinct properties governed by certain laws. Genres provide perhaps the most important information for analyzing fictional worlds, because their constitutive conventions set up relatively stable, predictable organizational rules and patterns that enable readers to navigate unfamiliar literary terrain. Whereas generic conventions encourage the audience to adopt certain values and expectations in approaching a text, such norms remain sufficiently flexible and open to change to keep fictional types from petrifying into sources of boredom and nonsignification. As I indicated in Chapter 1, however, the green world of the *Soledades* has defied ready generic identification from the beginning, supporting Rosalie Colie's assertion that the Renaissance system of genres was a fluid "place of convergence" in which varied forms and ideas mixed to produce new concepts and kinds of literature. Indeed, Góngora's contemporaries most frequently regarded the poems as a sort of pastoral hybrid, beautiful or bizarre, or both, which in turn spawned debate over the seriousness of bucolic literature, the merits of this fictional type, and its status in the hierarchy of genres. According to Colie, Renaissance pastoral's agonic dynamics of competitive interaction and resolution, both thematic and structural, served as a typological mark of distinction.[2] Góngora's pastoral masterpiece certainly dramatizes the agonic interplay of competing worlds and values, and the ludic combat of games and love play, but in the *Soledades*, the locus of conflictive resolution shifts from the context of community to the isolated domain of individual consciousness as represented by the pilgrim and his doubles, and as actualized by the lone reader in working through the poems. Even as the protagonist wrestles with the new life and land before him, so too does the "green thought in a green shade" generated within the active mind of the reader take command of the pastoral paradoxes created and struggle to solve the enigmas posed, thus transforming the thought process itself into a thematic focal point.

In the *Carta en respuesta*, Góngora himself emphasized the connection between reading his masterpiece and the stimulation of the inner activity of *entendimiento*, of intellection and understanding. Some of the earliest commentators of the aptly named *Soledades* followed suit and recognized the strikingly introspective, contemplative quality of the poems. Pedro Díaz de Rivas, for example, stated that the poet meant to compose four *Soledades:* the first featuring the fields; the second, the shores; the third, the woods; and the fourth, the desert. Similarly, José Pellicer maintained that Góngora planned four *Solitudes*, each corresponding to one of the ages of man, and ending with retreat into old age and contemplation of death. It is unlikely we shall ever know for certain whether these observations are accurate, but the trajectory outlined by both commentators, in terms of topography and stages of human life, respectively, conveys the impression of a gradual movement in the compositions toward withdrawal and isolation. This pattern runs counter to the traditional structure of the pastoral genre, which climaxes with a return to the world of everyday experience in human society from the green world of Nature.[3] Neither of the *Soledades* offers the aristocratic pilgrim or the other self-styled exiles who inhabit the bucolic landscape the promise of restoration or reintegration into court society.

Poggioli is not the only twentieth-century critic who took the title of Góngora's masterpiece to heart, ascribing the experience of solitude to readers and the pilgrim protagonist alike. Leo Spitzer noted in his 1940 commentary on Dámaso Alonso's then new edition of the *Soledades* that the "somber notes amid the nuptial happiness [of *Soledad* I] are very Spanish, very characteristic of Góngora, and very appropriate to the tone of the disillusioned and melancholy *Soledad*." In his 1946 article on the baroque in Spain, Stephen Gilman remarked in passing the unexpected presence of asceticism in the beautiful, harmonious Nature of the *Soledades*. That same year Karl Vossler described the work as a pastoral anomaly, as poems "engendrado[s] en los sentimientos de soledad" (engendered in feelings of solitude), unique in their subjectivism and presentation of "un artificial teatro de la naturaleza" (an artificial theater of nature). He concluded that Góngora wished to inspire "una agitación y un enriquecimiento del ánimo" (enlivenment and enrichment of the [reader's] soul) with myths, intellectual games, and the stimuli of carefully crafted Nature.[4]

Given Góngora's famous penchant for experimentation, especially for creative engagement with extant literary genres, and his predilection for hybrid forms, one can hardly deem surprising the poet's reshaping of pastoral conventions in the *Soledades*. In fact, Góngora tips his hand in this regard in a decidedly unsubtle manner by choosing the *silva* as the verse form of the bucolic compositions. Unlike the *Polifemo*'s more rigorous *octava real*, associated with narrative poetry of epic or mythological content, the *silva* features a malleable, variable, structureless structure that enables the composer to include and develop virtually any topic under the sun with diverse tones of voice. The *silva* consists of an unfixed number of heptasyllables and hendecasyllables that may rhyme, and that the poet may organize in stanzas, although strictly speaking the *silva* is astrophic. During Góngora's lifetime, the *silva* was linked with the madrigal, but the poet undoubtedly also knew of the classical origins of the rubric, derived from *sylva*, signifying a forest of mixed vegetation, and he was likely familiar with some classical and more contemporary models employing the form, which would include works such as Statius's *Silvae* (Statius ca. 45–96), Poliziano's *Silvae* (1596), Tasso's *Aminta* (1573), and several poems by Quevedo, which apparently predate the composition of *Soledad* I by a few years. Góngora's use of the *silva* thus sends a clear message to readers of the poems that they have entered an imaginary pastoral space of freedom, variety, and openness to the unpredictable. Furthermore, although the poet seems to emulate the *silva*'s classical antecedents in celebrating Nature in mixed rhetorical forms (odes, epithalamia, lamentations, amoebic songs, and so on), in the *Soledades* he clearly rejects the verse's original image as a vehicle of facile, improvisational expression.[5]

As the *silva* traces its way across the pages of the *Soledades*, the poems acquire a sinuous, asymmetrical, meandering silhouette, the curvilinear, biomorphic shape prized by Mannerist artists, that, in a way reminiscent of the concrete poetry of George Herbert and Richard Crashaw, paints the thematic and structural outline of the works' artistic and natural landscape of labyrinthine sentences, wandering streams, abundant forests, rugged outcroppings, and diagonal directionals that generate the visual illusion of depth and the potential for perspectival shifts, spatial and psychological. Obviously, there is more to Góngora's cultivation of the *silva* than meets the eye, more than formal stylistic innovation of the pastoral. I would suggest that the *silva* also provides a visual analogue to the movement of the human mind absorbed in the act of reading, grappling with seemingly incongruous images and ideas that flow together in nonlinear, associative patterns produced by sensory impressions conjured by the poetic language of *gongorismo*. The *silva* outwardly manifests the activity of solitary introspection, of a mind striving to apprehend the elusive, essential truths that Góngora obliquely referred to in the *Carta en respuesta*.

Overemphasis on the more readily accessible, innovative surface structure of the *Soledades*, however, can lead to blindness regarding this pastoral of solitude's experimental deep structure. In other words, less inquiring readers run the risk of not seeing the whole pastoral forest for the brilliant, varied foliage of the sylvan trees. Wolfgang Iser stresses pastoral's receptivity to other forms of fiction, underscoring the genre's self-conscious awareness of its own fictional nature, foregrounded and thematized in the crossing of boundaries from the external to the fictive world, an act of fictionalization forged by the author and realized by the reader. Iser acknowledges pastoral's conformity to the generic rule of growth through the continuous reconfiguration of conventions, but attributes the special elasticity of the type not to agonic interplay, as Colie maintains, but rather to the inclusion and absorption of other literary forms. By embracing and embedding multiple genres and cultivating theatrical representation and performance as standard conventions, the pastoral claims closer proximity to the threshold of dreams and occupies a privileged position in accessing the imaginary, a realm of new possibilities extending beyond the limits of the text.[6] Iser situates the space of cohesion and convergence for the pastoral in the mind and imagination of the audience, activity replicated by the pilgrim protagonist and readers of the *Soledades*, who strive to understand the strange world before them.

Meditational literature constitutes one of the key literary forms buried in the deep structure of the poems that has been conspicuously absent from critical discourse on the masterpiece. In my opinion, the confluence of the pastoral and meditational traditions accounts in large part for the focus on solitude and interiority noted by Poggioli and others, and elucidates the *Soledades'* intricate texture of interwoven sensory and intellectual elements. Although Spanish pastoral classics such as Garcilaso's *Eglogas* (ca. 1532–1536) and Montemayor's *Diana* (1559) manifested a tendency toward lyrical introspection, Góngora's pastoral of solitude emerged in the context of the Counter Reformation ideological redirection of art, an impetus that had profound repercussions in Spain, England, and elsewhere in Europe. As José Antonio Maravall has explained, in the aftermath of the Council of Trent (1545–1563), the Catholic Church in Spain mobilized resources to maintain the faith, win converts, and defeat the encroaching Protestant enemy. Literary and plastic arts played a major role in this program of doctrinal reaffirmation, that of engaging readers-spectators by shocking or striking them with wonder, appealing to the senses in a fashion that bridged the gap between exterior experience and interior awareness, outer and inner worlds. Art was obliged to move humans and make them receptive to the official ideology of church and state. But as the socioeconomic situation worsened within Spain, and for Spain in the arena of seventeenth-century European politics, art began to serve another crucial function in society: that of repository and refuge for the true moral self that resides within the soul, the legacy of Christian Neoplatonism.[7]

With the advent of the Counter Reformation, numerous secular genres, among them the pastoral and romances of chivalry, found themselves under attack for their potentially corrupting influence on a large reading and listening public. As a result, morally redressed versions of these literary types began to appear, *libros de caballerías a lo divino* (divine romances of chivalry) such as Pedro Hernández de Villaumbrales's *Caballero del sol* (Knight of the sun) (1552) and Jerónimo San Pedro's *Caballería celestial del pie de la rosa fragante* (Celestial chivalry from the foot of the fragrant rose) (1554), and religious pastoral works such as Lope de Vega's sonnet "Pastor que con tus silbos amorosos" (Shepherd who with your loving whistles) (1614) and his romance *Los pastores de Belén* (Shepherds of Bethlehem) (1612).[8]

As both Louis L. Martz and Edward M. Wilson have shown, however, the impact of the Counter Reformation extended far beyond the process of legitimating secular literary genres by adapting them to religious needs, to the alteration of the popular perception of religion in everyday life. In the sixteenth and seventeenth centuries, Protestants and Catholics alike drew upon the long-standing Christian tradition of spiritual exercises and the many treatises on meditation to merge religious experience with daily life. Fernando R. de la Flor notes that the first manuals promulgating this new, revitalized spirituality began to spread through Spain before the beginning of the sixteenth century, with treatises explaining Augustinian thought—some of the notions apocryphal in nature—playing a pivotal role in the dissemination of meditational methods with a visual, imagistic orientation. Interest in popular devotional literature burgeoned as members of all levels of society used formal and informal meditational techniques in an individualized, inward probing of the soul that promoted greater self-awareness and self-analysis, and a subsequent movement toward God. The fact that Catholic Spain and Protestant England shared the same devotional bestseller, Saint Ignatius's *Spiritual Exercises* (1548), indicates that enthusiasm for meditational praxis eclipsed the most divisive issues of the day. Poets gradually translated this heightened sense of self, appreciation for introspection, and desire for transcendence into unique secular and religious poetry that attracted the senses and the intellect, advanced conceptual paradox (as evinced by Tesauro's and Gracián's notion of the conceit), and displayed a theatrical vision of self or the world or both.[9] Góngora's masterpiece is one of many great works of Spanish Golden Age literature that incorporate some of the conventions of devotional literature into their fictional worlds.

Those who look for the systematic application of a particular meditational technique to the pastoral conventions of the *Soledades* or the devolution of a clear-cut religious agenda through Góngora's masterpiece, however, will search in vain. What they will find is a fluid, dynamic structure composed of diverse elements that dovetail with a variety of meditational schema that committed readers tap into in *text play,* Iser's term for the game a Renaissance audience would recognize as that of *serio ludere,* and they will also discover evidence of a divine order immanent in Nature, and made visible through the prism of Gongorine language. Some of the principal "aleatory rules" that govern Góngora's pastoral of solitude reside in the performance codes common to most meditational methods. In his landmark book *The Poetry of Meditation* (1962), Louis L. Martz describes the meditational process as a form of creative experience that unites sensory, affective, and intellectual powers to achieve a superior state of spiritual consciousness. By design, meditational exercises focus participants' rational and emotive faculties, turning them toward solitude, away from the external world, redirecting them inward toward active contemplation of a spiritual matter or the performance of one's Christian duties in daily life. Analysis of the imagined situation leads to increased self-knowledge and, ultimately, to new resolve to direct one's will to positive action.[10]

Like the pastoral, meditational literature exhibits keen interest in staging boundary crossing between contrasting worlds and shows a similar propensity for theatricality and dramatic performance. Vivid sensory imagery, especially of a visual or auditory nature, figures prominently in the meditational process as the awakener of the contemplative mind and spur of its movement toward introspection. When the mind engages in visualization techniques, creating fictional worlds, and subsequently initiates critical analysis, the self divides in two, projecting one self into the imaginary scene and experiencing the fictional world firsthand, with the analytical self stepping back to witness and assess the experience of the other subjective consciousness. The meditative "I" becomes actor and audience in an internalized stage production of the self. As was the case in Maravall's observations regarding post-tridentine aesthetics, Martz emphasizes the Neoplatonic tradition inherent in meditational literature. Successful enactment of devotional techniques depends on shared belief in a system of correspondences in which the immediate and concrete holds up an emblematic reflection of the divine abstract.[11]

In the dedication to the *Soledades*, Góngora begins as he means to continue: alerting readers to the multiple literary codes operative in the text and issuing an invitation to meditate on the poems' green world. He achieves this goal by dramatizing pastoral and meditational boundary crossing in a theatrical scene in which poet and patron appear as fictional characters in a bucolic landscape created by the presence of well-known pastoral topoi. The human figures enact a transition from aristocratic activity to solitary contemplation in an intimate dialogue initiated by Góngora's pilgrim persona, an actor who announces his entrance onstage in what have become some of the most famous lines of poetry in the history of Spanish literature:

> Pasos de un peregrino son errante
>   cuantos me dictó versos dulce Musa,

                     en soledad confusa
              perdidos unos, otros inspirados.
                                    (Jammes, 1–4)

(Dictated by the Muse, these verses, know,
As many footsteps as the pilgrim made;
Though some in solitude confused have strayed
              Others inspired were born.
                                    [Wilson, 1–4])

To date, the majority of the critical analyses of these verses have highlighted their many ambiguities and great semantic richness, their self-referentiality and self-conscious literariness. Resonant with allusions to Lope, Camões, Petrarch, Góngora himself, and others, these words serve notice that literally and figuratively the game of poetry is afoot.[12] Yet, the prologue's opening sentence is also a speech in which the pilgrim-poet draws readers' attention to the theme and concept of solitude as spatialized experience, at first associated with poetic inspiration and creation, but that little by little expands to encompass members of the audience willing to enter into imaginative collaboration with Góngora's fictional alter ego. The pilgrim identifies himself and his verses, their composition and reception, with sound *(pasos* [imprint of sound]; *son* [sound], *musa* [muse]) and movement *(pasos . . . son* [are steps], *errante* [wandering and wayward]), dynamics that are then developed in the prologue's following scenes, featuring the duke of Béjar as reader and meditator. The pilgrim occupies the inner stage of the mind only briefly, however, disappearing from view in line 5 only to reappear in line 30. His entrances and exits generate a visual, theatrical frame of reference in the prologue, marking short sketches or *pasos* that form a counterpoint to the duke of Béjar scenes, which lure readers into the realm of pastoral, contemplative solitude. When the pilgrim fades into the background, and becomes instigator and observer of the duke's activities, Góngora introduces into the composition a pattern of perspectival shifts from actor to witness that will be repeated in different contexts throughout the *Soledades*.

As Mary Gaylord has pointed out, despite the fact that the pilgrim-poet vanishes momentarily in the prologue, his voice remains a constant presence in the work. The tone this voice assumes enables the pilgrim to seduce, mobilize, and direct the readers' powers of understanding toward meditational activity. The familiar I-thou dialogue of lines 1–4, for example, allows Góngora's persona to insinuate his voice into the interlocutor's consciousness. This voice is by turns playful, with clever word games and intertextual references; alluring, with outright flattery and less obvious cajolery; hortative, with compelling commands (*arrima* [lean], *templa* [cool], *déjate* [let thyself]); and, at the end of the prologue, oddly subdued yet full of promise. In discussing Marvell's "Garden," Harry Berger Jr. has labeled erroneous the tendency to interpret the poem's voice as if it were the subjective "I" of a nineteenth-century lyric poem. He likens Marvell's "I" to the "staging of the green-world sensibility."[13] Although Góngora's poetic voice shares a certain kinship with that of "The Garden," the assertive "I" of the *Soledades* seems more concerned with designating a select audience possessing the appropriate state of mind to accompany him down the garden path, an audience that will also participate in the sketches he devises. The poet's persona prepares this dynamic partnership in the prologue by removing the reader from society, vacating the stage temporarily to let the reader trod the boards, and finally reappearing primarily as vocal rather than physical presence to lead the reader into meditation in the pastoral landscape through the power of his world-making voice.

The structural dynamics of staging that Góngora establishes in the opening lines of the prologue, in which he fuses imagery of sight and sound to move his patron and the rest of his audience into a solitary, reflective space, bear a striking resemblance to that of the first prelude of Saint Ignatius's *Spiritual Exercises*. This preparatory section, which precedes the main body of the Ignatian meditational model, commonly referred to as "composition of place" or "finding the spot," concentrates the meditator's mind on a certain subject by creating an imaginary scene in which dramatic mental activity can unfold. To set the psychological stage, Saint Ignatius employs powerful systems of imagery to mount a production replete with sensory details that function as a symbolic counterpart to the elusive kingdom of the spirit. Composition of place lays the foundation for meditational experience by one or more of the following: situating the meditator at the locus of the psychological drama, making the meditator envision events occurring at that spot, or transforming the meditator into a participant in the events happening at the imaginary spot. Saint Ignatius states:

> El primer preámbulo es composición viendo el lugar. Aquí es de notar que en la contemplación o meditación visible, la composición será ver con la vista de la imaginación el lugar corpóreo donde se halla la cosa que quiero contemplar. Digo el lugar corpóreo, así como un templo o monte, donde se halla Jesu Christo o Nuestra Señora, según lo que quiero contemplar.
>
> (*The first prelude* is a mental image of the place. It should be noted at this point that when the meditation or contemplation is on a visible object, for example, contemplating Christ our Lord during His life on earth, the image will consist of seeing with the mind's eye the physical place where the object that we wish to contemplate is present. By the physical place I mean, for instance, a temple, or

mountain where Jesus or the Blessed Virgin is, depending on the subject of the contemplation.)

Ignatian mobilization of the senses of the mind becomes most apparent later, in the Fifth Exercise, in which meditators are asked to imagine Hell. Then they are exhorted to see the fires, hear the cries of the damned, smell the smoke and corruption, taste bitter things, and touch Hell's burning flames.[14]

At the beginning, the primary concern of Góngora's persona seems to be that of distancing the audience from worldly cares and ambitions. The pilgrim-poet urges the duke-reader to move away from the violent, aristocratic activity of the hunt in the fictional present, which seems to coincide with the historical present outside the text, toward peaceful repose in a pastoral setting further removed in time and space. References to warfare initially crowd the inner theater of the mind:

> ¡Oh tú que, de venablos impedido,
> muros de abeto, almenas de diamante,
> bates los montes que, de nieve armados,
> gigantes de cristal los teme el cielo.
> (Jammes, 5–8)

> (O thou, whom hindering javelins surround
> —Diamond battlements, of fir the walls—
> Who beatest the high mountains [armed with snow
> This crystal giant crew the heavens appals].
> [Wilson, 5–8])

The duke-reader appears surrounded by hunters, represented synecdochally by javelins, with parts that in turn evoke castles prepared for fighting ("walls," "battlements"). Use of synecdoche within synecdoche to refer to the other members of the hunting party and their weapons casts the duke's companions in a supporting role in which they blend into the background, even as Góngora's patron emerges as the physical and psychological focal point of the scene. As the retinue scours the mountaintops in search of ferocious game, the earth seems to rise up to threaten the heavens, which opens the text up to the literary world of classical mythology in an allusion to the clash of the Titans with Zeus. The poet adds the sound of a hunting horn to this carefully orchestrated drama of death and destruction (9) before he returns readers to the external world with a topographical reference to the river Tormes, its color altered by the blood of the slain wild beasts (10–12). Yet, no sooner does Góngora complete this portrait of the duke-reader engaged in the noble pastime of the hunt than he asks the same actor-audience to abandon violent activity and cross the border from a fictional space with recognizable geographical and historical coordinates into a new locus available only to inward-turning readers acquainted with the furnishings of pastoral literature. The pilgrim-poet instructs the reader to leave behind the hunting implement, a symbol of combat—"arrima a un fresno el fresno" (lean by an ash thine ashen spear) (13)—to move into a space dominated by oaks, pines, and a cool mountain spring. These features automatically suggest a pastoral landscape, the Golden Age, and the *locus amoenus* of Platonic tradition.[15] Then the duke-reader withdraws into solitude, completing his separation from the rest of the hunting party, who *surrounded* him when he rode out, but whose presence *impedes* (implied by the ambiguous "de venablos impedido" [hindering javelins]) his progress toward quiet rest, that is, a contemplative state. From this point onward the audience is attuned only to the voice and footsteps of the pilgrim-poet, who pays homage to his patron and joins the duke in the dramatic space that straddles the line between exterior and fictional worlds.

As in the Ignatian model, Góngora relies on sensory vividness to help his audience of meditators create fictional scenes and then lure them into the settings they have imaginatively constructed according to his specifications. The call to the hunt of the horn in line 9 eventually gives way to the soothing melodies of Euterpe's flute (35–37). Readers feel cool water calm and refresh a body hot from exertion, restoring mental and physical equipoise—"templa en sus ondas tu fatiga ardiente" (Burning fatigue shall soon sweet coolness find) (27)—and afterward lie on ground softened by thick grass—"y entregados tus miembros al reposo / sobre el de grama césped no desnudo" (And to repose thy limbs delivered here / Upon the turfy ground) (28–29). The prologue's spectacular visual effects, however, outstrip those of an auditory or tactile nature to provide the most compelling, powerful weapons in the arsenal of imagery designed to aid readers in "finding the spot." Javelin points shine like diamonds (6), and snowcapped peaks sparkle like glass (7–8), as blood drips off a spear, dying the pristine white snow a majestic, if messy, purple (13–15). The hard, glittering, jewel-like surfaces and striking color contrasts attract the eye but forbid relaxation, whereas the fountain, grass carpet, and leafy canopy of the Golden Age's sacred oak soothe the eye, mind, and spirit as they draw the audience into a plein-air pastoral throne room (22–25). The poet incorporates directional movement into the visual imagery as well, shifting from the vertical motion of hunters, who climb mountains in pursuit of game, to the horizontal stasis of the lone figure reclining on the ground. The two axes cross at a point that traces a border within the confines of the prologue's fictional world and that functions as a psychological signpost ushering readers into a contemplative state and space: "del oso que aun besaba, atravesado, / la asta de tu luciente jabalina" (Of bears transfixed before by thy proud shaft / [They even then would kiss the shining haft]) (20–21). In these lines, a thrown horizontal javelin shaft has pierced and fixed the vertical bear, freezing the frame of the action sequence with death and ending visual contact with the hunting scene. Góngora effectively pins his readers to a new spot and focus, too, placing them under the spell of his pilgrim-poet. The aqueous centers on either side of this line of demarcation stress the psychological distance traversed by the audience since the beginning of the dedicatory prologue. As Góngora replaces the view of the frenzied Tormes crashing down the mountain slopes with the gentle waves of the forest spring, emblem of both poetic inspiration and the dynamics of the active mind, he reshapes his readers into a receptive group of meditators.

In retrospect, all three aspects of Ignatian composition of place figure in the prologue, permitting Góngora to lead the duke-reader, playing the part of meditator, into an inward state of contemplation, represented visually by a rest taken in bucolic surroundings. In harmony with Platonic tradition, repose liberates the subconscious mind from the tyranny of the material world, enabling the subconscious to wander and refocus its imaginative resources, piqued as it is by the sensory stimuli that form the basis of the inner, fictive microcosm. Góngora deftly projects the duke-reader into the fictional space, effortlessly shifting his role from that of principal actor in a hunting scene to that of passive, solitary individual supine before the spring, but whose active, disembodied mind dances attendance on the pilgrim-poet. The change in verbal registers from martial exploits to pastoral peace cues readers regarding their own mental preparation before they enter the text and world of the *Soledades*.

Góngora by no means, however, limits composition of place to the prologue, employing the same meditational technique as a cuing device for readers at the beginning of *Soledad* I and II. In both instances, the poet strives to separate and isolate the pilgrim (and, metaphorically, the audience) from his customary physical surroundings, usual companions, and previous psychological state, once again relocating the protagonist and reader at an imaginary spot far removed from daily life at court and inserting them into a new pastoral context of contemplative experience. *Soledad* I opens in medias res with the shipwrecked pilgrim protagonist, conveniently blessed with a pine-plank flotation cushion, washing up on the shore of an unknown land. With a paucity of background information, Góngora essentially sets the hero adrift in the fictional world, acknowledging only his handsomeness by comparing him to Ganymede ("cuando el que ministrar podia la copa / a Júpiter mejor que el garzón de Ida" [Jammes, 7–

8] [When, fitter cupbearer than Ganymede / For Jupiter, the lovesick boy gave tears Wilson, 6–7]), and his distance from the lady who disdains his love ("náufrago y desdeñado" [Jammes, 9] [Absent, disdained Wilson, 8]). Deprived of his inamorata's presence, the pilgrim gives voice to lovesick laments and finds that Nature offers him musical solace in the rhythmic sound of the wind and waves:

> lagrimosas de amor dulces querellas
> da al mar, que condolido,
> fue a las ondas, fue al viento
> el mísero gemido
> segundo de Arïon dulce instrumento.
> (Jammes, 10–14)

> (For Jupiter, the lovesick boy gave tears
> [Absent, disdained and shipwrecked] to the tide
> And winds, which moved by his complaining lays
> As to a new Arion's harp gave heed.
> [Wilson, 7–10])

The soothing complementarity of a personified, harmonious Nature underscores that the protagonist has crossed a fictional boundary and that fate has intervened to remove him from the city, the court, and the turbulent emotions of unrequited love. Marvelous sights accompany the auditory response of the sea in the form of a welcoming beach that quickly gives way to another physical barrier to be traversed:

> Del Ocëano pues antes sorbido,
> y luego vomitado
> no lejos de un escollo coronado
> de secos juncos, de calientes plumas,
> (alga todo y espumas)
> halló hospitalidad donde halló nido
> de Júpiter el ave.
> (Jammes, 22–28)

> (Close by a headland, crowned
> With sheltering feathers and dry rushes, he,
> Engulfed before, then spewed up by the sea,
> [Covered with foam, with seaweed girded] found
> A hospitable rest,
> Where built the bird of Jupiter his nest.
> [Wilson, 17–22])

Góngora's visual and acoustic details inspire readers to re-create imaginatively the pilgrim's near-death experience and rebirth into a different realm of existence. As in the prologue, the poet engages the mind's eye immediately by introducing a vertical shift into the narrative flow, panning upward and away from the beach to an eagle's aerie high atop a promontory. The perspective change has a literal and figurative function, for it indicates the direction of the pilgrim's steps as he moves inland into the heart of the pastoral landscape, and signals the moral and intellectual elevation to which the protagonist and reader can aspire through encounters with symbolically encoded tableaux and sophisticated, challenging verses. The shift identifies the pilgrim's movement inland and upward, and the reader's progress inward, into the inner space of the text and its fictional world, with spiritual ascent, an equation typical of Renaissance Neoplatonism.[16] When twilight falls, the pilgrim scales boulders in the gathering gloom only to face the next boundary in a vast expanse of unfamiliar, unilluminated territory. The glimpse of a faraway light—

> farol de una cabaña
> que sobre el ferro está, en aquel incierto
> golfo de sombras anunciando el puerto.
> (Jammes, 59–61)

> (The lantern of a cottage, stood displayed,
> At anchor in the uncertain gulf of shade,
> Showing the port at hand.
> [Wilson, 52–54])

—guides his once hesitant footsteps quickly and safely across uneven ground and the threshold of darkness to refuge and renewed human contact in a goatherd's hut. Just as the pilgrim must redirect all of his energy toward struggling against the dark to reach the light, so too must readers focus the powers of the mind inward, using the inner light of understanding to unravel Góngora's obscure conceits and disclose their hidden mysteries. The fade-out–fade-in scenario devised by the poet marks the completion of *Soledad* I's rites of initiation into the pastoral fictional world and passage to the contemplative life, and signifies that protagonist and audience have found the inner spot for meditation.

Chiaroscuro effects saturate these opening scenes (Jammes, 42–83; Wilson, 35–77), punctuating the pilgrim's physical and psychological transition. The blackness of night, reified by the rough ocean and forbidding rocks, recedes as the faint twinkle of a lantern magically metamorphoses into the North Star, which finally resolves into a blazing campfire that drops glowing embers as it burns:

> y la que desvïada
> luz poca pareció, tanta es vecina,

> que yace en ella la robusta encina,
> mariposa en cenizas desatada.
> (Jammes, 86–89)

> (That which far off he deemed
> A little lantern now much greater seemed:
> The holm-oak, sturdy, bare,
> Huge butterfly in cinders lay untied.
> [Wilson, 80–83])

The dazzling light imagery betrays an almost allegorical enactment of the roving Augustinian mind in pursuit of divine illumination, a process that moves in stages from the sensory to the intelligible, from exterior to interior, from lower to higher, and, eventually, to God. One can also detect in this flickering trail of light the searching focus of Augustinian meditation, as the mind gropes uncertainly toward Truth, wandering over fields of imagery in which momentary flashes of illumination provide glimmers of God, the realm of Ideas, and the resting place of the soul.[17] Although it would be erroneous to equate the humble community of goatherds the pilgrim finds with the presence of God, Góngora makes it clear that the protagonist has encountered a morally superior group of people who live simply and harmoniously with Nature, in contrast to the circle of vain courtiers identified with the hero's original milieu. In this sense, readers witness the pilgrim's first steps in the direction of a higher order of being in the opening scene of *Soledad* I.

The protagonist's quest for solitude and inner peace appears to intensify at the beginning of *Soledad* II. Here the boundary he crosses, an estuary, leads to the even greater isolation of an island, where he is doubly removed from aristocratic surroundings, first separated by the shipwreck from his ties to the court, and then separated by choice from the wedding guests *(serranos)* and festivities of *Soledad* I. As the pilgrim traverses the aquatic barrier in a small fishing boat, Góngora employs auditory and visual decor to set the stage for another pastoral fictional tableau, a piscatory landscape inhabited by young, enamored fishermen and -women, and a retired fisherman who cultivates the islet as if it were a garden. The poet transforms the hero's floating transport and the rhythmic motion of its oars into a stringed instrument that serves as a musical backdrop for the pilgrim's tuneful plaints:

> El peregrino pues, haciendo en tanto
> instrumento el bajel, cuerdas los remos,
> al Céfiro encomienda los extremos
> deste métrico llanto. . . .
> (Jammes, 112–15)

(The youth, as they were furrowing along,
—His instrument the boat, a string each oar—
Began unto the zephyr to outpour
The extremities of this his metric song. . . .
[Wilson, 105–8])

Horizontal movement on the diagonal through the water and away from the shore and the reflection of morning sunlight on the land replace the vertical motion and dusk chiaroscuro of *Soledad* I's opening scene. Nevertheless, the pilgrim undergoes a symbolic death and rebirth similar to that which occurs when he first washes up from the shipwreck. In his only soliloquy in the *Soledades,* delivered midstream when he is a passenger in the fishing boat, the hero looks inward and meditates on the vanity of his former existence, renounces his love and worldly desires, and proclaims his intentions to devote the remainder of his life to the sea, at peace with nature and in juxtaposition to the ceaseless strife of ambitious courtiers (Jammes, 116–71; Wilson, 109–64):

"Túmulo tanto debe
       agradecido Amor a mi pie errante;
       líquido pues diamante
       calle mis huesos, y llevada cima
       selle sí, mas no oprima
       esta que le fiaré ceniza breve,
       si hay ondas mudas y si hay tierra leve."
                    (Jammes, 165–71)

("In gratitude Love owes
So fine a tomb unto my wandering feet;
       Let liquid diamond meet
To calm my bones, and mountains' loftiness
       To seal, but not oppress,
The ashes few that I to them dispose,
If lightness, Earth—if silence, Ocean—knows."
                    [Wilson, 159–64])

The paradoxical imagistic mix of earth and water, hard and liquid substances, recalls the composition of place of *Soledad* I, in which the verbal registers of land and sea infiltrate and contaminate each other, just as the *pie errante* (wandering feet) that seem to find their final resting place beneath the estuary waves remind readers of the *pasos,* the pilgrim-poet's metric footsteps that mark the *Soledades'* dedication-prologue. Yet, in this context, the audience watches a scene of confession and conversion in which the pilgrim voices the *vanitas* theme and expresses sentiments of *desengaño,* severing ties to the outside world and espousing a quasi-ascetic code of human conduct predicated on withdrawal and self-denial.

As one might expect from poems that feature literal and figurative boundary crossing, promote heightened spiritual and intellectual consciousness for the protagonist and readers, and display a dynamic progression toward solitude and interiority, the *Soledades* frequently depict transitional zones and conditions that take the shape of hybrid people and scenery captured in the act of metamorphosis or in states of in-betweenness. *Soledad* I portrays the pilgrim's difficult rite of passage through a littoral region that blends ocean waves with rocky mountainsides and brilliant sources of fire and light, merging three of nature's four elements. *Soledad* II similarly opens in a transitional space, with the hero crossing an estuary ("Centauro ya espumoso el Ocëano, / medio mar, medio ría" [Jammes, 10–11] [The Ocean now a spumy centaur, see, / —Half sea, half estuary Wilson, 10–11]), a natural hybrid, to reach another hybrid destination, an island that seems to belong to both sea and earth:

> Yace en el mar, si no continüada,
>   isla mal de la tierra dividida,
>   cuya forma tortuga es perezosa:
>   díganlo cuantos siglos ha que nada,
>   sin besar de la playa espacïosa
>   la arena de las ondas repetida.
>   (Jammes, 190–95)
>
> (Lies in the sea, if no peninsula,
> An island hardly separate from the land,
> Whose shape a slothful turtle is to-day;
> How many centuries it swam, can say
> The tide so oft repeated on the sand,
> And never kissing the opposing strand.
>   [Wilson, 182–87])

Góngora transforms the islet, suspended between two worlds, that periodically increases or diminishes with the shifting tides, into an amphibian, a turtle, a terrestrial and aquatic creature who now submerges himself and now emerges from the water, thus constantly altering his size from the perspective of the human eye. These signs of perpetual transition and displacement coincide with the pilgrim's journey across a physical and psychological threshold in his soliloquy of confession and conversion that takes place midstream (Jammes, II:116–71; Wilson, II:109–64). Elsewhere in the poems, a goatherd who was once a soldier, "armado a Pan, o semicapro a Marte" (Jammes, I:234) (Satyr of Mars or warrior of Pan [Wilson, I:231]), draws attention to ivy-covered towers and battlements, silent, ruined monuments to war that briefly intrude upon the timeless peace of the green countryside with reminders of the armed conflict that lies outside the fictional microcosm of the text (Jammes, I:212–21; Wilson, I:208–17). An elderly mountaineer incongruously delivers (in this ahistorical realm) a didactic lecture on the voyages of discovery that seems more appropriate for a sermon or a formal discourse presented from a church pulpit or in a treatise on moral and political philosophy (Jammes, I:366–502; Wilson, I:356–486). In *Soledad II*, unpretentious fishing huts rub elbows with a Renaissance palace of Parian marble that issues a prince, his hunting party, and a magnificent procession of falcons—all about to engage in that most aristocratic sport of hawking (Jammes, 695–936; Wilson, 681–920).

Clearly, unlike Montemayor's *Diana*, in which the author configures juxtaposed worlds as separate spaces enjoying a degree of contiguity, Góngora has elected to organize his pastoral of solitude in a more oneiric pattern through the fusion or superimposition of contrasting worlds. Readers of the *Soledades* consequently experience the sensation of entering a dreamscape, a feeling consonant with the duke of Béjar's cued repose in the dedication-prologue and maintained by the almost geological disposition of the poems' referential fields. The textual landscape highlights the contours of liminality that arise along fissures and fault lines that permit buried substrata of consciousness to break through to the surface. What occasions such ruptures? As in the episodes described above, the rifts generally take place when Góngora blends antithetical systems of imagery or when he dramatizes agonic worlds through the representation of the conflicted consciousness of the pilgrim and other characters, whose displays of mixed emotions and identities are often triggered by memories. Significantly, these liminal episodes and moments manifest outwardly the contemplative modality of interiority that forms a part of the heritage of Platonic thought. According to Marsilio Ficino, to mention just one of the Renaissance Neoplatonists so influential in the age of Góngora, the mind cannot suddenly leap inward or upward to a superior level of knowledge. Nor can humans remain permanently in a heightened state of awareness. The contemplative mind undergoes the restless movement of consciousness as it slides up and down, in and out of, varying degrees of awareness. As Góngora hinted in his *Carta en respuesta*, this dynamic compositional profile of transient states and shifting, layered contexts of referentiality also mimics the structure of Augustinian meditational methods.[18]

The Pilgrim's Progress

The opening lines of the *Soledades* illustrate that Góngora's work fairly vibrates with intertextual echoes, another type of mimicry that has encouraged considerable speculation over the years concerning possible sources for the pastoral poems. María Rosa Lida de Malkiel appears to have found a major wellspring for narrative components of the *Soledades* in Dio Chrysostom's *Discourse* VII, in the section titled *The Hunters of Euboea*, which enjoyed a long, independent existence as a celebration of country life. Rearranged narrative fragments from this text combined with the Petrarchan tradition that portrays Nature as a place of solitude befitting a doleful lover in search of solace, or contemplative poets and philosophers in search of transcendent truths, may well have provided the preponderance of raw material that Góngora subsequently transformed into the oneiric world of his masterpiece.[19]

The issue of the internal organization of the text, of the concatenation of these same narrative and thematic elements within an identifiable, overarching structure, however, remains much more difficult to resolve. Recent criticism concerning this matter reveals the resurgence of the old debate pinning opposing labels on the *Soledades*—epic or pastoral, narrative or lyric—albeit recast in more modern rhetoric. Crystal Chemris, for example, concentrating primarily on the Gongorine tissue of conceits, views the poems' order in terms of a semantic pulse of deconstructionist bent that assumes an apocalyptic pattern of expansion and dissolution. Meanwhile, John Beverley sees the structure of the *Soledades* in terms of narrative schemata, essentially as a series of spatial-temporal cells that emerges from beneath the *silva* to take the shape of a succession of days and nights that in turn sets linear history against cyclic, cosmic myth and raises moral and economic issues in the Marxist vein. Antonio Vilanova, more attuned to the hybrid aspects of the work, observes that the poems feature an episodic configuration composed of a lyric hero placed in epic scenery.[20]

The sense of disjunction that Vilanova notes—the impression of different genres, tones, and structures loosely tied together or grafted onto one another—perhaps comes closest to capturing the sense of organization experienced by the *Soledades*' readers. And this is a case in which the audience's response to the text affords the best clues to the internal arrangement and cohesion of the fictional world. The visual and auditory stimuli of Góngora's pastoral impact so strongly on the mind of the audience that once readers have completed their garden journey with the protagonist, they perceive and remember that experience as a procession of *pasos*, dramatic sketches that seem to file by or approach the reader-spectator as if propelled by a will of their own or that of their creator. The pilgrim's movement through the landscape automatically strings the scenes together, like the beads of a necklace, in a narrative sequence that can be labeled "plot," but it is difficult to outline the pilgrim's progress because he frequently steps aside to listen and think about what he witnesses as a privileged spectator. Just such a shift occurs during the elderly *serrano*'s monologue on the voyages of discovery (Jammes, I:366–502; Wilson, I:356–486), when the protagonist momentarily vanishes from the stage as he listens and observes. In numerous catalog segments, in fact, the pilgrim becomes a disembodied focalizer paired with an extratextual vocalizer, somewhat like a series of movie close-ups combined with a voice-over. At other times he drops out of the drama completely and virtually falls into the reader's space, as in the hawking scenes of *Soledad* II (Jammes, 713–936; Wilson, 699–920). As a result, the pilgrim often appears to be a static figure watching a movie screen, who can, unlike the other members of the audience, actually project himself physically into a few frames, even if only in a passive role, whereas the reader must settle for imagined projection into the same fictional space, following in his wake. This quasi-theatrical disposition of the poems links them with the tradition of meditational literature, which relies on visual images—ranging from symbols drawn from the Augustinian book of Nature to the internalized stage sets of Ignatian composition of place—to focus the meditator's thought, convey spiritual messages and reveal hidden truths. The meditator's intellectual and affective faculties supply the analytical and intuitive thought that binds the discrete images and vignettes into a meaningful whole, just as Góngora's audience must harness intellect and intuition to assemble the pieces of his textual puzzle.

Curiously, the *Soledades* display such theatrical construction that one can block them for an imagined stage production more easily than Góngora's own *comedias*, *Las firmezas de Isabela* (1610) and *El doctor Carlino* (1613).[21] For example:

Soledad I: Mountains
Scene
Scenery—Goatherd's hut. Night campfire, then dawn light.
Action—The pilgrim is welcomed by goatherds, spends the night with them, and enjoys the generous hospitality of his rustic hosts. The *beatus ille* topos comes to the fore, accompanied by a catalog of rustic food and furnishings. (Jammes, 84–181; Wilson, 78–173)

Soledad II: Shores
Scene
Scenery—A series of natural wonders, artfully cultivated. Tame swans, a dove-

cote in a poplar, a hillock rabbit hutch, a beehive, a herd of goats on a rocky hillside overlooking the ocean.
Action—The host takes his guest on an island tour showing him wonders that offer a perfect blend of art and nature. (Jammes, 248–313; Wilson, 240–305)

An anatomy of this sort lays bare the influence of what Frances Yates calls the "art of memory," one of the major classical traditions that nourished meditational thought and technique in the age of Góngora. The poet would have received this component of Europe's rich Greco-Roman heritage by various means, among them through the standard rhetorical curriculum familiar to every student. As an aspect of formal education, the art of memory provided a system for the construction, organization, and use of visual images as mnemonic devices and aids for oratory and written composition. Three authoritative sources supplied the guidelines for instruction in this rhetorical technique: Cicero's *De oratore*, Quintilian's *Institutio oratoria*, and the anonymous *Ad Herennium*.[22]

The Greco-Roman art of memory imparted to Góngora and his contemporaries consists of two basic steps. First, the orator thinks of a place well known to him, usually a building or a defined space, such as a garden, that contains several rooms or subsections. Because sight dominates the other senses, the orator then visualizes unusual, striking images, which facilitate recollection and inspire wonderment in both the speaker and the audience, if the orator chooses to share the image with them. Second, the speaker mentally affixes each image to a specific location or architectural detail within a given room or compartment. With the schema established, the speaker can now recall a topic, and perhaps anecdotes or a set of positions on the topic, by imaginatively entering the room and examining the images in a certain order by roving through the space in a preset, invariable pattern.

Although the classical world regarded the art of memory as a type of cerebral writing, the inherently dramatic potential of the rhetorical strategy cannot have gone unnoticed. Góngora has maximized that potential in the blocked scenes of his pastoral, a genre already noted for theatrical propensities. The poet visualizes and creates a contained structural space, the pages of a pastoral of solitude and a fictive green world, that he subsequently subdivides into two poems and two bucolic microcosms, respectively, visually anchored by a natural background common to all scenarios that take place in each small world. Thus, the reader encounters not the rooms of a house, but a verdant cosmos split into a Solitude of Mountains and a Solitude of Shores. Each of the *Soledades* fragments into separate but connected scenes, in which topographical features, and frequently some sort of edifice, serve as ocular focal points, privileged locations to which Góngora attaches striking images and vignettes with encoded morals and themes. For instance, when readers reach the second scene in the poems, they focus the inner eye on the goatherd's hut, highlighted initially by a campfire and the next day by the rising sun. The goatherd's hut scene remains etched in memory as the most direct *beatus ille* segment of the work. Each item in the catalog of plain food and furnishings contributes to and strengthens the celebration of the simple life led in harmony with nature and human limitations, and simultaneously condemns court life, which foments vanity, avarice, and overweening pride. The reader's progress through the list is analogous to the orator's mental tour of the imaginary room in which select spots framing memorable images bear the fruitful weight of meaning. In such a context, even a bed can acquire aesthetic stature and serve a didactic purpose:

> Sobre corchos después, más regalado
> sueño le solicitan pieles blandas
> que al Príncipe entre holandas
> púrpura tiria o milanés brocado.
> (Jammes, I:163–66)

> (Then the soft skins upon the cork-bed laid
> Invited him to take more gentle rest,
> Than to the prince between his Holland sheets
> Purple of Tyre or Milanese brocade.
> [Wilson, I:156–59])

The audience learns that the pilgrim will sleep better on a bed of cork blanketed with animal skins than a prince between holland sheets covered with brocade because the humble bed represents warm, sincere generosity of spirit received in peaceful surroundings undisturbed by envy, selfishness, and empty flattery. In short, the moral superiority of innocence and unburdened conscience supercedes physical comfort burdened by immorality. Góngora merges contrasting values and worlds in victuals such as the dried goat meat, which he metamorphoses into rich cloth, "purpúreos hilos es de grana fina" (Jammes, I:162) ([t]he purple threads displayed of scarlet fine [Wilson, I:155]). The poet suggests that honest human labor invested in making a product that satisfies a basic need (in this case, hunger) ennobles the object and endows it with a spiritual value greater than the material worth of an extravagant possession that temporarily quiets a frivolous craving.[23] The quantity of items and the vibrancy of the images that figure in the inventory of the goatherd's hut and hospitality overwhelm readers with irrefutable evidence advancing the *beatus ille* topos.

The complex aesthetic and didactic dimensions entwined in the *Soledades*' dramatic enactment of the art of memory disclose the fact that two Christianized currents of the tradition lie embedded in the structural and conceptual backbone of the poems. Scholastic and Platonic ideas on mental imaging, well integrated into the meditational literature of the era, converge in Góngora's *Soledades* to further poetry's potential as an instrument in the spiritual and epistemological quest for Truth. Both strains of thought continue the expansion of the classical notion of "memory" to include not only the recollection of things past, but also the creative genesis of images, which the modern world might roughly equate with "imagination." At the heart of the Scholastic view of memory lies Aquinas's belief that images constitute the foundation of human thought: *"[N]ihil potest homo intelligere sine phantasmate"* (Man cannot know anything without images.)[24] Góngora's work indicates he subscribes to that belief and regards creative memory as one of the three powers of the soul. Moreover, in the *Soledades* the poet follows several of the Thomist precepts of memory, in particular, the use of wondrous corporeal forms and images to aid in remembering spiritual matters, the organization of images so that one can move readily from one picture to the next, and advocacy of solitude as the optimal state for the function of memory, thereby linking solitude with cognitive and devotional activity. On one level, Góngora ties the dazzling images of the *Soledades* together in a linear, processional order, like jeweled ornaments hung on the tenuous wire of the pilgrim's progress. This ordering principle preserves the relative independence of the dramatic scenes molded by the art of memory and encourages analysis and interpretation of the individual tableaux, yet at the same time engenders a loose, unifying narrative logic. Góngora has also designated solitude the space and experience of contemplation and analytical thought, made evident in the poems' title, isolated hero and his refracted doubles, and implied reader, set adrift alone in the pastoral world of *culto* language.

Still, the Platonic tradition of the art of memory that grew out of Saint Augustine's study of the book of Nature to pursue God is a much more potent cohesive force in the *Soledades*. In contrast to the linear, rational construct of Thomist thought, the Hermetic philosophy developed by Neoplatonists such as Marsilio Ficino, Giordano Bruno, and Pico della Mirandola views the divine *mens* as a supreme ordering power that exhibits an intuitive, synthetic disposition. As a result, Martz maintains that poetry with a substratum of Augustinian meditation tends to display a rambling, digressive structure lacking immediate, obvious coherence. The reader-meditator must let the mind struggle to synthesize the many into one and recognize the one inherent in each of the many, pulling fragmentary hints of truth into a whole. Most any reader of the *Soledades* can attest that the work epitomizes the rambling poetic trajectory aligned with the Platonic tradition of Augustinian meditation. Only in retrospect, given the opportunity to recollect and reflect on their disjointed impressions of the poems through the powers of memory and understanding, can readers then activate will, the synthesizing power of the mind, to formulate conclusions about the text as a whole. When readers finish the exercise in reading and meditation, images and scenes begin to coalesce along certain thematic lines, among them the ones that R. O. Jones argues constitute the spiritual nucleus of the *Soledades*, namely, "the continuity of Nature, Nature's harmony and Nature's plenty."[25]

The poems' central circulatory system of aquatic imagery seems to supply the intuitive, binding glue that makes apparent the Platonic principle of synthetic cohesion at work in Góngora's masterpiece. Of the four elements, water overshadows the others in the *Soledades,* providing readers with an emblematic representative of the pansophical ideal at work, the fluid activity of the mind engrossed in assimilating and combining isolated bits of knowledge into Truth. This omnipresent force of nature assumes many guises in the text, but the one concept visible in each of the many identities the element adopts is its life-giving, life-sustaining power. At the time Góngora composed this pastoral of solitude, the nourishing, self-replenishing water cycle had just been discovered, that is, the fact that this single element undergoes a natural, infinitely renewable series of radical metamorphoses, from water to water vapor to rain to water—illustrative of the one in the many and the many in the one. The *Soledades'* rivers, natural and artificial springs, marshes, and estuary similarly testify to the enduring beauty and vitality not only of water but also of Nature in general, an outward manifestation of the immanence of God's grace.[26]

In a sense, the hermeneutics involved in reading the *Soledades* parallels the Thomist and Platonic currents of the art of memory that I have identified as unifying aspects of the poems. As members of the perplexed audience work their way through the text, striving to unravel its enigmas, they search for rational connections within and between scenes, seeking a logical order that the pilgrim's progress appears to reinforce in narrative shape. Once readers have completed a poem or both poems, however, they tend to reconfigure the work in their minds in nonlinear, thematic terms, at which point the pilgrim's journey dwindles in significance. Góngora foregrounds the act of reading as an epistemological problem in this way, pitting intuitive and ratiocinative thought against each other.[27]

Yet, Góngora has staged an unequal match between these agonic but complementary forces that shape the structure and hermeneutic dynamics of the *Soledades*. In the poet's hands, the magical, talismanic power of the image, another facet of the Platonic art of memory, emerges the clear victor in this epistemological tug-of-war. Renaissance philosophers of the occult, such as Ficino, believed that the objects, elements, and entities of the natural universe possessed a latent spirit or soul, a nexus between upper and lower worlds that the artist-magus perceived in inspired flights of divine frenzy. The artificer then made the connection accessible to readers, spectators, or meditators through image-laden artifacts that enabled them to apprehend the incomprehensible in sudden, intuitive acts of discovery. Frances Yates describes this artistry as a "magico-religious technique for grasping and unifying the world of appearances through arrangements of significant images." The *Soledades* elicit a more cerebral than emotional response from readers to the relentless parade of visual imagery; nevertheless, the densely woven text of images within images brings to the surface hidden correspondences that Góngora the *vates* has perceived. He has chosen *culto* poetry as the medium to bring to his discerning audience glimpses of the system of beauty and harmony that animates the entire universe, the Platonic ideal that pervades his pastoral of solitude. The poet intuits the animating principle lying dormant in the most simple, ordinary objects and reveals the true beauty of the whole cosmos to the reader through the fragmentary beauty inherent in the many. Like others who subscribe to the Platonic philosophy of the occult, Góngora wishes "[t]o see the whole universe as a radiant hieroglyph, or rather to strip away the veil and see it all at once in angelic vision," in short, to unveil the hidden, divine *telos*, the cosmic design that lies beyond the corporeal world.[28]

Analysis of several "radiant hieroglyphs" illustrates how Góngora achieves this goal in his masterpiece. Consider, for instance, the catalog detailing the wedding-banquet fare of *Soledad* I:

> Manjares que el veneno
> y el apetito ignoran igualmente
> les sirvieron; y en oro no luciente
> confuso Baco, ni en bruñida plata,
> su néctar les desata,
> sino en vidrio topacios carmesíes
> y pálidos rubíes.
> Sellar del fuego quiso regalado
> los gulosos estómagos el rubio
> imitador süave de la cera,
> quesillo dulcemente apremïado
> de rústica, vaquera,
> blanca, hermosa mano, cuyas venas
> la distinguieron de la leche apenas;
> mas ni la encarcelada nuez esquiva,

>   ni el membrillo pudieran anudado,
>   si la sabrosa oliva
>   no serenara el bacanal diluvio.
> >   (Jammes, I:865–82)
>
> (Food, that to poison and lewd appetite
>   Was unknown equally,
> They served. Confused Bacchus did not try
> In burnished silver, no, nor shining gold
>   His liquor to supply,
> The pallid rubies and the topaz bright
>   In simple glass behold.
>
> To abate the greedy stomachs' genial fire
> The gentle waxy cheeses might desire,
>   (And Oh! when these were pressed
> How white the rustic milk-maid's hand did seem
> That veins alone distinguished from the cream!)
> The coy imprisoned nut and wrinkled quince
> Unto like task in vain themselves addressed,
> Only the savoury olives could aspire
> To appease the drunken flood, like that long since.
> >   [Wilson, I:843–58])

In this passage, the poet exalts and ennobles the values and virtues of the mythic Golden Age embodied in simple foods and warm, genuine hospitality, paradoxically couched in rich, sensuous language presented in a harmonious, contrapuntal composition. The series of images represents a spectacular case of "bilateral symmetry," the compositional characteristic typical of Gongorine style studied and made famous by Dámaso Alonso:[29]

Pagan scene—Bacchanalian orgy flood of wine, tempers flood of wine	Biblical scene—olive (branch) signals end of Flood,
Thirst satisfied by wine (liquid)	Hunger satisfied by food (solid)—cheese, nuts, quinces, and olives
Gold, silver, red, white	White predominates—cheese, hand
Hard, polished, reflecting surfaces—ruby, topaz, metal, glass	Soft, waxlike and spongy textures—waxy cheese, lovely hand, knotty quince
Liquid metaphorically hardened—winelike glass or metal container	Solids animated or personified—milkmaid's soul animates cheese
(Jammes, I:865–71; Wilson, I:843–49)	(Jammes, I:872–82; Wilson, I:850–58)

The menu divides readily into two major sections, separate sentences that function as counterweights to create a pleasing impression of balance, symmetry, and proportion. Rhyme reinforces both division between the sections and unity within each of the two, in the first sentence striking the reader's ear like couplets—*igualmente / luciente, plata / desata, carmesíes / rubíes* (rectifying the semantic mismatch). In the second and much longer sentence, Góngora employs rhymes across greater intervals, as in *regalado, apremïado, anudado* or *rubio,* and *diluvio,* as if to imply that more time, effort, and dishes were required to counteract the wine successfully. Phonetic contrast also underscores the semantic juxtaposition between the two sentences, although they share a similar phonetic and syntactic conclusion in "no . . . ni . . . sino" and "ni . . . ni . . . si . . . no," respectively (a familiar Gongorine construction), and alliteration and repetition contribute to a smooth transition from one section to another with *rubíes, regalado,* and *rubio.* Nevertheless, in the first division, voiced and unvoiced stops produce the predominant alliterative pattern, generating harsh, explosive sounds: *p* in *plata* and *pálidos; k* in *que, confuso,* and *carmesíes;* and *b* in *veneno, Baco,* and *bruñida.* Between the stops and the rhymed couplets, the audience conjures the image of clinking glasses and a crowd consuming wine at a galumphing pace. When the semantics shifts to temperance and moderation in the second sentence, Góngora graces the reader's ear with soothing sibilants and liquids: *s* in *sellar, süave, sabrosa,* and *serenara* (with additional support from *estómago* and *esquiva*); and *r* in *regalado, rubio,* and *rústica.* The first section concentrates on the satisfaction of thirst with wine, referred to periphrastically (and metonymically) as Bacchus's nectar, which immediately changes the portrait of the unpretentious feast into that of a Bacchanalian revelry, suddenly inviting the world of pagan myth to sit at the table. The audience envisions wine flowing so fast and furiously that red and white varieties blur together, whether from the fast-forward motion of imbibition or the speed with which the guests indiscriminately top off partially consumed glasses.[30] Góngora utilizes hypallage to capture the resultant strange mélange as *topacios carmesíes* (topaz bright) and *pálidos rubíes* (pallid rubies), emphasizing the disorderly flood of liquor unleashed by a "confused Bacchus" in the mismatched, crisscrossed nouns and adjectives. Despite the oenological mix-up, Góngora pauses to capture the beauty he finds dormant in an unexpected place, a common beverage in an ordinary container that he abruptly transmutes into hard, precious gems by means of a magical poetic trick, that is, by passing light through the refracting prism of glass colored by wine. A host of foods steps up to the plate in section 2 to bank the fires of intoxication and satisfy the fiery pangs of hunger suffered by the guests. The parade of victuals includes cheese that metonymically recalls the hands of its milkmaid maker whose skin is so fair that only her veins distinguish her from the milk (synecdochally, of course, the readers paint the maiden's entire portrait, not just her hands, in their minds), as well as nuts, quinces, and olives. Góngora animates Nature's bounty, giving each dish a personality, which in turn merges human and natural worlds. He depicts the cosmos of the Golden Age as a magic universe in which each figure and object possesses a lively animus, transforming the ordinary into the extraordinary. The milkmaid appears to have transfused part of her soul into the cheese (which now has her softness and innocent loveliness), the nuts shyly hide in their shells, and the knotty skin of the quince bears the wear-and-tear of outdoor life and labor. Although each displays a unique personality brought to light by the poet-seer, neither individually nor collectively can they stay the flood of wine, even though they end the guests' hunger. The waxy cheese, for instance, cannot withstand the burning flames of the formerly inhibited emotions unleashed by the wine. Only the olive, synecdochic representative of the peace symbol that signaled the end of the biblical Flood, can calm the Bacchanalian revelry, sacred and pagan myth linked by a tasty but commonplace fruit. This passage of the *Soledades* and the procession of banquet foods and drink thus conclude with restoration of peaceful equilibrium to the unbalanced, joyous celebration that began with the unstoppable flow of wine.

What is remarkable about this list of images is that it is a rather unremarkable sample of a thoroughly remarkable poetic work. Góngora starts with circumstances amazing to an aristocratic audience for what they lack: the material wealth and luxury to which the intended readers are accustomed. He then uses imagery that appeals powerfully to the senses, as in Ignatian meditation, and employs exquisitely tangible details to portray spiritual wealth in the physical terms of material splendor. Readers see the colorful wine, touch the wrinkly quince, and hear the sounds of laughter and happy eating and drinking. Even wine appears in a semantic field laden with aristocratic points of reference: gold and silver tableware, precious gems, faceted crystals—in short, the stuff of princes and palaces. As described, the dairymaid and cheese belong in a portrait of a fine lady draped in ermine who exhibits elegant, fine white hands. With a wave of the magic wand of artistry, Góngora the magus reveals the hidden connections that he suggests have always been there, written into the book of Nature, awaiting the moment in which he reveals their occult, universal design to readers in sudden glimpses of insight that he provides them through *culto* language. The superiority of the long-standing pastoral ethos leaps into the reader's mind: the peace, harmony, and abundance of the green world, and the almost prelapsarian purity and innocence of the Golden Age. In this mythic context, humans and nature are attuned to one another, and each person and thing pulses with the vibrancy of the beauty immanent in the divine cosmos. Góngora suggests to the members of his sophisticated audience that they can recover that idyllic world by shutting out the moral and physical distractions of court life, focusing the powers of the mind inward through his imagistic language, and traveling upward through that inspired poetry to the realm of Truth.

The poet's ability to provide readers with an imagistic conduit, a passage to the contemplative life to experience the beauty and harmony of the macrocosm, extends even to subjects that seem unable to sustain such a view. Near the end of *Soledad* II, the pilgrim stares transfixed as trained falcons bring down a crow:

> Breve esfera de viento,
> negra circunvestida piel, al duro
> alterno impulso de valientes palas
> la avecilla parece,
> en el de muros líquidos que ofrece
> corredor el dïáfano elemento
> al gémino rigor, en cuyas alas su vista libra toda el
>   estranjero.
>   (Jammes, II:923–30)

> (Brief tennis-ball of air,
> In black skin clad around, tossed to and fro
> Alternate by the hard and valiant pair,
> So seemed the little bird, seen from below,
> Between the liquid walls where courts were laid,
> By the pellucid element displayed
> To the twin rigour of the hawks. His sight
> The stranger fixed entirely on their flight.
>   [Wilson, II:907–14])

Jones notes that Góngora frequently organizes a sequence of images such that they crescendo in impact to a climactic image that concludes the series in exceptionally dramatic fashion.[31] Here the poet ends the parade of aviary hunting scenes with a morality play in miniature, which he cues readers, through the protagonist's reaction, to examine attentively. Crows are traditionally pictured as sinister birds with ugly voices cloaked in the mourning dress of black, iridescent feathers. This crow's own greed has caused her demise because like the rest of the covetous band, she cannot resist the lure of the gold eyes of the owl carried by the hunting party. Her quest for riches meets with disaster in an entrancing spectacle in which Góngora transforms her into a ball buffeted by the rackets of two feathered players, a gyrfalcon above and a saker below her, utilizing an aristocratic sport familiar to his elite audience for this key image. The positions of the birds metaphorically trace the boundaries of a walled court in the boundless, fluid medium of air. The impression of enclosure and compression emphasizes the smallness and defenselessness of the little bird *(avecilla)* in the grips of forces beyond her control. The poet packages a didactic message in this emblematic scene: an admonition regarding the dangers of avarice, one of the seven deadly sins. Yet, Góngora's use of the diminutive *avecilla* not only refers to size, but also indicates a level of subjective involvement, of sympathetic identification with the dying crow. After all, humans, too, have hastened the arrival of death with reckless, sinful behavior, and even blameless people find themselves inevitably, helplessly entrapped by the natural law of mortality. Death strips all living creatures of the adornments of physical beauty and noble social station, whether in the form of a shiny, plumed coat or a costly brocaded one, reducing both entities to a skin-covered bag of air fighting for and finally relinquishing a last, gasping breath. The span of life seems as infinite as the expanse of sky above, but eventually everyone must confront the limits that belie that illusion. Góngora offers for the perusal of pilgrim and reader a memento mori and an eloquent, meditative spectacle that underscore the poignancy and mystery of God's cyclic plan of life and death embodied as a somewhat frightening but also awe-inspiring tennis match played according to divine, omnipotent rules.

Góngora may in part have found inspiration for the dramatic staging of the art of memory, so apparent in the examples above, in Giulio Camillo's Venetian Memory Theater, a fanciful wooden edifice known throughout the courts of Europe in the second half of the sixteenth century from visitors' descriptions and written accounts of the structure's ornamentation and design. According to Frances Yates, Camillo sought to synthesize the macrocosm of the universe in the microcosm of the theater by means of a complex, multitiered exhibit of emblematic paintings, statuary, and astrological signs that would permit numerous visual groupings and interpretations. A solitary spectator activated the overlapping imagistic systems by entering the theater, stepping onto a small platform (what would be the stage in a traditional theater), and contemplating the spectacle surrounding him or her. The one-person audience focused the powers of the divine *mens* on the artistic representations, animating them, bringing their sleeping souls to life, and, through synthesis, symbolically linking lower and upper worlds in varied combinations of images. The viewer experiences moments of magical transcendence, tapping into the secrets of the cosmos made accessible in the theater of wonder. The same spirit of occult philosophy informs Góngora's memory theater: the *Soledades*. Substitute hybrid genres and multimedia effects for multileveled space and diverse plastic art forms, a solitary reader or pilgrim for a sole spectator, and a system of concomitant scenarios and images that demands varied readings for a system of interlocking figures and images that encourages different interpretations, and the basic structure and dynamics of the pastoral masterpiece emerge. Góngora, however, extends the opportunity to his readers to create an entire cosmic theater in their own imagination. They need go no further than to a quiet, comfortable space for reading and reflection to access the magical universe lurking beneath quotidian surroundings.

As the one constant in Góngora's memory theater, the pilgrim performs a crucial role in engaging and maintaining readers' interest, and subtly influencing the form that engagement takes. At the most pedestrian level, the hero's progress traces the poems' narrative line. His chance encounters and unpredictable adventures in the pastoral wonderland articulate the central, framing plot of the *Soledades* and mark the reader's path through the text. Yet, as the figural pivot in a unifying mode of emplotment, the pilgrim remains a rather mysterious, ambiguous, and somewhat fragile concoction to serve as the foundation for story or character development or both. The audience knows little about the protagonist. The poetic voice tells readers that he rivals Ganymede in youth and beauty, and suffers from unrequited love (Jammes, I:7–10; Wilson, I:6–8). The shipwreck of *Soledad* I occurs during an apparently self-imposed exile, and the pilgrim's clothes consistently identify him as an outsider and an aristocrat. The protagonist has painful memories of his beloved, and, eventually, in the plaintive soliloquy of *Soledad* II, he reveals the cause of his downfall in the vaguest of words. He resolves to lead a life of atonement dedicated to the sea in quiet semiretirement, distant from the unhappiness he found at court. Because Góngora never completed the *Soledades*, however, readers face the ultimate cliffhanger in regard to his fate. Yet, the protagonist compensates for what he lacks in personal history with an extremely rich literary ancestry. Antonio Vilanova, Jürgen Hahn, and others have noted that the pilgrim is really a composite of literary types: the wandering epic hero, like Ulysses and Aeneas; the *peregrino de amor* (pilgrim of love), that is, the solitary disillusioned lover who finds solace in nature as he roams the countryside, a tradition codified by Petrarch, Bembo, and Tasso; and the pilgrim of life, the wayward Christian wending his or her restless way back to God (to paraphrase Augustinian terminology), with important antecedents in the Bible, Dante, and, of course, Saint Augustine.[32] Góngora's pilgrim can also count among his fictional bloodlines the hero of Byzantine romance, the courtly lover; the protagonist of sentimental romance; and the sorrowful shepherd lover of eclogues and pastoral romances. Clearly, the *peregrino* may shed his personal past as easily as he does his water-stained clothes on the beach, at least from the audience's perspective, but he cannot divest himself of his basic literary nature.

For those reasons, the pilgrim is the perfect interlocutor to shuttle back and forth between extratextual and fictional worlds and occupy shifting distances and roles vis-à-vis the unfolding pastoral drama. The limited information the audience possesses about the nameless hero suffices to establish him as a special "Everyman," a courtier with a plethora of literary alter egos drawn from devotional literature and aristocratic fiction familiar to the intended readers. The protagonist, his creator, and the *Soledades*' audience thus appear to share a certain set of social and cultural experiences and expectations. Because the fashionable elite see the bucolic landscape filtered through an urban aristocratic consciousness and eyes similar to their own, they are drawn through the text by this other self. And by employing a hero with such a sketchy past, the author can mold him to function in many ways and assume multiple identities. This protean flexibility explains how Góngora can successfully merge pilgrim and poet in the prologue, and pilgrim and reader in the poems, in effect creating a multifaceted pilgrim complex that functions as a single compositional and hermeneutic unit.[33]

Although Góngora closely associates the pilgrim with the portrayal of voice and focalization in the *Soledades*, these relationships are obviously fraught with ambiguity and complexity. Whereas no one would expect the poet to adhere to anachronistic norms of consistency and precision in this regard, more often than not standard literary terminology fails to describe accurately the slippery disembodied persona, roughly identifiable with the implied author, who at times also shares the pilgrim's eyes and thoughts with readers. To my mind, only analogies to stage and screen prove helpful to characterize such intriguing but disquieting textual phenomena. It is certainly clear that Góngora the experimental poet was interested in exploring the use of shifting perspectives to create certain effects and stimulate the reader's mind. In the final tercet of his famous sonnet "De un caminante enfermo . . ." (On an ill traveler . . .), for example, a judgmental "I" appears out of nowhere, closes the gap between fictional and real space, and creates a sudden psychological and perspectival distortion—a jarring *admiratio* effect inspiring wonderment in the reader. Note that perspectival change and fluidity are also essential to meditational practice. Meditators must be able to see themselves float in and out of visions at will in their minds' eyes, effortlessly adjusting optical distance and contact with the imaginary worlds they concoct. Góngora's pilgrim does serve readers as a model of Augustinian self-education, as one who exercises the powers of the mind to accept his fate; reorient his values, in Epicurean fashion; and overcome his misfortunes by retiring into the self.[34] From the moment he awakens after his swoon on the beach, the pilgrim submits to an inward process of progressive change that Góngora manifests externally in word and deed. Memory, in the form of painful recollections of the past, rises up to smite him: "bueitre de pesares" (memory a vulture), to borrow a phrase from the old mountaineer's tale of woe (Jammes, I:502; Wilson, I:486). The sorrowful past visits him on several occasions: in the goatherd soldier's reminiscences of war; the *serrano*'s loss of his son; the presence of the bride, who resembles his beloved; and even in the dovecote woven into the poplar by the fisherman in his youth, a melancholy tribute to his former agility and daring. Understanding follows memory in the pilgrim's progress, when in his soliloquy of *Soledad* II the hero analyzes his current situation and confesses:

> "Audaz mi pensamiento
> el cenit escaló, plumas vestido,
> cuyo vuelo atrevido,
> si no ha dado su nombre a tus espumas,
> de sus vestidas plumas
> conservarán el desvanecimiento
> los anales diáfanos del viento."
> (Jammes, II:137–43)

> ("Once my audacious thought,
> In feathers clad, to scale the zenith sought,
> Though its bold flight assigned
> No second name unto a spumy wave,
> The dress of feathers gave
> The record of the dizzy fall to mind
> To the pellucid annal of the wind."
> [Wilson, II:130–36])

The protagonist compares himself to Icarus (periphrastically omitting an explicit reference to the mythic figure) in his former pursuit of a too lofty goal, his lady love, thus admitting the prideful error of his ways. No toponym remains to mark the tragic end of his dream; no Icarian sea records his mistake for all time. The pilgrim consigns his history to erasure in the annals of the wind. This cancellation of a past mistake symbolizes renunciation of life in what the elderly islander calls "'ese teatro de Fortuna'" (Jammes, II:401) ("this theatre of Fortune" [Wilson, II:392]), and signals the use of will to embrace a more ascetic, solitary, circumscribed existence:

> "¡Oh mar, oh tú, supremo
> moderador piadoso de mis daños!,
> tuyos serán mis años."
> (Jammes, II:123–25)
>
> ("O thou, o sea! supreme
> And piteous moderator of my tears!
> All thine shall be my years."
> [Wilson, II:116–18])

These lines of the protagonist's emotionally charged apostrophe to the sea resonate with prayerful humility and recognition of a higher, divine force. The pilgrim's interior progress appears to climax with the gift of his tears, a long-standing sign of contrition in Christian iconography, and a decisive bid for healing and self-improvement through rededication to a simpler and truer existence—a conversion to a different order of being exemplified by the poems' pastoral ethos and embodied by the protagonist's older doubles. At this point the progress of the pilgrim of love and that of the pilgrim of life converge to create a model of reading as a meditational, spiritual journey, symbolizing the substance and shape that the ideal reader's progress in the *Soledades* should assume: from the use of imaginative memory to internalize the images and scenes, to the exercise of analysis to ponder their significance, and, finally, to the use of will to act on the understanding achieved, to incorporate the lessons derived from the poems into everyday life and live with heightened awareness of the web of beauty and harmony implicit in the natural world.

A Symphony of Sight and Sound

The conceptual basis for the parallels I have drawn among the process of reading the *Soledades*, the pilgrim's progress, and meditational activity originates with Saint Augustine, who over the course of a lifetime redefined the act of reading as a pilgrimage, a journey made in varying stages of inwardness and ascent to a specific spiritual destination, the peaceful equilibrium sought by the restless soul and found in God, as mentioned in the *Carta en respuesta*. The trip begins when people first look at the book of Nature or readers encounter aural and visual stimuli in the form of written words, especially poetry, which serves as a second book of Nature. According to Brian Stock, Augustine considers the reader's engagement with inscribed language a rite of initiation, the crossing of a threshold from outer to inner worlds in which decipherment of the material text and internalized sensory experience lead to ever greater apprehension of the universe's inner design. All the senses contribute to this awakening of the mind and soul, but sight and hearing occupy the uppermost positions in the Augustinian hierarchy. Hearing provides indirect communication, as in the oral reading of a text to a group of listeners who hear, reflect, understand, and resolve to exercise what they have learned. Sight, however, unlike hearing, functions directly and perpetually, for even at night, even in sleep, the mind performs the work of memory (recollection and imagination) by inventing images. For this reason, sight lies closer to Truth, because the passage from outer to inner eye and the transformation from outward to inward vision occur instantly, with the silent text as the only intermediary.[35]

In accordance with the tradition of Augustinian thought and meditation, the poet deems sight and hearing the more powerful senses in their ability to stir readers' souls and move them across the boundary between outward experience and inward contemplation. Góngora provides his audience with a veritable symphony of sight and sound in the *Soledades*, executing a virtuoso performance in the confines of the written page and the solitary reader's mind. Renaissance Platonists prized poetry as a universal science that contained and transcended all other sciences, believing poetry could synthesize limitless subjects and imitate other artistic media, representing a sort of ideal, pansophic aesthetic form.[36] The *Soledades* adhere to this view in that visitors to Góngora's bucolic *Kunstschrank* will see a vast picture gallery among the marvels and listen to music all the while. In this way, the eyes and ears of the mind lead readers on their meditative odyssey.

Góngora's efforts to paint pictures made of poetry received impetus not just from Augustinian thought and the Platonic art of memory, but also from the related tradition of *ut pictura poesis*, the Horatian simile meaning "as is painting, so is poetry." The equation of poetry and painting reemerged in sixteenth-century Italy among humanists who asserted that these "sister arts" shared the same nature, content, and purpose. A century later, the notion had spread to such an extent that comparative systems of the arts proliferated throughout Europe, identifying plot with compositional design, metaphors with color, and so forth, marshaling poetry and painting in a common Platonic quest for Truth and Beauty.[37] Góngora cues readers to watch and listen to the festival of sight and sound early in the *Soledades*:

> De una encina embebido
> en lo cóncavo, el joven mantenía

> la vista de hermosura, y el oído
> de métrica armonía.
> (Jammes, I:267–70)
>
> (The hollow of an ilex was the nook,
> Where he his shelter took,
> Feeding on all their loveliness his eyes,
> His ears upon their metric harmonies.
> [Wilson, I:262–65])

The poet pushes the pilgrim into the audience's space by situating him in the natural box seat of a hollow oak and making the protagonist adopt the posture of a bedazzled viewer. The rhymes of *embebido* (absorbed) with *oído* (hearing) and *mantenía* (held) (Wilson's "feeding") with *armonía* (harmony) stress the degree of absorption or rapture elicited (or that should be elicited) by what the pilgrim and the reader see and hear. The writer also alerts readers to the function of these privileged senses as conduits that permit the Platonic ideals of beauty and harmony, dressed in human and natural form, to penetrate and transfix the soul. Góngora could hardly compose a more pointed proem to the spectacle that follows.

The impressive gallery of artwork that materializes near the beginning of the *Soledades* mirrors the taste of the members of Góngora's intended audience, many of whom would have owned or had access to private collections of pictures. Consider the subjects that dominate the poet's gallery and the painting collections of Golden Age Spain: mythology, genre scenes, portraiture, still lifes, and landscapes. Explicit and implicit mythological allusions abound in the *Soledades,* producing a continuous intertextual code that readers must master before they can appreciate the beauty or the ideas in the poems. The first one hundred lines alone of *Soledad* I introduce the classical topics of the rape of Europa, the rape of Ganymede, the rescue of Arion, the tale of Leda and the swan (with the subsequent birth of Castor and Pollux added for good measure), the story of Ursa Major or of Callisto and Arcas, along with casual references to Vulcan, Pales, and Flora. On occasion, Góngora renders classical mythology such that an actual painting comes to mind. *Soledad* I's opening lines (Jammes, 1–6; Wilson, 1–5), for example, recall Titian's *Rape of Europa* (1559–1562), which completed the series of mythological paintings titled *Poesie* commissioned by Prince Philip in 1550 and finished during his reign as Philip II.[38] An attentive reader might perform a little mental hocus-pocus to construe the following verses as an oblique quotation of Botticelli's *Birth of Venus* (ca. 1480):

> Dividiendo cristales,
> en la mitad de un óvalo de plata,
> venía a tiempo el nieto de la espuma
> que los mancebos daban alternantes
> al viento quejas. . . .
> (Jammes, II:519–23)
>
> (Parting the crystal seas
> The grandson of the foam
> In half a silver oval came, while they
> Gave their laments alternate to the wind.
> (Wilson, II:512–15])

The poet has painted a witty copy of the original (perhaps based on a print he had seen?), placing Venus's son, Cupid, on the oval half-shell (like mother, like son), and transforming Botticelli's personified wind (which blows a poised, weightless Venus along) into an evening breeze that carries only the sound of the amoebic song entoned by the enamored fishermen, while a busy, hardworking Cupid uses his arrows as oars to row ashore, poisoning the water with love as a result (Jammes, II:527–30; Wilson, II:519–22).

The *Soledades'* many scenes of everyday life in the country, albeit idealized as befits pastoral convention, have their pictorial counterparts in the genre paintings that appeared in the 1550s in Flanders where the tradition continued to develop, and then spread to northern Italy. Toward the end of the century, Flemish genre scenes began to surface in Madrid collections, and by the beginning of the seventeenth century, learned, trend-conscious Spanish collectors preferred genre pictures and still lifes to other types of paintings.[39] Frame any of the evening activities at the goatherd's hut, the wedding festivities, or the fishing and hunting sequences of *Soledad* II, and the resultant work of art would prove a welcome addition to these Golden Age collections. Góngora's most compelling genre scenes blend the ordinary and mythological in a strikingly incongruent fashion. Note how the author describes a heavy mountaineer, whose desire for glory drives him to enter the jumping competition:

> a un vaquero de aquellos montes, grueso,
> membrudo, fuerte roble,
> que, ágil a pesar de lo robusto,
> al aire se arrebata, violentando
> lo grave tanto, que lo precipita,
> Icaro montañés, su mismo peso,
> de la menuda hierba el seno blando
> piélago duro hecho a su ruïna.
> (Jammes, I:1004–11)

> (A peasant, a strong herdsman, sinewy,
> Robust as any oak, agile as well,
> Despite his sturdiness, now to rebel
> Against his hugeness, and the air defy;
>   Who should at last descend,
> A mountain Icarus, through his own weight,
> On the soft bosom of the grass to lie,
>   The hard sea of his fate.
>   [Wilson, I:980–87])

Góngora paints a humorous picture of an oak tree of a man who defies Nature by attempting to fly through the air, but meets the same fate as the winged Icarus. In contrast to the common response to the end of the tragic figure of yore, the solid trunk of the peasant herdsman hitting the ground elicits perhaps a slight wince and then tears of laughter, not pain, from onlookers in and outside the text. This blend of verbal and iconic registers anticipates paintings such as Velázquez's *Feast of Bacchus* (1629) and *Forge of Vulcan* (1630), in which the artist treats a classical theme with the naturalist style of Sevilla's late-sixteenth-century workshops.

In a sense, the toppling herdsman constitutes a portrait in the Gongorine art gallery. Numerous figural paintings of this sort hang in the *Soledades'* exhibition hall, serving, among other purposes, the ekphrastic principle of stopping the flow of the temporal medium of poetry. The portrait of a female lutenist spectacularly illustrates this point:

> rémora de sus pasos fue su oído,
> dulcemente impedido
> de canoro instrumento, que pulsado
> era de una serrana junto a un tronco,
> sobre un arroyo de quejarse ronco,
> mudo sus ondas, cuando no enfrenado.
>   (Jammes, I:237–42)

> (When remora to his footsteps was his ear
> By sweet canorous instrument constrained,
> Which, fingered by a mountain maiden near
> Above a streamlet from complaining hoarse,
> Silenced the ripples it had near restrained.
>   [Wilson, I:234–38])

This singing picture contrives to stop the pilgrim in his tracks, simultaneously silencing the personified stream and nearly halting its motion totally. Nature and human, united in a synchronous paralysis of wonderment, pay homage to the beautiful musician and her melodies, emblematic of the harmony of the universe, a familiar subject in northern Italian paintings of the sixteenth century. These artworks combine portraiture with genre scenes, as in the *Luteplayer*(s) of Veneto (1520), Caravaggio (ca. 1596), and Gentileschi (ca. 1615), respectively.[40] *Soledad* II provides perhaps the most memorable portrait in Góngora's collection, an equestrian painting reminiscent of Titian's *Charles V at the Battle of Mühlberg* (1548) and Rubens's *Equestrian Portrait of the Duke of Lerma* (1603):

> En sangre claro y en persona augusto,
> si en miembros no robusto
> príncipe les sucede, abrevïada
> en modestia civil real grandeza.
> La espumosa del Betis ligereza
> bebió no sólo, mas la desatada
> majestad en sus ondas el luciente
> caballo, que colérico mordía
> el oro que süave lo enfrenaba,
> arrogante, y no ya por las que daba
> estrellas su cerúlea piel al día,
> sino por lo que siente
> de esclarecido, y aun de soberano,
> en la rienda que besa la alta mano
> de sceptro digna. . . .
>   (Jammes, II:809–23)
>
> (August in person, and of ancient blood
> If not robust in limb,
> Followed a prince; and there combined in him
> With royal grandeur, civil modesty.
> His steed the spumy froth of Bætis' flood
> Not only drank, but the free majesty
> Inspiring every wave;
> This glowing stallion madly bit the gold
> That gently held him back; arrogant he,
> Though not because his hide cerulean gave
> New starlight to the day, but that the rein,
> In the illustrious and the sovereign hold
> Of sceptre-worthy hands, should him restrain.
>   [Wilson, II:796–808])

This passage made such an impact on Góngora's contemporaries that some asserted that the poet had portrayed a historical personage, either the duke of Béjar or the count of Niebla, the powerful duke of Lerma's son-in-law and the patron of the *Polifemo*.[41] I suspect Góngora relished speculation over the identity of the horseman, but I believe that in actuality he sought not to represent a specific individual, but rather to capture the essence, the universal ideas that form the conceptual core of this particular type of portraiture. Góngora emphasizes the contrast between the slight, elegant physique of the prince, who embodies nobility of blood and character, with the mythic grandeur of the colossal steed. He further juxtaposes the modest, unassuming composure of the noble, his *sprezzatura* (easy control and mastery), with the arrogant, choleric temperament of the horse, who does not wish to rein in his speed and strength, but does so out of respect for the inherent superiority he senses from the man who holds the reins. The poet-painter crystallizes all the physical and psychological tension of the relationship in a conventional visual focus of equestrian portraiture, the firm but refined hands that manage the horse and carry a sceptre, or some other symbol of power. On the most obvious level, the portrait delivers a paean to the social and political hierarchy of the time and the Renaissance ideal of the prince sovereign. Yet, Góngora has shown great skill in enlivening and enriching a standard topic in this colorful representation. The poet suggests that princes, and indeed all people, should let the noble and superior aspects of humanity, reason and the soul, rule the unbridled passions of the body—a riderless horse. The picture thus situates mind and flesh in their natural and appropriate order. Góngora may also have traced a schematic self-portrait of the artist in this passage, because poets and painters harness and train Nature (a wild, unruly, beautiful force), bringing the latent, hidden perfection it holds to light with hands that wield a pen or brush as if it were a sceptre. Far from putting artists and princes on equal footing, Góngora asserts that he and his peers surpass temporal rulers on account of their quasi-divine creative powers. The poet sketches the gestalt of the equestrian portrait so successfully that the reader-spectator finishes the canvas mentally, stroking in the sceptre that inevitably completes the painting. However, Góngora foils audience expectations when he declares the prince worthy of the powerful symbol and then leaves that sceptre unpainted and floating in conceptual limbo, reminding readers that the entire portrait the poet has drawn and they have visualized is a tenuous, magical illusion so strong that momentarily they invest the imagined image with reality. At the same time, the author reveals that his mind and hand will rule omnipotently in the poetic realm of the *Soledades*.

The validity and force of the *ut pictura poesis* comparison rest with the descriptive power of the poets, in the *enargeia* (pictorial vividness) that they infuse into their verses. Leonardo da Vinci found descriptive poetry analogous to still-life and landscape painting, precisely the types of artwork that dominate the *Soledades'* museum. Readers quickly discover that like his painter counterparts, Góngora demonstrates the virtuosity of a master illusionist in his still-life and landscape renditions. Still-life painting emerged independently in two locations, in northern Europe toward the end of the fifteenth century and in Italy roughly between 1500 and 1510.[42] The Hapsburgs' assiduous collection of Flemish and Italian art, along with the widespread dissemination of prints among Spanish painters, guaranteed exposure to the genre; nevertheless, still lifes did not gain entrée into Spanish collections until the 1590s, when they appeared in and around Toledo in the hands of a small group of educated elite who wanted to acquire the paintings most in vogue. Still lifes grew in popularity, gradually spreading southward through the peninsula, until by the 1630s they appeared in Sevilla. In his still lifes, his catalogs of food, fabrics, furnishings, falcons, and the like, Góngora lavishes so many details pertaining to light, color, and texture on each item that the objects and animals seem to step out of the frame of the page and into the extratextual world of the reader. Even a turkey headed for the village wedding merits the artist's touch and direct address by a narrative voice dripping with mocking familiarity:

> Tú, ave peregrina,
> arrogante esplendor, ya que no bello,
> del último Occidente
> penda el rugoso nácar de tu frente
> sobre el crespo zafiro de tu cuello,
> que Himeneo a sus mesas te destina.
> (Jammes, I:309–14)
>
> (Thou, migratory fowl, of farthest West
> Arrogant splendour in no lovely way;
> In vain the rugged nacre of thy crest
> In anger lower upon thy sapphire breast,
> Destined, for Hymeneal banquets, prey.
> [Wilson, I:302–6])

With several brush strokes, Góngora endows this strange *(peregrina)* fowl who has wandered *(peregrina* [migratory]) to the Old Country from the New World with body language that bespeaks outrage over his future as a main course at the banquet. The linguistic resemblance between *pavo* (turkey) and *pavo real* (peacock) implies character kinship, a shared arrogance unjustified by the ugliness of this bird, who does have a similarly impressive size and shape, lightly penciled by the artist. The poetic voice invites the ridiculously proud creature to indulge his indignation, because his efforts will prove futile and destiny awaits him at the dinner table. The poet employs color and texture to hone his portrayal of the turkey's most outstanding feature: a red, wrinkled snout that can swell in anger to cover his sapphire-blue neck.

Although Spanish artists eventually embraced still lifes enthusiastically, few specialized in landscape painting. Nevertheless, Golden Age painters assuredly knew the landscapes of Titian, Tintoretto, Veronese, and Bassano, as well as those of the Brueghels, and the hunting and animal pictures of Peter Snayers, Frans Snyders, and Paul de Vos.[43] In the *Soledades*, Góngora pays the same attention to detail in the sweeping vistas he pens for audience perusal as in the lines he dedicates to his still lifes, successfully evoking a tone or mood through landscape. The sight of the pilgrim's small, lonely figure atop dark, heavy boulders, silhouetted against the vast expanse of the starry night sky as he trudges upward and inland toward a distant light, conveys the sense of drama, solitude, melancholia, and otherworldliness appropriate for the opening scenes in the *Soledades* signaling boundary crossing. Chiaroscuro also contributes to the aura of welcome and grace in the next frame in which the goatherds' campfire, the visual focus, casts deep shadows and backlights the dog, humans, and their activities, adding a benedictory halo effect to the scene. In the hunting episodes near the end of *Soledad* II, the shimmering reflections of sunlight on water, the complementary ribbons of color of estuary, marsh reeds, and firmament, provide a tranquil, panoramic backdrop for the bold but isolated brush strokes marking the life-and-death interaction of falcons and prey, and the bright clothing of the human witnesses. Such sharp contrasts of color, light, and composition, with broad horizontal bands broken randomly by short verticals and sudden diagonal movements, communicate well the tension, excitement, and dynamism of the hunt.

Góngora's realization of *enargeia* in the *Soledades*, however, far exceeds the development of subject matter similar to that selected by contemporary painters. The author also shows artistic mastery in his adaptation of pictorial techniques to a poetic medium. His treatment of light offers a case in point. For this aspect of composition, Spanish painters and collections supplied Góngora with a plethora of examples of the correct use of light to generate the most powerful effects on viewers. Jonathan Brown has written of the emergence of a new reform style of devotional painting in Golden Age Spain that was tied to Counter Reformation goals and ideology and exploited light, as well as the contrast of light and shadow, for dramatic, spiritual impact. The brothers Bartolomé Carducho and Vicente Carducho became the principal proponents of this new style as royal painters at the court of Philip III. Vicente, a member of the duke of Lerma's coterie of artists and men of letters, counted among his friends two of Góngora's most vocal peers and adversaries: Lope de Vega and Juan de Jáuregui. The composer of the *Soledades* would also have known the works of Caravaggio's followers, who found an important patron in the duke of Lerma's uncle Bernardo Cardinal Sandoval y Rojas, archbishop of Toledo from 1599 to 1618, a figure of some significance in Góngora's advance at court.[44] The scenes of the pilgrim's nighttime arrival at the goatherd's hut illustrate the author's confidence in translating into poetry the Caravaggist style of tenebrism, in which a focused beam of klieglike brilliance illuminates a few figures and leaves others in darkness. In fact, Góngora betrays a fascination with light in myriad forms throughout the *Soledades,* such as the way light transforms a glass of wine into a sparkling gem, morning sunbeams generate mist and swathe a river valley in haze, chiaroscuro alters perception and mood as twilight sweeps over the land, or sunrise reflects off the burnished capitals of a palace's columns:

> Cuantas del Ocëano
> el Sol trenzas desata
> contaba en los rayados capiteles
> que, espejos (aunque esféricos) fieles,
> bruñidos eran óvalos de plata.
> (Jammes, II:701–5)
>
> (The tresses that the sun freed from the main
> He counted in each shining capital,
> That—faithful mirrors although spherical—
> Were shaped in burnished silver ovals plain.
> [Wilson, II:687–90])

As the sun comes up, the horizon acts as a prism that refracts the light, which, due to closeness to the horizon, waves on the ocean, atmospheric interference that viewers perceive as discrete rays, a phenomenon Góngora likens to a lady unbraiding her tresses in the morning. The sun lady can count (or perhaps the pilgrim performs this pleasant task) the unbraided rays of light in the faithful mirror of the polished, silvery capitals, which are *rayados* (striped) when hit by individual beams of light, and therefore accurately reflect the streams of light back to the viewer. The capitals also faithfully mirror the geometrical disposition of elements at the light source. To the human eye, the spherical sun appears to be an oval cut by the line of the horizon from which ribbons of light emanate. These rays in turn strike a striated, convex capital, which looks like an oval cut by lines, but if one extends the shapes imaginatively in volumetric space, the oval metamorphoses into a reflective sphere that returns the light prismlike, in bright bands. If the conceit seems too obscure, readers should keep in mind the epoch's enthusiasm for optical illusions, instruments, and experiments, and paintings that evolve from the camera obscura or emphasize optical effects, such as Parmigianino's *Self-Portrait in a Convex Mirror* (1524), Holbein's *French Ambassadors* (1533), or any of the magical interior scenes of Vermeer (1632–1675). Góngora's complex analogy sets up a self-contained system of harmonious correspondences that transforms art into a second mirror image of Nature, in which both congenially conspire to dazzle readers with the divine beauty of light.

Góngora also proves himself a supreme colorist in the *Soledades*, the equal of the great painters of the age. Eunice Joiner Gates has pointed out how the copious lists in the poems create an impression of mass and plasticity through variety and the sheer quantity of heterogeneous items cataloged.[45] I agree with her observations, but I also add that, like Titian, Góngora relies on vibrant colors and sensuous textures to emphasize mass and shapes and, conversely, to diffuse the outline of distinctive forms. Color's ability to define and distinguish stands out in the description of the procession of *serranos* burdened with wedding gifts, which quickly become the focus of a Gongorine still life of game and animals in the Flemish mode. The catalog begins with a heavy load of black-crested hens that the poet immediately contrasts with the proud rooster who rules the avian harem. Góngora portrays him as an exotic pasha with a coral beard, and a purple, rather than golden, turban (Jammes, I:291–96; Wilson, I:285–91). The red- or purple-on-black contrast separates rooster from hens, male from female, and attracts the inner eye of the reader. The patterned colors of spotted kids wearing garlands of flowers, numerous furry rabbits, and the turkey who exhibits his red snout against a sapphire-blue neck contribute additional visual interest overall, but each in a distinct manner—pattern, texture, or color contrast—that separates the creatures by type (Jammes, I:297–314; Wilson, I:307–24). The brilliant primary colors—red, blue, and gold—highlighted by the color black, rich patterns (spots or geometric honeycombs), and textures (fur or feathers) celebrate the uniqueness and integrity of each class of game or fowl and preserve the overwhelming feeling of the diversity, abundance, and luscious sensory appeal of the whole. However, Góngora also skillfully employs color to create the opposite visual effect in the *Soledades*, that of breaking down the boundaries traced between objects, and between things and beings. The poet imitates the technique of sfumato brilliantly executed by artists such as Leonardo, Correggio, and Titian, in which the painter mixes contiguous, contrasting shades of color to blur hard lines and dissolve the illusion of solid, separate masses. On a rudimentary level, a rhetorical structure such as hypallage can serve this purpose. For instance, the author characterizes a personified ocean as "coronado / de blancas ovas y de espuma verde" (Jammes, II:24–25) (crowned / With foam and weeds, in green and white display [Wilson, II:23–24]). The constant motion of the sea blends foam and algae so thoroughly that the colors run together indiscriminately, producing green spume and white algae.

Yet, Góngora manipulates sfumato in the poems for more profound purposes than just to capture visual phenomena accurately. The technique foregrounds the network of hidden correspondences in nature, permitting readers to sneak a peek at the superior cosmic order they could never otherwise see. In *Soledad* I, the author personifies a stream, transforming it into a sort of river god who steals glimpses of the crystalline beauty of the maidens' ankles and feet as they dance along the banks:

> en cuanto él hurta blando
> (entre los olmos que robustos besa)
> pedazos de cristal, que el movimiento
> libra en la falda, en el coturno ella,
> de la coluna bella
> ya que celosa basa,
> dispensadora del cristal no escasa.
> (Jammes, I:543–49)

> (So that by stealth it took
> (Kissing the robust elms on either side)
> The crystal fragments that their movements freed
> Between the skirt and buskin, which, indeed,
> Did jealous base for column fair provide,
> But scattered too, much crystal to the tide.
> [Wilson, I:526–31])

The river robs slivers of whiteness from the pure, alabaster skin of the *serranas* via reflections in which mirrored human porcelain blends indistinguishably with the crystalline water. Góngora merges male with female, human with nature, animate with inanimate, stressing the pastoral ethos of idyllic, harmonious coexistence between humankind and Nature.[46] Note that although the conceit turns on the shared color of purest white, the poet enacts another strategy to support the visual impact of the image and the Platonic ideals it conveys, namely, the humanization of the river and the aestheticization of the maidens. Góngora makes the brook into a dream lover who kisses the elms and clearly longs to do the same to the *serranas*. Simultaneously, the poet transforms the women, with their cothurni and their column legs, into the dancing maidens of a Greco-Roman frieze, ironically through ekphrasis frozen in time and motion, almost as if they were caryatids or amphora decorations. These transmutations bear witness to the magical fluidity of the pastoral world that Góngora has constructed and to the tremendous power the poet-magus wields.

Góngora's generous distribution of dramatic gestures in the poems represents another point of contact with pictorial art of the epoch. The sixteenth-century theorist Lomazzo stated that the sister arts shared the genius of expressive power. In fact, according to Leonardo, artists should transfer this most important aspect of the painter's art to the canvas in body gestures and movements. The works of Caravaggio and of El Greco perhaps best illustrate the implications of these notions realized in magnificent, moving paintings. Caravaggio's famous use of light contributes to the high dramatic quotient of his works, but other technical features add to their emotional impact as well. For example, he includes figures or features that break the picture plane, such as the jutting stone slab in *The Entombment of Christ* (1603–1604) or the dirty feet of the kneeling pilgrim in the *Madonna di Loreto* (1604–1605). Often, Caravaggio focuses on gesturing fingers and hands, as in the *Calling of St. Matthew* (1599–1600) and the *Conversion of St. Paul* (1600–1601). He even creates palpable tension through *contrapposto* (the counterbalancing of a twisted body or bodies around a central axis), as in the famous *Crucifixion of St. Peter* (1600–1601). Viewers will encounter similar techniques intended to engage and move viewers in the paintings of El Greco, such as the interlocutory figures and highlighted hands of *The Burial of the Count of Orgaz* (1586–1588), the illogical combination of two totally different perspectives in *Assumption of the Virgin* (1577–1578), and the energized, almost frenetic treatment of the human figure in *Adoration of the Shepherds* (ca. 1612–1614).[47] The shifting point of view of the narrator in the *Soledades,* moving in and out of the pilgrim's consciousness, and the constantly changing distance of the protagonist vis-à-vis the reader outside the text and the activity inside the pastoral world, has, to say the least, a disquieting effect on the audience, keeping them off-kilter, and perpetually struggling to reconcile imaginary distances and perspectives while trying to redefine their role in regards to the bucolic masterpiece and the inhabitants of that fictional landscape. In terms of the emphasis on gestures, Góngora rivals Caravaggio and El Greco in his focus on hands as symbolic and emotive human features. As the pilgrim gazes at the procession of maidens from his oak hiding spot, the *Soledades'* focalizer zooms in for a close-up of two beautiful gestures, one rendered as the metamorphosis of a lily-white hand into the elegant bucket of a water wheel ("por el arcaduz bello de una mano") and the other as lovely, nimble musician's fingers playing pieces of slatelike castanets ("Negras pizarras entre blancos dedos / ingeniosa hiere otra" [Jammes, I:245, 251–52; Wilson, I:241, 247–48]). Both sets of hands delight the eye, but they also emphasize human ingenuity and, at the same time, bridge the gap between human activity and Nature's beauty and harmony, here enhanced by the maidens' clever, artistic touch. In *Soledad* II, wedding guests raise their hands to hail a boat, the fingers of the islander's daughters sew labyrinthine fishing nets, one talented daughter spears a sea monster with a skilled hand, falcons rest on the gauntleted hands of hunters, and a prince's elegant hand controls all of Nature's power, energy, and beauty embodied in his horse (Jammes, II:42–44, 219, 480–81, 971–73, 820–23; Wilson, II:40–42, 210, 474–75, 954–56, 806–8). Unlike the hands painted by his artist contemporaries discussed above, the masterful fingers forged by Góngora pay tribute to human ingenuity, endeavor, and achievement in harnessing and shaping the God-given raw materials of this world. However, the poet, like the painters, clearly strives to inspire wonderment in his audience.

I suggested earlier in this chapter that the elements of emotionalism portrayed in the *Soledades* correspond to the pictorial taste of the day, but have a staged, theatrical quality that deprives them of the sense of spontaneity and the immediacy of impact of a Caravaggio or El Greco painting. In part due to the different media and the responses each arouses, in part due to the process of intellectual aestheticization to which Góngora submits virtually everything, the joy, laughter, tears, and melancholia that cross the pastoral stage inspire readers' analysis rather than intuitive empathy. When the old *serrano* of *Soledad* I sheds bitter tears over the loss of his son to the entire historical sweep of the voyages of discovery, puzzling out the allusions to famous navigators and conquistadores—an entertaining, cerebral game to be sure—consumes all the audience's attention to the point that any spontaneous, emotive potential that might have existed originally is lost. Such histrionic episodes indicate Góngora's commitment to techniques, albeit of a painterly nature, that inspire solitary contemplation, and hint that such self-conscious emotionalism functions more as a cuing mechanism, signifying that "this is the spot" where the reader should stop, listen, and meditate.

The varied landscapes that Góngora paints in the *Soledades*, with their complex interplay of perspectival and spatial relationships, show that the poet shared his artist contemporaries' fascination with recessional space and the problem of creating the illusion of depth.[48] The poet handles the issue by presenting people and objects in different scales of magnitude in the poems and by incorporating one of the primary focalizers, the pilgrim, into the text. However, the author also creates depth through dynamism painted as sudden, distant movement that frequently cuts across the field of vision on the diagonal, instantly catching the mind's eye: the flight of birds, the sparkle of fireworks, the downhill rush of a stream, or the hurried descent of a mounted hunting party:

> Lúbrica no tanto
> culebra se desliza tortüosa
> por el pendiente calvo escollo, cuanto
> la escuadra descendía presurosa
> por el peinado cerro a la campaña,
> que la mar debe, con término prescripto,
> más sabandijas de cristal que a Egipto
> horrores deja el Nilo que lo baña.
> (Jammes, II:823–30)
>
> (The smooth and twisting snake
> Cannot so rapidly go on its way
> Under a bald and hanging cliff, as they,
> The squadron, from the unequal summit make
> Their progress to the underlying strand,
> The plain that with prescribed boundary
> Owes far more crystal serpents to the sea
> Than all the horrors left upon the sand
> In Egypt, when the Nile has bathed the land.
> [Wilson, II:809–17])

Yet, even as Góngora attracts readers through their sense of sight with the rapid, zigzag progress of the hunters down the slope, a *serpentinata* that the poet wittily sketches as a snake's twisting slither, only to repeat the optical pun in the silvery puddles rendered as *sabandijas de cristal* (crystal serpents), he appeals to the audience's sense of hearing as well, stimulating the other sense privileged by Augustinian thought to draw his captive meditators into the *Soledades'* pastoral world. The passage's abundant sibilants—"*se*," "de*s*liza," "tortüo*s*a," "e*s*collo," "e*s*cuadra," "de*s*cendía," "*p*re*s*urosa," "*p*re*s*cripto," "*s*abandijas," "cri*s*tal," and "horrore*s*"—produce the hissing sound of a snake, a case of onomatopoeia that enlivens and completes the serpentine picture while delighting the reader's inner ear. The predominance of tonic front vowels (the *i* of "desl*i*za," "prescr*i*pto," "saband*i*jas," "Eg*i*pto," and "N*i*lo"; and the *e* of "cul*e*bra," "*se*," "c*e*rro," "d*e*be," "t*é*rmino," and "d*e*ja") lends tonal brightness and lightness to the image, just as the rapid succession of alliterated stops (the *p* of "*p*or," "*p*endiente," "*p*resurosa," "*p*einado," and "*p*rescripto"; the *t* of "*t*anto," "*t*ortüosa," and "*t*érmino"; and the *k* of "*c*ulebra," "*c*alvo," "*c*uanto," "*c*ampaña," "*c*ristal," and "*q*ue") contributes a brisk staccato rhythm to the whole that conveys the swift pace of the riders. The use of anaphora in lines 824 and 826 introduces an enhancing visual component, a verbal mirror image that underscores the repeated notion of descent of a steep incline. The alliteration, echoed words and semantics, and rhythmic repetition ("pór el pendiénte cálvo" and "pór el peinádo cérro") add an auditory complement to the horses' motion, seen by the mind's eye, that enables the inner ear to hear their hoofbeats. The caesura in line 823 that separates this landscape animated by human activity from the preceding equestrian portrait of the prince (Jammes, II:809–23; Wilson, II:796–808) breaks the flow of sound with a momentary silence that frames the shift in subject, scale, and focus, from the magnified close-up of the prince's hand to the glimpse of a distant, moving S-shape that the reflective viewer surmises consists of mounted hunters, although the focalizer cannot discern the individual figures from the current imaginary vantage point. Rhyme plays an important part in the sonority of the passage. The rhymed link between *tortüosa* (twisting) and *presurosa* (rapidly) highlights the seemingly impossible combination of winding movement and haste, *contrapposto* typical of a snake, but strikingly applied here to the human procession. The aural tie between *campaña* (plain) and *baña* (bathe) points out conceptual complementarity, that is, that the sea leaves saltwater imprints on the marshland periodically, with the changing tides, just as each year the Nile floods its riverbanks, giving the plain an ambiguous legacy of fertility and pestilence, an unexpected and memorable comparison, to be sure, for the reader. Góngora's attention to sonorous detail extends even to the manipulation of a single word, *tortüosa*, for onomatopoeic effect. The repetition of the plosive *t* forces the audience's inner voice to start and stammer, whereas the diaeresis over the *u* strengthens and diversifies the vowel sounds, and elongates the word's pronunciation by another syllable. Readers thus receive the audible impression of sustained, tense, but lithe sinuosity, the very essence of a serpent communicated through sound.

The observations above prove Góngora as adept at composing coloratura as at painting color. John Hollander has written that the basis for discussing the music of poetry lies in the belief that the sound patterns held in common by these artistic media have a similar, magical impact on their respective audiences. The remarkable musicality of the *Soledades*, another underappreciated aspect of the work, suggests that Góngora shares this belief. The author demonstrates such proficiency at wedding words, visual images, and sound effects in the pastoral masterpiece that he seems intent on re-creating and reclaiming the ancient symbiosis between music and poetry. These sister arts, after all, share the same Greco-Roman ancestry and a historical development in which they, at times, closely entwine and, at other times, diverge to move on parallel tracks. Both Hollander and James Winn note that over the years a persistent tension between constructive techniques, which emphasize structural and (almost visual) stylistic elements, and dramatic expressiveness, which stresses auditory impact, has characterized critical analysis and thought regarding music and poetry. However, in the epoch of Góngora, whereas new devotional practices advocated for greater commitment to affective, hearable communication, poets and composers refused to abandon their preoccupation with matters of form, choosing to tie expressivity and structure more tightly together. Belief in the reaffirmed and reinforced kinship between music and poetry spread at such a pace in Renaissance Europe that the previously mentioned comparative treatises on painting and poetry met with musicopoetic counterparts, such as Joachim Burmeister's *Musica Poetica* (1606), in which the author employs rhetorical terms to describe procedures of musical composition, with the object of moving the listener without neglecting proportion and design.[49]

New musical and poetic types arose during the Renaissance in which the sister arts actively engaged with or mimicked each other, flaunting the rediscovery of their close kinship. Near the beginning of this chapter, I referred to the *silva*'s association with the madrigal, perhaps the quintessential polyphonic musical composition of sixteenth- and seventeenth-century Europe. This musical invention originated as the composers' response to Petrarchan poetry lauded and imitated by Bembo and his disciples. *Bembismo* sought to recover the sonority and emotive power of Petrarch (and, in general, of classical poetry), which subsequently translated into musical text-setting as "chromatic harmonies, highly decorated vocal lines, contrapuntal imitation, and witty rhetorical 'word-painting.'"[50] The word *madrigal* appeared for the first time in print in connection with musical compositions in 1530. As the century advanced and the spate of new music continued, some composers created verses strictly for consumption as madrigals, whereas others, in works usually considered the best of the lot, fused extant texts of refined literary quality penned by prestigious authors with melodies of matching expressiveness—all intended to stir the audience's emotions. Petrarch's *Canzoniere* offered composers a wellspring of varied source material in this regard, including the *canzone petrarchesca*, which, although stanzaic, consists of the freely alternating hendecasyllables and heptasyllables with unset, irregular rhyme familiar to readers of the *Soledades* as the *silva*.[51]

In reality, however, Góngora's masterpiece resembles the madrigal in more ways than verse form. James Winn has outlined four analogues between poetic and musical technique to illustrate how composers adapted Petrarchan lyrics to music: rhythm, melody, harmony, and counterpoint.[52] These same categories serve equally well as the basis for analysis of the *Soledades*' musicality and their echo of madrigal conventions. Góngora cultivates diverse rhythmic beats in his pastoral, seemingly modifying the beat of the verse effortlessly for mimetic purposes. He uses alliterated stops and repeated stress patterns to generate the auditory impression of swiftly moving horses in the passage of the hunters' descent that I examined above. The poet signals a shift in the pilgrim's tread by inverting the stress schema of consecutive heptasyllables in *Soledad* I: "cón pié yá más segúro / declína al vacilánte" (Jammes, 56–57) (With safer foot he passed / Toward where tremblingly [Wilson, 49–50]). Five of the seven syllables bear an accent in the first line, including one for each of the four initial monosyllabic words, which captures the rhythm of a series of firm, discreet, confident steps taken after the pilgrim conquers the promontory en route to the distant, inland campfire. The next line, in which the protagonist proceeds downhill and draws closer to his destination, boasts only two accented syllables. The five unstressed syllables convey the notion of acceleration and quick, light footfalls as he nears the end of his journey. When the pilgrim hides in a hollow oak later in *Soledad* I, the rhythmic sound of music, "de métrica armonía" (Jammes, 270) (His ears upon their metric harmonies [Wilson, 265]), holds him enthralled.[53] The stress pattern traced by the accents creates a low-high-low (sustained)-high-low sine wave of sound that possesses a sensuous, alluring quality much like the music and dancing that the hero witnesses. Each of these examples reveals Góngora's concern with rhythmic detail on a line-by-line basis, but this preoccupation also characterizes the work as a whole. The alternation of narrative, descriptive, and lyric segments constantly changes the reader's perception of the pace of the text. Moreover, Góngora attenuates the temporal rhythms in the poems more familiar to courtiers (and other audience members), those of chronological and historical time, substituting diurnal cycles marked by the position of the sun and stars in the sky, and the ebb and flow of tides, temporal rhythms more attuned to Nature's own pulse and the conventions of the imaginary world of pastoral literature.

Winn equates vowel color with melody and the establishment of tone, musical or emotional. In the *serpentinata* selection previously discussed, the author's use of front vowels, especially the high-pitched *i*, communicates a mood of gaiety and sprightliness to readers. Góngora sets a totally different tone when he emphasizes the back vowel *o* and the open, low-pitched *a* to describe the crow's last gasp as he receives the mortal blow of the saker, "a un bote corvo del fatal acero" (Jammes, II:934) (by a curved and fatal steely claw [Wilson, II:918]), and then disappears from the sky. The enunciator of these vowels cannot avoid adapting a wide mouth that emits a sad, mournful noise reminiscent of both a final, weak caw and the "aw" or "oh" of a sympathetic, awestruck onlooker. Throughout the *Soledades,* Góngora plays major and minor keys against one another in order to produce poetry rich with subtle harmonies. The text is replete with harmonic contrasts born of rhetorical devices that yoke together opposing elements: antithesis, paradox, and oxymoron. These strategies range in scale from an oxymoronic metaphor labeling the sea "una Libia de ondas" (Jammes, I:20) (an Ocean's

Libya [Wilson, I:16]) to the numerous melancholy interludes (for example, the goatherd's soliloquy) that add a chromatic dimension to the pastoral thematic major of joy or peaceful contentment (or both) in life close to idealized Nature. Even *Soledad* II appears to rewrite some aspects of *Soledad* I, transposing them into another complementary key. Whereas *Soledad* I climaxes with a festive celebration of love and matrimony with the lonely, marginalized goatherd sounding a discordant note, *Soledad* II puts the happy solitude of the islander in the forefront, with the engagement of the couples, and the active lives they lead, in a secondary, supporting role.

Alfred Einstein has referred to Petrarch as a "contrapuntal" poet forever linked to polyphonic music.[54] Over the course of the *Soledades*, Góngora makes a successful bid for the same appellation and reputation. The many voices that flow into the poems' polyphonic river of music assume various guises. The inconsistent, divided narrative voice that moves in and out of the pilgrim's consciousness and continually alters its distance in regard to the fictional world traces a contrapuntal relationship that animates the pastoral work. The consonant-dissonant flux between the eye and voice(s) in the text, focalizer and vocalizer(s), adds greater depth to the *Soledades'* complex counterpoint. Other voices issue from characters' mouths, in direct discourse from the old goatherd, the aged islander, the young fishermen lovers, and the pilgrim himself. Intertextual echoes and dialogue with bucolic conventions constitute other important voices in Góngora's polyphonic poems. The author develops the traditional pastoral themes of *otium* (leisure), love, and Nature's beauty and abundance, but presents them in a different key, that is, with a new vocal identity. The goatherds, shepherds, and fishermen live well, and provide a model of hospitality worthy of any courtier, but they do not loll about expecting shelter and sustenance to drop into their laps. The poet strives to endow his characters and their environment with a serious work ethic, with implicit praise of human labor and ingenuity manifested in diverse tasks and accomplishments: carving a wooden spoon, making cheese from milk, harvesting the ocean's bounty with a net, or fashioning a dovecote from tree branches. Love figures in both *Soledades*, not erotic, illicit amorousness, but love sanctified and legitimated by marriage, which leads to a harmonious life of shared labor, companionship, and procreation. Gongorine love in these pastoral verses guarantees continuity of the species and the community, values that align the masterpiece more closely to the official views of the Church and Spanish society. Although Góngora celebrates Nature's beauty and vitality throughout the poems, he suggests that humankind can improve that beauty by harnessing and shaping the raw materials that Nature supplies, turning them into useful or artful projects and products or both. He holds up for approbation a symbiotic pairing of humans and Nature conspicuously absent from pastorals in which the bucolic setting functions only as lovely window dressing for the emotional outpouring of indolent shepherds and shepherdesses who have temporarily taken refuge from the court in an obligingly close *locus amoenus*.

Polyphony formed one of the principal flash points of the humanist debates over the sweeping changes in musical composition that occurred during the Renaissance. Traditionalists opposed elaborate counterpoint and advocated a return to the monody of ancient Greece. Other humanists, though, such as the University of Salamanca's Francisco Salinas, maintained that ancient music possessed a polyphonic character. The nascent musical form of opera emerged a clear winner from these arguments inasmuch as composers such as Monteverdi mixed contrapuntal pieces with updated versions of monody in the *stilo recitativo*, in which a solo voice sings dramatic lyrics (such as a soliloquy) set above a *basso continuo* accompaniment or figured bass, a style that imitates the sound of emotionally charged speech.[55] A monodic recitative appears at the beginning of *Soledad* II in the pilgrim's tearful plaint. The protagonist imaginatively transforms the rowing of the boat into the music of a stringed instrument that serves as the necessary figured-bass accompaniment for his "metric plaint": "El peregrino pues, haciendo en tanto / instrumento el bajel, cuerdas los remos" (Jammes, II:112–13) (The youth, as they were furrowing along, / —His instrument the boat, a string each oar— [Wilson, II:105–6]). Góngora applies the operatic paradigm to the pastoral's compositions, blending polyphony with the monodic soliloquies of the hero and his older doubles in dramatic representations of counterpoint in the antiphonal, hymeneal choruses of *Soledad* I, with their incantatory refrain of "Ven, Himeneo, ven; ven Himeneo" (Come Hymen, Hymen here), the subsequent epithalamial hymn blessing the newlyweds, as well as in the amoebic, interlocking voices of *Soledad* II's barcaroles.

Nature herself exhibits a marked preference for polyphony in the *Soledades*, revealing her underlying, contrapuntal design in impromptu concerts:

> Coros tejiendo, voces alternando,
> sigue la dulce escuadra montañesa
> del perezoso arroyo el paso lento,
> ....
> Pintadas aves, cítaras de pluma,
> coronaban la bárbara capilla.
> (Jammes, I:540–42, 556–57)
>
> (With weaving choirs and sweet alternate song,
> The mountain troop was following along

> The slow pace of the lazy flowing brook,
> ....
> Above, the feathered lyres,
> The painted linnets, crowned
> The untaught rustic choirs.
>
> [Wilson, I:523–25, 538–40])

The alternating voices of the choirs play different pitches and melodic lines against each other, sustained by the natural figured bass of the brook musician's *paso lento* (slow pace) below them. Nature contributes further to the polyphonic interlude in the birds of varied colors that, even as they occupy the higher reaches of the trees above the tuneful mountaineers, fill in the higher vocal registers that surpass the human range with additional song. Góngora invites readers to marvel at the spontaneous open-air concert, in which human and natural voices blend in an aural and visual representation of cosmic harmony. The poet implicitly aligns himself with humanists such as Francisco Salinas as an advocate of polyphony and more complex musical forms, thus translating a conventional pastoral theme and major tenet of Neoplatonic thought into the contemporary vernacular of critical discourse and cutting-edge artistic taste familiar to his sophisticated audience.

R. O. Jones has stated that Nature's harmony, rendered primarily through musical metaphors in the poems, constitutes one of the major themes of the *Soledades*.[56] Clearly, this theme transcends concerns with musical aesthetics specific to Góngora and his epoch. Still, I would modify Jones's view slightly in that I believe the poet wishes to unveil the secret, fundamental truth of Nature's (and the universe's) musical essence, making audible to the reader the melodies embedded in the pastoral landscape that would ordinarily escape the less finely tuned inner ear. Throughout the *Soledades*, Góngora strives to bring to light the dormant musicality in Nature that lies waiting for revelation and recognition. Song and dance pervade the work, magically animating objects as well as people in the harmonious reciprocity of universal music. Choral groups and dancers perform frequently during the wedding festivities that dominate *Soledad* I, setting a lively tone for the piece, whereas melancholy lovers (the pilgrim and the young fishermen) issue doleful or yearning songs, thus establishing the minor key of *Soledad* II's melody. A host of literal and figurative instruments dots the countryside, releasing the latent musicality that virtually everyone and everything seem to possess in the pastoral masterpiece. A *serrana* plays a stringed instrument that emits sounds of such aching loveliness that she stops the pilgrim cold in his tracks (Jammes, I:236–42; Wilson, I:649–50). Sonorous horns break the morning quiet and call humans and their animal attendants to the hunt, apparently wielding a mysterious power to open castle gates and lower drawbridges in an almost operatic fashion (Jammes, II:709–16; Wilson, II:695–702). Gongorine language also figuratively evokes musical instruments that lie hidden in the spiritual core of the natural world. Birds metamorphose into "(esquilas dulces de sonora pluma)" (Jammes, I:177) (sweet bells in sonorous feathers clad [Wilson, I:169]), as in the poet's hands, whereas in the hands of a fictional mountain maiden, an inert mass of black slate pieces unleashes the latent percussive beat of castanets, music not immediately evident to the reader's ear (Jammes, I:251; Wilson, I:247). The pilgrim's rhythmic plying of the oars transforms a boat into a stringed instrument (Jammes, II:112–13; Wilson, II:106–7), and even neighing horses and shrieking falcons broadcast an unexpected "ruda ... harmonía" (rude harmony) pleasing to the mind's ear (Jammes, II:736; Wilson, II:721). Aquatic music permeates the *Soledades*, as in the case of a gently plashing fountain that Góngora likens to the lilt of a theorbo (a double-necked lute) (Jammes, II:350; Wilson, II:343). Each one of these witty, tuneful images and events functions as a subliminal implant in the reader's mind, convincing the *Soledades*' audience through the sheer quantity of proof of the inherent musicality of the cosmos.

This plethora of melodious evidence explains in part the prominence in the poems of the word *canoro*, the adjective *canorous* meaning "musical," "tuneful," or "sweet-singing." Góngora serves notice in the prologue that the voice of Euterpe's oaten flute, the "canoro ... instrumento," will prevail over all others in the *Soledades* (36). Precisely this quality unites the most disparate elements in the work, from the "nuncio canoro del sol" (Jammes, I:294) (canorous herald to the sun [Wilson, I:287]) of a rooster to the "canoro / son de la Ninfa un tiempo, ahora caña" (Jammes, I:883–84) (canorous sound / Of her before a nymph but now a reed [Wilson, I:859–60]), the mellifluous legacy of Syrinx, including as well a "canoro ... bajel" (canorous bark) (Jammes, II:60; Wilson, II:56), a "canoro labrador" (canorous peasant) (Jammes, II:177; Wilson, II:170), and a "canoro río" (canorous stream) (Jammes, II:555; Wilson, II:546). To paraphrase Marshall McLuhan, "The medium and the metaphors are the message" in the *Soledades*. The music of poetry that resembles the madrigal and the development of the theme of *musica mundana* in verse represents an aesthetic replication of what Góngora perceives as the divine artistic medium that orders the potential chaos of the universe, binding its myriad parts (the many) into a coherent whole (the one).

Yet, significantly, as portrayed in the *Soledades*, cosmic music encompasses discordant notes, transforming latent dissonance into chromatic harmonies that blend into the predominantly sweet sound of the piece. In this regard, the author continues the tradition of the *concordia discors*, identified among others with Heraclitus, who maintained that harmony arises from integrated contrasts, thus allowing for conflict and violence as part of the tuneful equation. Saint Augustine subsequently regarded music as a medium of contemplative exploration that enables the individual to tune the inner ear to the fundamental universal music that unites the cosmos beneath its superficial diversity and strife. Closer to the age of Góngora, Ficino asserted that music and the visual arts provide humankind with a means of elevating the soul through refocusing the inner eyes and ears so that they perceive the divine essence of intellectual beauty that lies beneath mere sensory attractiveness.[57] The concept of *concordia discors* arises in one of the most famous passages of the *Soledades:*

> y las confusamente acordes aves,
> entre las verdes roscas de las yedras,
> muchas eran, y muchas veces nueve
> aladas musas, que, de pluma leve
> engañada su culta lira corva,
> metros inciertos sí, pero süaves,
> en idïomas cantan diferentes
> mientras cenando en pórfidos lucientes,
> lisonjean apenas
> al Júpiter marino tres Sirenas.
> (Jammes, II:351–60)

> (And the confusedly agreeing choirs,
> Among the spirals of the ivy green,
> Were many, many times winged Muses nine,
>   [Their feathers light the screen
> Deceitful that concealed their curvèd lyres]
> Who sweet although uncertain metres told
>   In language manifold;
> While, supping mid the porphyry, combined
>   Three Syrens' flattery,
> Offered unto the Jupiter of sea.
> [Wilson, II:344–53])

The juxtaposition of words in the description of "confusamente acordes" (confusedly agreeing) birds (birdsongs) conveys the paradoxical notions of dissonant consonance and diverse, unique voices that meld into one harmonious choir, which characterizes both the classical tradition of *musica mundana* and the fabric of the *Soledades*. A double disguise hides the winged lyres and deceives the lowly bodily senses. Ivy fronds mask the birds' presence, and people who do spy their feathers expect contrasting noises from fowls of clashing colors, shapes, and sizes. Those who ignore the exterior misdirection and refocus their inner auditory sense on what lies beneath the surface, however, experience a marvelous concert that defies conventional music theory with an unexpected combination of different pitches and rhythms, and a mysterious beauty that far exceeds even music fit for the gods. Góngora suggests that the divine music of the *Soledades* possesses the power to temper and move readers' souls to greater heights through an act of reading that is at the same time an act of meditation and contemplation, of inward turning and inner concentration of rational and affective powers.

Numerous memento mori provide a gauge of the repertoire of chromatic harmonies accommodated by the Gongorine vision of cosmic music. Although the Grim Reaper is no stranger to the pastoral landscape, death in the *Soledades* lacks the tragic dimension that some readers might associate with its presence.[58] The pilgrim, for example, finds the rather macabre sight of the crow's violent end an enthralling bit of entertainment, one episode in a series of "agradables casos" (agreeable sights) (Jammes, II:937; Wilson, II:922). More commonly, the subject of mortality appears in the context of the cycle of life, which perhaps should not surprise the audience given the work's proclivities for diurnal sequences and circadian rhythms. The chorus's reminder to the newlyweds that a gravestone bearing a brief inscription awaits them after a deceptively long life, one marked by hard work, fecundity, and the achievement of modest prosperity within the golden mean, seems a logical part of the happy occasion:

> "Cisne pues una y otra pluma, en esta
> tranquilidad os halle labradora
> la postrimera hora,
> cuya lámina cifre desengaños,
> que en letras pocas lean muchos años."
> (Jammes, I:939–43)

> ("And may the fatal hour your bones receive
> When swans in whiteness either one shall be,
> And in the labourers' tranquillity:
> Your epitaph shall travellers undeceive
> Who in few letters many years shall see."
> [Wilson, I:914–18])

Góngora depersonalizes and desensitizes the subject of human mutability with a forthright reference to death as the ultimate reality all people face. Simultaneously, he aestheticizes the topic by translating the experience into the graceful movement of two swans (the elderly white-haired couple) as they glide into the tranquil port of the tomb. Death simply figures as an integral part of life's eternal harmony, a part of Nature's continuity that Góngora addresses even more directly in yet another image focused on swans. Here the elegant birds, raised by the old fisherman as if they were chickens, enact a symbolic tableau accompanied by natural music:

> En la más seca, en la más limpia anea
> vivificando están muchos sus huevos,
> y mientras dulce aquél su muerte anuncia
>   entre la verde juncia,
> sus pollos éste al mar conduce nuevos,
>   de Espío y de Nesea
> (cuando más escurecen las espumas)
> nevada invidia sus nevadas plumas.
>   (Jammes, II:255–62)

> (Many the cat-tail grass, cleanest and dry,
> Harboured that they their eggs might vivify,
> And while one sweetly his own death foretold
>   In reeds and greenery,
> Another led her cygnets to the sea;
>   Of Galatea, behold,
> —When least her limbs beneath the sea-foam show—
> The snowy envy, in their plumes of snow.
>   [Wilson, II:246–53])

The Gongorine vision merges life and death into one beautiful, perpetual spectacle, an aristocratic, self-replenishing procession of swans garbed in snowy white. Individuals die, but new ones are born and grow to replace their elders in an infinitely repeated cycle that affirms mortality's role in Nature's immortality. Accordingly, no funeral dirge serves as the aural backdrop for the scene, but rather the pure, sweet sound of a swan song is proudly delivered by a dying vocalist nestled in comforting, green surroundings. The poet orchestrates discordant death to fit into a serene symphony, a paean to life.

The Quest for Silent Speech

If, as Wolfgang Iser maintains, the pastoral dramatizes "fictionality" more so than other literary genres, that is, the merger of mutually exclusive worlds that permits readers to shuttle back and forth in dreamlike fashion between textual and extratextual universes, then in the *Soledades*, Góngora has reshaped this urbane, aristocratic genre into a vehicle of solitary contemplation, transforming the act of reading into a meditational experience involving an ever shifting grasp of inner and outer selves and worlds that leads to transcendent apprehension of the divine telos beneath the superficial cosmos. By maximizing the theatrical propensities inherent in the pastoral, and by incorporating into the work forms of court culture familiar to his audience, the poet mobilizes the "fictional ecstasy" of reading, which "permits us to step outside the contexts that normally define what we are."[59] The pastoral stage production Góngora has mounted permits boundary-crossing readers to enter the bucolic world vicariously through the pilgrim protagonist, but once there they witness aural and visual spectacles closely akin to court entertainment: musicales and memory theater, art galleries and chambers of marvels, as well as imagistic language that quickly becomes a star performer. Yet, this tumultuous merger of court and country in extravaganzas of sight and sound takes place within the reader's mind as transmitted by the written words of poetic language that speak silently from the confines of the page to the boundless imagination of the audience.

The notion of poetry as refined, elevated language that mysteriously speaks to the reader-listener, much like God communicates directly to the human soul through interior discourse, boasts of a long, enduring presence in Western tradition. George Steiner observes that "[t]he poet makes in dangerous similitude to the gods," striving to emulate the divine logos, in which word and essence, rhetoric and world, are one. Steiner also remarks: "[I]t is decisively the fact that language does have its frontiers, that it borders on three other modes of statement—light, music, and silence—which gives proof of a transcendent presence in the fabric of the world." However, poetry, a finer and more volatile form of language, especially when molded by a virtuoso such as Góngora, actively engages those frontiers and, through a sort of artistic sublimation, emerges as language of light, music, and silence. In the *Soledades*, the poet continues the Augustinian quest for a "rhetoric of silence," language constituted of light and music that overcomes the limits of superficial verbal eloquence and speaks inwardly to the reader of truths through signs. Just as God communicates directly through the symbolic book of Nature, so too does Góngora the artist imitate that divine work in a book of pastoral poetry fused with his maker's tome—yet another merger of mutually exclusive worlds.[60] Although past critics have recognized the *Soledades*' importance as a codifier of the seventeenth-century Spanish yoking of pastoral poetry and solitude (for example, Vossler, Poggioli, and Egido), they have in large part left unexplored the connection between this occurrence and Góngora's adoption of the Augustinian model of writing and reading in the masterpiece, thus eliminating an important key to its structure and meaning.

Brian Stock opines that Saint Augustine deemed silent reading an otherworldly, meditational process in which words forged in silence return to silence in the contemplative reader's mind. In short, *lectio* metamorphoses into *meditatio*. The success of the rhetoric of silence paradoxically resides in the poet's ability to harness words to stimulate the reader's inner auditory and visual senses, which in the Augustinian reading model eventually frees ideas from images and liberates the mind and soul for ascent. Near the beginning of *Soledad* I, Góngora symbolically alludes to the rhetoric of silence that permeates the work, cuing his intended audience regarding the aesthetics at play in the text and the hermeneutics of interpretation they should employ to penetrate its mysteries. The morning of the pilgrim's first full day in the green world, the goatherd leads his guest to a cliff from which the protagonist gazes in mute wonderment at the panoramic vision of a river's course, "Muda la admiración habla callando" (Jammes, I:197) (Dumb Wonder speaks by silence [Wilson, I:188]). The pilgrim's speechless awe attests to the powerful impact of the book of Nature on the receptive human consciousness and the inadequacy of spoken language to express the beauty of Nature's wonders. With their careful orchestration of color, light, and music, the pastoral river and the *Soledades* speak silently to the solitary reader of a magical universe of infinite potential and possibilities.[61] The audience who gazes on Góngora's book of Nature perceives not a world governed by stringent laws and limits, but rather an animated, protean cosmos in which fire and water mix in boiling eddies; fluid and solid blend in the ocean's liquid jasper; art and nature fuse in a personified, prolix sentence stream; and nature eternally renews itself through a series of transmutations and metamorphoses that seemingly defy human logic, like the river water that assumes the complete cycle of transformative identities from mountain spring to rushing liquid, from salty sea to hazy water vapor. And Góngora, like the prophets of yore, summons all his visionary powers to communicate the elusive beauty and intricacy of the whole divine system to his readers through the medium of poetic wonderment.

3

A Poetics of Alchemy

> Couldn't one call this a work of magic, a true process of alchemy, which extracts the precious metal of poetry from the most coarse and common materials?
>
> —Pedro Salinas, *Reality and the Poet in Spanish Poetry*

Admiratio and the Paradox of Art and Nature

"Muda la admiración habla callando" (Dumb Wonder speaks by silence), the *Soledades*' poetic voice declares, echoing the phrase Plutarch attributed to Simonides of *poesia pictura loquens*, usually translated as either "Poetry is a speaking painting" or the corollary "Painting is mute poetry" (Jammes, I:197; Wilson, I:188). Wonderment may well speak silently in the *Soledades*, but *admiración*'s mute voice still makes an indelible impression on readers of the poems. *Admiratio* spawns a major semantic field in the work and marks the pilgrim-reader's path of marvels through the landscape, which provides some idea why *admiración* impacts so powerfully on the solitary visitor of the Gongorine pastoral universe. As the riverscape sequence of *Soledad* I illustrates, *admiratio* activates a figurative switch that closes the metonymic circuit linking cause and effect, which in turn permits the books of Nature and Poetry to speak silently and, at the same time, triggers audience awareness of and receptivity to a transcendent realm. Góngora shapes words to forge an experience that exceeds words and goes beyond corporeal limits with stimulation that communicates directly to the mind and soul of the audience. Literal and figurative evocations of *admiratio* maintain such a persistent presence in the poems that wonderment not only functions as the conceptual pivot for this particular episode of discovery and revelation, but in fact also serves as an imaginary axis of reader engagement on which actualization of the work as a whole turns.

Góngora litters the verbal countryside of the *Soledades* with linguistic variants of *admiratio*, displaying all the enthusiasm of a rookie stagehand waving an applause sign at a studio audience. Demonstrations of wonderment's unforgettable imprint on fictional counterparts of the readers remind the extratextual spectators what the proper response to the marvels they witness should be. Perhaps more accurately, literal mentions of *admiratio* represent one of the poems' many self-referential gestures that draw attention to the fact that marvels constitute the metapoetic backbone of the *Soledades,* and convince good readers that they should never lose sight of this important point, no matter how compelling the specific wonders at hand and how enraptured they may become at any given moment. This stylized, literal flaunting of *admiratio* could be compared to the use of self-consciously dramatic components—gesturing hands, pointing fingers, figures that engage visually with viewers or slide into their space—in sixteenth- and seventeenth-century painting. The linguistic paradigm of *admiración* in the poems also indicates conditions or qualities that consistently produce wonderment within the context of the work's dramatic vignettes. When the pilgrim finds a blend of present bucolic rusticity and past military might, humble dress and sophisticated speech in his goatherd guide, the protagonist reacts with amazement to this surprising turn of events:

> Bajaba (entre sí) el joven admirando
> armado a Pan o semicapro a Marte
> en el pastor mentidos . . .
> (Jammes, I:233–35)

> (Alone the youth descended, —on his course
> Satyr of Mars or warrior of Pan
> Admiring in the herdsman . . .
> [Wilson, I:230–32])

Of course, the hero himself poses an unlikely figure in these surroundings, as he soon discovers when he becomes the target of dumbstruck gazes after leaving his oak hiding spot to join the wedding procession:

> Saludólos a todos cortésmente,
> y, admirado no menos
> de los serranos que correspondido.
> (Jammes, I:356–58)

> (The youth saluted all with courtesy,
> And then [admired was he
> As well as answered by the mountaineers].
> [Wilson, I:346–48])

An unexpected confrontation with the incongruous, here in the form of a sudden eruption of the court in the pastoral (a common occurrence in the *Soledades*), supplies the awe-inspiring thread that ties these two scenes of wonderment together.

Spectacles also engender *admiración* in the *Soledades*. The superhuman jump of an athlete at the postnuptial festivities leaves the fictional audience and other competitors transfixed, paralyzed with amazement:

> La admiración, vestida un mármol frío,
> apenas arquear las cejas pudo;
> la emulación, calzada un duro hielo,
> torpe se arraiga . . .
> (Jammes, I:999–1002)
>
> (Wonder in marble cold
> Was clad, and hardly could her eye-brows bend;
> Envy, shod in hard snow,
> Was almost motionless . . .
> [Wilson, I:975–78])

Góngora metonymically transforms the crowd into a collective, personified embodiment of frozen Wonder, as cold as marble and as hard as ice, and so rigidly immobile that this peculiar entity can scarcely arch his or her brows in amazement. The spectacle of great beauty elicits a similar response in the *Soledades*. In *Soledad* II, for example, the pilgrim reacts with astonishment when he accidentally douses himself in the spray of a secret water trap. He responds in like fashion a little later when he spies the lovely perfection of the fisherman's daughters:

> La vista saltearon poco menos
> del huésped admirado
> las no líquidas perlas . . .
> (Jammes, II:230–32)
>
> (The wandering guest was hardly less amazed,
> By these [not liquid] pearls on whom he gazed . . .
> [Wilson, II:223–24])

The pilgrim's wonderment grows as he ponders these female marvels whose celestial radiance rivals that of the sun and the stars:

> Ponderador saluda afectüoso
> del esplendor que admira el estranjero
> al Sol en seis luceros dividido.
> > (Jammes, II:239–41)
>
> (Marking their splendour, did the young man greet
> The sun divided in six planets fair.
> > [Wilson, II:231–32])

The hero's greeting, charged with the affect of amazement, reifies the women, and makes the reader envision these human distillations of the glory of the firmament as animated exhibits in the Gongorine *Wunderkammer*, beautiful human specimens that defy normal standards.

These staged cases of *admiratio* literally inscribed in the *Soledades* show the extent of Góngora's exuberant cultivation of Golden Age Spain's aesthetics of wonderment. Michael J. Woods, the critic who has contributed the most to the understanding of the importance of wonder in Góngora's works, characterizes this epoch as the "Age of Wonderment." As a cultural phenomenon, this obsession with wonderment extended beyond the limits of Catholic Europe. Kitty Scoular, for instance, describes *admiratio* as a contemplative perquisite common to readers in Protestant England of the sixteenth and seventeenth centuries. By all accounts, Spanish authors and orators of the period sought to move their audiences to *admiración* through style or content or both, with a variety of classical and contemporary sources supplying an authoritative theoretical basis for this aesthetic ideal. E. C. Riley traces the origins of *admiratio* to Aristotle, who identified the marvelous as subject matter integral to the epic and to tragedy, and to Cicero, who noted that rhetoric should stimulate and move the listener. Riley observes that Longinus's treatise on the sublime, at first glance a likely source of inspiration for the Golden Age aesthetics of *admiración*, was actually familiar only to a select few prior to the end of the seventeenth century, despite the fact that translations and commentaries of *On the Sublime* were available as early as the middle of the sixteenth century. Significantly, Pedro de Valencia mentions Longinus in correspondence to Góngora, which means it is possible, but by no means certain, that the author of the *Soledades* knew this important work in some form.[1] Regardless of their lingering doubts about this particular source, critics can rest assured that Góngora had more than a passing acquaintance with a number of the many Renaissance treatises on poetics that embraced the Aristotelian or Ciceronian (or both) strains of *admiratio* as a precept.

The spate of Italian commentaries on Horace's *Ars poetica* that appeared in the 1550s expanded the objectives of poetry to include not only those of "instruct" and "delight," but also that of "infuse *admiratio*," a Ciceronian end that may also have contributed to the search for parallels between Horatian aesthetics and Aristotelian poetics. Francesco Robortello concluded in his immensely influential 1548 interpretation of Aristotle's *Poetics* that poetry offers "three bases of pleasure": "imitation, the *difficulté vaincue*, and admiration." Bernard Weinberg states that "[o]f these three bases, perhaps the most important is admiration, that feeling of wonder and amazement which comes from the spectacle of the unexpected, the extraordinary, the marvelous." In Góngora's Spain, El Pinciano and Francisco Cascales, one of the author's most mordant critics, expressed the same point of view, advocating, in *Philosophía antigua poética* (1596) and *Tablas poéticas* (1617), respectively, *admiración* as the proper aim of heroic poetry. Without wonderment, they maintained, the poet cannot stir the soul and may also fail to teach and entertain. Antonio Minturno's *De poeta* (1559) likely provided another theoretical spur and support for Góngora's quest to amaze his readers. The multivolume *De poeta* blends material from Cicero, Quintilian, Horace, Plato, and Aristotle into a varied, comprehensive metapoetics. Minturno places *admiratio* under the classifying rubric of *officium*, that is, what poetry ought to do. According to Minturno, wonderment should arise from verisimilar portrayal of the unreal and from general stylistic excellence. Moreover, *admiratio* plays a role in the cathartic function of poetry by overwhelming and displacing other passions. Minturno regards wonderment as a desirable, salutary effect of poetry, at once moral and pleasurable in impact.[2]

Góngora clearly shared the belief that *admiratio* elevates and ennobles poetic representation, and possesses a unique capacity to move readers and improve their minds and souls by honing their internal perception after their initial affective response to potent stimuli passes. The literal references to *admiración* in the *Soledades* discussed above and the notions on *admiratio* advanced by well-known Renaissance poetic treatises yield some understanding of how Góngora's aesthetics of wonderment perform in his masterpiece. *Admiratio* involves a sudden encounter with the exceptional, such as meeting a courtly goatherd, seeing a courtier in a rustic setting surrounded by ordinary herdsmen, witnessing a display of unparalleled athleticism, or contemplating quasi-divine feminine beauty. In the two latter cases, wonderment affords pleasure and glimpses of qualities that defy human limitations. The former cases conclude and introduce, respectively, didactic, purgative episodes in which expressions of intense grief move the pilgrim to pity the sufferers. Simultaneously, the older, more experienced characters teach the protagonist and readers lessons on the devastating consequences of war and avarice. In writing of *admiratio* as a favored technique of Golden Age literature, B. W. Ife stresses that wonderment depends not on "a total breech of illusion, but rather [on] a sudden shift of focus which gives the reader a fleeting awareness of the work's otherness before the illusion settles in again around his adjusted scale of values." Ife likens *admiratio* to the use of *Verfremdungseffekte* (alienation effects) that emphasize the artifice of literature while denying the audience none of literature's artful pleasures.[3] One could also describe *admiratio* as a linguistic strategy analogous to the painterly technique of anamorphosis. Both ploys require the skillful manipulation of mutually exclusive perspectives such that against all odds the reader-viewer can momentarily suspend natural law or conventional thought and simultaneously perceive and grasp the multiple perspectives as if they formed a coherent construct. The sensation of double vision that readers of the *Soledades* experience does indeed precipitate a feeling of "alienation," of being perpetually off-balance and out-of-sync in the reading process.

The oscillation between unmediated and mediated *admiratio* in the poems also contributes to the disquieting impact of the *Soledades* on their select audience. When Góngora employs variants of the word *admiratio* to prod readers unsubtly into recognition of occasions of wonderment, he seems to remove the element of surprise requisite to cue *admiración*. He eliminates spontaneity from the response, almost as if he were a poet-playwright handing out the script to spectators to make them privy to the same stage directions as the actors. As a result, the pilgrim and his fictional companions may stop suddenly in astonishment, dumbfounded by what they see or hear, but readers enjoy a certain analytical distance from the immediate experiences of their poetic guide(s) and end up in the same intermediate imaginary space occupied by the (at such times) disembodied voice of the *Soledades*. In these cases, the author qualifies *admiración*, transforming it into a somewhat detached, vicarious aesthetic experience that disrupts identification with the hero. Readers tend to forget, however, that these instances may be necessary to remind them of the interpretive resistance of the *Soledades* in a "momentary withdrawal by the author of his words from the reader's grasp."[4]

The poems' enigmas and puzzles exercise a peculiar, hypnotic pull of their own on the audience in which unmediated wonderment becomes the normative, standard response elicited by a thoroughly astonishing text. Ife has noted the potential of peripeteia, the resolution of a complicated plot, and the evocation of the marvelous to create *admiratio*. Góngora sets a smorgasbord of these literary concoctions before readers of the *Soledades*. Although I have analyzed the poems' narrative structure as basically that of a plotless plot and as a dreamlike sequence of theatrical scenarios loosely stitched together, unexpected twists and turns, the unraveling of complex situations, and marvel upon marvel account for much of the pastoral world portrayed by Góngora. Consider the amazingly good fortune of the shipwrecked protagonist, who stumbles onto hospitality that satisfies his physical needs, offers moral therapy for a disillusioned courtier, and serves up (along with breakfast) ruins and views worthy of a discerning aristocrat. Furthermore, the protagonist moves from the goatherd's bed-and-breakfast to lavish wedding entertainments that happily accommodate outlander party crashers, and from that invitation to an impromptu banquet in his honor generously sponsored by an old man who no longer wants anything to do with the world the pilgrim represents. As if these bizarre peripetal twists did not suffice to meet the cravings of the most jaded consumer of the aesthetics of wonderment, unlikely denouements greet *Soledades* readers at each turn in the narrative road. The pilgrim cuts the Gordian knot of an impossible love affair in a highly stylized, tearful renunciation of the past. He also successfully ventures into a new career as marriage broker, arranging matches that happily resolve the melancholy plaints of yearning lovers. Readers and protagonist bump into marvels everywhere in the poetic *Wunderkammer:* fireworks, a rustic arena, a palace of Parian marble, a goatherd-warrior, a tidal island, lovely female harpooners, and a hawking party. Linking all of these elements of wonderment together is the sustained marvel of Góngora's *culto* language, which overwhelms readers of the *Soledades* from beginning to end with what Ife summarizes as the stylistic analogues of the techniques of narrative *admiratio*, namely, "virtuoso writing and visual vividness *(energia)*."[5]

The unsettling effects of *admiratio* that Góngora has incorporated into the poems disclose two major fonts of awe-inspiring marvels in the text: art and nature. The poet has developed the potential of these forces to create wonder to such an extent in the *Soledades* that one could almost imagine the masterpiece inspiring Emanuele Tesauro nearly fifty years later (in *Il Cannocchiale Aristotelico* [1654]) to include *mirabile per arte* and *mirabile per natura* in his list of four types of marvels.[6] Throughout the work, art incites *admiración,* as the composer takes pains to show:

> La admiración que al arte se le debe,
>   áncora del batel fue, perdonando
>   poco a lo fuerte, y a lo bello nada
>   del edificio . . .
>   (Jammes, II:706–9)

> (The admiration that is due to art
> Became the vessel's anchor, noticing
> The strength and beauty that in every part
>   Of the great building lay . . .
>   [Wilson, II:691–94])

Art exudes sufficient power to stop a boat midstream. Moreover, the poetic voice asserts, the passengers held enthralled by the spectacle owe art this strange form of homage, perhaps suggesting to the *Soledades'* aristocratic audience that they should set aside court imbroglios and pay full attention to the skill and loveliness of Góngora's poetry. The voice also informs readers that these proper spectators appreciate not just the strength of the fortress, but, more important, its palatial beauty, noting almost every detail of the edifice's practicality, and each and every element that contributes to a pleasing impression on the eyes. The poet insinuates that the most minute aspects of his pastoral compositions merit examination and appreciation, observing too that exceptional aesthetic appeal does not preclude pragmatic function. This rule of Gongorine aesthetics applies throughout the *Soledades*, regardless of the scale of the source of wonderment, from the monumental grandeur of a Renaissance palazzo to the humble accoutrements of a table setting in a goatherd's hut:

> Limpio sayal (en vez de blanco lino)
> cubrió el cuadrado pino;
> y en boj, aunque rebelde, a quien el torno
> forma elegante dio sin culto adorno,
> leche que exprimir vio la Alba aquel día,
> mientras perdían con ella
> los blancos de su frente bella,
> gruesa le dan y fría,
> impenetrable casi a la cuchara,
> del viejo Alcimedón invención rara.
> (Jammes, I:143–52)
>
> (Instead of linen white, their sackcloth clean
>   Covered the squared pine soon;
> In boxwood [which, though rebel to the wheel,
> Did elegance, not ornament reveal]
> Milk—which pressed out that day the Dawn had seen,
> Whose lilies white beneath her brow of gold
>   With it could not compare—
>   They gave him thick and cold,
> Impenetrable almost to the spoon,
> Ancient Alcimedon's invention rare.
> [Wilson, I:136–45])

Contrast forms the structural core of this excerpt from a literary set piece, a cross between the *beatus ille* topos and "Menosprecio de la corte, alabanza de la aldea" (Scorn for the court, praise for the village), in which the poetic voice praises the moral superiority of a simple country existence over the sinful corruption of lavish court life. Yet, even in these circumstances, Góngora highlights the sophisticated artistry apparent in articles made invisible by daily use. He defamiliarizes them and casts the light of wonderment on them by means of synecdoche, rendering the table covering as a clean sackcloth, the table as a squared pine, and the bowl as boxwood resistant to the lathe. The author ennobles a common spoon, glorifying the implement poetically by identifying it with classical genius and tradition, as the "rare invention" of Alcimedon.[7] Note that although the bowl lacks ornamentation, the dish still exhibits the elegance wrought by a skilled artisan. Although the gifted workers here may eschew embellishments, and the frivolity and excessive pride they symbolize in this context, the artificers still possess the magic to extract from the wood the objet d'art that lies hidden, dormant in nature's raw material, waiting to blossom through human intervention. As an artifact whose beauty has been brought to life by humans, a spoon or bowl deserves the same *admiración* as a more elaborate artwork such as a palace. Thanks to Góngora's creative intervention, readers see an ordinary utensil and container transformed into marvels through the poet's visionary lens. The elegant simplicity of these domestic artifacts makes them worthy counterparts of Nature's marvels, embodied in the fresh, rich, cold milk that rivals a personified Dawn's whiteness and purity, an image Góngora invokes by playing with the double meaning of *alba*, which signifies both "dawn" and "white." As readers can detect from the milk description, the poet captures the idealized essence of this natural liquid, capitalizing on the qualities that render milk most worthy of admiration and drawing an implicit contrast with the corrupting influence of the liquor consumed immoderately by debauched courtiers.

When R. O. Jones wrote of unifying aspects of the poems in "Neoplatonism and the *Soledades*," he noted the role of three major themes in that regard: "the continuity of Nature, Nature's harmony and Nature's plenty."[8] I agree with his statement to a point, but I would rearticulate his insightful observation, stressing that Góngora simply focuses on Nature's wonders in whatever shape they might take—the eternal cycle of life; nature's harmony (even in the musical equilibrium of *concordia discors*); or the variety, vitality, and abundance of the natural world—and whichever ones might move the discerning viewer to *admiratio*. One would, of course, expect a pastoral that also doubles as a literary chamber of marvels to offer a paean to Nature's wonders. However, the stylistic measures Góngora employs distort Nature artfully and, in the process, unearth the marvels buried in the quotidian world of sensory experience, providing readers with an added source of amazement.

The power of artificially recontoured nature to command attention becomes apparent in the opening scene of *Soledad* I, which with the dramatic juxtapositions of pounding waves, a welcoming expanse of beach, and a forbidding rise of boulders and cliffs seems more like a theatrical set imitating a rearranged nature or a setting mediated by the literary tradition of Byzantine romance. The sentence river valley examined in Chapter 2 offers another case of nature's wonders altered, heightened, and brought to the fore through stylistic virtuosity. Góngora's defamiliarization techniques also include mythological periphrasis, which in the passage below enables the poet to give his audience stars that shine with unusual brightness and splendor:

> piedra, indigna tïara
> (si tradición apócrifa no miente)
> de animal tenebroso, cuya frente
> carro es brillante de nocturno día.
> (Jammes, I:73–76)

> (The stone, unworthily
> [If apocryphal tradition does not lie]
> The crown of a dark animal whose brow
> Is the bright chariot of nocturnal day.
> [Wilson, I:66–69])

Allusions to ancient tales and dazzling chiaroscuro effects resensitize the audience, skewing their normal vision so that they can marvel anew at the once familiar sight reconfigured by Góngora's poetic wand. The pilgrim's guiding star glows with greater brilliance thanks to the lucent incongruities and oxymorons painted in a mythological context that the reader must unravel.[9] The dark animal, the Great Bear, refers to the nymph Callisto, whom Jupiter transformed into a constellation along with her son (who became Ursa Minor) before the boy could kill his mother, whom an envious Juno had previously changed into a bear. A portion of Ursa Major points to the North Star, which the author of the *Soledades* reconstitutes as the imaginary crown jewel in the astral diadem placed on the head of this ferocious beast. Such puzzling, oblique references suffice to whet the contemporary audience's love of verbal and visual enigmas and stimulate *admiratio* for both the stars and the poet's wit. However, Góngora, who steadfastly rejected the "less is more" maxim of good taste for a "more is more" personal aesthetics, ups the ante on luminescence with a more accessible allusion to Apollo's chariot, implying that the North Star effectively transmutes night into day, and that just as the sun's apparent movement through the sky provides a sure path for the needy wayfarer, so too does Polaris offer a reliable compass for the lost and weary traveler.

Góngora clearly exploits the potential of art and nature to function independently and together as coconspirators in a plot to perpetrate *admiratio* on the *Soledades*' audience, habituated to wonders by the spectacle-mad court and culture of Golden Age Spain. The poet's vested interest in exploring the relationship between art and nature, however, also represents his personal interpretation of a traditional pastoral theme with classical antecedents. Richard Cody has characterized the pastoral as a "symbolic mental landscape" in which the sentient and intelligible world and experiences meet, in which Nature and nature shaped by art converge. One of the pastoral's long-standing disputes pertains precisely to the aesthetic articulation of that convergence, which over the centuries has assumed the shape of conflict, reconciliation, and everything in between. Edward Tayler notes that Plato portrays the pair in opposition to one another, whereas Cicero promotes the image of art and nature as a complementary twosome. Theocritus's *Idylls* paint country life in which art and nature balance and harmonize each other, yet Virgil's *Eclogues* celebrate an aestheticized and moralized treatment of the pastoral.[10]

The sixteenth and seventeenth centuries witnessed a major revival of this classical debate. As Rosalie Colie has indicated, Castiglione situates the sophisticated dialogues of *The Courtier*, some involving discussion of the relationship between art and nature, in a pastoral milieu in which a lovely, fertile, and healthful countryside frames elegant, artful discourse that takes place in the rich, beautiful court of Urbino. Such a delicate balance of art and nature supports Cody's claim that pastoral poets of the Italian Renaissance enact a compromise between artifice and naturalness, transcendence and immanence—literary and philosophical concepts of harmony and equilibrium akin to the behavioral notion of *sprezzatura*. Tayler expresses a similar view, identifying the complementarity of art and nature with Christian humanism, but commenting as well on literature's dramatization of the duality of the pair as a moral issue, a function of the use or misuse of human reason.[11]

In terms of complexity, Góngora's engagement with this familiar pastoral theme in the *Soledades* bears some resemblance to that of Garcilaso in his *Eglogas*. Elias Rivers has shown that with each *Eclogue*, art's presence in the bucolic landscape grows more pronounced. By the time the audience reaches *Egloga* III, which features the famous ekphrastic interlude of the nymphs weaving a tapestry, art has become an integral part of the bucolic world, something that can compete or even improve on nature. Garcilaso's aesthetic position appears to change from regarding art and nature as separate and conflictive forces to seeing the pair as intricately interwoven threads in the tapestry of pastoral verse. Although undoubtedly few contemporary critics would question labeling Góngora's treatment of the art-nature connection complex, many have debated the complexion that relationship acquires, whether it is adversarial or complementary. R. O. Jones oversimplifies and overstates the case for nature when he contends: "[Góngora] is asserting that the artificial is transient and that only natural values are permanent in a changing world." Jones further argues: "The underlying theme of the *Soledades* is the vanity of opposing Nature, which destroys artifice and punishes presumption. Only Nature herself is immutable."[12]

For the most part, subsequent analyses of the wonder-inducing pair express the relationship in a more nuanced manner, focusing on the subtle and suggestive implications of the art-nature tie in the *Soledades*. Bruce Wardropper, who limits his study to *Soledad* I, believes the poet presents art in a much more positive light, as a necessary, symbiotic partner of nature in the quest for transcendent ideals. He rightly maintains that Góngora's poem depicts rural life through the filter of an urban sensibility. Gwynne Edwards sees a gradual erosion and darkening of the author's "celebration in a particularly intense and rapturous manner of the pastoral ideal" from *Soledad* I to *Soledad* II, paralleled by increasingly stronger criticism of court aesthetics. Michael Woods wisely emphasizes that art and nature in the work take place in the context of a human community devoid of hubris and avarice. In this situation, Woods stresses, Góngora praises human skill and creativity without diminishing the *admiratio* evoked by nature's marvels. John Beverley adds a sociopolitical agenda into the critical mix, viewing the *Soledades*' bucolic nature as "a landscape tableau to be read on the panels of the Court where its redemptive value as a social and moral prescription will have to be deciphered."[13]

Art about art, art about nature, art about art and nature, art about human values, art and nature, art about nature and political reform—the *Soledades*' dynamic duo have elicited a wide variety of critical responses and have proved themselves extremely malleable in support of these different points of view. The importance of the relationship in the *Soledades* forms about the only area of accord among this circle of critics. I believe, though, that much more is at stake here. To my mind, *admiratio*, art, and nature lie at the very heart of Góngora's poetics. Understanding the intimate links between them will bring readers one step closer not just to apprehending the truths concealed in his pastoral masterpiece, but also to grasping the essence of the Gongorine literary revolution of *cultismo*. In the *Carta en respuesta*, which has served for generations as an enigmatic *culto* manifesto, Góngora defends his revision of the poetic canon as an attempt to ennoble the Castilian language, sharpen readers' wits, and provoke thought. The poet may not have known Longinus's *On the Sublime* directly, but the *culto* aesthetics outlined in his letter and practiced in his compositions coincides with this classical treatise on wonderment to a remarkable degree. The Greek *auctor*, for example, informs his audience that true sublimity elevates, exalts, predisposes to greatness, and inspires meditation: "Real sublimity contains much food for reflection, is difficult or rather impossible to resist, and makes a strong and ineffaceable impression on the memory." Then consider that Góngora promises the committed reader access to hidden truths, tantalizes his audience with language that challenges with witty conundrums and verbal enigmas while making a strong appeal to the senses, and stages memory theater in the reader's mind. Longinus reminds readers that "sublimity raises us towards the spiritual greatness of god"; Gongorine *admiratio* stimulates and focuses the audience's powers of the mind on a spiritual and intellectual quest for a higher realm. The Spanish master employs myriad defamiliarization techniques to produce wonderment; the classical theorist observes that whereas "the useful and necessary are readily available to man, it is the unusual which always excites our wonder."[14]

Longinus lists five sources of sublimity, instances of which appear throughout the *Soledades*: "the power to conceive great thoughts" (for example, the poems' celebration of the eternal cycle of life, which subsumes death); "strong and inspired emotion" (such as Góngora's staging of affect in scenes of love and lamentation); certain figures of thought or speech (for instance, the poet's enthusiasm for hyperbaton, periphrasis, and the challenging *culto* conceit); refined diction (including Góngora's Latinate Spanish and mythological allusions); and noble composition (as in the poems' rhythmic musicality and varied verse and sentence lengths). Even some of the more puzzling features of the *Soledades* obtain felicitous support in Longinus's treatise on the sublime. The sudden shift from third-person narration to first-person direct discourse, as in the monologues of the *serrano*, fisherman, and the pilgrim, charges the language with intense, powerful emotion, the *auctor* asserts. Longinus also states that rhetorical questions add credibility to sublimity: "For emotion carries away more easily when it seems to be generated by the occasion rather than deliberately assumed by the speaker, and the self-directed question and its answer represent precisely this momentary quality of emotion."[15] Góngora employs this type of sublimity in *Soledad* II, when the poetic voice abruptly shifts into first person. He then compounds this bit of *admiratio* when the speaker questions Love in apostrophic fashion, only to answer his own question immediately afterward:

> ¡Cuán dulces te adjudicas ocasiones
> para favorecer, . . .
>
> . . . a dos entre cáñamo garzones!
> ¿Por qué? Por escultores quizá vanos
> de tantos de tu madre bultos canos
> cuantas al mar espumas dan sus remos.
> (Jammes, II:658–64)
>
> (How happily thy disposition falls
> To favour, . . .
>
> . . . two poor youths among their nets and line!
> And why? Perhaps because as sculptors vain,
> With all the foam their oars give to the sea,
> They snowy figures of thy mother feign.
> [Wilson, II:646–52])

Faithful to his "more is more" credo, Góngora raises the quotient of sublimity to an even higher power by using periphrasis to allude to Venus and Cupid, whose names never cross the speaker's lips. Unlike the obscure reference to Ursa Major of *Soledad* I, however, these lines readily yield their "secrets" to readers, functioning not so much as a puzzle, but rather as a lighthearted, witty verbal tease that contributes to the wonderment elicited by the unexpected switch to direct discourse and the rapid-fire response to a rhetorical query.

Most significant for understanding Góngora's poetics, however, is the fact that throughout *On the Sublime,* Longinus lauds sublimity that arises from the merger of art and nature. Thus the Greek *auctor* comments on hyperbaton, a hallmark of Gongorine *cultismo:* "[People experiencing strong emotions] seem to be blown this way and that by their excitement, as if by a veering wind. They inflict innumerable variations on the expression, the thought, and the natural sequence. Thus hyperbaton is a means by which, in the best authors, imitation approaches the effect of nature. Art is perfect when it looks like nature, nature is felicitous when it embraces concealed art."[16] A "veering wind" describes both the convoluted syntax of the *Soledades'* sentences and the audience's experience of reading the verses, moving back and forth across fused and confusing fields of imagery, allusions, paradoxes, and ambiguous words, and grammar replete not only with hyperbaton but also with hypallage and chiastic structures. The blend of the prolix Gongorine sentence with a meandering river shows the merger of art and nature that Longinus and the Spanish poet associate with the elevated thought and style of the sublime and *admiratio,* respectively. Even the weaving course of the *silva* across the page with varying combinations of heptasyllables and hendecasyllables reveals art at work imitating nature from the beginning to the end of the *Soledades*. Góngora also employs striking conceits to highlight the poetic ideal of mixing art and nature together in a symbiotic relationship:

> Hermana de Faetón, verde el cabello,
> les ofrece el que, joven y gallardo,
> de flexüosas mimbres garbín pardo
> tosco le ha encordonado, pero bello.
> Lo más liso trepó, lo más sublime
> venció su agilidad, y artificiosa
> tejió en sus ramas inconstantes nidos,
> donde celosa arrulla y ronca gime
> la ave lasciva de la cipria diosa.
> Mástiles coronó menos crecidos
> gavia no tan capaz: estraño todo,
> el designio, la fábrica y el modo.
> *A pocos pasos lo admiró no menos*
> montecillo, las sienes laureado,
> traviesos despidiendo moradores
> de sus confusos senos,
> conejuelos que (el viento consultado)
> salieron retozando a pisar flores,
> el más tímido al fin más ignorante
> del plomo fulminante.
> (Jammes, II:263–82; emphasis added)

> (Next Phaethon's sister, splendid with green hair,
> Displayed a dovecote, which his host had made
>   When he was young and gay,
> Plaited, of bending osiers, a coif grey,
> And yet though roughly corded it was fair.
> The smoothest trunk he'd climbed, the height obeyed,
> Conquered by his agility, and there
> Wove in her boughs the nests inconstant, where
> Lascivious fledgelings of the Cypriot queen
> Should coo and hoarsely moan with jealousy.
> No greater crowsnest crowned a mainmast high
>   Upon a warship fine.
>   And all strange to be seen.
> In workmanship, conception and design.
> *Few paces distant, no less wondered he*
> At a small hill with laurels on its brow,
>   Which from its bosom now
> Dismissed its population festively,
> The coneys that had sniffed the wind that day
> Then scurried out to tread on flowers and play;

> Even the most timid ignorant, be it said,
> Of fulminating lead.
> [Wilson, II:254–75; emphasis added])

These lines posit an equation of identity (A = B) that epitomizes sublimity, the unusual uplifted and ennobled: "... strange to be seen. / In workmanship, conception and design." Conceit A, lines 263–74 (254–67), represents natural art. In his youth, the islander artist spotted the raw material of an artifact buried in the flexible, intertwining boughs of the poplar, because his visionary powers enabled him to spy the artistic potential hidden in nature. The islander then proceeded to exercise heroic skill, labor, and courage to climb the tall tree and extract and develop that potential into a functional objet d'art, a dovecote. Góngora increases the element of wonderment even more with a periphrastic allusion to the myth of Phaethon, in particular to the story of his sisters, who turned into poplars while weeping for his tragic death. The poet draws a crisscrossed, chiastic analogy between two metamorphoses with this allusion. The classical tale transforms a woman into a tree, whereas the islander transmutes a tree into a snood, a net for a woman's hair—the poplar's green foliage. In a sense, Góngora's metamorphosis brings out the buried essence of the tree, like Michelangelo's calling forth a statue from a block of stone. The author also alludes to Venus in the conceit, labeling her the "Cypriot goddess," and through metonymy compares the "inconstant nests" of the doves, who flit about and whose roosts shift with the breeze, to the fickleness of love, which continuously changes allegiances. The poet further enhances *admiratio* when he incorporates a new field of imagery into the conceit in references to the sea, topsail masts, and a crow's nest, perhaps suggested by the mention of Cyprus or the thought of the island kingdom that the old artificer now rules. Line 275 (268) provides the equal sign in the equation that functions as a fulcrum of *admiración*, almost as a zeugma yoking the two component metaphors together. After the extreme heights of conceit A, the word *pasos* (paces) sends the reader's inner eye plummeting earthward, visually refocusing the imagination on the ground after it has soared skyward with Phaethon. Conceit B, lines 276–82 (269–75), symbolizes artful nature in the form of a rabbit warren, a work of art not created by a human being, although the poetic voice does not actually make that declaration. This natural maze does, however, possess distinctly anthropomorphic features, including "brows" that wear a victory crown of laurels and a protective "bosom" whose maternal depths release their charges only at propitious moments. The poet informs the audience that these bunnies enjoy an innocent, Edenic life free of the fear of hunters armed with guns.

In addition to the transitional pivot of line 275 (268), the author employs the natural system of the four elements to unite the two conceits into a sublime whole: earth—tree and hillock; water—mast and crow's nest; air—doves and rabbits sniffing the breeze; and fire—"fulminating lead" and the lightning flash of a fired gun. Natural art and artful nature, unified imagistically, disclose a shared conceptual basis that reveals important elements of Gongorine *culto* aesthetics. Both symbiotic artifacts harness and contain nature in a discernible, albeit intricate, labyrinthine framework, transforming the patterns of nature into an organized and fruitful design. The constructs arise from the recognition of the artful potential inherent in the natural medium and the realization of that potential. As a result, the perfect essential telos of the cosmos surfaces in works of art as does the godlike potential of the artist. Such creations shape and channel nature's vitality without imposing paralyzing rigidity on life. Both cages in this passage exhibit a plasticity that allows for movement, the dynamic processes of life, and the abrupt changes of *admiratio*. Moreover, Góngora has chosen two notoriously prolific species, doves and rabbits, to imply that cultivated nature flourishes and perhaps finds the natural immortality of cyclic continuity denied creatures in the wild who may meet their ends at the end of a gun. Artifacts born of the symbiosis of art and nature bear the unmistakable stamp of Longinus's sublime, as the supreme embodiment of beauty, magic, and wonder.

Moral concerns migrate into Góngora's development of the art-nature thematic paradox in the *Soledades,* belying the notion that the author and his *culto* style promote poetry devoid of serious or spiritual issues or both. The author qualifies his acclamation of the art-nature bond with periodic admonitions against the misapplication of human ingenuity to corrupt the natural world for selfish, immoral reasons. Through the voice of the old *serrano,* he roundly condemns the perverted metamorphosis of the once glorious voyages of discovery into handmaidens of insatiable avarice: "'Piloto hoy la Cudicia, no de errantes / árboles, mas de selvas inconstantes'" (Jammes, I:403–4) ("Covetousness the pilot is to-day / Of wandering forests not of shifting trees" [Wilson, I:392–93]). Fleets of ships, identified metonymically with forests, invade the ocean's realm to the point that the earth expands to usurp water's dominion, thus upsetting cosmic order.[17] In a symmetrical manner, the fisherman of *Soledad* II, another character cast in the conventional role of elderly *desengañador* (undeceiver), echoes these sentiments. He calls the ocean "'ese teatro de Fortuna'" (Jammes, 401) ("[that] theater of Fortune" [Wilson, 392]) that rewards greed with nameless, watery graves:

> "cuanto en vasos de abeto Nuevo Mundo
> (tributos digo américos) se bebe
> en túmulos de espuma paga breve."
>
> (Jammes, 404–6)
>
> ("drinks in wooden goblets all
> That the new world lets fall,
> —The tributes of America I say—
> Granting brief monuments of foam in pay."
>
> [Wilson, 394–97])

Elsewhere the poems' voice seems to speak almost directly to artists, although Góngora compresses matters of art, life, and ethics into the same conceptual frame. The author extols the virtue of humility symbolized by a simple goatherd's hut:

> No moderno artificio
> borró designios, bosquejó modelos,
> al cóncavo ajustando de los cielos
> el sublime edificio . . .
>
> (Jammes, I:97–100)
>
> (No artificer new
> Models designed for thee, or sketches drew,
> Adjusting to the skies' concavity
> An edifice sublime . . .
>
> [Wilson, I:91–94])

Contrary to their initial impression, these lines do not promote a return to rustic life and primitive architecture. Rather, they introduce an emblematic, moral counterweight to the high-flying pride represented by city life and grand architecture that challenge and threaten to displace the designs of the divine artificer above. Góngora warns readers in general and artists in particular against hubris, the pilgrim's apparent transgression in love. Later in *Soledad* I, the poet reminds his audience that excessive pride, a mortal sin, can precipitate tragic retribution:

> "ilustren obeliscos las ciudades,
> a los rayos de Júpiter expuesta,
> aun más que a los de Febo, su corona,
> cuando a la choza pastoral perdona
> el cielo, fulminando la floresta."
>
> (Jammes, I:934–38)

> ("For though the mighty towns
> Adorn themselves with obelisks, their crowns
> Are to the rays of Jupiter displayed
> Even more than to the sun's
> The thunderbolt the rustic hovel spares
> But fires the forest glade."
> [Wilson, I:908–13])

The juxtapositions, stated and implied, resemble those of the previous passage: city-country, urban-rustic life, art-artlessness, and pride-humility. Here, though, the tone of condemnation grows stronger with the insertion of an oblique reference to the Tower of Babel, in that the builders of obelisks seem to indulge their vanity by trying to touch heaven. While they incur God's wrath, those who wisely acknowledge human limitations possess a natural (divine) shield that protects them from disaster.

Góngora may invite his elite listeners to exercise and refresh their minds by leaving the court behind imaginatively for the solitary pleasure of reading his pastoral poems, but he does not advise his readers to abandon city comforts for a hovel in the woods. Yet, the conventional pastoral oppositions discussed above leave the *Soledades'* audience with a moral dilemma in regards to life and art that unfolds in paradoxical terms. Throughout the masterpiece, the author seems to advocate balance, a dynamic working through of the diametrically opposed positions of paradox as the only viable solution to the ethical quandaries posed. In terms of human existence, that solution assumes the shape of the golden mean. The warning about the deadly consequences of pride constitutes part of an epithalamial hymn sung to the newlyweds of *Soledad* I. Just before the friendly reminders about lightning bolts aimed by a divine hand, the chorus blesses the couple and their descendants with the legacy of the golden mean:

> "Entre opulencias y necesidades,
> medianías vinculen competentes
> a vuestros descendientes
> (previniendo ambos daños) las edades" . . .
> (Jammes, I:930–33)
>
> ("Twixt opulence and hard necessities,
> Avoiding either evil, may the years
> Furnish their modest fortune to your sons."
> [Wilson, I:905–7])

Either extreme is undesirable, and the young people should therefore steer a middle course to achieve genuine good fortune, which they can then pass along to their descendants. This ideal, a well-known literary topos, resurfaces in *Soledad* II when the poetic voice praises the island kingdom as the embodiment of the golden mean: "los extremos de fausto y de miseria / moderando" (Jammes, II:207–8) (to moderate / Extremes of poverty and wealth too great [Wilson, II:198–99]). The recommendation "all things in moderation" offers a practical solution to existential dilemmas, but the art-nature tension resists an easy resolution, despite the sublime complementarity Góngora elects to develop in the dovecote–rabbit warren analogies. Art possesses a dual, ambiguous quality vis-à-vis nature that at times endows it with an inevitably, irresolubly conflictive character. Two diametrically opposed reactions to a fireworks display demonstrate this point:

> Los fuegos pues el joven solemniza,
> mientras el viejo tanta acusa tea
> al de las bodas dios, no alguna sea
> de nocturno Faetón carroza ardiente,
> y miserablemente
> campo amanezca estéril de ceniza
> la que anocheció aldea.
> (Jammes, I:652–58)

> (The youth extolled the gay and fiery sight,
> But the old man deplored the excess of light
> Unto the wedding god, lest one should be,
> Of a nocturnal Phaethon, carriage vain,
> Lest that, which slept a village, miserably
> Should wake, a sterile and a cindery plain.
> [Wilson, I:633–38])

The pilgrim gazes on the evanescent, luminous art with the eyes of wonderment, whereas the aged mountaineer, Cassandra-like, views the spectacle as a latent prelude to a conflagration unleashed by an artificer who cannot control his own creation—the very image of Phaethon. The protagonist sees only beauty, whereas the *serrano* anticipates the loss of the town, perhaps of human lives, and the despoilment of the green world. One could interpret the juxtaposed perspectives as a function of age, the naïveté of youth contrasted with the elderly wisdom of disillusioned experience. As perspectives on art, though, neither view invalidates the other. If Góngora wishes to teach a subtle lesson, that instruction appears to take the shape of a warning that those who tap nature to produce artifacts must control and manipulate nature's beautiful and powerful forces without turning them back on the source of inspiration itself or on humankind—like the hand of the prince in *Soledad* II who masters the magnificent horse he rides by perfecting, not annihilating, the innate grace, beauty, and strength of the beast.

Longinus upholds as the ultimate in sublimity the blending of art and nature, although art plays the crucial role in lifting nature to new heights of wonderment: "[A]rt must always come to the aid of nature, and *the combination of the two may well be perfection*" (emphasis added). Anyone who reads the *Soledades* would emerge from the experience with an image of Góngora as a poet who advocates this aesthetic principle of *admiratio* with great alacrity. Perhaps no conceit better demonstrates the composer's quest to generate *admiración* by merging art and nature in the *Soledades* than that of the fishing net:

> Dando el huésped licencia para ello,
> recurren no a las redes que, mayores,
> mucho Océano y pocas aguas prenden,
> sino a las ambiciosas menos penden,
> laberinto nudoso, de marino
> Dédalo, si de leño no, de lino
> fábrica escrupulosa, y aunque incierta,
> siempre murada, pero siempre abierta.
> (Jammes, II:73–80)
>
> (With the permission of their guest, they chose
> To fish, not with their greater nets—for those
> Much ocean but small depth of water hold—
> But those that less ambitiously enfold,
> The knotty labyrinth of some marine
> Daedalus, but whose wood had fibre been,
> Fabric exact, in an uncertain way,
> That always walled, yet always open lay.
> [Wilson, II:68–75])

The striking, immediate impact of the words and imagery obscures the fact that Góngora has actually revitalized a conventional pastoral topos: the *griphos* (fishing net). Traditionally, the *griphos* represents a maze, a puzzlelike construct that engages the mind, but steadfastly resists facile, linear, rational resolution and cedes only to mental agility, flexibility, and persistence—certainly requirements for the audience of the *Soledades*. As John Beverley observes, this conceit, one of several in the text that allude to labyrinths, offers readers a microcosmic symbol of the poems as a whole, and the hermeneutic challenge of deciphering them. I find it most significant that Góngora couches this metapoetic symbiosis of art and nature in paradoxical terms, as a praxis of *synoeciosis*, which embraces paradox and oxymoron not as paradigms of opposing thoughts that obliterate meaning through mutual cancellation, but rather as paradigms that encourage meditation after the initial startling shift in viewpoint incurred by *admiratio*, and eventually spur the reading public to speculate about the dialectical interplay of conflicting ideas and values.[18]

The conundrums posed by the fishing-net conceit shed light on Góngora's *culto* poetry as well as on the *Soledades*' aesthetics of enigma. The artifact contains water, but cannot hold it; flaunts exacting, virtuoso craftsmanship, but displays an ever shifting, protean form; and resembles the walled, wooden, land-based labyrinth of Daedalus, but consists of an open, aquatic maze crafted of thread. In short, a fishing net, Góngora's masterpiece, or *cultismo* answers the riddle: "What artifact, work of poetry, or type of poetry features volumeless volume and wall-less walls, shows intricate design and formless form, and captures and intensifies nature's beauty, vitality, variety, and abundance without asphyxiating its vibrant essence?" Note that the poet also embeds a moral stance in this metapoetic metaphor that reiterates the abhorrence of vanity, especially that of the egotistical artificer, voiced throughout the *Soledades*. Daedalus, the quintessential, mythological ancestor of all artists, brought about his own imprisonment and that of his son, Icarus, and eventually his offspring's demise, by proud artistic invention unmoderated by prudent considerations or a proper degree of humility. Góngora's fishermen, by contrast, wisely and modestly elect not to cast a large, wide net into the sea—the piscatory equivalent of flashy, superficial, pretentious verse disseminated in haste and with a "catch" of dubious worth. These craftsmen employ smaller, artfully woven nets that reach greater depths as they hang in the water for a longer period of time. Góngora, too, sets out a stunning array of labyrinthine nets or conceits in the liquid medium of the *silvas*, wall-less walls with formless form, suspended on the page, that ensnare the rich marvels of nature even as they plumb the intellectual depths and imaginative profundity of an elite audience. The multiple paradoxes of the fishing-net conceit convey the notion of Gongorine poetics as a dynamic, creative balance of tensions in which the poet artificer shapes and controls nature through the sinuous, elastic mold of art, whereas nature continuously strives to break free of art's confines. The author seems to place before himself the task of fabricating a complex, multidimensional, linguistic grid that fits nature like a glove and, in a sense, becomes one with nature, actualizing Longinus's concept of the highest level of sublimity. The catalog of sea creatures entrapped by the net, which follows this descriptive tribute to Daedalian ingenuity, appears to support this supposition. Góngora portrays the net and its bountiful harvest as a volatile compound, a lively mix of oysters that hide in their shells, a slippery conger eel that tries to slide out of his knotty jail, and a noble salmon and a feisty sea bass who struggle to break the tough threads that bind them. The readers witness here on a small scale the same type of spectacle they encounter on a grand scale in the *Soledades* and other Gongorine works: the generative, dramatic conflict between a controlling art and a recalcitrant nature forever seeking to escape art's bounds.

With his obvious interest in depicting littoral regions, and other areas and states of "in-betweenness," it should come as no surprise that Góngora conceives of poetry as a liminal zone in which he explores and explodes the boundaries between art and nature. The author alerts readers to poetry's function as a place of convergence in scenes such as *Soledad* I's flight of cranes against the sky, figuratively rendered as letters marching across paper or mysterious hieroglyphs emblazoned on papyrus:

> caracteres tal vez formando alados
> en el papel dïáfano del cielo
> las plumas de su vuelo.
> (Jammes, I:609–11)
>
> (winged characters they feign
> Upon the sky diaphanous to write
> As parchment, for the feathers of their flight.
> [Wilson, I:591–93])

The poems' voice and eyes enable the audience to see nature transmogrified, reshaped into the art of writing by imaginative refocalization. Other episodes in the *Soledades* also serve as an almost allegorical representation of poetry as an artificial space of perpetual transmutation in which art merges with nature to produce astonishing hybrid forms that force the reading audience to rethink the relations between humans and their world. In a moment in which he magically acquires telescopic optical powers, the pilgrim observes the hand of a *serrana* dip into a cool, crystalline stream, and then carry the water to her face:

> juntaba el cristal líquido al humano
> por el arcaduz bello de una mano
> que al uno menosprecia, al otro iguala.
> (Jammes, I:244–46)
>
> (Who, to her human, liquid crystal gave;
> Her hand, sweet aqueduct for such a wave,
> Equalled the one but far outdid the other.
> [Wilson, I:240–42])

The hand, a familiar motif associated with Mannerist painting and literature, and the appendage most identified with writing, artisanry, and the plastic arts, metamorphoses into a conduit or channel, an implement and mediating agent that links human and natural worlds in a dynamic, organic, and beautiful way. I believe that Góngora viewed poetry in a similar fashion, as a glorious aqueduct that conducts and focuses the cosmic elixir of life, permitting humans to tap into the fluid essence of the universe while denying none of its vigor, in the process merging art, nature, and humankind into a harmonious whole, worthy indeed of *admiración*.

The Gongorine Conceit

The treasure of meaning entwined in the *griphos* metaphor illustrates how Góngora achieves the seemingly impossible task of merging art and nature in the construction of a poetic universe of more than two thousand lines of sustained marvels in the *Soledades*. The author deploys such conceits in the poems with a boundless zeal that still amazes readers today. As the poet's chief stratagem of *admiratio,* the Gongorine conceit implements what Longinus terms *phantasia,* that is, image production or rhetorical visualization techniques designed to generate "grandeur, magnificence and urgency," and, perhaps most important, "astonishment." In regards to metaphor in particular, Longinus asserts that "tropes are naturally grand, that metaphors conduce to sublimity, and that passages involving emotion and description are the most suitable field for them."[19] Whether or not Góngora knew Longinus's views on sublimity, here again his high opinion of yet another tactic of *admiración* parallels that of the Greek *auctor.*

Hindsight reveals that the complex Gongorine metaphor has provided much of the fuel for the controversy surrounding the poet's reception by readers and critics, and has contributed greatly to his movement in and out of the canon. Even close to Góngora's lifetime, thoughts on metaphor varied widely. Whereas Erasmus and Castiglione valued metaphor for its aesthetic and pedagogical potential, Gracián and Tesauro saw metaphor as a purveyor of wonderment, especially through the depiction of unexpected conceptual correspondences. In his rhetorical manual *Agudeza y arte de ingenio* (Acuity and the art of wit) (1642, 1648), Gracián, a writer not frequently identified with effusiveness, borders on idolatry in his praise of Góngora as a master of wit, lauding the Gongorine conceit among other tropes employed by the author of the *Soledades.*[20] Yet, this technique of the elaborate grafting of several systems of connections onto one another and the mixing of their constituent parts in a hybrid metasystem of meaning undoubtedly bears more of the burden than any other aspect of the *culto* style for the poet's subsequent relegation to the noncanonical blacklist as the "prince of darkness" during the eighteenth and nineteenth centuries.

This same rhetorical culprit, however, has played the role of prime mover in Góngora's resurrection, recanonization, and current near apotheosis. Consider Federico García Lorca's pivotal lecture "La imagen poética de Don Luis de Góngora" (The poetic image of Luis de Góngora), a discourse written in 1925–1926 that performed double duty as manifesto of the *culto* poet's self-proclaimed heirs, the Generation of '27, and as an essay that revolutionized critical analysis of Góngora's poetry. Lorca regards the Golden Age poet's major innovation as the reshaping of Spanish into a language of new beauty, "una nueva torre de gemas y piedras, inventadas" (a new tower of invented gems and stones), that stands on a firm foundation of metaphors and imagery: "Inventa por primera vez en el castellano un nuevo método para cazar y plasmar las metáforas y piensa sin decirlo que la eternidad de un poema depende de la calidad y trabazón de sus imágenes" (He invents for the first time in Spanish a new method for hunting and molding metaphors and he thinks without saying it that a poem's eternity depends on the quality and union of its images). Lorca also emphasizes that although Góngora proves himself keenly attuned to all five senses, sight, the primary sense of the artificer of metaphors, dominates his poetic imagery: "La metáfora está siempre regida por la vista (a veces por una vista sublimada), pero es la vista la que la hace limitada y le da su realidad" (Metaphor is always governed by sight [at times by sublimated sight], but it is sight that limits it [metaphor] and gives it its reality).[21] As a peerless hunter-gatherer of conceits (some form of the word *cazar* [to hunt] appears repeatedly in this lecture), Góngora, according to Lorca, envisions the world as a gigantic game preserve of metaphors, which he must cull, limit, and define, following his instincts as a metaphor hunter.

Just as I pointed out earlier in the analysis of the *griphos* conceit as a metapoetic commentary on art, and as a construct of irresoluble tensions and paradoxical parameters such as "wall-less walls," Lorca portrays the typical Gongorine landscape as a symbolic visual representation of the poet's dynamics of creative conflicts. He notes Góngora's love of an endless expanse of mountains or the sea or both, but observes that the Golden Age poet also obsesses over artistic control, projected as the imposition of invented optical limits, containment fields superimposed on these sweeping vistas:

> Y tanto deseo tiene de dominarlo y redondearlo [el mar] que ama inconscientemente las islas, porque piensa, y con mucha razón, que un hombre puede gobernar

y poseer mejor que ninguna otra tierra, el orbe definido, visible de la redonda roca limitada por las aguas.

(And he has so much desire to dominate and round it [the sea] out that he unconsciously loves islands, because he thinks, and very rightly so, that a man can better govern and possess more than any other land, the visible, defined orb of a round rock bounded by tides.)[22]

Lorca deliberately compares Góngora to the old fisherman of *Soledad* II, stressing the poet's need to demarcate and refashion nature artistically, as well as his desire to dominate his aesthetic microcosmos the way a king, even a disillusioned fisherman monarch, would govern his realm—all of which Lorca communicates in imagery that mimics the language of Gongorine conceits.

Although Lorca does not address the interplay of metaphor and generic conventions as a function of *admiratio,* he does recognize that Góngora faced the challenge in the *Soledades* of penning a lyric poem that could compete in quality with the great epics of the day. Lorca articulates the problem as one of maintaining suspense in a long lyric poem, that is, a work that traditionally suppresses reliance on narrative or narrative tension for aesthetic appeal. Gongorine metaphors solve that problem: "Góngora entonces elige su narración y la cubre de metáforas. Ya es difícil encontrarla. Está transformada. La narración es como un esqueleto del poema, envuelto en la carne magnífica de las imágenes" (Góngora then chooses his narrative and covers it with metaphors. Now it is difficult to find it. It is transformed. The narrative is like the poem's skeleton, wrapped in the magnificent flesh of the images). As an element of camouflage, the Gongorine conceit brings about a profound change in the reader's perception of the poetic entity. Suddenly, the bare bones of plot acquire the living, breathing dimensions of a palpable organism. Throughout the lecture, in fact, the twentieth-century author relates the magical transformations realized by Góngora's metaphors as visual and volumetric in nature, endowing his poems with a quality at once organic and plastic or architectonic. Lorca attributes the timelessness of Góngora's works to the "preocupación arquitectónica" (architectonic concern) displayed by verses that are "estatuas pequeñas" (small statues).[23]

Another member of the Generation of '27, Dámaso Alonso, has labeled Gongorine poetics "fundamentalmente, pero no únicamente, metafórica" (fundamentally, but not solely, metaphorical), and in his 1927 essay "Claridad y belleza de las *Soledades*" (Clarity and beauty of the *Solitudes*), he invited comparisons between Gongorism and cubism. The forceful, visual bias of Lorca's insights and Alonso's early essay has nourished a "painterly" critical approach to the Gongorine conceit that Michael Woods has rejected, repudiating literary analysis based on analogies between poetry and painting. Woods supports instead a rhetorical approach to metaphor, stressing that, in the *Soledades*, Góngora uses the conceit as a unifying, rhetorical mechanism that strikes readers with wonderment and creates a bond between the poems' protagonist and their audience: "The contribution made by the accumulation of individual conceits to the poem as a whole is to create a kind of emotional unity by means of the sense of amazement they generate. . . . The presence of so many conceits manoeuvres the reader into sharing this sense of wonderment."[24]

Maintaining a strict dichotomy between visual and rhetorical approaches to the Gongorine conceit, however, seems to me to run counter to the actual impact of the *culto* metaphor on readers. Verbal strategies encourage readers, in rhetorical fashion, to conjure images perceived by the mind's eye, in keeping with the traditions of memory theater and meditational literature. Why divorce two parts integral to a continuous process that involves both moving the reading public to *admiración* and supplying sufficient sensory stimuli for this same public to generate mental images? As Nicolae Babuts has suggested, the creation and interpretation of literary texts require linguistic and nonlinguistic sources of information. He has introduced the concept of "mnemonic potentials" into critical discourse on the hermeneutics of reading to capture the notion of "internal representational patterns that reflect memories of previous events, of oral communications, and of readings," which can operate as "partially bonded linguistic and perceptual sequences." Metaphors, Babuts asserts, "are in effect dynamic patterns harking back to the perceptible forces of the visible reality. Being the products of a metaperceptual impulse, metaphors are epistemologically indirect. Yet, they refer to, and communicate, their incontrovertible truth directly in epiphanic moments and offer the only privileged way to knowledge." In this sense, *admiratio* functions as an inherent component in the interpretation of metaphors, as the experience initiated when rhetoric mobilizes readers' minds and affects to the takeoff point when epistemological leaps, dependent at least partially on recollections of perceptual data, become possible. Conceits inspire imaginative machinations in a liminal space of unique referential power: "[Metaphors] are dynamic, and their semantic complexity and nuances and their referential mode often take them beyond the limits of concepts. Metaphors fall midway between directly perceived images and abstract concepts."[25]

Góngora and his peers grasped intuitively what Babuts expresses in phenomenological terms, because they were accustomed to Neoplatonic thought and cosmology. Certainly, the author of the *Soledades*, living among a cultural elite who almost universally espoused the principle of *ut pictura poesis*, would have found puzzling the separation of visual and rhetorical approaches to metaphor. After all, one of the dominant art forms of the epoch that made a profound impact on his work and that of other Golden Age poets relies specifically on the nurturing symbiosis of the verbal and the visual to relay meaning extending beyond the perceptual and into the conceptual realm of Ideas. I refer to emblem literature, a rich, complex forerunner of today's much simpler picture books. In Góngora's time, emblems already lay claim to an illustrious heritage with roots reaching back to classical antiquity. Sebastián de Covarrubias's *Tesoro de la lengua castellana o española* (Treasury of the Spanish or Castilian language) (1611), a dictionary published shortly before *Soledad I* began circulating at court, supplies a revealing etymological account of the word *emblem:*

> Es nombre griego, "emblēma," significa entretenimiento o enlazamiento de diferentes pedrecitas o esmaltes de varias colores de que forman flores, animales y varias figuras enlosados de diferentes mármoles, enlazados unos con otros, y en las mesas ricas de jaspes y pórfidos, en cuyos compartimientos suelen engastar piedras preciosas.
>
> (It is a Greek noun, *emblēma*, [that] means inlay work of different pebbles or enamels of varied colors that form flowers, animals and varied figures in flagstones of different marbles, some linked with others, and in rich tables of veined marbles and porphyries in whose compartments they customarily set precious stones.)

Well into the seventeenth century, when they had traveled from stone to the printed page, emblems retained this ancient connection with the decorative arts, as indicated by their prominence in set designs for plays, masques, and pageants.[26] The notion of small, precious, heterogeneous materials artfully linked together in figures and patterns, which in turn frequently interlock with one another and form part of a larger, encompassing design, carried over as well into emblem literature. Here one finds precious wit and wisdom communicated by verbal and visual arts skillfully conjoined in intricate, interlaced conceptual patterns. Góngora's conceits also bear the stamp of the mosaic and of inlay artistry with their multiple tropological systems whose components interlock in unforeseeable ways to function as part of a larger, hybrid construct.[27]

Covarrubias duly notes the ties between older heraldic devices and mottoes, as well as coins and medallions struck with images and epigrams, and his contemporaries' emblems, all of which compress sophisticated concepts into a form of ideographic writing that approximates that of the sacred, mysterious Egyptian hieroglyphs. Heraldic devices originated in France, where in the fourteenth century this combination of adage and picture emphasized love and military themes, only to acquire a more esoteric and philosophical bent as the device, or *empresa,* traveled to Italy, where humanists steeped in the aesthetics of enigma transformed *emprese* into vehicles of occult knowledge. Covarrubias remarks, just as literary critics hundreds of years later have observed, that Andrea Alciati created the first book of emblems, published in Augsburg in 1531. However, Góngora's contemporary could not have gauged the astounding success of the *emblemata.* Between 1534 and 1545, the printer Wechel alone generated 13 editions of Alciati's work. Records document the existence of more than 150 editions of the book, which seemed to grow with each successive edition as emblems were added.[28]

What exactly constituted an emblem remained a matter of intense speculation and theoretical debate. Covarrubias at least could boast of a blessedly decisive opinion on this matter:

> Metafóricamente se llaman emblemas los versos que se subscriben a alguna pintura o talla, con que significamos algún concepto bélico, moral, amoroso o en otra manera, ayudando a declarar el intento del emblema y de su autor. Este nombre se suele confundir con el de símbolo, hieroglífico, pegma, empresa, insignia, enigma, etc. Verás al obispo de Guadix, mi hermano, en el primer libro de sus *Emblemas,* a donde está todo muy a la larga dicho, con erudición y distinción.

> (Metaphorically the verses written under a picture or carving are called emblems, with which we make known an amorous, moral or martial concept [or conceit] or in some way, helping to state the intention of the emblem or its author. This noun is customarily confused with that of symbol, hieroglyph, pegma [a movable stage or scaffolding, sometimes bearing a written phrase, frequently found in pageants], device, standard, enigma, etc. Consult the Bishop of Guadix, my brother, in the first book of his *Emblems,* where everything is said fully, with erudition and distinction.)[29]

Before deferring to his brother's literary accomplishments, in particular Juan de Horozco y Covarrubias's *Emblemas morales* (1591), as a sort of free, fraternal publicity stunt as well as a sort of deus ex machina to rescue himself from a definition turned problematic, Sebastián de Covarrubias abandons his initial tone of total confidence. At first he identifies only the subscript verses as emblems in the metaphorical sense, because they communicate the essential thought of image and verses in the succinct, witty fashion of a conceit. Yet, when Covarrubias repeats the word *emblem* at the end of the same sentence, the reference clearly encompasses both visual and verbal elements.

This ambiguity in regards to what fits under the umbrella term *emblema* has important implications for understanding the Gongorine conceit. Renaissance emblem theorists often argued about which component had primacy, or if either one did in fact have primacy, in the hybrid medium. Did image outweigh words, or did the verbal sway the visual? As Peter Daly has indicated, the emblem presumed a preexisting tradition of imagery already familiar to emblematists and many members of their audience. Authors of emblem books and their readers carried an internal, mental catalog of pictures and ideas that gave them an interpretive head start when approaching a new set of emblems. Daly observes that a number of the Alciati editions were published without pictures, probably in many cases to save money, but they were also produced with the certainty that the readers already knew the images and had no need of an optical prompt to recall them. Such collections of *emblemata nuda* appeared in various countries, including Spain, as Alonso Ledesma's *Enigmas hechas para honesta recreación* (Enigmas made for honest recreation) (Madrid, 1611) attests.[30] Ledesma challenged readers to exercise the image-making powers of the mind to draw the pictures described on an internal, cerebral page, and then apply intellectual powers to grasp the hidden meaning of the author's words and the image in the mind's eye. Intentionally or not, such cases of *serio ludere* lend credence to the notion that the linguistic component of the emblem reigns supreme over the pictorial element, because language appears to function as the key that unlocks the emblem's symbiotic sign system. The same ambiguous statement demonstrates how readily the notions of "metaphor" ("metaphorically" operating here almost as a synonym for "synecdochally"), "concept," and "conceit" creep into discussions on emblems. The immediacy of the reference suggests a fundamental link that Góngora chose to explore, intensify, and develop. The list of terms and art forms frequently used interchangeably with *emblem* gives some idea of the fluidity of both word and medium at the time the poet composed the *Soledades*.

Covarrubias's lengthy definition hints at the considerable success emblem books met in the Iberian peninsula. The first Spanish edition of Alciati appeared in 1549, although Latin editions of the Italian humanist's work were common in Spain, including the annotated version of El Brocense (1573), the famous humanist at the University of Salamanca who shortly afterward, in 1576, published an extremely influential, annotated edition of Garcilaso. In 1615, Diego López, knight of Alcántara, teacher of Latin rhetoric, and former student of El Brocense, wrote what would perhaps become the best-selling edition of Alciati, that is, of a version accompanied by a Spanish translation. Between 1549 and 1615, about sixty-five emblem books directed at a Spanish-speaking public were published in or outside Spain. Yet, despite the obvious popularity of the medium or, more likely, because of it, the Spanish emblem tradition diverged markedly from the original model born in Italy.

From the beginning, most emblematists were compelled to subject readers to an introductory treatise on the medium to establish their authority, position themselves rhetorically and ideologically vis-à-vis the audience, and prepare that group of readers for their meditative encounter with the emblems. Italian humanists, who closely identified hieroglyphics and the aesthetics of enigma with the emblem tradition, emphasized that an aura of mystery constitutes an essential part of the medium:

> Para los tratadistas italianos, la insistencia en la necesidad de la presencia de algo misterioso e ingenioso en el emblema se hizo particularmente persistente, hasta el punto de que algunos afirmaban que la principal característica del emblema había de ser lo enigmático. El mismo Alciato escribe que un emblema es «aliquid ingeniose ab ingeniosis excogitatum.»
>
> (For the Italian treatise writers, the insistence on the necessity of the presence of something mysterious and witty in the emblem became particularly persistent to the point that some affirmed that the principal characteristic of the emblem had to be the enigmatic. Alciati himself writes that an emblem is "something witty devised by wit.")[31]

Yet, in Spain, this view of the emblem as a complex, compact form of brainteaser became the normative standard of only a small but powerful group of elitist counterparts with connections in learned cliques and court circles. On the whole, Spanish emblematists, many of whom were priests, saw in the medium a didactic vehicle that, if exploited properly, could serve to instruct a large audience in morality and official church doctrine. To achieve this pedagogical end, however, they had to tone down or eliminate altogether the emblem's quality of enigma. The select minority represented by El Brocense and Diego López regarded the emblems of Alciati, and the symbiotic form itself, as a means of preserving through direct contact the hermetic, classical wisdom contained in hieroglyphs, adagia, and epigrams. Pedro Campa rightly states that this position anticipates the paradoxical, conservative modernity of Góngora, the poet who proclaimed his intention to restore propinquity between Castilian and classical Latin, even if the endeavor involved the puzzling process of distortion to make a less analytic and more synthetic language that engaged solely the intellectually intrepid. The conflicted Spanish response to Alciati, divided between moralists and pedagogues in search of a larger, more passive audience, on the one hand, and the elitist humanists in search of a small, active audience, on the other, set the stage for the great battle over Gongorism. In fact, Gracián's treatise on *agudeza* (wit) cites Góngora and emblem books frequently as illustrations of the same style of writing: compressed ("much in little"), mysterious, and intellectually challenging. Because Gracián maintained the elitist view of the emblem developed by the Italian humanists, he naturally connected Gongorine *cultismo* with emblem literature not of the popular strain.[32]

The emphasis that Covarrubias and Gracián place on the linguistic component of the emblem and the fact that some emblem books appeared without drawings seem to settle the issue of which component of the form deserves the title of "most important." Nevertheless, there is another side to this story. According to Neoplatonic thought, the image performs the significant function of merging symbolic revelation with a flash of intellectual intuition in a moment of insight, when the viewer's meditative perception leaps to the higher realm of Ideas. With such a strong philosophical tradition invoked on behalf of images, one can well imagine how the split over the supremacy of words or images escalated into a full-scale war in England, where author Ben Jonson battled stage designer Inigo Jones over this very issue. Yet, after all is said and done, Peter Daly points out that the argument lacks relevance in terms of how emblems function, because the art form relies on an interdependent relationship of the verbal and the visual, even in "emblematic poems" in which language paints both the picture and the rhetorical portion of the emblem tradition. Daly coins the term *word-emblem* to describe a "verbal structure in which words convey both pictures and meaning" based upon qualities perceived through meditation and communicated as an intellectual message, whether recondite or unsubtly didactic in intention.[33] Like the metaphor, the "word-emblem" operates within a liminal, conceptual space merging the literal and the figurative.

Emanuele Tesauro noted such similarities in 1655 when he wrote in *Il cannocchiale aristotelico* (The Aristotelian binocular) that all types of wit *(agudeza)*—poetry, painting, and emblems—share a unifying rhetorical principle and conceptual process. Metaphor constitutes that nexus, the dynamic common denominator that enables humans to decipher meaning in emblems, and the emblematic poetry and painting so familiar to Tesauro. Góngora, however, clearly pushed the envelope on the emblematic principle by creating metaphors that simultaneously run several systems of imagery, while incorporating links that permit signification across sign systems. Tesauro's notion of metaphor relies on a thorough knowledge of source materials, presumably shared by the author and audience alike: hieroglyphics, catalogs of adages, devices, and emblems. Of course, both the inventor and the reader of metaphors must also be able to categorize that information by semantic fields, organizing the data into paradigms that allow for imaginative and unexpected combinations.[34] To say the least, Góngora possessed superior, highly original combinatory skills in this regard.

This particular aspect of Gongorine creative genius comes to light through what David N. Taylor terms an *emblemorphic* interpretation of some of the poet's works, that is, in reading a selection of his compositions as poetic analogues of existing emblems based on structural and thematic similarities. As Taylor acknowledges, Góngora employs such a variety of literary techniques to remake emblems into "emblemorphic poems" that the resultant poetic transformation bears a highly personalized stamp.[35] I suspect, however, that a number of Góngora's works, and many of the conceits in the *Soledades*, may lack clearly identifiable analogues, yet betray the influence of the emblem tradition in what I call the poet's "emblems of fantasy," which require the complexity of a focused human mind to unravel the multilayered meshing of verbal and visual elements.

In "The Rhetoric of the Image," Roland Barthes contrasts the noncoded messages of photographs with the coded iconic messages of a medium such as *emblemata*, which features interactive pictures and texts. Such combinations generate connotations as well as denotations, and they do so in a culturally and ideologically specific way. The linguistic and iconic messages together both fix or anchor meaning and simultaneously open the interpretive process of reading to different levels of signification. Emblems typically display two or three components: the *pictura*, the picture representing people, objects, or events (or all three) in a fashion that blends the unreal and the real, sometimes referred to as the emblem, plate, device, or image, and regarded in Platonic terms as the body; the *inscriptio*, the short, interpretive motto or posy, often in verse, generally placed above the *pictura*, and considered the Platonic soul of the iconic body; and the *subscriptio*, a prose or verse addition from the emblematist or an *auctor*, a feature not always present that offers a more literal description of the device and provides a verbal transition from the iconic to the discursive.[36]

Alciati's emblem "Que la bienaventuranza de esta vida no dura más de un momento" (The good fortune of this life only lasts a moment) illustrates the creative interplay of word and image, denotation and connotation, that characterizes the medium. Despite its position above the device, the title functions almost as a *subscriptio*, providing the audience with a succinct explanation of the relationship between the picture and moralistic text. The plate is relatively simple and straightforward, and easy to read, offering visual interest in the leafy, sinuous vine curling upward along the trunk in search of greater heights, and in the healthy, abundant fruit poised precariously above the earth and whose very robustness contrives to hasten their demise. In the motto, the personified pine tree actually warns the vain gourd that pride goeth before a fall, life is short, and old age and death quickly vanquish the splendor and pride of youth.[37] The posy identifies the discrete features of Alciati's device (pine tree, gourd, and spring-summer season) and announces the moral lesson regarding the brief, transitory nature of life. However, the visual simplicity of the image and the accompanying didactic verse do not deprive the emblem of a certain suggested, connotative richness. On the Richter scale of vegetative aggression, these gourds cannot hold a candle to the fruits of Marvell's "Garden," which attack the poetic speaker with overpowering, amorous zeal. Nonetheless, this nonfigural representation of a tree full of voluptuous fruit ripe for a fall, and described as guilty of overweening pride, also reminds the reader of the forbidden fruit in the Garden of Eden, original sin, the Fall, and the divine sentence of mortality received by the guilty parties.

Góngora's emblems of fantasy show decidedly more complex and challenging characteristics. Consider the conceit occasioned by the pilgrim's introduction to the bride in *Soledad* I, a passage that has proved both compelling and difficult to readers from Pedro Díaz de Rivas to Robert Jammes:

> Al galán novio el montañés presenta
>   su forastero, luego al venerable
>   padre de la que en sí bella se esconde
> con ceño dulce, y, con silencio afable,
> beldad parlera, gracia muda ostenta,
> cual del rizado verde botón, donde
> abrevia su hermosura virgen rosa,
>   las cisuras cairela
>   un color, que la púrpura que cela
> por brújula concede vergonzosa.
> Digna la juzga esposa
> de un héroe, si no augusto, esclarecido,
> el joven, al instante arrebatado
> a la que, naufragante y desterrado,
>   lo condenó a su olvido.
> Este pues Sol que a olvido lo condena,
> cenizas hizo las que su memoria
> negras plumas vistió, que infelizmente
> sordo engendran gusano, cuyo diente,
> minador antes lento de su gloria,
> inmortal arador fue de su pena.
> Y en la sombra no más de la azucena,
> que del clavel procura acompañada
>   imitar en la bella labradora
> el templado color de la que adora,
> víbora pisa tal el pensamiento,
> que el alma, por los ojos desatada,

> señas diera de su arrebatamiento,
> si...
> (Jammes, I:722–50; pp. 342–49)

> (To the gay bridegroom first the mountaineer
> Presented him, and to the sire of her,
> Who in her beauty had herself concealed
> With charming silence and with modest gaze,
> Whose speaking beauty her dumb grace revealed:
> As in its green and frizzled bud the rose
> Abbreviates its loveliness, but shows
> The fringe of an incision, and displays,
> Through modest spy-hole, the rich purple hue
>   It strives in vain to hide.
>   He judged her worthy bride
> If for no prince, still for a hero great,
> And suddenly he her resemblance knew
> To one, who shipwreck and an exile's fate
> And her oblivion him decreed of late.
> That sun, who sentenced him to her disdain,
> Made ashes of black feathers that he wore,
> The Phoenix feathers of her memory,
> And the deaf worm begat unhappily,
> Whose tooth should slowly through his pleasures bore,
> Then the inmortal ploughman of his pain.
>   And in the lily's shade,
>   By the carnation there accompanied,
>   Producing in the maid
> The fair complexion of his love to be—
> His thoughts on such a viper trod that he
>   His soul would have untied
> And show of his affliction plain betrayed,
> Had not...
> [Wilson, I:702–30])

Readers can sympathize with a frustrated Dámaso Alonso, who offers his interpretation of these lines (pp. 133–44) only to conclude: "Ninguna explicación me satisface" (No explanation satisfies me) (p. 184). What this simile that expands outward into an enigmatic conceit does satisfy are the two circumstances Longinus judges perfect for realization of the sublime through metaphor. The verses proffer descriptive richness of physical beauty and psychological process as well as expressive power in capturing the pilgrim's intense suffering that arises from painful memories, albeit in dramatic, representational form rather than in a lyric mode that invites audience identification. The predominant senses in Augustinian meditation and the *Soledades*, sight and hearing, play major roles in this conceit, for visual stimuli set the experience of memory in motion and the sound of music releases the pilgrim from being swept away *(arrebatado, arrebatamiento)* by the powerful sorrow of lost love. Two common hieroglyphic figures, the phoenix and the snake (viper), with two somewhat oblique allusions to the mythological figures of Flora and Icarus, constitute the basis for several overlapping systems of emblems that merge subject and object, and provide a surprisingly sophisticated anatomy of how painful memories function. The conceit begins with the hero meeting the bride and apprehension of her shy demeanor and physical beauty, likened to that of a rosebud that partly reveals and partly discloses her charms. Her reticent, silent splendor speaks mutely to the protagonist, just as *Soledad* I's river valley strikes the pilgrim dumb with amazement. Appropriately, the virgin bride–rosebud's modesty permits only glimpses of her latent passion, represented through the hints of purple that a bud on the verge of blooming reveals through natural peepholes *(brújula[s])*. The paradoxical mixtures of silent speech and innocent eroticism establish the tone for the entire conceit, which repeatedly forces the reader to fuse mutually exclusive semantic universes. In line 732 (712), focalization and narrative perspective shift from the immediate sensory impact of the bride's magnificence, the object of *admiratio* perceived from a point somewhere outside the human figures, even outside the protagonist, to the internal realm of the pilgrim's consciousness. Now readers learn that the subjective viewer deems the bride worthy of a hero, with adjectives such as *augusto* (majestic) and *esclarecido* (noble) stimulating the audience's memory of the *Soledades*' dedication and opening scene, where these attributes appeared in relation to the duke of Béjar and the shipwrecked hero. Furthermore, even as Góngora cues readers' memory with semantic echoes of verses past, the stunning beauty of the maiden triggers the protagonist's memory of rejection by his beloved, who consigned him to "her oblivion" of forgetfulness and the oblivion of a shipwrecked exile.

The new focus on the internal experience of painful memories also signals movement from the Flora-rosebud *pictura* to an even more complicated device superimposing the images of Icarus and the phoenix on one another. The remembered disdainful lady, now merged with the present shy bride, metamorphoses into the sun, which metonymically allies itself with *naufragante* (shipwreck[ed] or sinking) and *desterrado* (exiled) to suggest the blackened wings of Icarus's fatal flight in line 739 (718). The phoenix *pictura*, however, supersedes that of the doomed youth of Greek myth, who does, in fact, sink into oblivion as readers move on to wrestle with the conceit's next conundrum. Translator E. M. Wilson simplifies matters when he actually mentions the phoenix by name (719), a hint Góngora does not provide in the original text. The poet presents a rather detailed account of the immortal bird's perpetual cycle of death and rebirth. Medieval bestiaries relate that when the phoenix grows old, the bird constructs its own funeral pyre, turns toward the sun, and sets itself on fire by beating its wings. A worm emerges from the decaying ooze and eventually grows into the phoenix that repeats the cycle.[38] Note the ambiguity of this Gongorine worm, however, that does not connote the promise of renewal and resurrection traditionally embodied in the phoenix's avian chrysalis, and that one might identify with the passion latent in the earlier image of the bride rosebud, so much as the cruel gnawing of painful, parasitic memories that rob the pilgrim of his former identity and happiness, and prepare the fields of his imagination for a bitter harvest of constant sorrow. Whereas the lovely maiden awaits fulfillment, fertility, and harmony in marriage, the pilgrim expects only an endless cycle of suffering.

The final lines of the conceit remit audience and hero alike, in cyclic fashion, to the initial, external cause of these sorrowful reveries. The pilgrim sees the bride at this juncture as an almost ghostly apparition of his lost lady, rendered once again as Flora, whose skin harmoniously blends lily whiteness and carnation red, a fitting combination for an innocent about to consummate wedding vows. For the protagonist, however, a viper accompanies this particular vision of the flower goddess. The ambiguous worm has undergone a deadly metamorphosis. According to bestiary lore, the viper is synonymous with self-destructive violence because the female viper bites off the male's head after copulation, and the offspring literally rip their mother's body apart during birth.[39] The viper also has associations with original sin, the Garden of Eden, and human mortality. The use of *arrebatado* conveys the notion of forceful seizure against one's will, indicating that the pilgrim remains in the grip of powerful, painful memories beyond his control. Only the timely, disruptive intervention of the rustic, hymeneal choruses prevents him from dissolving into tears.

This multifaceted emblem of fantasy recalls the origins of the tradition in mosaic and inlay work. The intricate interweaving of shifting optical and psychological perspectives, the exploration of the relations between sensory experience and mental process, the simultaneous activation of an image's positive and negative polarities (immortal phoenix of rebirth and renewal versus immortal phoenix of undying, painful memories), and the creation of symbolic language that occupies a dynamic space somewhere between the iconic and the discursive (the locus of emblem and metaphor) show Góngora the innovator reshaping the conceit to generate wonderment and let readers experience the sublime through the process of analysis—in essence, writing their own *subscriptio*. The multiple linked images make it difficult to formulate a succinct motto that captures the conceptually unified device. Several *refranes* (popular Spanish sayings) seem to apply in part: "Espaldas vueltas, memorias muertas" (Out of sight, out of mind); "Quien bien quiere, tarde olvida" (He who loves well, forgets late); and "Música y flores, galas de amores" (Music and flowers, the trappings of love). The posy of an Alciati emblem attributed to Theocritus might also fit this conceit: "Que por pequeño que sea el amor da gran pena" (No matter how small love might be, it produces great pain).[40] Yet, none alone suffices to communicate in full Góngora's apparently intuitive grasp of the way in which bad memories and mixed emotions can possess the human mind, although clearly literary conventions have influenced this portrayal as well. Nevertheless, the poet affords readers a glimpse into the Augustinian "restless heart," to which he refers in the *Carta en respuesta*.

Another emblem of fantasy from *Soledad* I demonstrates just how quickly and effectively Góngora moves readers from immediate sensory appeal and impact to intellectual stimulation and conceptualization. In this case, the poet transforms the bride into a glorious phoenix in an extended simile:

>   la novia sale de villanas ciento
>   a la verde florida palizada,
>   cual nueva Fénix en flamantes plumas
>   matutinos del Sol rayos vestida,
>   de cuanta surca el aire acompañada
>   monarquía canora,
>   y, vadeando nubes, las espumas
>   del Rey corona de los otros ríos,
>   en cuya orilla el viento hereda ahora
>   pequeños no vacíos
>   de funerales bárbaros trofeos
>   que el Egipto erigió a sus Ptolomeos.
>   (Jammes, I:946–57)

>   (. . . when the bride,
>   A hundred maidens following beside,
>   Entered the green and flowery palisade:
>   So the young Phoenix in his flaming plume,
>   Clothed in the glory of the morning sun,
>   [By all canorous monarchy, that plough
>   The air, accompanied]
>   Conquers the clouds at last to crown the spume
>   Of that famed river, king o'erall declared;
>   Upon whose shore the wind inherits now
>   The wide expanse, before no vacant one,
>   Where grand funereal monuments appeared
>   That Egypt to her Ptolomies had reared.
>   [Wilson, I:920–32])[41]

Comparatively, *pictura* and *inscriptio* seem much easier to assign to this conceit. One can imagine "A bride is like a phoenix" atop a device that superimposes the image of a phoenix on a bride in a way that strikes the viewer with wonderment at her magnificence without a trace of sphinxlike monstrosity. The *subscriptio* of the device, however, poses a bit of a problem, and takes readers rather far afield from the initial encounter with a dazzling bride and her wedding attendants. In typically Gongorine style, the poet yokes together apparently conflicting figures, frames of reference, and temporal systems. The verdant, flowery palisade and the comparison between the bride and the immortal phoenix underscore the maiden's beauty and her association with fertility, rebirth, renewal, and the cyclic continuity of nature. The reader jumps from physical, perceived beauty to the dazzling, imagined beauty of the mythic bird that represents eternal life. As the conceit progresses, though, discordant elements gradually seep into the celebrative poetic context. The *flamantes plumas* (flaming plumes) can either ambiguously signify the bright reflection of the morning sun's rays off the phoenix's wings, a dazzling visual impression, or remind the audience of the destructive potential of the wedding torches as well as of the bird's death through a process of self-consumption, roughly analogous to human consumption of life through time. While the bride takes her place in the scheme of nature's continuity, her marriage marks a new phase of life and yet another step toward death, and the maidenly retinue will inevitably follow her march toward mortality just as the other birds follow the phoenix. The love and beauty envisioned in the bride-phoenix contain the seeds of destruction and death. In the mind's eye, readers pursue the *monarquía canora*, that is, the avian monarch and the rest of the melodious, feathered retainers, across the clouds and into the mysterious realm of thought and meditation, from the kingdom of birds into the king of rivers, the Nile, and finally to the kings' monuments, the pyramids of the pharaohs, a mental excursion linked metonymically by the phoenix's return to the exotic land of its origin (and the birthplace of hieroglyphics). The audience has moved from admiration for material beauty to contemplation of conjured monuments to human vanity and mortality, for the wind inherits the fame and wealth of monarchs the same as that of any other human. The linear, chronological march toward death appears to supplant the phoenix's ceaseless rebirth, but in actuality Góngora circumscribes the two within the cycle of nature, which, like the water cycle, he explores with boundless fascination in the *Soledades*. Even the presentation of the four elements in the conceit suggests the cycle of water, changing from the green enclosure (earth), to sun and phoenix (fire), to flying birds and clouds (air), to the foam of the Nile (water). Yet, this emblem of fantasy ends with a memento mori on a grand scale, in which the poet exchanges the promise of fertility for the pharaohs' giant funerary urns set in a barren landscape of death. It is as if Góngora has compressed into a deceptively straightforward device the bittersweet law of life; the individual inevitably confronts mortality, but the species survives as each generation gives way to the next. Marriage, of course, symbolized by the bride, legitimates and celebrates that form of immortality.

Yet, Góngora's emblems of fantasy need not display overt didacticism or intricate iconic and linguistic interweaving. Nor do they necessarily generate a multiphasic response involving wonderment, meditation, and abstract conceptualization on the part of readers. The simpler Gongorine emblems produce appreciation for the poet's wit and altered perception of the world that correlates with a sudden epistemological jolt of discovery. At the wedding banquet of *Soledad* I, for example, only telltale blue veins distinguish a milkmaid's hands from the cream she has used to press the cheese:

> de rústica vaquera,
> blanca, hermosa mano, cuyas venas
> la distinguieron de la leche apenas.
> (Jammes, I:876–78)

> (when these were pressed
> How white the rustic milk-maid's hand did seem
> That veins alone distinguished from the cream!
> [Wilson, I:852–54])

Metonymically, the *vaquera* (cowherdess) becomes a *lechera* (milkmaid), literally a woman made of milk. This literalization of the figurative likely brings a smile to the reader's face, but at the same time merges human and natural worlds, animate limb and inanimate object, in a rhypographic construct that invites the audience to view the person in a new light—she is what she does.[42] Similarly, the poet reveals that the essence of a bride-Flora resides in her innocent potential to flower into legitimate passion in marriage, whereas the heart of an equestrian prince (Jammes, II:809–23; Wilson, II:796–808) lies in his ability to rein in the unbridled passions symbolized by the horse he rides. Man and horse form one continuous image, but Góngora focuses attention in the emblem on the controlling, powerful hand, which establishes the proper relationship between the rational and irrational facets of human nature and upholds the social hierarchy of the status quo.

Such rhypographic emblems transform even the decor of pastoral convention into a magic universe, ready for reexamination by eyes opened by *admiración*. With a wave of his magic wand, cleverly disguised as a pen,

Góngora defamiliarizes and transmutes an estuary, a rather common topographical feature in piscatory pastoral tradition, and in Spanish geography, into a living, breathing force. The first symbolic transparency the poet affixes over the rivulet rushing to meet the sea anthropomorphizes the natural phenomenon:

> Éntrase el mar por un arroyo breve
>> que a recebillo con sediento paso
>> de su roca natal se precipita,
>> y mucha sal no sólo en poco vaso.
>> mas su rüina bebe,
>> y su fin (cristalina mariposa,
>> no alada, sino undosa)
>> en el farol de Tetis solicita.
>>> (Jammes, II:1–8)

> (The sea through a brief streamlet seeks to pass,
> Which with a thirsty pace to meet it flows
> As from the natal rock itself it throws;
> Much salt not only in a little glass
>> It drinks, but ruin too,
>> A crystal butterfly
>> —Not winged, but wavy—who
> Begs that it may in Tethys' lantern die.
>> [Wilson, II:1–8])

This brook wears a distinctly human face, that of a thirsty being with a death wish who eagerly drinks doom in saltwater form, like the proverbial moth, here a butterfly, drawn to the flame, in this case, the lantern of the sea nymph Tethys. Góngora not only encourages his audience to read a human shape into the landscape, but also invites readers to see the aquatic medium as figuratively composed of entirely different elements, as a creature of air bursting into fire. The next transmutation continues this process, shifting the confluence of two bodies of water into the terrestrial elemental register:

> Centauro ya espumoso el Océano,
> medio mar, medio ría,
> dos veces huella la campaña al día,
> escalar pretendiendo el monte en vano,
> de quien es dulce vena
> el tarde ya torrente
> arrepentido, y aun retrocedente.
>> (Jammes, II:10–16)

> (The Ocean now a spumy centaur, see,
> —Half sea, half estuary—
> Twice in a day tread underfoot the plain,
> Pretending too to scale the mount, in vain,
> Whose gentle vein the tardy torrent falls,
> Repentant, even drawing back again.
> [Wilson, II:10–15])[43]

In this clash of animal forces, the rushing stream retains its quasi-human character, repenting too late its precipitous pursuit of destruction. The poet's depiction of the ocean as a conquering centaur frothing with aggression seems especially apt, given the mythological beings' reputation for violence as well as their hybrid nature, readily comparable to the mix of sea and brackish water at this liminal spot. Furthermore, even though the brook must concede defeat to the overwhelming force of this galloping warrior ocean, the victorious centaur must also face defeat because the beast still lacks the power to take the mountain he attacks during the periodic land incursions of high tide. As a matter of fact, land appears to encroach poetically on water in Góngora's next transformation of the estuary:

> Eral lozano así, novillo tierno
> (de bien nacido cuerno
> mal lunada la frente)
> retrógrado cedió en desigual lucha
> a duro toro, aun contra el viento armado . . .
> (Jammes, II:17–21)
>
> (And thus might we a lusty bullock find,
> Young two-year-old—whose noble horns have now
> Hardly their crescent set upon his brow—
> Receding in unequal fight, give way
> To a fierce bull, armed even against the wind . . .
> [Wilson, II:16–20])

The uneven contest metamorphoses into a generational conflict that pits a two-year-old bull against a fierce adult counterpart with horns mighty enough to challenge the wind. The outcome of this battle is a foregone conclusion, with the youngster backing away from the awe-inspiring elder, letting the salty ocean claim dominion over the shoreline. This animate terrestrial overlay appears almost to supplant the watery estuary scene, but no sooner does Góngora create that vision than he strips all the transparencies away, restoring the original marine landscape:

> no pues de otra manera
> a la violencia mucha
> del Padre de las aguas, coronado
> de blancas ovas y de espuma verde,
> resiste obedeciendo, y tierra pierde.
> (Jammes, II:22–26)
>
> (The stream, no other way,
> Resists obeying, as it loses ground
> The violence of the watery father, crowned
> With foam and weeds, in green and white display.
> [Wilson, II:21–24])

This fifth and final metamorphosis brings the Gongorine magic show full circle in a way, with Tethys's father, Neptune, adopting the position of supreme power. The succession of metaphorical identities assumed by the estuary encourages readers to reconfigure the scene optically, to project or read human, mythic, or animal figures—Tethys, Neptune, a thirsty drinker, a butterfly, a repentant torrent, a centaur, and young and mature bulls—into the landscape in an almost anamorphic fashion. Góngora's imaginative visual reconstructions bring to the surface certain essential truths perhaps otherwise lost in a scene framed by literary and experiential conventions. The poet awakens readers to the interconnectedness of aquatic forms, linked by fundamental similarities and differences. He dramatizes the tidal cycle as a repetitive battle of natural elements in which the same temporary victory must be won again and again, highlighting the natural order beneath the constant flux. As always, he emphasizes the unique beauty of hybrid, liminal zones, spaces in which the elements freely mix to create an impossibly harmonious whole in obedience to the logic of a higher force.

Góngora was by no means the first or only artist at the time to develop the aesthetic and epistemological implications afforded by double vision or double reading, that is, interpretation involving analysis of discrete image units, like clusters of tesserae in a mosaic, that in turn, as in emblem tradition, require reinterpretation within the context of a larger, encompassing system or systems of imagery. The Spanish poet had a kindred spirit in Giuseppe Arcimboldo (1527–1593), painter of Emperors Maximilian II and Rudolf II. As the unofficial *magister ludi* of the Hapsburg court in Vienna and Prague, Arcimboldo painted portraits; designed tapestries, windows, coats-of-arms; and staged tournaments and dramatic performances. The following observation by Thomas Kaufmann indicates that this Mannerist artist shared with Góngora the guiding principles of *serio ludere* and the aesthetics of enigma: "Arcimboldo's images are one production of a court which like many other centers of the time, cherished the display of wit and playful forms of expression that lead to deeper truths. There learned painters and witty poets alike favored such forms as the epigram, the most popular poetic genre in Rudolfine Prague, the emblem, and many other types of painting which evinced *ingenium* (wit) at the same time that they imparted a message."[44]

Just a glance at some of Arcimboldo's works reveals similarities with Góngora's emblems of fantasy despite the difference in the medium of expression. Like the poet's dairymaid made of milk, the painter's *Cook* (ca. 1587) is composed of some of the raw ingredients of his trade. He wears a dish helmet *(sallade)* filled with *salad(e)* ingredients that delineate his face. Cooks make dishes; Arcimboldo defines his cook with a dish that crowns him and marks his profession. Note that the painting relies at least in part on a pun and the literalization of the figurative to convey meaning to the viewer. The gallery also includes rhypographic paintings that lack the complexity of *Soledad* II's centaur-estuary, but that likewise dwell on metamorphosis, and the liminality of animate and inanimate worlds. Arcimboldo's topographical heads display a fascination with the resemblance between a brooding human countenance and a craggy outcropping, which more closely parallels Góngora's rendering of the grotesque Cyclops Polyphemus as an animated version of the dark, cavernous lair he inhabits.[45] Assigning a posy to these images is a difficult task once the reader-viewer moves beyond initial admiration before the show of wit. Nevertheless, the emblems do seem to embody the gloomy, melancholy, earthbound aspect of human nature with the emphasis on grim, rugged features suggesting the depiction of the darker, more instinctual side of the soul.

Arcimboldo also painted an allegorical representation of *Flora* or *Spring* (ca. 1589) based on rhetorical propositions. Flora is the goddess of flowers (metaphor), and flowers bloom in the spring (metonymy). These clichés provide the unwritten motto for the painting as a whole, but each constituent flower of the figure poses the riddle of an emblem within an emblem, an image in search of a posy that only thinking spectators can discern. The portrait skillfully communicates the beauty, abundance, and colorful variety associated with spring flowers or spring itself, but the almost garish contrast between her lead-white, floral skin and rose-red lips and cheeks adds a disquieting undercurrent to the picture. As in the case of Góngora's bride-Flora, which juxtaposes lilies and carnations, Arcimboldo's Flora boldly mixes together symbols of passion and innocence: roses and lilies. Contrary to the Spanish poet's version of the goddess, however, which sanctifies and legitimates budding passion, this image seems to consist of the superimposition of two common iconographic representations in one, that of Flora as goddess of flowers and that of Flora as courtesan, *Flora*

*Meretrix.*⁴⁶ Consideration of the visual palimpsest encourages reformulation of the assumed motto. Arcimboldo's Flora, with a surprisingly direct gaze at odds with the shy demeanor of *Soledad* I's bride, perhaps reminds the audience that in spring, pristine white snow gives way to Nature's riotous display of color, just as innocent young people yield to the urge for passionate love and procreation. Arcimboldo does approach the intricate complexity of Góngora's emblems of fantasy in his allegorical paintings of the seasons and elements created for the Hapsburg court. The most accomplished of these works is the portrait of Rudolf II as *Vertumnus* (1590), in which the emperor metamorphoses into a human cornucopia, an iconic realization of the metonymic cliché of the autumn harvest of Nature's bounty. With his crown of grapes and wheat, *Vertumnus* exudes a distinctly Dionysian aura underscored by the figure's bright, ripe plum cheeks. Yet, surely the artist did not intend to comment obliquely on the drinking habits of his royal patron. More likely, he advances another metonymic proposition through this composite head: that the reign of the robust, smiling monarch ushers in another Golden Age for his subjects and realm, a joyous time and place of harmony and fecundity. The shiny wheat that radiates from Rudolf II's head sketches an encircling halo that links him to the mythic rulers of ancient Greece and Rome, transforming him into the godlike sovereign of an idyllic land. As Thomas Kaufmann points out, *Vertumnus* marks the culmination of Arcimboldo's allegorical series. Contemporary poems written by Giovanni Fonteo and Gregorio Comanini regarding the pictures shape interpretation of these works as symbolic of the view "that as the emperor rules over the body politic, so he rules over the seasons and elements." A poem by Comanini supports the notion that *Vertumnus* identifies Rudolf II with the return of the Golden Age.⁴⁷ The fact that writers composed poetry in conjunction with the wonder-inspiring portraits adds another curious note to this imperial phenomenon, for in essence the poets supplied the mottoes for Arcimboldo's odd devices, performing emblems for the Hapsburg court. Yet, before storing the portrait of Rudolf II in a cabinet of curiosities, one should bear in mind that the artist also enriches understanding of this anthropomorphic, allegorical version of the season, for each and every autumn humankind regains spiritual and physical contact with the Golden Age through the celebration of Nature's variety and abundance.

The Gongorine Philosophers' Stone

The iconographic backbone for many of Arcimboldo's painterly hieroglyphs and Góngora's verbal enigmas alike lies in classical mythology, with

Ovid providing the lion's share of the most frequently cited material. Thomas Kaufmann considers Ovid's tales of Vertumnus from the *Metamorphoses* and *Fasti* as well as Propertius's elegy to Vertumnus the best candidates as sources for the portrait of Rudolf II. In the case of Góngora, not only does the *Polifemo* (1613) attest to the influence of Ovid, but so does the post-*Soledades* parodic ballad on Pyramus and Thisbe, "La ciudad de Babilonia" (The city of Babylon) (1618). Pamela Waley sees numerous parallels between Sannazaro's myth-laden *Arcadia* and the Spanish pastoral masterpiece, but observes that Góngora "uses myth in his pastoral for atmospheric purposes, but more figuratively than directly. Allusions to mythology lie thick upon the ground in the *Soledades,* but they are intrinsic to his expression rather than to his matter." Waley analyzes the pervasive role of classical mythology in the poems in such rhetorical constructs as metonymy, hyperbole, periphrasis, and metaphor, concluding that the plethora of mythological allusions enables the author to realize the purpose expressly stated in the *Carta en respuesta* of latinizing Castilian in order to ennoble the national language by bringing it closer to the mother tongue. The interweaving of a treasure trove of mythological references into the *Soledades* doubtlessly contributes also to what Elias Rivers has described as the *Soledades*' revitalization of worn pastoral conventions, creation of an artificial world dense with natural materials and cultural artifacts, and formation of an elite, educated reading public, the select few who can unravel the literary conundrums, mythological or otherwise.[48]

Regarding the impact of Ovid on Góngora, Waley notes: "Few are the classical allusions in his poetry as a whole which cannot be referred to Ovid's works, even if detail is sometimes added from other authors; and Ovid was perhaps the classical author most dear and with closest affinity to the Spaniard." Significantly, aspects of critical response to Góngora parallel reaction to Ovid, who some say wields a superficial stylistic brilliance that masks an underlying lack of substance. Whether or not one agrees with me that both writers merit a better critical fate, Góngora's enthusiasm for mythology in general and his fascination bordering on obsession with Ovidian tales of metamorphosis and change in particular mark him as a man of his time. The large number of editions of Spanish translations of the *Metamorphoses* document well sixteenth-century Spain's embrace of Ovid. These renditions include the prose version of Jorge de Bustamante (ca. 1546) and the translation in verse of Pedro Sánchez de Viana (1589). Góngora's *Polifemo* offers just one of several Spanish versions of the story, and the discerning reader of the *Soledades* may detect faint echoes of the *Remedia amoris* in the text. For example, Ovid deems solitude the best remedy for lovesickness and recommends retreat to the country and engagement in leisure activities such as gardening, hunting, and fishing as cures for this emotional malady. Recovery requires that the patient absent himself from the object of his affections for a long period of time and not let his thoughts wander to the past. These Ovidian cures blend with pastoral conventions in the *Soledades*, in which the lovesick pilgrim finds himself stranded in solitude, exposed to all the aforementioned prophylactic endeavors, determined to forget painful memories of his cruel beloved, and committed to a new life of pastoral meditation far removed from the court and the lady in question. It is also important to bear in mind that Góngora likely received as part of his educational heritage a catalog of fables already encrypted with meaning, the result of the contemporary tendency to yoke myth and emblem. As Jean Seznec has pointed out, during the Renaissance the Jesuits, formidable pedagogues, combined teaching classical mythology with teaching the art of emblems. The Greco-Roman stories of the pagan gods thus acquired a hieroglyphic dimension that legitimated them for Christian artists, especially those who created with didactic intentions in mind.[49]

But what of the assertion that separates form and content in the *Soledades*, relegating the proliferation of mythological allusions to atmospheric and expressive functions? Such a stance ignores the fact that from the beginning to the end of the *Soledades*, Góngora places before his readers a jungle of myths and metamorphoses that perpetually tests their familiarity with Ovid and other purveyors of mythological tales. At the risk of imitating Gongorine prolixity, I offer the following partial list of allusions to metamorphoses in the *Soledades:* Jupiter's pursuit of Europa (Jammes, I:1–6, Wilson, I:1–5), Ganymede (Jammes, I:7–8, Wilson, I:6–7), Danae (Jammes, I:840–43, Wilson, I:820–22), and Leda (Jammes, I:840–43, Wilson, I:820–22); the tales of Actaeon (Jammes, I:481–90, Wilson, I:465–74), Daphne and Apollo (Jammes, I:1054–60, Wilson, I:1029–34), Venus and Adonis (Jammes, II:581–83, Wilson, II:572–74), and Cupid and Psyche (Jammes, I:767–79, Wilson, I:746–58); and mention of Clytie (Jammes, I:372–73, Wilson, I:361–62), Phaethon's sisters (Jammes, I:659–62, Wilson, I:639–42; Jammes, II:263–66, Wilson, II:254–58), Syrinx (Jammes, I:884, Wilson, I:860; Jammes, II:831, Wilson, II:818–19), Ascalaphus (Jammes, I:990–91, Wilson, I:965–66; Jammes, II:886–92, 974–79; Wilson, II:872–78; 957–62), Icarus (Jammes, II:137–43, Wilson, II:130–36), and Echo (Jammes, II:185–89, Wilson, II:177–81). This intertextual embedding of myriad transformations recalls the association between emblem tradition and decorative, interlocking inlay work, establishing a correspondence between the text in microcosm and macrocosm. Readers who pause to think about the matter will discover that the poems are actually all about metamorphosis. The major human figures in the *Soledades,* the pilgrim and his older doubles, display hybrid qualities that arise from a shared, transitional pattern of life that can be traced to initial disillusionment or *desengaño* (undeceivedness) or both with the court, or at the least an outside world ruled by avarice and hypocrisy, which in turn leads to retreat into a more solitary, meditative, passive, yet more harmonious existence at one with the beauty and balance of the Gongorine landscape. Complementing these characters in metamorphosis, and providing a sort of transelemental cosmic backdrop, readers find the merging of earth and water at the beginning of each poem, coupled with the mixing of earth and fire at the goatherd's campfire and the wedding celebration of *Soledad* I, and of air and water as the piscatory world of *Soledad* II yields to the hawking party of the marshlands. Perhaps most significantly, however, the pastoral genre undergoes a startling metamorphosis in the poems in that Góngora constructs a liminal bucolic universe melding furnishings of contemporary Spain, classical fables, and literary conventions, elevating his work with constant references to transmutations from antiquity, a time and place alive with the magic of pagan gods. As I suggested in the previous chapter, the composition based on metamorphoses provides one more instance of the poet's transformation of the pastoral into a polyphonic text, consisting of the pilgrim's principal melodic line accompanied by harmonizing submelodies belonging to the poems' atmosphere, events, and inhabitants, all built on a *basso continuo* of mythological references, which supply the masterpiece with a unifying, dynamic, driving, underlying conceptual force.

The intaglio work of metamorphoses in the *Soledades* infuses the pastoral world with *admiratio* and enables the audience to view that world with eyes of wonderment. The conceits bring about a sort of perceptual deflection that spawns epistemological realignment, which in turn allows the select public access to hidden truths and the heightened realities of a magical, animate Nature while permitting the artist to reclaim the godlike powers of the *vates.* Góngora achieves such conceptual reconfiguration in large part by employing unexpected transformations to defamiliarize and exalt the commonplace in the reader's mind. Consider the wordplay involved in his description of the fisherman's daughters, who abandon fieldwork to welcome the pilgrim to their island home:

> y de Vertumno al término labrado
> el breve hierro, cuyo corvo diente
> las plantas le mordía cultamente.
> (Jammes, II:236–38)

> (Who to Vertumnus had once more consigned
> The iron tool, by whose sharp tooth has grown
> The trees that it could cultivate alone.
> [Wilson, II:228–30])

The conceit turns on the axis of the pun on *plantas* (plants or feet), in this case the feet of Vertumnus, the god of vegetation whose offspring are plants. However, Góngora also transmutes the rake into a toothed creature, who paradoxically bites into the plants or feet, but in such a fashion as to cultivate rather than devour those plants. The maidens' activity pays tribute to Vertumnus even as the multiple metamorphoses remake simple manual labor into an experience simultaneously sacral, playful, productive, and celebrative. Góngora invites his reading public to see crop tending in a totally different light, for the fields and instruments of cultivation come alive in these lines, in essence gaining a quasi-human, quasi-divine face. Note, too, that the poet uses the verb *morder* (to bite) artfully to tie the conceit to the verbal context that lies beyond its limits, introducing the notion of eating, which subsequently leads into a description of luncheon preparations for the pilgrim guest.

A few verses later, Góngora achieves defamiliarization by reversing the process, transforming the extraordinary into the ordinary, again in an unexpected way:

> armonïoso número se esconde
> de blancos cisnes, de la misma suerte
> que gallinas domésticas al grano,
> a la voz concurrientes del anciano.
> (Jammes, II:251–54)

> (The number of harmonious swans away,
> Which, like domestic fowls to take their grain,
> Came hurrying up unto the old man's side.
> [Wilson, II:243–45])

The incongruousness of the imagery that strikes readers with wonder resides in the fact that here birds associated with princes and palaces act like farmyard chickens trained to the human hand. The old fisherman has established a unique, intimate, harmonious relationship with these prized fowl, hinting at what the ideal relationship between humans and Nature should be and suggesting that this close bond of interrelatedness reflects some sort of higher, more truthful order that is always present in an essential, potential form. Góngora may well have in mind the image of the swan as a hieroglyph of music or may recall Horapollo's identification of the swan with a musical old man, a reference supported by the pilgrim's veneration for the old fisherman's withdrawal into a small, happy, self-sustaining kingdom that embodies the golden mean.[50] Whatever the case, the representation is consistent with the traditional values upheld by pastoral convention of an idyllic Nature inextricably linked to an ideal human presence.

Góngora recontextualizes familiar mythological allusions, revitalizing conventional references and restoring their awe-inspiring power. For example, the poet renews the myth of Clytie, transforming the tale of the nymph's metamorphosis into a sunflower forever in search of her lover, Apollo, who abandoned her, into a metaphor for the ships of discovery:

> el campo undoso en mal nacido pino,
> vaga Clicie del viento
> en telas hecho, antes que en flor, el lino?
> (Jammes, I:371–73)

> (The spumy country in ill-destined bark,
> Vague Clytie of the breeze
> Transformed to canvas rather than a flower?
> [Wilson, I:360–62])

Góngora locates Clytie in a new element, the *campo undoso* (wavy field) of the sea, thus achieving a shift of elements from earth to water as the backdrop for metamorphosis. In this different frame of reference, the Gongorine Clytie is no longer rooted to the spot, but rather wanders (*vaga* [wandering]) in accordance with the changing air currents, the movement of the sails imitating the heliotrope's turning toward the sun. Although the conceit's ability to inspire wonder relies on readers' knowledge of the original myth, Góngora's version is nevertheless far from a slavish imitation of the original and requires as well a degree of interpretive skill and imaginative engagement on the part of those readers. Note, too, that the poet metamorphoses an object of human construction into a beautiful natural object, blending artifice and nature through a poetic device that surprises and delights.

In yet another case of Gongorine magic, Echo becomes a spectator and listener, garbed and hidden by a cave, who keeps the tuneful plaint of the pilgrim:

> Eco, vestida una cavada roca,
> solicitó curiosa y guardó avara
> la más dulce, si no la menos clara
> sílaba, siendo en tanto

> la vista de las chozas fin del canto.
> (Jammes, II:185–89)
>
> (Echo, who in a concave rock was decked,
> Sought, curious, and, like a miser, kept
> The sweetest, though perhaps not the least clear
>   Syllable, till ere long
> Sight of the hovels made an end of song.
> [Wilson, II:177–81])

Here the poet reverses the familiar myth, restoring her body to the nymph whose very name signifies a disembodied voice. Moreover, this Echo, metonymically garbed in a rocky dress, seems disinclined to return the voice she hears, preferring instead to hoard the sweet sound in her lair-vestment. Sound cedes to sight at the end of the conceit, which appropriately marks the transition from one scene to another.

Virtually all the conceits with imagery of metamorphosis share a common emphasis on the interconnectedness of human and natural worlds through correspondences that link different elements and realms of existence together. Góngora changes the competitors in a footrace, one of the sporting events in the wedding festival of *Soledad* I, into latter-day Apollos in pursuit of Daphne:

> De la Peneida virgen desdeñosa
> los dulces fugitivos miembros bellos
> en la corteza no abrazó reciente
> más firme Apolo, más estrechamente,
> que de una y de otra meta glorïosa
> las duras basas abrazaron ellos
> con triplicado nudo.
> (Jammes, I:1054–60)
>
> (Apollo once before with fervour burned
> For old Peneus' scornful daughter, clasped
> Her flying limbs as to fresh bark they turned,
>   But with more vigour these
>   In threefold knot now grasped
> Their winning-posts, the hard trunks of the trees.
> [Wilson, I:1029–34])

To grasp the conceit, readers must puzzle out the maiden's identity from the periphrastic reference based on metonymic allusion to her father. Both the classical metamorphosis and Góngora's more modern analogue describe a race with a specific, eagerly sought goal: on the one hand, Daphne, and, on the other, the trees that designate the finish line. Yet, the sun god and the runners actually reach something besides the particular desired end. Apollo seizes only a laurel, a symbol of his frustrated desire, whereas the running contestants figuratively attain the victor's laurels, the crowning glory of winners in the Pythian games of ancient Greece, which were dedicated to Apollo. Góngora bridges an enormous gap that lies between the pagan sun god and the fleet but rustic athletes, likening the eager clasp of a thwarted lover to the muscled grip of the pastoral runners, and inviting comparisons between the agitated, but beautiful, flying limbs of Daphne and the blurred motion of masculine racers' arms and legs. Part of the well-crafted, imaginative refashioning of the mythological allusion pertains, too, to its fit within a network of related imagery that extends beyond the confines of the conceit. While the finalists await the decision regarding who won the contest, Hymen stages a race of his own because he knows the eagerness of love to run its course:

> En tanto pues que el palio neutro pende
> y la carroza de la luz desciende
> a templarse en las ondas, Himeneo,
> por templar en los brazos el deseo
> del galán novio, de la esposa bella,
> los rayos anticipa de la estrella,
> cerúlea ahora, ya purpúrea guía
> de los dudosos términos del día.
> (Jammes, I:1065–72)

> (And while the prize was hanging neutrally,
> Apollo sought to moderate his fire
> Declining to the sea,
> Hymen, to temper in locked arms desire
> Of handsome lover and of lovely bride,
> Anticipated now the planet's ray,
> Cerulean, though before a purple, guide
> To the uncertain boundaries of the day.
> [Wilson, I:1039–46])

One can tell from these verses how carefully Góngora composed the *Soledades* such that although the conceits retain a certain autonomy as independent verbal puzzles or linguistic emblems, their conceptual foundation and imagery spill over and infiltrate neighboring lines, coloring their meaning both literally and figuratively. "La carroza de la luz" (The chariot of light) recalls Apollo, who here seeks to quench the flames of his desire in the sea's embrace. His mad chase of Daphne metamorphoses into the setting sun's pursuit of the horizon and the newlyweds' rush to consummate their marriage. Hymen accommodates their haste by bringing out Venus, the evening and morning star, the planet consecrated to the goddess of love and whose appearance and disappearance mark the limits of their time to love. Nature acts in harmony with humans to satisfy, not frustrate, their wishes, but Góngora continues the imagery of competition to the last line of *Soledad* I, in which the nuptial bed becomes a *campo de pluma* (a feathered field) for *batallas de amor* (love battles).

Such an intricate network of conceits, imagery, and correspondences lends credence to José Ortega y Gasset's assertion in 1925 that "[l]a metáfora es probablemente la potencia más fértil que el hombre posee" ([m]etaphor is probably the most fertile power that man possesses). Although Ortega clearly had twentieth-century, avant-garde artists in mind, the confidence and consistency with which Góngora employs the power of metaphor throughout his work suggest that he would subscribe to that opinion. The poet would probably object, however, to Ortega's identification of metaphor with avoidance of reality: "Sólo la metáfora nos facilita la evasión y crea entre las cosas reales arrecifes imaginarios, florecimiento de islas ingrávidas" (Only metaphor facilitates evasion for us and creates imaginary reefs between real things, the flowering of weightless islands). For Góngora, a poet with an "emblematic world view" in which hidden meanings and connections pervade the universe, conceits enable artist and audience to perceive the interlocking reefs that actually are there, once the eyes of the mind have been awakened and illuminated by *admiratio*. Ortega approximates this notion in an earlier essay (1914), in which he states: "Cada metáfora es el descubrimiento de una ley del universo" (Each metaphor is the discovery of a law of the universe).[51]

Michael Woods has rightly stressed the capacity of wonderment induced by Gongorine conceits to generate such moments of discovery, including flux and metamorphoses among the qualities or properties applicable to art and nature that can trigger *admiratio* and newfound insight and knowledge. Woods regards Gongorine conceits as a type of epistemological tool employed in a quest for truth, as well as beauty, that links the practice of poetry to that of natural magic. An imprecise, grab-bag term at best, natural magic merges with the notions of hermeticism and occultism, associated also with hieroglyphics, emblems, and the aesthetics of enigma, encompassing as well "the working of marvelous effects, which may seem preternatural, by a knowledge of occult forces in nature without resort to supernatural assistance." The rubric subsumes a wide range of human endeavors and natural phenomena: from alchemy to fountain hydraulics, from automata to celestial bodies, and from exotic flora to unusual fauna. The magus who understands how to activate the connections between terrestrial and higher forces, or a poet-magus such as Góngora who grasps the fundamental interconnectedness of the cosmos, knows how to perform natural magic to inspire wonder and make those hidden reefs appear between real things, bringing occult truths to light. Góngora may well have been invoking the praxis of natural magic in the *Carta en respuesta* in his defense of the *Soledades*, for practitioners of natural magic sought not to elicit superficial, razzle-dazzle effects, but to stimulate inner enlightenment of the mind and soul, bringing the individual closer to God.[52]

Of the activities and phenomena associated with natural magic, I believe that alchemy provides the closest analogues to the artistic forces at play in the creation and impact of the Gongorine conceit, the foundation for the *Soledades* and the master's poetics. By some accounts, this hermetic discipline dates back to the first centuries of the common era, originating in ancient Egypt, and linked with the divine Greek patron Hermes Trismegistus and Zosimos of Panoplis. Even the earliest alchemical manuscripts evinced a challenging elliptical style full of riddles, enigmas, and metaphors, which closer to the age of Góngora would develop into a quasi-allegorical rhetoric likening alchemical methods to classical mythology. Ovid's *Metamorphoses* figured among the most frequently employed tales for narrative symbolism in such documents. Interest in alchemy continued through the Middle Ages and into the Renaissance, but the second half of the sixteenth century experienced what Lynn Thorndike has called a "Paracelsan revival," which started in Italy with the publication of Paracelsus's works, renewed curiosity about the writing of fourteenth-century Catalonians such as Ramón Llull, and prompted the appearance of a spate of new alchemical treatises, a burst of activity that quickly spread to other parts of Europe.[53]

To understand the cultural context in which Góngora lived and wrote, one should bear in mind that the Iberian peninsula maintained a more liberal attitude toward natural magic and manifested a stronger disinclination to condemn its praxis as demonic than elsewhere in Europe. Arabic schools of necromancy reportedly existed in Toledo and Salamanca during the Middle Ages, and astrology survived as a discipline at the University of Salamanca, which Góngora attended, later than at any other European university. Francisco Torreblanca, a contemporary of Góngora and, like the poet, a native of Córdoba and acquaintance of the duke of Lerma, defined natural magic as "an exacter knowledge of secret things in which, by observing the course and influence of the stars and the sympathies and antipathies of particular things, they are applied to one another at the proper time and place and in the proper manner, so that marvels are worked." It would be difficult to imagine Gongorine advocacy for the astrological component of this definition, but the poet would beyond a doubt envision himself as the possessor of more exact, esoteric knowledge of interrelated sympathies and antipathies in nature, and as a person who can apply that knowledge to produce poetic marvels. Yet another contemporary of Góngora, Gerónimo Cortés of Valencia, authored an important work titled *Phisonomia y varios secretos de naturaleza* (Physiognomy and various secrets of nature). First published in 1601, in subsequent editions between 1603 and 1614, and in different locales, from Córdoba to Alcalá to Tarragona, Cortés discusses in the work the marvelous effects of nature, ranging from the occult virtues of gems, to the function of fountains, to recipes for solutions and elixirs. The fascination of the Hapsburg court of Rudolf II with natural magic is well documented, and one can readily suppose that along with the constant interchange of nobles and official representatives between the Austrian and Iberian courts of the Hapsburgs flowed an accompanying stream of ideas and changing aesthetics. Certainly, both centers of the empire displayed similar enthusiasm for alchemy and alchemical experimentation. David C. Goodman notes that El Escorial boasted an impressive collection of treatises on alchemy, actively fomented by Philip II, whose curiosity about the potential of alchemy to maintain good health waxed even as his belief in the promise of alchemy to increase the wealth of the royal coffers waned. Still, the palaces of El Escorial and Aranjuez featured laboratories equipped to prepare distilled water and mix medicines for the benefit of the royal family.[54]

Traditionally, mention of alchemy conjures almost exclusively the process of the transmutation of base metals into the noble ones of gold and silver, or of Mickey Mouse clothed in a star-and-moon-spangled gown trying to control dancing brooms, but in actuality a spiritual agenda of purification paralleled the material applications of the discipline. Evidence indicates that most alchemists spent as much time philosophizing and engaging in rhetorical speculation as they did experimenting in laboratories with alembics and retorts. Harry J. Sheppard synthesizes the multiple aims of European alchemy:

> Alchemy is the art of liberating parts of the Cosmos from temporal existence and achieving perfection which, for metals is gold, and for man, longevity, then immortality and, finally redemption. Material perfection was sought through the action of a preparation (Philosopher's Stone for metals; Elixir of Life for humans), while spiritual ennoblement resulted from some form of inner revelation or other enlightenment (Gnosis, for example, in Hellenistic and western practices).

Belief in the transmutation and perfectibility of spirit and matter is the foundation of alchemy, and, perhaps surprisingly, the quest for the elixir of life predates the search for the philosophers' stone. According to alchemists, the metals commonly found in the earth were mutable and undergoing a long gestation period in which they would gradually change toward perfection. The philosophers' stone, a form of pure matter made perfect by art, had the power to accelerate that natural process by artificial means. The alchemist could realize an immediate transmutation by projection of the philosophers' stone, or its tincture, over the base metal, which then instantly reconfigured the imperfect material to match the perfect interior design of the stone.[55]

On close examination, the Gongorine conceit functions in a way analogous to that of the philosophers' stone. With their emphasis on hybridization, embedded metamorphoses, liminal states, and transelemental metaphors, the *Soledades* provide ample evidence of Góngora's belief in and fascination with universal change and transformation, which once again marks him as a man of his time. The conceit provides an artificial, rhetorical construct and conceptual design that the poet casts linguistically onto the world that allows him instantly to bring to the fore the hidden connections he intuits in the cosmos in a latent, embryonic state. Projection of the conceit onto the imaginary world of the *Soledades* results in material and conceptual realignment, precipitates *admiratio,* and, it is hoped, among the select few, leads to spiritual alembication—a transmutation of the reader's mind and soul, refined and ennobled through Gongorine intellectual exercises, in short, made more perfect perforce in adjusting their internal models and patterns to fit the superior ones of the poet.

In enacting his poetics of alchemy in the *Soledades,* Góngora tops himself at the end of the work with an act of alembication that inspires as much puzzlement as *admiración*. No one knows for certain whether the rather abrupt final lines constitute a definitive conclusion to the poems or an incomplete ending that simply trails off after sounding a foreboding note perhaps meant to segue into more episodes of *Soledad* II or into a *Soledad* III. I do not presume to resolve that issue, but regardless of what the correct response might be, one could scarcely imagine setting, imagery, or a series of lines more typical of the wonder-making work as a whole. After witnessing the hawking scene, the pilgrim and fishermen travel by boat to a primitive riverbank settlement dominated by a game warden's watchtower, a liminal community that mixes shepherds' huts with fishermen's shacks. Although the village lies too far inland to experience the effects of shifting tides, coves invade and mesh with the land, with the rustic dwellings built out into the stream contributing to the impression of a transelemental mix of earth and water. The poetic voice conveys an atmosphere of solitary, vulnerable abandonment by informing readers that the inhabitants have left the village to pursue their daily labor, some fishing under the vigilant eye of Glaucus and others tending the herd under the protection of Pales. Meanwhile, focalization changes from the initial panoramic view of the town to a magnified close-up of a cluster of featherless chicks safely sheltered by the wings of a mother hen, which in emblem lore is frequently a symbol of health, security, and fertility, an animate version of the lookout that seemingly shields the village as well as the hunting game.[56] The poetic "I" informs readers of the failed attempts by avian *corsario(s)* (corsairs)—*milano(s)* (kites)—to pirate away *la infantería* (infants or infantry), a pun that underscores the imagistic parallels established between several protectors (tower, Glaucus, Pales, and hen) and protected (dwellings, fishermen, shepherds, and chicks), as well as continuing the notion of water-based incursions into land. Góngora metamorphoses and reifies the hen, transforming her into a fortress:

> . . . la infantería, que pïante
> en su madre se esconde, donde halla
> voz que es trompeta, pluma que es muralla.
> (Jammes, II:963–65)

> (. . . the infantry
> Who chirping 'neath their mother flew to hide,
> Where in her feathers they a rampart found,
> Her voice a trumpet sound.
> [Wilson, II:945–48])

Stressing paradoxical analogues between animate and inanimate, the *Soledades*' voice then announces the arrival of the tired hawking party, communicated by the panting horses and the personified falcons, who are complaining of fatigue *(quejándose venían)* even though borne along on gauntleted hands. The audience learns that whereas the hen merits the attributes of a fortress, the sheltering walls of the human edifices do not deserve the title (especially given the exalted nature of the visiting party): "a los indignos de ser muros llega / céspedes, de las ovas mal atados" (Jammes, II:969–70) (Came to the worthless walls together bound / —Though ill— the turf and weed [Wilson, II:952–53]).

Having moved from images of watchfulness, protectiveness, and security to those of vulnerability, followed by a parade of new aviary pirates in the form of hunting birds, Góngora unifies the scene and closes the poem with one final, climactic emblem of metamorphosis:

> Con sordo luego estrépito despliega
> (injurias de la luz, horror del viento)
> sus alas el testigo que en prolija
> desconfianza a la sicana Diosa

                dejó sin dulce hija,
                y a la stigia Deidad con bella esposa.
                            (Jammes, II:974–79)

    (Then with a deafening noise his wings displayed
    —Light's injury, the horror of the day—
                The witness, who betrayed
    Sicanian goddess to prolix despair,
                    Of daughter sweet deprived,
    And gave the Stygian god a consort fair.
                            [Wilson, II:957–62])

The poet narrates through periphrastic indirection the tale of Ascalaphus ("the witness"), who deprived Ceres ("Sicanian goddess") of Proserpine ("her daughter") and gave Pluto ("the Stygian god") a wife when he revealed that the fair queen had eaten a pomegranate in the Underworld. Jupiter, who had promised to restore Proserpine to her mother if the daughter had eaten nothing while in Hell, was forced to make her spend a portion of the year with Pluto and the other part with Ceres. The angry Proserpine transformed Ascalaphus into an owl to punish him for the betrayal.

As always, Góngora has appropriated the myth in a unique way, revitalizing the metamorphosis within the context of the *Soledades*. The story offers a narrative counterpoint to the guardianship of the tower and the hen, for, in this case, the mother-protector loses her offspring to the piratical Pluto. The poet alludes to yet another liminal space in Proserpine's shuttling back and forth between upper and lower worlds. And in the grander scheme of things, the marriage of the reluctant goddess to the king of Hell contrasts with the newlyweds' joyful indulgence in marital bliss at the end of *Soledad* I. The owl itself adds another level of complexity to this final conceit, because in the emblem tradition this fowl is an extremely ambiguous symbol. Although the allusion to the myth of Ascalaphus and mention of the bird's frightening looks as he blots out the light with his wings support the owl's reputation as a sinister harbinger of doom and darkness, and as the last figure described in the procession of hunters, this predator seems to hasten the gloom and melancholy of nightfall; nonetheless, the owl also has a long-standing reputation as Athena's bird, associated with magic, wisdom, and occult powers.[57] Naturally, Góngora complicates matters by providing ambiguous or insufficient information or both to guide the audience to a universally satisfying interpretation.

Yet, what remains in the reader's mind, in addition to the classical tale of betrayal and transmutation embedded in a bird of prey of dual and somewhat conflictive symbolism, is the manner in which Góngora almost completely effaces the human presence from the pastoral landscape at the end of the *Soledades*. The audience of spectators has at this point all but forgotten their fictional doubles: the pilgrim and fishermen observing the settlement from the small craft. The village itself is a ghost town abandoned by the inhabitants during the workday. Even the arriving hunters appear in only a fragmented, synecdochic fashion, represented by weary horses and a gloved falconer's hand. Of course, elimination of human mediating agents from the fictional space of the *Soledades* forces the reader to concentrate on the difficult task of interpretation itself, increasing the intellectual intimacy between reader and text. In this sense, regardless of what the poet's original intentions may have been in composing this final conceit, the owl does serve to focus the reader's attention on a single, solitary, perplexing figure that celebrates intellectual and occult powers, providing a sort of visual and linguistic summation of these pastoral poems that pays tribute to solitude and to the artistry of their *vates*, the master of a poetics of alchemy who utilizes a rhetorical philosophers' stone to create a spectacle of enduring wonder.

4

The Masque of the Imagination

> For this purpose poplar groves are planted, fountains are sought, hills are smoothed, and gardens are cultivated with curious skill.
>
> —Cervantes, prologue to the *Exemplary Tales*
>
> God *Almightie* first Planted a *Garden.* And indeed, it is the Purest of Humane pleasure.
>
> —Bacon, "Of Gardens"

In the Garden of the Mind

Outside Rome in Tivoli lie the magnificent Renaissance villa and water garden of the powerful Este family. At dusk on a warm summer evening, when tourist voices are muted and the shimmering, silvery green of the olive trees fades and darkens, even less fanciful visitors can detect the rustle of silk skirts, sudden outbursts of laughter, the eerie music of the water organ, and, against the aural backdrop of fountains and flowing streams, the low hum of conversations of kindred visitors from a time long ago. To latter-day readers of Góngora's *Soledades,* these ghosts of the distant past, perpetually engaged in the ludic delights afforded them by the garden's artful nature, might appear strange and decidedly unhelpful companions. In actuality, the reverse is true, for these phantom guests in another land may well constitute the closest facsimile of a key that will unlock the Spanish poet's pastoral virtual reality.

The formal gardens of Renaissance Italy offer a three-dimensional counterpart to the competitive relationship between art and nature that Rosalie Colie identifies with the pastoral, and that Góngora explores in such startling and paradoxical ways in the *Soledades*. The Villa d'Este's cultivated grounds, the Boboli Gardens in Florence, and the Sacro Bosco of Bomarzo exemplify a third nature, in which art and nature work in tandem to display to full advantage the hidden order beneath the raw, wild landscape for the recreation of the mind and senses. Gongorine poetics and the gardenist aesthetics of sixteenth-century Italy alike espouse this guiding principle, among others, but not all such commonalities manifest this specifically Platonic cast. The enjoyment evoked by the green spaces enhanced by human design represents a creative merger of Epicurean pleasure with Stoic ideals of reflective solitude shared by insightful discourse with friends and a life lived in harmony with nature, a philosophical blend apparent in Góngora's masterpiece as well.[1]

Moreover, just as Góngora's innovative, "modern" Castilian imitates and pays homage to classical Latin, so too do the Italian gardens provide "modern" versions of ancient models, reviving the Roman retreats of antiquity with their sophisticated yet playful vocabulary of mazes, grottoes, topiary, mosaics, waterworks, and automatons. The tendency to quote classical sources seems especially conspicuous at Tivoli, where a mere stone's throw from the Este enclave, Hadrian's Villa stands in monumental architectural splendor, providing Renaissance visitors with a blueprint for the latest fashion in house and garden design, and, in the case of the Villa d'Este, with actual raw materials.[2] One can assume that the target audience members for Góngora's poems and the Italian gardens doubtless resembled each other in many respects as well. Readers and garden guests alike belonged to a small, wealthy, powerful, aristocratic elite, that is, they were privileged people blessed with leisure time and the opportunity to indulge in urbane and elegant forms of entertainment.

The gardens also show a markedly self-conscious literary sensibility sufficient to rival Góngora's. The Italian garden aesthetic arose in the same locales that nurtured the revival of interest in classical epic, theater, and pastoral poetry, which frequently inspired garden topoi and settings, along with their ubiquitous mythological scenarios. Some fifteenth-century works such as Boiardo's *Orlando Innamorato*, Colonna's mysterious *Hypnerotomachia Poliphili*, and Sannazaro's *Arcadia* encouraged the erudite to view the natural world in a new light, as a medium that lends itself to artistic shaping that will sustain symbolic and narrative weight. Thus, most garden architects and spectators designed and experienced these elaborate horticultural delights under the influence of the written word. Just as I earlier noted the parallels between *emblemata* and memory theater in the *Soledades*, so also have garden critics observed the influence of imprese, conceits, and mnemotechnic theater in the iconographic and spatial deployment of Renaissance gardens. The presence of such a strong literary and rhetorical heritage in the remapping of landscape in Italy, England, and elsewhere in Europe has led John Dixon Hunt to state that formal Renaissance gardens can be read and interpreted as if they were literary texts.[3]

Like the *Soledades,* which convey to the educated reader a wealth of meaning in the many genres, authors, and conventions invoked, from pastoral to epic, from Ovid to Petrarch, from romance heroes to the pilgrim of love and more, Renaissance gardens bear an intricate, embedded system of signification with potential meanings that, as in Góngora's masterpiece, may seem to contradict one another. Gardens embody the *locus amoenus,* the site of love's pleasure and pain, but also symbolize a space of intellectual retreat and stimulation, the setting chosen for the rebirth of Plato's Academy being the Medici Villa at Careggi. The *Soledades* often juxtapose court and country, with aristocratic taste and pastimes popping up regularly in the bucolic landscape. Italian villas similarly counterbalanced city palaces, although the monied owners spared no expense to ensure themselves and their guests in the country all the comforts of an urban home with a lavish lifestyle relocated in healthier environs. Góngora's pastoral combines the ideal of solitude and solitary contemplation with collective entertainments such as sports, hunting, dancing, and banquets. Architects of Renaissance gardens designed villa grounds to accommodate these same amusements, but also planned isolated spots and nearly autonomous venues that would allow individuals to dedicate themselves to quiet study and meditation. As I discussed in Chapter 2, the *Soledades* offer the discerning eye a veritable art gallery in verbal form, with all the major types of paintings encompassed within the poems' confines. Renaissance gardens provided a natural frame for collections of great diversity from paintings and sculptures to flowers and seashells, from herbs and exotic fruit trees to crystals and unusual rock formations. These collections would eventually serve as the foundation for genuine scientific discovery as alchemy and natural magic gave way to botany and geology.[4]

Although Góngora never set foot outside the Iberian peninsula, he probably knew about the Italian gardens mentioned above, for even during the poet's lifetime the Villa Medici north of Florence at Pratolino, along with Tivoli's Villa d'Este and Hadrian's Villa, boasted numerous foreign travelers who left vivid descriptions of these wondrous places in letters and memoirs. Influential personages such as Giorgio Vasari and Michel Montaigne share their impressions of the Medici villas at Castello and Pratolino, and though Montaigne sings praises of the Medici gardens' automatons as well as those at Tivoli, he seems less excited about the Este water organ, with its extremely limited musical range. With ready access to the court, and the powerful and well-traveled nobles and members of the elite who flourished in that rarefied atmosphere, the Spanish poet likely met more than a few people who could supply him with eyewitness accounts of such experiences. In addition, paintings and engravings that cataloged the formal gardens circulated widely outside Italy, drawings of fountains and automatons turning up in illustrated books and architectural studies that established the guidelines for similar garden focal points in countries such as England and France. Many compositional elements identified as quintessential components of the Italian gardens, such as geometric patterns, side-by-side placement of flowers (ornamental nature) and vineyards (agricultural nature), and extravagant use of water, were actually of Moorish origin and may have first reached the courts of Florence and Rome through the influence of Spain's Islamic culture, the long arm of the Spanish crown at one time encompassing Sardinia, Sicily, and Naples. The modern tourist could not possibly miss the resemblance between the water steps and fountains of the Court of the Pool in the Generalife of Granada's Alhambra and the Villa d'Este's famous water chain and Terrace of the One Hundred Fountains. In fact, Spanish gardens made a profound impact on foreign visitors even during the Renaissance. As early as 1556, an awed Venetian diplomat at the court of Charles V communicated in a letter his amazement at the extraordinary fountains he had seen in the Moorish gardens of Spain. Góngora, a native of Córdoba, a major center of the once Islamic Andalusia, must have possessed a certain knowledge of the gardens of his region, especially when an entire contingent of Andalusian noblemen graced the court of Philip III.[5]

Nonetheless, in case the elaborate planning and ornamentation of those gardens momentarily slipped his mind while serving the king, the royal palace and grounds of Aranjuez lay close at hand to remind him of the intricacies of formal garden design. Before Aranjuez's current incarnation as a miniature Versailles, which coincided with the Bourbon dynasty's ascent to the Spanish throne in the eighteenth century, the palace grounds resembled an Italian Renaissance garden. As early as the late fifteenth century, a residence occupied the meadow by the Tagus River known as Aranjuez, which became royal property in 1523, during the reign of Charles V. The holdings underwent extensive renovation under his successor, Philip II, whose principal architects for El Escorial, Juan Bautista de Toledo and Juan de Herrera, designed the king's new palace in the country, which became a royal retreat for meditation, hunting, and other forms of recreational activity: "Covered with woods, parks and gardens, in which an immense variety of trees, plants, fruits and, above all, flowers flourished, Aranjuez was a source of wonder to visitors and of unremitting pleasure to the monarch. He fled there to escape from his papers and to fish in the lakes." History credits Juan Bautista with the improvements in harnessing the waters at the confluence of the Tagus and the Jarama to transform Aranjuez into a huge garden of flowers and fruit trees nourished by channels and irrigation ditches fed in turn by millraces and water diverted from the streams. However, if Juan Bautista could claim responsibility for these feats of engineering, including making the Tagus navigable at the king's behest, then Philip II himself assumed the role of landscape architect here and elsewhere. The Aranjuez expansion and refurbishing formed just one component in the king's ambitious construction and rebuilding plan, which also included the palace of El Pardo, the Alcázar of Toledo and of Madrid, hunting lodges at Fuenfría and Torrelodones, and the monumental palace-monastery El Escorial. The king deemed no task too small for his attention, from reviewing lists of flowers ordered to dispensing advice on how to water orange trees. Philip's love of garden design arose from his esteem for the cultivated landscape of the Netherlands, particularly from his admiration for the country's lovely, healthy flowers and plants, and his interest in the formal gardens of Italian nobles. He established a veritable international exchange program on the subject, bringing experts from Italy and the Netherlands to advise him on garden landscaping and sending his own specialists abroad to bring back new and creative ideas on the same subject. In all likelihood, Philip II acquired the concept of the palace and garden grounds as a unified architectural construct from the Italian Renaissance view of the villa and garden as a single, harmonious unit. The palace gardens conceived by the king paid tribute to Italian Mannerism, a label applied perhaps most often to the water garden of the Villa d'Este. After the monarch's death, Philip III continued the architectural project at Aranjuez, adding more fountains and thoroughfares to the avenues lined by willows, elms, and orange trees, and increasing the number of sites of flowers, statues, and waterworks laid out by his father. These ornate locales became familiar places to members of the peripatetic court of Philip III and to those who aspired to enter that inner circle of privilege, men like Góngora.[6]

Whether Italian garden design or its Spanish kin influenced the author of the *Soledades* directly or indirectly remains a matter of conjecture. Clearly, however, similar, and in some instances identical, literary conventions and classical and contemporary aesthetic principles impinged on both the construction of formal Renaissance gardens and the creation of Góngora's masterpiece, making for striking and informative parallels that can enlighten the hermeneutic process for the audience of the *Soledades*. John Dixon Hunt has written that "classical allusions . . . [in] the gardenist experience . . . also contributed to larger patterns of psychological and intellectual response," the same sorts of allusions that require active engagement from sophisticated readers of the *Soledades*. So if gardens of such complexity invite reading and interpretation as if they were literary texts, as Hunt has suggested, perhaps hermetic, compelling poems with a strong foundation in classical literature such as Góngora's work might yield their secrets when read and interpreted as if they were imaginary gardenist experiences. Comparisons between the configuration of space and the disposition of central elements in Renaissance gardens and the *Soledades* indicate that this analytical exercise might work to the readers' advantage. Consider the poet's organization of narrative space, which, as I discussed in Chapter 2, blocks into quasi-autonomous vignettes that unfold in a specific setting in an almost theatrical fashion. The pilgrim himself provides in large part the active, dynamic link that moves the reader from one scenario to the next, pulling the audience into and through the mental, bucolic landscape. By the mid-sixteenth century, garden architects divided the parcel of land targeted for creative design into nearly discrete units, niches, or compartments deployed in axial arrangements. The major directional paths enabled the mobile spectator to connect the independent spaces experientially as a series of successive frames. This plan allowed the fanciful architect to conceive movement through the garden as an episodic narrative in which the visitor plays the part Góngora reserves for the reader-pilgrim of his poems. Like the audience of the *Soledades*, visitors to formal gardens could not immediately discern an overarching pattern of spatial deployment, but they most certainly could have spied thematic landscape clusters: vineyards, woods, water, and the like. Góngora's poems foreground such divisions, too, mapped out as changing topography—mountains, fields, estuary, and marshlands—that taken as a whole reveals a certain tendency toward bilateral symmetry (*Soledad* I—land; *Soledad* II—water), as previously discussed in Chapter 2. Bilateralism typified the epoch's formal gardens as well, with sculpture and fountains echoing or uniting (or both) the parts of the plan.[7]

Another concept of mutual interest concerns the cohesiveness of artifice and green world. Landscape architects sought to integrate villa, garden, and countryside, successfully blending art and nature into a pleasing whole. Góngora's impulse toward spatial integration of art and nature also emerges upon reflection. While the poet refashions the riverscape of *Soledad* I into a prolix sentence or a cornucopia, that is, the horn of Amaltheia, and offers, literally in microcosm, an example of the villa and landscape symbiosis in the palace on the hillside that gives way to the marsh in *Soledad* II, he also ennobles the fisherman turned landscape architect who has artfully transformed his island kingdom into a miniature garden equipped with tame swans, a dovecote, a rabbit warren, flowers, crowning poplars, a meandering stream, and an outdoor dining alcove (a customary horticultural furnishing at the time). Italian garden design turned the natural lay of the land to best advantage, posing the villa on top of a hill and employing the steep, vertical drop to frame open, dramatic, panoramic views alternating with fabricated, enclosed spaces, such as groves and grottoes.[8] The pilgrim and his fisherman host dine in such a grove in *Soledad* II, and, in the same poem, the protagonist watches as the hunting party wends its way down the slope of the hill from the palace gates. In *Soledad* I, a rock outcropping offers the pilgrim a broad vista of the river valley below, a spectacle so expansive that the inner eye can visualize the stream originating in a mountain cavern and emptying into the ocean, yet in other places the foliage is so dense and visually limiting that the protagonist can only gaze on the path and the wedding guests before him, or at other times the pilgrim can see strictly only what a campfire illuminates or what the walls of a goatherd's hut contain. Furthermore, despite the *Soledades*' suggestion of symmetry, one cannot perceive a simple, immediately accessible, coherent spatial plan, given that formal and informal components mix so freely together and because even the constraining verse form of the poems themselves takes on the sinuous, loose, curvilinear, quasi-vegetal quality of the *silva*. This imperfect symmetry with ambiguous delineation and closure also characterizes the Mannerist style of artful landscape found at Tivoli and at other gardens in Europe.

The same principle of *admiratio* that plays such a pivotal role in the *Soledades* and Gongorine aesthetics constitutes the touchstone for successful design in formal Renaissance garden architecture, too. Employing the Villa d'Este as a model, Hunt emphasizes the landscape architect's intention to engage the visitor in an act of discovery and exploration through unpredictability.[9] To generate surprise and maintain the expectation of the unexpected, the designer incorporates features that produce rich sensory stimuli, mixing aural and visual effects in the sounds of varied birds, running water, and musical instruments driven by cutting-edge hydraulics with a wealth of species of plants, trees, and flowers, elements comparable to the *Soledades*' literal and figurative musicality in verse and fictional world, and the rich, gallery-like display of painterly effects and images that unfolds during the course of the pilgrim-reader's voyage of discovery. Games form part and parcel of the journey in both cases, whether the ludic component assumes the shape, on the one hand, of the wedding celebration's sports contests of *Soledad* I or the enigmatic linguistic puzzles that compose Góngora's masterpiece, or, on the other hand, of the *scherzi d'acqua*—the surprise showers released by hidden water jets in the garden—or the alternate turns and paths that make the wanderer choose between spatial programs mapped out by the landscaper.

Perspectival shifts also contribute to the objective to inspire and maintain wonderment, whether in formal gardens or Góngora's literary garden. The *Soledades* flaunt an ever changing viewpoint—linguistic, visual or auditory, natural or cultivated spaces, internal or external to the protagonist—whereas the cultivated landscape generates an integrated flux of artful or natural spaces, panoramic or directed perspective. Spatial arrangements evolved in Renaissance gardens such that the visitors' steps and eyes moved toward a focal point, sometimes enclosed, that contained a spring or sculptural grouping. Occasionally, one finds a similarly emphatic directional statement in Góngora's poems, as when the wedding guests converge on a *glorieta* (rotary) built around a fountain, an architectonic set piece common to pastoral literature and garden design alike:[10]

> Centro apacible un círculo espacioso
>   a más caminos que una estrella rayos
>   hacía, bien de pobos, bien de alisos,
> donde la Primavera,
> calzada abriles y vestida mayos,
> centellas saca de cristal undoso
> a un pedernal orlado de narcisos.
>   (Jammes, I:573–79)

> (A spacious circle pleasant centre made
> To more road-ends than planet to its rays,
> With alder-trees and poplars white about;
>   And there the Spring essayed
> —In April's glory shod and clad in May's—
> To draw the sparks of wavy crystal out
> From a hard flint that the narcissi crowned.
>   [Wilson, I:556–62])

This colorful, luxuriant visual focus literally marks the end of the road(s) to the village of the wedding festival, but it also signals a psychological shift in *Soledad* I from the more solitary scenes in which nature subsumes a limited number of human figures in the landscape to the scenes of collective celebration in which humans mold nature to their own purposes, anything from serving a simple but satisfying banquet to building a rustic sports arena. *Soledad* II offers numerous examples of converging lines of vision that actualize an optical and dramatic transition in the poem. The island adorns the intersection of ocean and stream, and a boat creates the link that bridges mainland shore and island, transporting pilgrim and reader from the forest to an aquatic realm:

> a la turba, que dar quisiera voces
> a la que de un ancón segunda haya
> (cristal pisando azul con pies veloces)
> salió improvisa, de una y otra playa
> vínculo desatado, instable puente.
> (Jammes, II:44–48)

> (Who wished to call a second bark to land,
> That from an inlet sudden came in view,
> Treading with rapid feet the crystal blue,
> Free link, unstable bridge between each strand.
> [Wilson, II:42–45])

Later in the same poem, the sliding movement of an S curve, the synecdochic representation of the hunting party leaving the palace, draws the pilgrim-reader's eye down the hillside and into the marshlands, where the rest of the poem takes place:

> la escuadra descendía presurosa
> por el peinado cerro a la campaña,
> que al mar debe, con término prescripto.
> (Jammes, II:826–28)

> (The squadron, from the unequal summit make
> Their progress to the underlying strand,
> The plain that with prescribed boundary.
> [Wilson, II:812–14])

The celebration of variety foments the *admiratio* effects of the gardens and the *Soledades*. The abundance of collections prominently displayed in both venues provides an objective correlative to this notion. By all accounts, formal gardens functioned in part as museums showcasing antiquities, a mixture of flora and fauna, and diverse objects, natural and fabricated, that would catch the spectator's attention by means either auditory or visual or both.[11] The *Soledades* likewise serve readers a smorgasbord of collections in catalog form, from the movable still life of rustic wedding gifts presented in procession for the pilgrim-reader's viewing pleasure in *Soledad* I to the extensive lists of fish and fowl in *Soledad* II.

However, resemblances between the fictional worlds of Renaissance gardens and the *Soledades* actually extend beyond matters of the overall compositional plan and strategic objective of inspiring wonderment in the reader-spectator to include resemblances in the furnishings that occupy the respective imaginary spaces. For instance, as Claudia Lazzaro points out, horticultural designs accommodated aviaries and fishponds, exotic and domestic animals, as essential aspects of the garden showcase. Góngora, too, goes to considerable lengths to depict a full spectrum of fauna in his poems. In addition to the potential candidates for catch of the day and the parade of hunting birds in *Soledad* II, the reader vicariously experiences, through the old islander's account of his daughter's exploits, the less mundane activity of seal hunting and a triumphant victory over a sea monster so hideous as to defy description:

> «en la ribera vimos convecina
> dada al través el monstro, donde apenas
> su género noticia, pias arenas
> en tanta playa halló tanta rüina.»
> (Jammes, II:508–11)

> ("Even before next sunrise we could see
> Stretched out upon the neighbouring shore, pierced through,
> The monster whose strange form we hardly knew;
> And even pitying sand
> Such ruin hardly knew, on such a strand."
> [Wilson, II:501–5])

The passage is best understood in the context of the age's fascination with the monstrous and grotesque, which inspired *admiración*. Therefore, anomalous figures and forms turned up in *Wunderkammern* on a regular basis and even made their way into texts such as Góngora's *Polifemo*, in which the poet affords the Cyclops loving attention. Here the creature's gargantuan size (mountains of churning water as he fights the harpoon; no one has seen his like in the neighborhood) and his strength (scales like plates of armor) may remain sufficiently vague to render the beast's species indeterminate, but they appeal to the awestruck reader, proving as irresistible to the imagination as the legendary chimera or the Loch Ness monster. In addition, some of the poems' more arcane, apparently unique furnishings have precedents in garden models. Góngora may declare the net the fisherman wove into the poplar tree's branches to fashion a swaying dovecote "estraño todo, / el designio, la fábrica y el modo" (Jammes, II:273–74) (And all strange to be seen / In workmanship, conception and design [Wilson, II:266–67]), but at the time, the aviaries of the Villa d'Este, Villa Lante at Bagnaia, and Rome's Villa di Papa Giulio retained birds by means of draped nets imaginatively not that distant from the poet's creation.[12]

Moreover, many of the architectonic elements that turn up in the landscape of the *Soledades* also have antecedents in the gardenist vocabulary of the epoch. Lazzaro has written of the impact of classical sources and of pastoral literature such as the *Arcadia* on the imagination of Renaissance landscapers in regard to nature's malleability to reshaping as an artistic medium. Nature lent itself to the collaborative enterprise of forging a third nature, and, in the process, disclosed its underlying potential as a new building material. Thus, in the late sixteenth century, garden visitors could find before their wondering eyes all manner of pavilions, temples, loggias, theaters, and so on, made of greenery constructed of classically inspired wooden trelliswork subsequently covered by vegetation or by clever placement of trees and intertwining foliage.[13] Readers of the *Soledades* do not have to search long or hard to find counterparts of these fragile monuments. In *Soledad* I, branches create a leafy vault that shades the resting *serranas* ensconced on a grassy carpet that rivals those of the finest Turkish looms:

> Ellas en tanto en bóvedas de sombras,
> (pintadas siempre al fresco)
> cubren las que Sidón, telar turquesco,
> no ha sabido imitar verdes alfombras.
> (Jammes, I:612–15)

> (The maidens paused beneath the vaults of shade
>   In the fresh painted glade,
> Reclining on green carpets there, that grew
> With tints the looms of Sydon never knew.
> [Wilson, I:594–97])

The words *al fresco* provide the linguistic axis of a pun that supports the art-nature symbiosis, as the phrase can mean either "in open air" or "in the fresco style of painting." The former meaning conjures an outdoor, natural bower of overarching trees, whereas the latter suggests the architectural construct of a vaulted ceiling ripe for painting in plaster, which in turn requires a suitably grand carpet underneath to complement the artistic marvel above.

This implicit merger of art and nature in a spontaneous or accidental pastoral monument achieves explicit, literal realization in the preparations for the wedding. On this occasion, strong peasants chop down trees to fabricate a decorative, artificial landscape:

> Estos árboles pues ve la mañana
> mentir florestas y emular viales,
> cuantos muró de líquidos cristales
> agricultura urbana.
> (Jammes, I:701–4)

> (So morning saw the trees
> Feigning a forest, avenues beseem,
> While urbane agriculture bounded these
> With liquid crystal stream.
> [Wilson, I:680–83])

The villagers show surprisingly sophisticated taste in emulating the garden design of their more aristocratic landscaping kin, who plant groves and fabricate byways that demarcate flowing water channels. Indeed, the pilgrim marvels at woven greenery that equals the elegant tapestries at court and wonders at the carefully crafted hanging gardens of varied flowers that compare with those of Babylon:

> con su huésped, que admira cortesano,
> a pesar del estambre y de la seda,
> el que tapiz frondoso
> tejió de verdes hojas la arboleda,
> y los que por las calles espaciosas
> fabrican arcos, rosas:
> oblicuos, nuevos, pénsiles jardines,
> de tantos como víolas jazmines.
> (Jammes, I:714–21)

> (When with his youthful guest
> The ancient onward pressed
> Through the well-peopled village, there to see,
> Admiring courteously
> —What might with silken stuffs have well compared—
> The carpets, that the grove,
> Of leaves and greenery, wove,
> Arches that over spacious streets divided
> And roses fresh provided;
> Fair hanging gardens, new obliquities,
> Of jasmine as of violets were these.
> [Wilson, I:691–701])

The courtly gardenist aesthetic readily adopted by the protagonist's rustic hosts might dictate linking and enclosing garden axials overhead with arches of red, yellow, and violet blooms forming slanting lines that cut the street at oblique angles. This high level of geometric and architectural expertise distinguishes poet, pilgrim, and reader as members of the intellectual elite and reveals the extent to which Góngora projects urban and court culture onto the bucolic, literary countryside. The *Soledades*' audience can even visit a clever, poetic double of the hippodromes and amphitheaters common in formal gardens of the time:[14]

> Los árboles que el bosque habian fingido,
>   umbroso coliseo ya formando,
>   despejan el ejido,
>   olímpica palestra
> de valientes desnudos labradores.
>   (Jammes, I:958–62)

> (Trees that before a feigning forest made,
>   And from the common cleared,
> Now formed a coliseum in the shade;
>   Olympic wrestling ground
> For valiant naked men.
>   [Wilson, I:933–37])

Amenable nature and human artifice conspire to build ephemeral monuments to the occasion, as they did in the special celebrations staged in the grand gardens of the age.

Góngora and landscape architects alike also exercise their construction skills in altering the natural terrain for artistic effect. Artificial mounts *(montagnettes)* became familiar terms in horticultural vocabulary by the mid-fifteenth century. They find a literary counterpart in *Soledad* II's rabbit warren, which inspires the same wonderment as the ingenious dovecote: "A pocos pasos lo admiró no menos / montecillo . . ." (Jammes, 275–76) (Few paces distant, no less wondered he / At a small hill . . . [Wilson, 268–69]). On a much bigger scale one encounters *Soledad* II's island, cultivated with devotion by the venerable old fisherman, a locale that imaginatively imitates one of the key topographical features of Renaissance water gardens. Such famous sites as the Boboli Gardens' *isolotto* and Aranjuez's Jardín de la Isla, along with grottoes, alcoves, fountains, and pavilions, constitute focal points, stopping places, or destinations in the visitor's garden itinerary. These aquatic nuclei share a common ancestor: the renowned island villa or enclosure, often called the maritime theater, of Hadrian's Villa. The ancients regarded islands as places of refuge and solitary contemplation; humans favored by the gods traveled after death to the Isles of the Blessed. With these traditions in mind, critics have asserted that Hadrian's island retreat may have served as a private studio for work and relaxation, the moat functioning as a swimming pool, and the overall design of concentric circles perhaps conveying in an arcane, oblique fashion an idealizing signification involving geometric and cosmological perfection.[15] Góngora seems to cite such island iconography deliberately in the *Soledades*. After all, the shipwrecked pilgrim washes ashore onto an unknown land, which may not be an island, but is defined by the watery border the hero crosses. Furthermore, this new world offers him a haven from the dangers of the sea and the court, even as it consigns him to solitude in a different environment, the narrative space of the *Soledades*. The poet evokes the same iconography at the beginning of *Soledad* II, in which the pilgrim disembarks onto the island rather than being cast ashore. Here he enters a locus that honors humility, offering a respite from the exhausting demands of aristocratic vanity, and that exalts horticulture, the cult of Pomona: "donde la humildad contenta / mora, y Pomona se venera culta" (Jammes, II:198–99) (wherein Humility did dwell / Content, and where Pomona's shrine was laid [Wilson, II:190–91]). The protagonist refers to the island as "esta esmeralda bruta" (Jammes, 367) (this emerald rough [Wilson, 360]), a wise retreat for the person grown weary of excess ambition and overweening pride who wishes to lead a quiet, measured life in isolation from the wide world's "teatro de Fortuna" (Jammes, 401) (theater of Fortune [Wilson, 392]). As the hero exhorts his elderly host:

> "Del pobre albergue a la barquilla pobre
> geómetra prudente, el orbe mida
> vuestra planta . . ."
>
> (Jammes, 380–82)
>
> ("From your poor shelter to your vessel poor,
> Prudent geometer your foot and sure
> Shall measure all your world . . ."
>
> [Wilson, 372–74])

Just as this carefully tended jewel encrusted in the confluence of river and ocean mimics the juxtaposition of rustic and artful nature often incorporated into formal landscape design during the age of Góngora, so too do *Soledad* I's contrasting complements of forest and village scenery. There are gardenist parallels in this respect as well, for landscape architects frequently designed rustic groves to coexist in aesthetic equipoise with more cultivated sections overtly marked by human artifice. The Sacro Bosco of Bomarzo, one of the most famous created forests of Renaissance Italy, draws on the sacred wood of Sannazaro's *Arcadia* and the sacred groves of classical literature for inspiration, seeking to move visitors to reverent reflection as nature commemorates Vicino Orsini's dead wife, Giulia Farnese. An elaborate program that alludes to numerous literary and architectural sources, and quotes emblem books and romances of chivalry, pulls the guest into the landscape and into a paradoxical experience at once playful, witty, and cathartic. Góngora can certainly match the conceptual complexity of Bomarzo, but his fictional words lack the pervasively elegiac quality of the Orsini groves, even as they foster the silence, repose, tranquillity, and solitude associated with the *bosco* convention. Under the influence of *Arcadia,* landscape architects frequently incorporated ruins into the invented woods to celebrate the presence of the past and also to remind viewers of time's fleeting essence. These crumbling structures could be genuine or simulated and lent the garden an air of solitary abandonment. At Bomarzo, for instance, these monuments to temporality assume the shape of rocks cut to resemble Etruscan tombs.[16] Architectural memento mori make cameo appearances in *Soledad* I, when the disillusioned, *desengañado* (undeceived) goatherd allows the pilgrim and the reader a glimpse into his past life as a warrior:

>   «Aquellas que los árboles apenas
>   dejan ser torres hoy—dijo el cabrero
>   con muestras de dolor extraordinarias—,
>   las estrellas nocturnas luminarias
>   eran de sus almenas,
>   cuando el que ves sayal fue limpio acero.
>   Yacen ahora, y sus desnudas piedras
>   visten piadosas yedras,
>   que a rüinas y a estragos
>   sabe el tiempo hacer verdes halagos.»
>   (Jammes, 212–21)

("Those towers, that the trees to-day conceal
Almost from sight," the goat-herd said, with show
Of more than common grief, "were tall before,
So that as nocturnal luminaries o'er
Their battlements the stars appeared alone,
Ere sackcloth had replaced my suit of steel.
Then lie they now, and clad the naked stone
    With pitying ivy is;
    For wastes or ruins, know,
Time can console with green cajoleries."
                [Wilson, 208–17])

In Góngora's hands, a language of substitution—*árboles* (trees) for *torres* (towers); *sayal* (sackcloth) for *acero* (steel); *desnudas piedras* (naked stone[s]) dressed in *piadosas yedras* (pitying ivy) for *almenas* (battlements); and *verdes halagos* (green cajoleries) for *rüinas* (ruins)—deconstructs the world of battles and strife, and signals the triumph of a pastoral ethos of peace, harmony, and bucolic leisure. The pattern reiterates the structure of the *Soledades'* dedication, in which the poet invites the duke of Béjar to cross the border from the untamed woods and mountains full of hunting game into the peaceful garden niche of a pastoral fountain, from a wild forest in which one bears arms and kills bears to a *bosco* landscape of solitude and repose, the space of the poems, marked by the arboreal transformation from the land of the *robre* (oak) and *pino* (pine) (17) to the dominion of the *encina* (ilex or evergreen oak) (22), the acorn-producing tree of the mythic Golden Age, yet another sign of entry into a pastoral world.

Given that Góngora begins the *Soledades* with a transformation of this sort, it seems only fitting that the poems are replete with imagery of metamorphosis and change fundamental to the narrative flow and to the functioning of his multilayered conceits. Like the literary masterpiece, formal gardens of the time betray the Renaissance enthusiasm for Ovid's *Metamorphoses*, weaving their way into sculpture and statuary, visual focal points, even as they are entwined into the linguistic fabric of the Gongorine verses, where they become focal points for the eyes of the mind. Reliefs among the Villa d'Este's Terrace of the One Hundred Fountains depict scenes from Ovid's work, and episodes such as those that relate the transformation of Daphne, Syrinx, Narcissus, and others emerge as favorite motifs for the automated sculptures that prove an awe-inspiring, integral part of the gardenist experience.[17] Góngora's readers will recognize other motifs from the daily lives of humans considered appropriate for garden decorum and landscape design: rustic figures, such as peasants, farmers, shepherds, and the animals they tend, along with genre scenes, stylized renditions of their habits and routines. The *Soledades*' goatherds, mountain dwellers, and fishermen, their work and leisure portrayed in the poems, honor the established pastoral and horticultural conventions, but Góngora endows his figures and their lives with a distinctive, courtly cast and an aristocratic substratum that continuously remind the audience of the elitist tenor of the genre and of the author's own bucolic fictional world.

Yet, of all the elements of the gardenist aesthetic that pervade the *Soledades*, the signature feature of Góngora's garden of the mind remains water in abundant quantities and a variety of forms, from the harrowing sea that shipwrecks the pilgrim and tempts the avaricious to set off on voyages of discovery to a meandering mountain stream; from a forest spring to the marshlands; and from a long, winding river to a tame, nourishing rivulet. The poet's enthusiasm for aquatic imagery doubtless sprang in part from the spirit and concerns of the times. The growth of urbanization in the sixteenth century spurred public interest and discourse on the availability of water, how to access this vital resource and transport it to where it was needed. Celebration of the element reached the point that poets wrote encomiastic verses to honor water, fountains, and gardens, and bas-relief carved into fountains garnered the title of *poesie*. The second half of the century also witnessed a resurgence of water and fountains as key components in garden design. Not surprisingly, this phenomenon in turn coincided with the recovery of Hero of Alexandria's *Pneumatics,* which provided the hydraulic technology to power the water organs; moving statues; varying sizes of jets; and surprise water sprays, tricks, and traps that induced wonderment among visitors to famous Renaissance water gardens.[18]

Pirro Ligorio, the antiquarian and architect chosen by Ippolito Cardinal d'Este to design the garden of the Villa d'Este at Tivoli, found a blueprint for successful aquatic landscaping nearby at Hadrian's Villa. As William MacDonald and John Pinto note, at Hadrian's Villa

> [w]ater was deployed and shaped not only as a functional necessity but also as an artistic medium in its own right, equal, in the major fountain displays, of the architecture and sculpture that enframed and embellished it. Water in motion, with its attendant range of familiar, reassuring sounds and lightstruck corruscations, is a palpable thing, stimulating sensations fixed media cannot. Waterworks were indispensable to the Arcadian leisure country estates provided, but the prodigious quantity of water that spent itself across the Villa was also an integral part of the Villa's statement about the sophisticated, knowing Greco-Roman culture of the age.

Ligorio studied and translated the aquatic idiom of the ancient Roman villa, a huge, sprawling complex, loosely united by waterworks—pools, grottoes, fountains, statuary, and mosaics—into a compartmentalized, axial pattern that exploits the dramatic drop-off from the Este manor perched on the hilltop to create a spectacle of noisy water, with aquatic steps, fish pools, the water organ, the Dragons Fountain, the immense Oval Fountain, and more, all of which at once titillate and soothe visitors' senses. As at Hadrian's Villa, water served in part to link the quasi-autonomous sections of the garden at Tivoli and elsewhere, water steps and chains imitating the flow of streams in nature and directing viewers to search for the river's source. Architects such as Ligorio strove to integrate fountain statues with the movement of the fluid medium, engendering maidens crafted to wring out their hair or their laundry, young males who relieve themselves, women who squeeze their breasts, urns that spill their contents, and so on. Some automatons mechanically followed elaborate scripts, such as at Tivoli's Owl Fountain, a favorite with Góngora's contemporaries who visited the Este gardens. Guests watched a show in which hydraulically manipulated birds sang until an automated screeching owl appeared on the scene, bringing the chirping musicale to an abrupt close. Whether or not the poet alludes obliquely to this well-known fountain at the conclusion of the *Soledades*—in which an owl moves to center stage visually and conceptually, his heavy, brooding presence emphasized by association with the myth of Proserpine and Ascalaphus and by usurpation of the focus on his lighter, if equally lethal, falcon cousins—will stay a matter of speculation, but the owl's arrival does impose silence on the pastoral world and end the musical sound and visual feast of Góngora's verses. Like the Owl Fountain's designer, the composer conceived the poems' final image as a set piece, a self-contained unit still linked intellectually and aesthetically to the rest of the pastoral garden. In all likelihood, Góngora drew on one of the same sources as Ligorio for the creation of his owl, because the architect adapted the automatons for the Owl Fountain in a literal fashion from the writings of Hero of Alexandria. Góngora reveals his own fascination with hydraulic devices in the play *Las firmezas de Isabela*, in which he makes several references to the marvelous Toledo aqueduct designed by Janelo Turriano, whose machine lifted water from the Tagus River and, defying gravity, delivered it to the city's castle.[19]

To what extent Góngora consciously incorporates the aquatic aspect of the gardenist experience into the *Soledades* is a mystery I cannot solve, but the poet seems sufficiently aware of the visual and aural impact of water landscaping so highly prized by ancient Rome and Renaissance Italy as to summon its power to induce the *admiratio* effect throughout the poems. In *Soledad* II, the poet compares the pilgrim's surprise as he suddenly beholds the islander's daughters, "las no líquidas perlas" (Jammes, 232) (these [not liquid] pearls [Wilson, 224]), that is, pearls, but not liquid like water droplets, to a *scherzo d'acqua* situated in an artificial grotto:

> De jardín culto así en fingida gruta
> salteó al labrador pluvia improvisa
> de cristales inciertos, a la seña,
> o a la que torció llave el fontanero:
> urna de Acuario la imitada peña,
> lo embiste incauto, y si con pie grosero
> para la fuga apela, nubes pisa,
> burlándolo aun la parte más enjuta.
> (Jammes, 222–29)

> (Thus in a princely garden, in feigned cave,
> The peasant is surprised by unforeseen
> And crystal torrents of uncertain rain,
> [When the dissembling masters' sign is seen
> By him who with his key lets loose the wave].
> Aquarius' pitcher, the pretending walls
> Attack him unprepared: and clouds to tread
> If with his clumsy foot for flight he calls,
>   Deceiving him again
> The dryest path by which he would have fled.
> [Wilson, 213–22])

Note that artifice underscores the interconnectedness of the elements, merging earth and water even as hidden jets beneath the path of egress catch the shocked peasant unaware. Shortly afterward, the pilgrim stumbles across a redirected stream that may not exhibit the elaborate workmanship of the grotto water trap alluded to by the poet, but still functions in a similar manner, surprising the protagonist with a spontaneous aquatic display reshaped and rechanneled by human hands, or so it seems, to nourish a beautiful bed of flowers, painting yet another familiar garden scene for the poems' readers:

>   cuando los suyos enfrenó de un pino
>   el pie villano, que groseramente
>   los cristales pisaba de una fuente.
>   Ella pues sierpe, y sierpe al fin pisada
>   (aljófar vomitando fugitivo
>   en lugar de veneno),
>   torcida esconde, ya que no enroscada,
>   las flores que de un parto dio lascivo
>   aura fecunda al matizado seno
>   del huerto, en cuyos troncos se desata
>   de las escamas que vistió de plata.
>   (Jammes, 317–27)
>
> (When curbed they found their footsteps by a tree
> That trod with rustic foot discourteously
>   The crystals of a stream.
> The stream, a trodden snake, itself displayed
> —Spitting instead of venom, liquid pearl—
>   Hiding, mid twist and curl,
>   Flowers, [that the fertile gales
> In joyful birth gave to the tinted shade,
> The garden's heart], leaving within the glade
>   Its dress of silver scales.
>   [Wilson, 310–19])

Consonant with formal garden aesthetics, the brook matches beauty with pragmatism, bubbling to the surface, meandering in a Mannerist serpentine shape through the garden plot, which Góngora playfully renders in an almost literal, animated transformation that captures water's silvery reflection of light as the movement of a slithering snake's scales before the metamorphosed stream recovers its original form to disappear into the ground. This magnificent irrigation canal contributes to the visual effect of the colorful patch, even as it provides the flowers with life-giving sustenance.

The *Soledades* demonstrate as well Góngora's awareness of the pleasing auditory properties of moving water, qualities prominent in aquatic landscaping at least since the construction of Hadrian's Villa. The poet transmutes the gliding of a boat through water and the stroking of the oars into the sound of a stringed instrument: "El peregrino pues, haciendo en tanto / instrumento el bajel, cuerdas los remos" (Jammes, II:112–13) (The youth, as they were furrowing along, / —His instrument the boat, a string each oar— [Wilson, II:105–6]). The dulcet tones of a *serrana* playing a lute cause a mountain stream to damper its own loud song, as in the muting of a *basso continuo* to allow the melodic line to stand out from the accompaniment: "sobre un arroyo de quejarse ronco, / mudo sus ondas, cuando no enfrenado" (Jammes, I:241–42) (Above a streamlet from complaining hoarse, / Silenced the ripples it had near restrained [Wilson, I:237–38]). One could also maintain that the human figures who merge with the sonorous, watery landscape bear more than a passing resemblance to the fountain sculptures and automatons of formal gardens. The amorous fishermen suitors Micón and Lícidas, who sing barcaroles to their respective ladyloves in *Soledad* II, linked to the image of Cupid in a skiff made of silver shell beside them, and to the pilgrim, his host and his family intent on every tuneful plea, recall the marvels of garden water displays that form mechanized, independent spectacles for the audience's delight and wonderment. Góngora in effect stages a fountain spectacle writ large in this garden of the mind.

The *Soledades* also tap into the rich iconographic tradition identified with aquatic landscaping, in which water, the natural decoration most valued by humans, provides the scaffolding for mounting multiple layers of meaning that add life, spirit, sound, dynamism, and significance to the Gongorine text as readily as to the third nature of the garden. The deployment of water at the Medici Villa in Pratolino gives some idea of the intricacy of aquatic iconography and the arcane appeal the artfully shaped natural medium held for Renaissance aristocrats. At Pratolino, water flows from the top of the park, originating at the fountain of Jupiter Pluvius, the god of rain residing in heaven, slides downhill along a central axis to the statue of Appennino below, the allegorical representation of the mountain range, and from there enters a network of grottoes occupied by statues of river gods, which symbolize the streams that feed the fountains, power the automatons, and fertilize the estate. The system as a whole illustrates the metamorphic cycle of water, from water vapor, to rain, to rivers, to the sea. At the same time, this aquatic nucleus in the garden alludes to the flow of poetic inspiration from on high, from the divine powers on Mount Parnassus, into earthbound mountains and grottoes where river gods and nymphs, guardians of poetic inspiration, dwell. In fact, traditionally, all pools, fountains, and grottoes inhabited by nymphs, equated with the Muses, symbolically evoke the spring of Hippocrene, the source of poetry on Mount Helicon. These contained aquatic spaces of artistic inspiration became associated with sleep and solitude, a detail obviously not lost on Góngora. Water supplies the soul of Renaissance gardens and, likened to the lymph moving through human veins, endows the gardenist experience with the potential to become an intimate encounter with a palpable, living being. Alchemical lore offers another symbolic dimension to the aquatic landscape, because according to conventional belief, water undergoes a transformation as it passes through the earth's stones into precious metals, which generates the seeds for the elixir of life. Moreover, the argent reflection of light off water transmutes the element imaginatively into mercury, the principal metal linked to the philosophers' stone and the life-giving quintessence.[20] The water that circulates throughout Góngora's garden landscape, inscribed within the poems' overall system of verses and emerging in individual conceits, such as the metamorphic cycle of water in the style of Pratolino captured in *Soledad* I's river valley, imaginatively transmutes the *Soledades* into works of art that have at their core a celebration of life, poetry, contemplation, and inspiration.

Returning to Chapter 2's discussion of meditational literature, the relationship between the meditational subject and the locus mentally constructed by the subject plays a vital role in the successful actualization of composition of place. With that thought close at hand, if Góngora has induced the *Soledades*' audience to build a formal garden in the mind, then he has also created in the pilgrim an imaginary counterpart to readers-meditators who project themselves into the cultivated third nature and, as in a meditational exercise, move through a fictional world in a manner that resembles that of the gardenist experience. Hunt has noted that landscapers strove to engage visitors actively in reading, analyzing, and connecting the decor and furnishings of the garden, effectively transforming spectators into actors in a drama in which they had to move from vignette to vignette, assembling the entire *comedia* from a succession of tableaux or intermezzi mounted as garden set pieces. Architects sometimes elected to emphasize the playful aspect of this engagement in spatial discovery and narrative formation by offering guests a choice in paths to follow with all sorts of surprises planned along the way. At times a narrative program awaited, such as at Tivoli, where the enterprising spectator reenacted the choice of Hercules, patron saint of the village and the Este family, who after following a straight, quiet road in life had to decide between the path of virtue and that of vice. At the Villa d'Este, a long, straight axis leads to the statue of Hercules, whereupon the course splits into two diverging routes, one an easy path that ends at the Grotto of Venus, roughly at the same level as the monument to Hercules, the other a steep pathway that ascends the hillside to the Grotto of Diana. Thus, the visitor chooses between the arduous road to chastity or virtue and the easy route to voluptuous pleasure.[21]

Although Góngora does not incorporate a strict, programmatic pattern of this sort into the *Soledades,* he nevertheless guides the reader and the reader's representative, the pilgrim, through the garden landscape, utilizing directional signs along the way, such as the goatherds' beaconlike night campfire or the landmark island in the stream, or even actual guides who provide directions, such as the old *serrano* or the islander. The poet situates the reader's alter ego vis-à-vis the landscape and drama, identifying his location—perched atop a high boulder, hidden in a hollow tree, or in a boat close to the riverbank—and qualifying his stance as active or passive. The pilgrim watches the wedding procession before joining the guests after he receives an invitation to do so. He observes a hunting party and listens to lovers' plaints, and then acts as a marriage broker for the young couples. The Gongorine landscape also displays pathways, often defined by nature's topographical features, such as a route through the forest traced by the twisted course of a stream or an inland waterway shaped by a riverbank, but at times crafted by human hands, such as the final approach to the nuptial village or the decorated paths to the sites of the marriage celebration. As in gardenist aesthetics, the *Soledades'* audience must also parse together a cohesive narrative or work of art out of vignettes stitched together by the pilgrim's movement and out of complex conceits shot through with fragmenting hyperbata that force readers to backtrack on the paths they doggedly pursue and choose alternate routes. At times, they may elect to zigzag back and forth between paths, attempting psychologically to follow two or more syntactic trails simultaneously.

Performing the Masque

From the vantage point of hundreds of years of hindsight, one can only marvel at the extremely dynamic, interactive demands Góngora imposes on his readers, demands that frequently locate the audience in an intense, performative role. Nonetheless, one could scarcely expect less of a masterpiece of such marked theatricality, a quality of the *Soledades* that has surfaced repeatedly in my study of his work. The audience will find upon reflection that in the text, the poet inscribes dramatic performance into the garden of the mind with references suggestive of the theater, providing additional cues regarding the reader's task of composition of place.[22] Near the beginning of *Soledad* I, the goatherd leads the pilgrim to the sylvan equivalent of a royal theater box:

> distante pocos pasos del camino,
> imperïoso mira la campaña
> un escollo apacible, galería
> que festivo teatro fue algún día
> de cuantos pisan Faunos la montaña.
> (Jammes, I:185–89)

> (For where, few paces distant from the way
> Imperiously dominates the land
> A cliff, a pleasant gallery to-day,
> Before a joyful theatre to the band
> Of numerous fawns [fauns] who trod the mountainside.
> [Wilson, I:176–80])

The cliff, which enjoys a commanding view of the land, serves as a loggia, a gallery on an open court, usually in an urban setting, in which plays and spectacles were frequently staged. This natural watch post's strategic effect garners the qualifier *imperïoso* (imperiously), recalling the adjective *imperial*, which in turn links Hapsburg court entertainment to the more rustic fêtes of fauns during the mythic Golden Age. The apparent paradox of the comparison, so typical of the *Soledades*, in actuality confirms the existence of aristocratic underpinnings beneath the edifice of contrived pastoral simplicity. The protagonist steps into the space of the theater as a spectator: "inmóvil se quedó sobre un lentisco, / verde balcón del agradable risco" (Jammes, I:192–93) (Immobile stood, above a mastic tree, / Green balcony upon the pleasant height [Wilson, I:183–84]). Nature affords a vegetative double of an architectural feature appropriate for the audience of a dramatic performance in the green mastic tree, which juts out from the height of the rocky platform like a balcony.

References to the theater grow as the sequence of wedding scenes takes over *Soledad* I's narrative line. Two groups of chattering peasant maidens converge before the final stretch of the journey to the wedding village. They form a noisy and colorful tableau in a compact space, a defined scene pleasing to the eyes and ears:

> Mezcladas hacen todas
> teatro dulce, no de scena muda,
> el apacible sitio: espacio breve
> en que, a pesar del sol cuajada nieve,
> y nieve de colores mil vestida,
> la sombra vio florida
> en la hierba menuda.
> (Jammes, I:623–29)

> (They, mixed together, made
> A pleasant theatre—but for no dumb show—
> Of that delightful place;
> Resting a little space,
> In which despite the sun their curded snow,
> And snow in many hundred colours dressed,
> Beneath the flowery shade,
> The slender grass oppressed.
> [Wilson, I:605–12])

Such allusions culminate with the performance-oriented scenes of collective singing and dancing, and of games staged in a venue labeled both an "umbroso coliseo" (Jammes, 959) (a coliseum in the shade [Wilson, 935]) and a "teatro" (Jammes, 981) (theatre [Wilson, 955])—all of which characterize the marriage celebration.

This propensity for theatricality continues in *Soledad* II, in which the island in the estuary becomes a natural theater box from which to observe the tragedies caused by human greed that take place in the Atlantic, Fortune's theater. The banquet scene, punctuated by the dialogue between the pilgrim and his host, and the yearning *barquillas* of the suitors Micón and Lícidas share the same performative, dramatic aura as the festival of *Soledad* I. And the air of theatricality recurs near the end of *Soledad* II, when Góngora transforms the hawking episode into a spectacle at which the protagonist and his fishermen guides gaze enthralled until their eyes falter from sheer weariness, "Destos pendientes agradables casos / vencida se apeó la vista apenas" (Jammes, 937–38) (Hardly did they forbear / On pendent and agreeable sights to look [Wilson, 921–22]), as the boat's audience slowly follows the exhausted hunting party, matching their oars to the tired pace of the performers:

> cuantos da la cansada turba pasos,
> tantos en las arenas
> el remo perezosamente raya.
> (Jammes, 940–42)

> (As there the weary crowd its paces took,
> So often on the sand
> Shone slothfully their oar.
> [Wilson, 924–26])

Readers of the *Soledades* can find a precedent for Góngora's theatrical high jinks once again in the formal Italian garden design of the epoch. As Germain Bazin describes them, these architectural marvels—which wed palace and gardens, featuring, on the de rigueur slope, terraces, fountains, islands, grottoes, hidden shrines, and aquatic conduits and containers of varying sizes and shapes—create a protean space, perpetually in transformation, the perfect setting for balls, intermezzi, plays, operas, fireworks displays, naumachiae, and masques. Claudia Lazzaro similarly notes that many gardens "functioned as a theater for the spectacle of nature beyond," in which the green world itself becomes an artful performer whose dramatic potential the interactive visitor-spectator sets in motion. And John Dixon Hunt observes that "[t]he instructional motive of gardens, teaching their visitors through an elaborate system of images and inscriptions, together with the strongly metamorphic impulse of their designs, transformed whole gardens into magical peripatetic theatres, locations for a *commedia improvvisa* as the spectators strolled through their spaces." Hunt finds the garden-as-theater concept so universal that he holds the principles of *theatrum mundi* valid for third nature's domain as well, making the garden a microcosm and a stage in which humans slip into the roles of actors and spectators.[23]

As one might predict from the more general identification of gardens with the theater, actual theaters frequently turned up in these cultivated green worlds. Loggias on one or more sides of the garden served as stages for performances in the fifteenth century, but, over the course of time, such provisions for dramatic displays evolved into theaters or amphitheaters, as in the Boboli gardens. The increasing theatricalization of the garden climaxes with monuments such as the Villa Aldobrandini's *nympheum* with artificially rustic fountains, underground rooms, and asymmetrical frame of ilex trees, which in essence demarcate the open-air theater's stage left and right, and the Villa Mondragone's water theater, an apsidal structure with niches, statues, and fountains that set the stage for games of water tag played with leather tubes, the object being to see who could soak whom first, but clearly the winners ended up nearly as drenched as the losers. Note that in this aquatic diversion, visitors alternated parts as actors and spectators, taking "star" turns as others watched the ludic drama unfold. Closer to home for Góngora, but years after his death, Philip IV's Madrid Palace of the Buen Retiro boasted a theater of Italian design with a breakaway back wall that at the proper moment—for instance, when a scenery flat portrayed an imaginary garden—would collapse to make the real, three-dimensional third nature part of the spectacle, generating a typical seventeenth-century game of witty illusions in which a garden like a theater contains a theater that frames a painted garden scene that frames a real garden scene that constitutes a section of the larger garden that resembles a theater, which contains a theater, and so on, ad infinitum.[24]

Recently, notions of an inner theater of the mind and of an imaginary *theatrum mundi* have surfaced in a different but related context: that of theories of reading as a process of visualization. Ellen Esrock and Christopher Collins observe that twentieth-century logocentrism focused interpretive attention in an almost literal way on the mediating graphic symbols of the page. As a result, critics often lose sight of the audience's role of enactive interpretation, in which readers conceptualize what they read through mental visualization, construction of images in the *theatron* (viewing place) of the mind. As Esrock points out, this particular approach to reading is not truly innovative, as one can trace it back at least to Aristotle, who regarded images as the essential link between sensory perception and abstract thought. Despite Góngora's intricate, witty wordplay, the poet's regard for imagery, and for reading as an act that ties visualization to conceptualization, allies him much more closely to this ancient tradition than more modern linguistic theories that leap from the level of discourse to semiotic dissemination or the blocking of signification. Contemporary research indicates that imaging plays a vital role in cognitive and affective functions of apprehension, providing a scientific basis for what artists such as Góngora knew intuitively or inherited from Aristotelian, Platonic, and Thomistic theories of images; from meditational literature, emblem books, and memory theater; from Longinus's notion of the sublime; and from sixteenth- and seventeenth-century definitions of metaphor.[25] Curiously, or perhaps not so curiously, Western thought has rediscovered imaging and visualization along with the emergence of telecommunications and computer-generated virtual realities that, according to some, threaten the reign of the printed word. Yet, ironically, this rediscovery may bring readers of Góngora's *Soledades* back into the magical theater he has constructed through the medium of poetic language.

Art historian Rudolf Arnheim has similarly argued that even art forms that appear inherently sequential or linear must be comprehended in terms of images: "[A] piece of music, a drama, novel, or dance must be perceived as some kind of visual image if it is to be understood as a structural whole." In his seminal essay "A Plea for Visual Thinking," Arnheim maintains:

> [T]here is no break between the arts and sciences; nor is there a break between the uses of pictures and the uses of words. The affinity between language and images is demonstrated first of all by the fact that many so-called abstract terms still contain the perceivable practical qualities and activities from which they were originally derived. Such words are mementos of the close kinship between perceptual experience and theoretical reasoning.[26]

No writer could demonstrate a more acute awareness of such affinities than the wordsmith Góngora, whose neologisms drew such harsh commentary from some quarters only to receive vindication with the passage of time as many such coinages entered the mainstream of the Castilian language. The astute scholar will find that the newly minted words reveal a keen knowledge of their classical Latin etymology and revitalize contact between the cultures of Imperial Spain and the ancient Golden Age of learning.

Arnheim recognizes a special power in poetry, which "would make language, our principal medium for communicating thought fit for thinking in images." He compares the reading of a poem to analysis of a painting: "The progression in time, which runs from the beginning to the end of the poem like the story in narrative prose, is overlaid by an equally important second structural pattern, a coordination rather than a sequence of elements. The attentive reading of a poem requires much going back and forth, not unlike the scrutinizing of a painting, because the poem reveals itself only in the simultaneous presence of all its parts."[27] Arnheim focuses on short, contained poems such as haiku or twentieth-century concrete poetry, but his comparison offers rich and intriguing implications for grasping the reader's experience of the *Soledades*. Góngora elects to push the "going-back-and-forth" aspect of reading to the maximum in his masterpiece, relegating the sequential, narrative progression to the background in reading comprehension. The reader must visit and revisit sentences in the poems, trying out various syntactic and semantic possibilities, entertaining multiple alternatives simultaneously, and producing layers of imagery that complicate, complement, or contradict (or all three) one another all the while.

Christopher Collins also ascribes a shuttling dynamic to the reading process, envisioning the reader navigating between "peripheral awareness," in which the text encourages unconscious merger of the audience with the fictional world, and "focal awareness," in which the reader tends to narrow the mental field of vision, objectifying the text under scrutiny. Poems, Collins asserts, invite objectification, leading to *poiesis,* an act of reading that is a performance of the act of making and analyzing, merging artist and audience in collaborative creation.[28] Góngora chooses to emphasize the focal awareness bias of poetry with a vengeance in his pastoral poems, calling attention to the word puzzles he has created and demanding that the reader perform the act of decipherment, which is clearly a poetic act of "making," an act of fabrication. Peripheral awareness becomes a manufactured afterthought of the reading process, arising from the multilayered imaging systems spawned by Gongorine conceits, and triggered by the pilgrim's progress through the landscape.

Yet, even the protagonist dramatizes the dynamics of reading in this text as he enters the space of the pastoral inhabitants' lives, joining in their activities in moments of peripheral awareness, and as he distances himself to observe and objectify the strangers, at times recalling his former life at court in moments of focal awareness. This enactment of the reading process serves all the more to objectify the *Soledades* as a literary artifact and to invite the audience to read, perform, and analyze, to achieve unconscious merger with the fictional world only in the mind's eye of crafted mental images, removed from the letters on the page. Góngora's rhetorical strategies of dislocation and reconfiguration reach such extremes that they liberate the mind, spurring readers to imagine the unimaginable in paradoxical concepts that sometimes defy natural laws, leading to the unsuspected discoveries, the unveiling of hidden truths, that the author promises the reading elite in the *Carta en respuesta*.

Although I have drawn a parallel between today's computer-based virtual worlds and the imaging process sparked by Gongorine conceits, important distinctions between the two remain. Perhaps foremost among these is the fact that the poet's visualization techniques stimulate the reader's mind to jump from sensory specificity to philosophical abstraction in the arena of the individual's *theatron* of the mind. Computer programming conversely dictates the same sensory specificity for each and every viewer who selects the same options, bombarding the spectator with set images in a predetermined order that fixes certain visual and auditory impressions on the brain, leaving little time or incentive for reflection, much less philosophical abstraction dependent on idiosyncratic intellectual proclivities.

If one agrees that reading "is an activity that reinstates a ritual showing place, a place of agonistic combat, of sacrifice, of offerings, and of witnesses to the powers that rule our lives," in which "we form mental images in response to verbal cues," making the reader's mind a *theatron*, then visitors to formal Renaissance gardens naturally "read" and interpreted the gardenist landscape narrative in a particular way that conformed to a type of court entertainment familiar to aristocratic audiences of the epoch. I refer to the court masque, which apparently served as an unconscious mediating agent for those who experienced the elaborate gardens of the time firsthand. Hunt reports that English visitors to Italian gardens often described their recollections in the idiom of the masque, that is, as an encounter best captured and communicated to others in the language of court spectacle and dramatic performance. Henry Wotton, British ambassador to Venice (1604–1612, 1621–1624) and author of *The Elements of Architecture* (1624), recalls an awe-inspiring entry into the "very wilde *Regularitie*" of an Italian garden:

> [T]he first Accesse was a high walke like a *Tarrace*, from whence might bee taken a generall view of the whole *Plott* below but rather in a delightfull confusion,

then with any plaine distinction of the pieces. From this the *Beholder* descending many steps, was afterwards conveyed againe, by several *mountings* and *valings*, to various entertainements of his *sent*, and *sight:* which I shall not neede to describe (for that were poeticall) let me onely note this, that every one of these diversities, was as if hee had beene *Magically* transported into a new Garden.[29]

Admiratio saturates Wotton's reaction to the variety in the garden spectacle that assails his senses as diverse entertainments arranged at various levels on the slope. His impression of controlled descent and magical transportation is reminiscent of eyewitness accounts of moving cloud machines and other hydraulic devices employed to convey masquers or members of the exalted audience back and forth from stage to observation space, whether the performance takes place outside or in an enclosed theater. Note the effusive emphasis, too, on being both spectator and participant in a process of metamorphosis and transformation, and in an adventure of precipitate discoveries.

As an aesthetic response to the third nature typical of the age of Góngora, Wotton's comments hold hermeneutic promise for readers of the *Soledades* who wish to understand the poems better by approaching them with greater knowledge of the court culture to which they belong. Góngora's masterpiece is in fact a garden of the mind shot through with theatrical elements and references to theater that upon reflection mold themselves into a court spectacle in the guise of a literary text. This configuration to a remarkable degree assumes the shape of a masque to be performed in the reader's imagination. Although the court masque unfortunately resists facile definition and categorization, that characteristic alone suffices to establish a vague kinship with Góngora's *Soledades*. Like the Spanish masterpiece, the masque is a generic hybrid composed of music, dance, drama, narrative, and spectacle. Destined for a court audience, again like the *Soledades,* the genre has become virtually synonymous with the masques of Ben Jonson, codifier and canonizer of the form in England. Northrop Frye's broad-based definition of the masque betrays the profound impact of the Jonsonian model in shaping critical thought about the genre:

> The masque proper was a stately and elaborate ceremonial in honor of a distinguished person, frequently royal. The theme was usually allegorical or Classical, of a kind that often required a good deal of explanation when printed, especially when Ben Jonson was the author. Such a theme was appropriate to the elitism of the setting, the Classical deities clearly having been originally created on the analogy of an aristocracy. The actors of the later and more elaborate antimasques [a feature of Jonsonian masque] were often professionals; those in the masque proper more likely to be lords and ladies whose names were proudly listed in the printed versions.[30]

Variations of this type of court entertainment could be found throughout Europe in the second half of the sixteenth and first half of the seventeenth centuries, the zenith of such lavish aristocratic spectacles. Because other countries lacked a major artist identifiable as the one who consolidated and fixed their respective counterparts of the genre, Jonsonian masque has become the normative model and the most familiar basis for critical comparisons, although diversity characterizes approaches to defining the masque. David Lindley, for example, maintains that the "heart" of the masque "is the appearance of a group of noble personages dressed in elaborate disguise to celebrate a particular occasion and to honour their monarch." Meanwhile, Alastair Fowler identifies masque by its unique (that is, unique to Ben Jonson) structure: "poetic induction / antimasque / masque / epilogue." Stephen Orgel emphasizes the political aspect of the genre: "Masques were essential to the life of the Renaissance court; their allegories gave a higher meaning to the realities of politics and power, their fictions created heroic roles for the leaders of society." More recently, however, Jerzy Limon has urged critics to consider dimensions of the masque other than their function as tools with a political or ideological purpose.[31]

In actuality, this aristocratic performance art originated in Italy during carnival time, in which bands of masked revelers paraded through the streets joking, singing, and dancing. Before too long the *mascherata* (masquerade) entered the courts of the Medici, where it became more formal, stylized, complex, and attuned to court ritual and protocol. The masque in its simplest incarnation merged with the intimate evening entertainments such as those described in *The Courtier*, to which I referred in Chapter 1, in which games of riddle and emblem divination might lead to shared performances of music, singing, and dancing. Nevertheless, as one might expect of the Medici, who like Góngora espoused the principle that "more is more," the *mascherata* grew ever more intricate in design and execution, embellished with elaborate costumes and scenery as well as allegorical symbolism that by all accounts at times reached near impenetrability. Increasingly, the masquerade became just one component in a cycle of festivities created to celebrate and commemorate a special event in the lives of noble families—part of the legacy passed on to the masque. The spectacles that marked the wedding of Ferdinando de' Medici and Christine de Lorraine in 1589 included not only a *mascherata*, but also musical compositions by various composers, intermezzi laden with classical allusions, sets and costumes alluring to the mind and senses, machine-made marvels, a fireworks display, and a naumachia in the flooded courtyard of the Pitti Palace with twenty ships of different types and sizes enacting a battle between Christians and Turks. Choral performances and dances capped the extravaganza, as noteworthy for conspicuous consumption as for the extraordinary planning and design, ten months' worth recorded in impressive detail to be exact, required to integrate the diverse art forms and myriad details into a successful, wonder-inducing whole. In the tradition of *theatrum mundi*, this final, stupefying cycle of events culminated another cycle of events that began with a welcoming ceremony for Christine's arrival in Livorno in April 1589. Other events leading up to the grand climax included a triumphal entry, a soccer match between teams of nobles, theatrical performances, the investiture of a knight, religious processions, animal baiting in a public square, a joust, and a tournament. The 1589 wedding as performance remained a high-water mark in court spectacle known and emulated throughout Europe.[32]

Although the scale of this production was unique and unprecedented, the circumstances surrounding the appearance of the masquerade at court, and its subsequent evolution into the entertainment known as the masque, were not. In France, England, and Spain, for example, an occasion fêted by nobles might culminate with the arrival of masqued aristocrats who performed a specially prepared dance. The performance might conclude with the masquers drawing the audience into the final dances, effectively breaking the barrier between actor and spectator, an action that would become another characteristic of the masque. Regardless of the country, the masque inevitably evolved toward greater and greater complexity. The masquers became allegorical figures incorporated into an emblematic tableau. A presenter appeared before the dance performance, offering a contrived plot to explain the presence of the masquers. Similar to romance, a kindred genre, the masque proved a protean type ready to absorb and accommodate other art forms, readily growing by accretion. And so pageants and processions, musical compositions and staged *emblemata*, tournaments and battles, machinery and other spectacular devices, songs and dramatic interludes, which had once been separate components in a cycle in which a masked dance had been just one element, all came together in the conglomerate, hybrid masque—a theatrical manifestation of the pansophical ideal of Renaissance humanism.[33]

In France, the masque emerged in the late sixteenth century as the *ballet de cour*, a title that emphasizes the central importance of the dance in the art form as well as its inherently aristocratic nature. The influential *Ballet Comique de la Reine* of 1581 synthesized a variety of arts, including music; allegorical tableaux; elaborate, gardenlike scenery; and poetry, all of which led up to the spectacle of dances in geometric figures, doubtless demonstrating the divine correspondence between celestial music and the moral virtues and harmonious reign embodied by the monarch. The *ballet de cour*'s intricate design and stagecraft had a strong impact on the brilliant productions of Inigo Jones, who partnered with dramatist Ben Jonson to create arguably the most fully realized, mature examples of the court masque. In the hands of this incomparable, and eventually incompatible, team, the components of the hybrid genre seem to have become more closely integrated. Their artistry transformed the masque into a visual and auditory feast of complex iconography that served as a communal paean to the monarch and an ideological tribute to the values of absolute monarchy and the divine right of kings.[34]

Of all the *mascherata*'s progeny, however, the Spanish masque perhaps deviates most from the pattern of the genre's evolution found elsewhere in Europe. Public and court precedents for the masque in Spain predate the appearance of the mature version of the genre, meaning that as a public and aristocratic ritual and type of entertainment, masque had a cultural foothold in the Iberian peninsula before the sixteenth-century Italian models revived and altered the genre. Moreover, Spain never adhered to the fairly strict division between secular and religious drama found in other national theaters, which means that secular and religious counterparts of the masque coexisted in the peninsula under the Hapsburgs. And unlike other countries that set music and dance apart from dramatic representation, from the earliest times Spain included both in theatrical performances, even going so far as to put the musicians onstage at times, and this irrespective of the venue or social class of the audience. Mummeries and masked dances can be traced back to the early fifteenth century in the Iberian peninsula and may originate with celebrations of the Saturnalia or the Christmas Ludi, when masked persons played dice at the church altars. Fifteenth-century Corpus Christi pageants were lavish public events with processions, singing, dancing, and tableaux. Similar festivities also turned up in the households of nobles. Even a young Princess Isabel, the future famous Queen Isabel la Católica, acted as patron of and participant in a masque composed for the fourteenth birthday of Prince Alfonso. True to the genre's early form, a presenter narrated a prose prologue to the dance of the masquers, who were all court ladies, and this simple performance composed part of a cycle of special events for the occasion.

Without the impetus of a Spanish equivalent of the Jones-Jonson artistic collaboration, the masque languished under the Hapsburgs until the reign of Philip III, whose patronage revitalized the genre as court entertainment. This renewed cultivation of the masque seems to owe more to the influence of Italian models than the earlier masques and mummeries of Iberian tradition. The court masque enjoyed a tremendous vogue in Spain for roughly the first decade of the sixteenth century, a period during which Góngora maneuvered himself into royal circles and that also coincided with the duration of Philip III's marriage to Margaret of Austria. The young Queen Margarita proved a great enthusiast of theater and spectacle in general and the masque in particular. Lope de Vega participated in a masque honoring the marriage of Philip and Margarita performed as part of Valencia's festivities for the monarchs' wedding held during the 1599 carnival season. Both sovereigns patronized masques and at times performed in them; other distinguished nobles followed suit as sponsors and actors in aristocratic entertainments. A special masque commemorating Queen Margarita's birthday took place in 1601. The next year Margarita herself danced in yet another masque. Two such spectacles sponsored by the monarchs were mounted in 1604, one at El Escorial in March and one in Madrid in May, the latter meriting construction of a special hall adorned with tapestries. Contemporary accounts indicate that these Hapsburg fêtes were sumptuous events with exquisite scenery and costumes, and the latest theatrical machinery. As in other European courts, performances sometimes were mounted outdoors in a formal garden, which explains in part Wotton's readiness to project the conventions of masque onto the cultivated nature before his eyes. As I mentioned in Chapter 1, Philip III and Margaret of Austria weaned the future Philip IV on these costly extravaganzas, which may have determined to a large extent the splendor of court theater during his reign. In fact, the masque held in 1605 in Valladolid to honor his birth may have sealed his fate as royal patron from the beginning. Whatever the case, the spate of court masques came abruptly to a close with Queen Margarita's death in 1611 and the ensuing two-year hiatus of performances before the king.[35]

Some speculation exists regarding the fate of the Spanish masque after the genre's temporary demise following the mourning period. N. D. Shergold suggests that the genre was reborn in and subsumed by the court play, in vestigial form as an interval of singing and dancing added to the end of the drama, or that it survived in the spectacular settings, costumes, machinery, and special effects of the plays themselves. These dramatic works also feature the allegorical and mythological characters identified with court masques. In the years after the death of Góngora and under the aegis of thespian enthusiast Philip IV, magnificent court productions on a grand, new scale were mounted in a variety of locales on the grounds of the Palace of the Buen Retiro, including on the island of a large lake. As the audience, which at times might extend to the general public, watched from boats or from the shore, the latest machine-driven tricks and illusions wove their magic spell into visual spectacles far more impressive than mere words could convey. Readers of *Soledad* II, of course, imaginatively adopt this pose along with the pilgrim and his fishermen guides as they gaze from the water in wonderment at the hunting pageant of the nobleman, hunters, and hawks. The protean nature of Spanish theater with its mixture of the secular and the religious also suggests another place of refuge and development for the masque after 1611—in the religious plays financed by municipalities. Stephen Rupp has explored this possibility, noting the numerous similarities between Calderón's *autos,* written for Madrid's Corpus Christi celebration, and Jonson's masques. The shared characteristics include symbolic costumes, allegorical characters, elaborate settings and stage machinery, contrasts of speech and song, emphasis on scenes of discovery and metamorphosis, and the aesthetic intention of arousing *admiratio* in spectators. Despite the differences in patronage and audience, the moral values encoded into *auto* and masque resemble each other in that good and the earthly representatives of order and virtue invariably triumph over evil and chaos. If both Rupp and Shergold are right regarding the fate of the Spanish court masque, and I believe they are, then Spain actually did have a codifier of the masque of sorts in the great dramatist Calderón, who after his ordination in 1651 wrote exclusively *autos* and court plays, the two Spanish variants of the genre. Curiously, the splitting of the masque's development in Spain between court theater and the religious *autos* after 1611 signals the genre's return to the circumstances of its initial fifteenth-century appearance, which featured a dichotomy of performative contexts, divided between public religious fêtes and court pageantry.[36]

In *The Masque of Stuart Culture* (1990), Jerzy Limon distinguishes between what he terms the *emblematic masque* and the *literary masque.* The former rubric belongs to the ephemeral event, the "masque-in-performance" that "may be seen as a theatrical equivalent of a book of emblems. In a sequence of 'openings' the 'book' unfolds its pages on the illusionistic stage, which functions as the emblem icon. The verbal elements of the performance function as the emblem motto." Limon notes that the emblematic masque blends with the rituals of court life, tends to constitute part of a cycle of courtly events, and fuses all the arts—"poetry, painting, music, architecture, sculpture, dancing, and acting"—into a symbol of Stuart values and culture as well as of the king, whose patronage makes possible both the art form and the performance. The literary masque "tries to create an imaginary performance in the reader's mind," relying on the audience's knowledge of the latest techniques in theatrical production and on the choice of elements of the production to evoke a performance in the reader-spectator's mental *theatron* by purely literary means. In regards to this type of masque, Limon focuses almost exclusively on the printed counterparts of the masque in performance, which in style ranged from perfunctory, eyewitness narrative accounts to the increasingly detailed, annotated publications of Jonsonian masques: "[I]n the vast majority of printed masques there also are . . . prefaces, addresses, introductions, dedications, plot summaries, and even elaborate footnotes and marginal notes; sometimes there are also digressions or even replies to criticism."[37] If one considers this observation against the backdrop of seventeenth-century reactions to the *Soledades*, then the cumbersome, didactic, ostentatiously erudite, annotated editions of Díaz de Rivas, Pellicer, and Salcedo Coronel seem kindred literary souls.

Limon identifies Ben Jonson as "the only masque writer who tried at one point to abandon the narrative character of printed masques in order to create a new literary form that would be autonomous, or independent from the past theater realization. This resulted in amalgamated works composed of poetic, dramatic, and narrative elements." A step beyond this creative practice, however, lies a masque with no connections past or present to actual theatrical dramatization, the only production being the one cued and suggested by a text, mounted on the inner stage of the mind, and visualized and performed in the act of reading. Although Jonson may have been the only masque writer to push the genre in that direction in England, the Spanish poet Góngora has actually composed a masque in literary form in the *Soledades*, a masterpiece that, true to the genre's conventions, upholds the values of Spain's intellectual and aristocratic elite, and confirms that ethos in a solitary relationship between author and reader forged through collaborative, performative reading of the text in a daring reduction of a grandiose spectacle of the court community to the recesses of the individual imagination.[38] After all, the *Polifemo* and the *Soledades* sprang from Góngora's pen in the interval between 1610 and 1614, just as the vogue of the court masque came to an end, only to metamorphose into a different type of theater in Spain. Composition of *Soledad* I, in 1612, follows closely upon the death of Queen Margarita, which indicates that the poet and his intended readers possessed more than a passing acquaintance with court masques and spectacles. The author, ever an experimenter, gave his target audience the full panoply of a theatrical production similar to the ones enjoyed before the young queen's demise, but the note of melancholia and of life's transitoriness (a standard feature in pastoral, but stronger here), though subsumed by nature's harmony and the replenishing cycle of life, might owe something to awareness of a change in court rituals and culture concomitant with the loss of this royal patroness of the arts.

As occasional works, masques traditionally commemorate birthdays, weddings, investitures, and the like of members of the nobility. Although the *Soledades* do not foreground a link with a specific event of this kind, they possibly bear an encrypted reference to the duke of Béjar's aspirations at court. In 1609, the young nobleman to whom Góngora dedicated his masterpiece tactlessly requested a royal appointment as Philip III' s *cazador mayor* (grand huntsman), an office already occupied by the count of Alba, whom Zúñiga y Sotomayor labeled "enfermo y viejo" (sick and old). He received nothing but disdain for seeking to usurp someone else's position at court, and eventually the king's *privado*, the duke of Lerma, bestowed the appointment on one of his own favorites, leaving the duke of Béjar without the coveted court position. Significantly, Góngora flatters his patron in the dedication by portraying him as a great hunter, perhaps alluding to the duke's aspirations at court, and, in essence, imaginatively "investing" him with a compensatory literary equivalent of the appointment denied him by the monarch's favorite. As if to underscore this connection, the sights and sounds of hunting pervade the *Soledades*, generating one of the poems' most prominent fields of imagery.[39] Readers will recall that the sudden eruption of a party of hunters and hounds on the scene in *Soledad* I (Jammes, 222–32; Wilson, 218–29) signals a shift away from the melancholy reflections of the old goatherd's monologue into the sequence of tableaux leading up to the wedding celebration, marking an important transition in the text. Much of *Soledad* II highlights hunting scenes, from the fishing episodes at the beginning to the magnificent procession of the noble equestrian and his hawks, from the descriptions of the birds of prey at work to the game warden's watchtower and the final, elliptical image of the owl, the nocturnal hunter. The abundance of venatic references creates a bond between the text and the elite audience, because after all, with the exception of fishing, formal hunting of the sort dramatized in the poems pertains to the realm of aristocratic privilege and diversion, and creates a link among poet, reader, and patron through the poems' mediation, subliminally identifying the duke of Béjar as the perfect, noble huntsman. Although paying tribute to his patron's special skills, Góngora encodes an insiders' joke into the work that unifies a small circle of readers in and around the court.

Whether such speculation seems plausible or far-fetched, the superstructure of the *Soledades* individually and collectively assumes the shape of a masque cycle, which Limon describes as a sequence of spectacles or a festival of signifying events that celebrates a special occasion. A heterogeneous mixture of court entertainments composed of events from different systems of signification blend together in a syncretic spectacle, or in this case syncretic text of meaning, combining processions, competitive games, displays of martial arts, and a variety of performing arts: drama, singing, dancing, and, of course, masques. In Góngora's masterpiece, two events supply the key occasions for organization of the cycle(s): the wedding of *Soledad* I and the engagement of *Soledad* II. These focus episodes also coincide with intervals in the poems in which the physical and psychological distance between the pilgrim and the bucolic world disappears, facilitating readers' imaginary entry into the text. The pastoral-gardenist setting, typical of the masque, provides an overarching, unifying auditory and visual backdrop that contributes to the sense of continuity between the two poems. Indeed, pastoral and masque share a marked affinity:

> The union was a natural one, for the pastoral, whether in its Arcadian or chivalric guise, was well suited to supply the framework for graceful poetry and elaborate dances alike, while the rustic and burlesque elements were equally capable of furnishing matter for the anti-masque, when the form had reached that stage of structural elaboration. The allusive and allegorical features which had long been traditional in the pastoral likewise suited the topical and occasional nature of the masque.[40]

The masque cycle of *Soledad* I begins with the glimpse of the distant campfire, a guiding light that leads the pilgrim to the humble goatherd's hut. He and readers experience genuine hospitality, in contrast to the empty flattery of the court. The emblematic tableau introduces and celebrates the pastoral values of simplicity and harmony with nature. The next morning, the lyric apostrophe of the *beatus ille* passage, description, and narrative gives way to a short, dramatic monologue in which the goatherd host shares his sorrowful reflections on a military past. Then Góngora treats the protagonist and the reading audience to a procession of mountain youths and maidens who make their way to a wedding. The plaintive monologue of the aged *serrano* interjects aural, theatrical counterpoint into the visual processional spectacle, and on the journey to the wedding, the poet adds music, singing, and dancing to the mixture of performing arts. The entire wedding sequence with which *Soledad* I concludes functions in itself as a mini-masque cycle that encompasses the following events: a fireworks display, music and dancing, a choral concert accompanied by dancing, presentation of the bridal couple, a banquet, singing and dancing, sports competition, and a procession and illumination ceremony of the newlyweds' abode. If one discounts the contrived rusticity of the scenarios, then Góngora has staged a wedding masque festival in the poem's imaginary garden, inviting the audience to gaze inwardly at the spectacle and join the celebration.

Soledad II presents a different concatenation of events that together constitute another masque cycle. In this case, the cycle in microcosm takes place at the outset of the poem with the double engagement of the fisherman's daughters serving as the climax of the sequence of events. Adhering to the conventions of the aristocratic genre, which mixes dramatic, lyric, and narrative elements, Góngora juxtaposes poetic narrative and descriptive passages with dramatic monologue and dialogue at the beginning with the pilgrim's tuneful plaint and conversion, followed shortly afterward by exchanges in direct discourse between the protagonist and his venerable host. The opening tableaux also include fishing described as a hunting ritual, presentation of the islander's daughters, a tour of the island garden, a banquet with avian background music, speeches by honored guest and host, a heroic narrative highlighting the venatic prowess of the daughters, an amoebic singing performance of barcaroles, and formalization of the engagement. The minicycle establishes the tone that will permeate the rest of the events in *Soledad* II, which has more of an active, martial, hunting focus as opposed to the celebrative performing-arts bias of *Soledad* I. Whereas the protagonist of *Soledad* I is drawn into the heart of the pastoral world, where he subsequently makes the transition into a piscatory counterpart, he then moves away from that island world in the remaining scenarios of *Soledad* II. Góngora first dazzles the protagonist and the audience with the elegant procession of hunters and hawks, after which spectators witness the birds acting the part of dancers in a beautiful but deadly aerial ballet. Finally, reader and pilgrim watch another procession as the hunting party enters the simple village at the end of the poem. The dark, brooding owl contrasts powerfully with the image of the honeymoon cottage ablaze with light at the end of *Soledad* I.

Keeping with the masque tradition, many of the processions and episodes of singing and dancing serve a ritualistic, symbolic function in Góngora's work. For example, the music of a rustic lute and flute announces the appearance on the forest stage in *Soledad* I of the processions of mountain maidens and youths, respectively, who make their way to the wedding celebration. The male-female division, which the hymeneal choruses reiterate on the day of the marriage, is overcome, linked by the melodious sounds of the instruments and songs, and the rhythmic dancing, to which Nature, the embodiment of cosmic music and harmony, responds empathetically, with the birds giving voice to natural song and an anthropomorphized stream listening enthralled to the concert:

> Pintadas aves, cítaras de pluma,
> coronaban la bárbara capilla,
> mientras el arroyuelo para oílla
> hace de blanca espuma
> tantas orejas cuantas guijas lava,
> de donde es fuente a donde arroyo acaba.
> (Jammes, 556–61)
>
> (Above, the feathered lyres,
> The painted linnets, crowned
> The untaught rustic choirs;
> Meanwhile the stream a means to hear them found,

>   Shaping in ears the milk-white foam around
>   The pebbles in its course,
>   From where it rose to where it lost its force.
>   [Wilson, 538–44])

The gifts from Nature's bounty that the young *serranos* carry to the wedding, perhaps also an allusion to the early masques when disguised guests brought offerings to the hosts of the celebration, pay tribute to the fertility of Nature, at the same time foreshadowing the choral petition to Hymen to bestow numerous offspring on the newlyweds:

> CORO 1   Ven, Himeneo, y nuestra agricultura
>   de copia tal a estrellas deba amigas
>   progenie tan robusta, que su mano
>   toros dome, y de un rubio mar de espigas
>   inunde liberal la tierra dura.
>   (Jammes, 819–23)
>
> (SEMICHORUS 1 Come Hymen come, our agriculture heap
>   With plenty that from friendly stars is due,
>   A progeny robust, so that their hand
>   Shall tame wild bulls, and a red sea of grain
>   Shall liberally flood the stubborn land.
>   [Wilson, 798–802])

The blessings should include daughters to match the sons, shepherdesses and weavers to accompany the masculine tamers and cultivators of nature:

> CORO 2   Ven, Himeneo, y tantas le dé a Pales
>   cuantas a Palas dulces prendas ésta,
>   apenas hija hoy, madre mañana.
>   (Jammes, 832–34)
>
> (SEMICHORUS 2 Come Hymen come, and may she also pay
>   To Pales as to Pallas pledges sweet,
>   A mother then hardly a girl to-day.
>   [Wilson, 811–13])

A shared symbolic code ties the procession of guests and the hymeneal choruses together, the identification of the sacrament of marriage with fertility, and with Nature's abundance and continuity, the combining of the male and female principles representing cosmic harmony and the natural, ideal order of the universe. The alternation of the male and female choruses with their complementary invocations forms an auditory, emblematic background for the busy-bee Hymen to do his job of tying the marital knot around the symbols of yin and yang:

> El lazo de ambos cuellos
> entre un lascivo enjambre iba de amores
> Himeneo añudando,
> mientras invocan su deidad la alterna
> de zagalejas cándidas voz tierna
> y de garzones este acento blando . . .
> (Jammes, 761–66)

> (Hymen began straightway,
> In a lascivious swarm of loves, to tie
> On either neck his band.
> Alternate choirs invoked his deity:
> The tender voices of the maidens and
> Of youths this accent bland . . .
> [Wilson, 740–45])

Góngora provides a variation of the image at the conclusion of the choral concert, which coincides with the return of the newlyweds from their nuptials. The echoing, contrasting male and female voices of "[e]l dulce alterno canto" ([t]he soft alternate lay) set off the young couple, who for the first time feel the yoke of their new bond, like oxen just trained to plow: "[d]el yugo aun no domadas las cervices, / novillos" (Jammes, 848–49) ([w]ith still half-tamèd neck, young oxen so [Wilson, 827]). The official joining of the couple now separates them from the serenading ranks of youths and maidens.

To underscore the point, Góngora once again resorts to the symbolic use of song and dance. After the banquet, the sylvan flute initiates another interlude of entertainment:

> Levantadas las mesas, al canoro
>   son de la Ninfa un tiempo, ahora caña,
>   seis de los montes, seis de la campaña,
>   (sus espaldas rayando el sutil oro
>   que negó al viento el nácar bien tejido)
>   terno de Gracias bello, repetido
>   cuatro veces en doce labradoras,
>   entró bailando numerosamente . . .
>   (Jammes, 883–90)

> (The tables cleared, to the canorous sound
> Of her before a nymph but now a reed,
> Six mountain girls, six from the plains around,

> Triad of graces these
> Four times repeated in twelve maidens, see,
> —Their shoulders gleaming with the subtle gold
> That woven nacre guarded from the breeze—
> Now entered dancing to that melody . . .
> 			[Wilson, 859–66])

Although the dance lacks the geometric complexity of the *ballet de cour*, it follows the metric beat of the flute's melody, and Góngora arranges the dancers imaginatively in patterns, the six-plus-six symmetry of maidens from mountains to maidens from fields and four groups of three Graces. These representatives of beauty, harmony, and equilibrium dance as a unified group, unlike the antiphonal choruses who perform earlier in the wedding festival. Significantly, the song that accompanies the dance addresses the couple as a unit and the shared life that lies before them instead of the special province of male or female, husband or wife. The singer exhorts the newlyweds to live in accordance with the golden mean, to avoid the extremes of poverty and excess—a moral well suited to a dance of measured beats and dancers organized in signifying numerical arrangements.

At first glance, the disguised performers and allegorical figures that the audience expects from the masque seem conspicuously absent from the *Soledades*. Close inspection reveals, however, that Góngora has given this central characteristic of the genre an especially cunning twist in his masterpiece. All of the pilgrim's older guides display courtly grace and dignity, and bear vestiges of a former life as a courtier. The goatherd of *Soledad* I informs his guest that although he now wears a humble shepherd's *sayal* (sackcloth), once he wore *limpio acero*, the "shiny steel" of armor. Thus, the goatherd becomes in the mind's eye of the protagonist and reader *armado a Pan o semicapro a Marte*, a "soldier of Pan" or "satyr of Mars," a noble warrior who has chosen a pastoral identity. Similarly, Góngora labels the elderly leader of the band of wedding guests a *político serrano* (politic mountain man) in the sense of a sagacious, cultured, urbane individual, more of a city dweller than a rustic, sylvan inhabitant. His long monologue on the voyages of discovery, a poetic narrative articulated as a discursive morality play, discloses his former identity as a rich man who has lost his son and considerable wealth to the lure of avarice, which rendered him subject to the vagaries of fortune and the notoriously changeable ocean. The aged island host of *Soledad* II conforms to the established pattern. He greets the protagonist in courtly fashion, *con urbano estilo*, in an "urbane" or "polished manner" that belies the relative material poverty of his minikingdom of fishing huts and cultivated garden plots. Góngora dignifies him with the labels of *sagrado Nereo* (sacred Nereus) and *venerable isleño* (venerable islander) and endows him with an adventurous, ambitious past history out on the wide waters of the sea. The poet singles out these elder statesmen and the protagonist to deliver the speeches or direct discourse that, in masquelike style, set them apart as an expressly dramatic component in juxtaposition to the lyric and narrative components of the rest of the work. Moreover, though masques traditionally move toward a climactic moment of anagnorisis, when the disguised nobles unmask themselves to unveil their true identities as members of the elite, Góngora's masque of the imagination moves inexorably toward willful renunciation of the past, the original identity of the foregrounded personages and the adaptation of a "disguise" more consonant with a new, simple, more measured, and meditative life, more consistent with the morality of the pastoral ethos. The pilgrim's soliloquy at the beginning of *Soledad* II suggests that he has elected to pursue the solitary path of his older guides.

Góngora has also submitted the classical and allegorical figures that populate masques to a creative process of renovation and innovation. In the more traditional vein of court spectacle, Love personified as Cupid accompanies the smitten fishermen of *Soledad* II on their marriage quest:

> Dividiendo cristales,
> en la mitad de un óvalo de plata,
> venía a tiempo el nieto de la espuma...
> (Jammes, 519–21)
>
> (Parting the crystal seas
> The grandson of the foam
> In half a silver oval came...
> [Wilson, 512–14])

Góngora develops the figure further, making Cupid into a visual counterpart of the auditory, lovelorn serenade by Micón and Lícidas: "Inficionando pues süavemente / las ondas El Amor (sus flechas remos)" (Jammes, 527–28) (Love had his oars of his own arrows made, / And, sweetly poisoning the waters... [Wilson, 519–20]). As the youths' song permeates the air, Love delivers his sweet poison through the aquatic medium. When the petitions of Micón and Lícidas meet with acceptance by the islander, the poet transposes one winged divine into another, from Cupid into Mercury, bearer of the good news and transporter of the lovers:

> Mercurio destas nuevas diligente,
> coronados traslada de favores
> de sus barcas Amor los pescadores.
> (Jammes, 648–50)

(Love, now the Mercury of tidings sweet,
Brought from their boats the boys, with favours crowned.
           [Wilson, 638–39])

More frequently, however, Góngora incorporates classical myth or classical allusions or both into the rhetoric of the poems, assigning readers the task of imaginary reconfiguration along the lines suggested by these references. For instance, the patriarch compares his daughters Éfire and Filódoces, the seal huntresses, to goddesses: "'cazar a Tetis veo / y pescar a Dïana en dos barquillas'" (Jammes, 419–20) ("I Tethys hunting see / Besides Diana fishing, in two skiffs" [Wilson, 411–12]). The poet employs a chiastic structure to blend land and sea, to transform the goddess of the hunt into a fisherwoman and the goddess of the sea into a huntress, superimposing images from classical mythology onto the young women. Literary representations of the goddesses become visual mediators in the process of reading as imaging, and the resultant figures in the mind's eye will be hybrid constructions of mythological entities with their attendant accoutrements, an ideal of feminine beauty. In Góngora's poems, and in readers' imaginations, such associations enjoy much greater fluidity than the fixed identity of allegorical figures onstage. During the course of the seal-hunt narrative, one of the brave daughters metamorphoses into two of the three Fates, meting out death to a scaly sea monster: "'Láquesis nueva mi gallarda hija, / si Cloto no de la escamada fiera'" (Jammes, 435–36) ("New Lachesis my daughter did appear, / If not the Clotho of the scaled beast she" [Wilson, 429–30]). The fisherwoman measures out the line (thread) of the harpoon like Lachesis, but in a sense the beast himself spins the line like Clotho by thrashing about in a blur of motion. The visual image conjured acquires a much more somber tone, subtly altering readers' imaginary perception of the beautiful huntress, now refashioned as a death-dealing maiden who triumphs over a monster. The audience encounters these layers of mythological allusions and potentially allegorical references throughout the text. They come at readers so fast and furiously that virtually every image becomes a creative exercise in assimilating a poetic palimpsest.

As I explored in Chapter 3, the *Soledades*' conceits tend to function as *emblemata* strung together by a tenuous narrative line. Masque displays this same characteristic, as does romance, but the preference for emblematic pastoral tableaux seems the special sphere of the court entertainment genre.[41] Instead of a highly motivated plot, the reader-spectator ambles through a garden gallery of speaking pictures, all rendered through the medium of Gongorine language. The poet has also successfully translated the theatrical representation of perspectival space to his text with broad panoramic vistas; slashing, diagonal movement; and jumps in optical scale that cause readers to readjust the lens of the inner eye. The lavish detail of sets and costumes typical of masques emerges in the *Soledades* as well in the intricate, formal garden ambiance of the wedding celebration, the loving attention paid to the marble palace and the huntsman prince who commands it, and the luxurious visual feast that overwhelms the reader in the catalog of epithalamial gifts and vast array of fish and birds.

Masques have always exhibited a decided preference for scenes of transformation, discovery, and anagnorisis—as one would expect from a genre that climaxes with unmasking and disclosure of identity.[42] Góngora has woven this predilection for metamorphosis into the very fabric of the *Soledades* with conceits replete with Ovidian allusions. Even on the most literal level, though, moments of revelation and discovery add a note of theatricality to poems with much spectacle and little in the way of plot-driven suspense. The poet describes the sudden appearance of the procession of the mountain maids, the *serranas*, in the following way:

> Tantas al fin el arroyuelo, y tantas
> montañesas da el prado, que dirías
> ser menos las que verdes Hamadrías
> abortaron las plantas . . .
> (Jammes, I:259–62)

> (So many maids the meadows had revealed,
> So many, too, the brook, that you would say,
>   That in their number, they
> Surpassed the hamadryads green, concealed
> In every tree . . .
> [Wilson, I:254–58])

The passage could almost serve as a verse rendition capturing the unexpected emergence of a troupe of dancers from the wings of the theater or from behind scenery flats depicting a dense, green forest. Whereas the dryads were originally oak nymphs, a term whose meaning subsequently expanded to encompass all tree nymphs, the hamadryads were nature spirits who lived and died in the trees they inhabited. In an implicit comparison, Góngora invites readers to superimpose a mental image of otherworldly feminine beauty on the *serranas*, suggestively veiling and unveiling them in the imaginary garb of forest spirits who have magically sprung from their tree homes. The poet then proceeds to play with the conceit, for even as the maidens intimate the disclosure of a supernatural presence, the pilgrim hides in an ilex, the holm or evergreen oak that would likely serve as the abode just abandoned by one of the hamadryads: "De una encina embebido

/ en lo cóncavo, el joven . . ." (Jammes, I:267–68) (The hollow of an ilex was the nook, / Where he his shelter took [Wilson, I:262–63]). At this juncture, the discovery scene may seem like a clever, witty game that reveals more about Góngora's poetic gifts than about profound, hidden truths. Nevertheless, this ludic passage soon modulates into a much more serious tableau of anagnorisis when the protagonist leaves his hiding place, much to the amazement of the *serranos,* and the young man and elder mountaineer share their identities with each other and the audience. The water-stained clothing marks the pilgrim as a seafaring traveler, an outlander, who reminds the old man of his former days as an outlander, as well as of the loss of his son and fortune to the sea. Quasi-comedic discovery cedes to sad revelations and rhetorical denunciation of avarice highly charged with stylized emotions. As readers watch, the simple mountaineer metamorphoses into a skilled, articulate orator who shares a moral lesson wrapped in the historical narrative of the voyages of discovery.

Vertical movement, especially rapid ascents and descents, enlivens masques' scenes of discovery and contributes to the symbolic associations between upper and lower worlds.[43] Góngora saturates the *Soledades* with this particular type of dynamism, pulling the pilgrim and reader into the imaginary space of the pastoral world. The protagonist crosses the border from the troubled cosmos of shipwrecks and disdained love to harmonious nature by means of an arduous climb:

> entre espinas crepúsculos pisando,
> riscos que aun igualara mal volando
> veloz, intrépida ala,
> menos cansado que confuso, escala.
> (Jammes, I:48–51)

> (He trod the twilight down 'mid many a thorn;
> Rocks, which to equal hardly had availed
> A swift intrepid wing,
> He—more confused than he was weary—scaled.
> [Wilson, I:41–44])

Góngora challenges the audience to imagine simultaneous opposing motions in part through the spatialization of time. As the pilgrim expends the twilight hours, he leaves them underfoot, down and behind him during the steep ascent, which distances him from the horizon, where the sun descends, and from the court. The rocky, thorny climb delineates an almost clichéd representation of the lover's difficult recovery from the sorrow of loss and rejection, and of psychological distancing from past memories. Often in the poems, an ascent or descent signals a shift in point of view and in scenario. The pilgrim gazes at the river valley in *Soledad* I from a promontory, and at the end of the reflective passage, his goatherd guide runs uphill in pursuit of a hunting party that threatens to wash the mountains down:

> torrente de armas y de perros
> (que si precipitados no los cerros,
> las personas tras de un lobo traía)
> (Jammes, 223–25)

> (when torrent great nearby,
> [Hunters and arms and dogs composed its train]
> That almost washing down the mountains high,
> Carried, to hunt the wolf, the people there.
> [Wilson, 219–22])

Meanwhile, the pilgrim descends from nature's balcony and on the way hears the *serrana*'s lute, which completes the transition from the domain of the goatherds to the wedding-festival scenarios, as if Góngora had drawn the curtain to allow the production crew to change the scenery onstage. The poet captivates the inner eye of the reader-spectator in a similar manner in *Soledad* II, in which the rapid descent of the hunting party off the hillside initiates a transitional focus away from the islander's microcosm to the nobleman's venatic adventures. The hawking scenes foreground optical dynamism with the speedy rise and fall of the birds, tracing sharp verticals and slashing, swooping diagonals and loops on the skylike projection of the mind—acrobatics laden with meaning as well as visual interest.

Ellen Esrock has stated that "imaging can situate a reader within the perceptual sphere of a particular character or narrative voice" through "the textual crafting of a point of view." One of the cuing mechanisms Góngora employs in the *Soledades* to situate pilgrim and reader in the text, perhaps borrowed consciously or unconsciously from the court masque, is the sudden movement up or down I have just described. Curiously, though Góngora lacked the modern physiological expertise to articulate the way in which eyes function in a visual field, like any good "poet of perceptual imagery" he possessed the "ability to portray not only objects but the 'disguised rituals' by which those objects are perceived." The author of the *Soledades* imaginatively dramatizes and instigates saccadic movement, that is, the sudden, restless darting of the eyes, "unidirectional jerks" that refocalize optical interest on salient objects or details. Saccades occur within the circle of a peripheral field of vision, which blurs out of focus, as the eyes flash to new focal points, where they rest for varying amounts of time in optical fixation.[44] In Góngora's *Soledades,* saccadic movements not only aid the reader to visualize the masque in performance as it flows and develops in the theater of the mind, but also trigger shifts in the reader's performance of the literary masque, which involves textual interpretation as a performative art symbolically imaged in the fictional world through the pilgrim's activities.

So frequently in *The* Soledades, *Góngora's Masque of the Imagination,* Gongorine conundrums and complexities have behaved like homing pigeons, inevitably wending their way back to roost on the doorstep of astute, active, attentive readers. In his *Carta en respuesta,* Góngora defended himself against charges of gratuitous obscurantism in large part by placing the burden of interpretive responsibility on the shoulders of this special audience. Predictably, court masques also received criticism for the cultivation of excessively hermetic language and symbolism. To counter similar accusations of deliberate obfuscation, masque canonizer Ben Jonson advanced a similar line of defense in the preface to *Hymenaei* (1605): "It is a noble and just advantage that the things subjected to understanding have of those which are objected to sense that the one sort are but momentary and merely taking, the other impressing and lasting. Else the glory of all these solemnities had perished like a blaze and gone out in the beholder's eyes. So short lived are the bodies of all things in comparison of their souls." Like Góngora's later *Carta,* and in keeping with the praxis of literary criticism at the time, Jonson couches his reply in Neoplatonic terms, the standard critical approach to *emblemata* as well. Although he appreciates the power of sensory appeal, the body of things, he recognizes the ephemeral quality of such material spectacles, comparing physical razzle-dazzle to a short-lived blaze that makes no lasting impact on the viewer. What the mind must struggle with in order to understand impresses or imprints itself on the mind and endures like the soul. Jonson encourages his reader-spectator to search beneath the surface for underlying meaning, an exhortation Góngora also extends to his potential audience. As in the case of his Spanish contemporary, Jonson identifies his ideal reader-spectator as an aristocrat, a member of the social and cultural elite:

> This it is hath made the most royal princes and greatest persons, who are commonly the personators of these actions, not only studious of riches and magnificence in the outward celebration or show, which rightly becomes them, but curious after the most high and hearty inventions to furnish the inward parts and those grounded upon antiquity and solid learnings; which though their voice be taught to sound to present occasions their sense or doth or should always lay hold on more removed mysteries.

Jonson stresses, as does Góngora, that outward beauty and sensory stimulation should arouse intellectual curiosity to go beyond the superficial on a quest for higher truths, for enigmas and mysteries that lie beyond the simple, immediate, more literal level of understanding. Like his Spanish counterpart, the English artist emphasizes that his poetics is firmly grounded in the learning of classical antiquity and is more readily accessible to an audience who has this cultural foundation. Góngora cannot resist some rather pointed, snide remarks directed at his critics in the *Carta*. Similarly, a testy Jonson has recourse to biting wit to express his disdain for the numskulls who cannot or will not accept the challenge of his masques' artistry:

> And howsoever some may squeamishly cry out that all endeavor of learning and sharpness in these transitory devices, especially where it steps beyond their little or (let me not wrong 'em) no brain at all, is superfluous, I am contented these fastidious stomachs should leave my full tables and enjoy at home their clean empty trenchers, fittest for such airy tastes, where perhaps a few Italian herbs picked up and made into a salad may find sweeter acceptance than all the most nourishing and sound meats of the world. For these men's palates let me not answer, O muses. It is not my fault if I fill them out nectar and they run to metheglin.[45]

Just as some readers of the *Soledades* attacked the author for lack of decorum in lavishing classical learning and elegant style on nonepic, lowly, bucolic poems, so too have detractors targeted Jonson for devoting such superior intellect and intricate skill to the cultivation of a transitory art form. The dramatist remains content that those intelligent and active enough to seek out what his masques will reveal when subject to scrutiny will appreciate the feast set before them and the nectar of the gods poured for them to drink. He dismisses the taste of his attackers as distinctly inferior, distinguishing his followers as bright, discerning individuals of impeccable taste, a bias an equally acerbic Góngora displays in the *Carta en respuesta*.

At performances of Stuart masques, the king occupied the most privileged space among the exceptional audience of nobles and notables. Much of the masque's activity, including dances, speeches, and songs, unfolded below the stage in an area known as the dancing place, located close to the king, who sat on a throne on a dais situated directly opposite center stage. The king's throne lay aligned with the vanishing point of the perspectival scenery, and when figures descended from on high, they converged on the monarch. The stage provided the pictorial backdrop, the mute device or body of the emblem, whereas the soul or motto of the iconic representation belonged closer to the quasi-divine figure of the sovereign. Clearly, the king presided at the heart of these spectacles, cast in the multiple roles of spectator, magician who unmasks or summons forth the true nobles behind the disguises, author of the order and cosmic harmony at court and elsewhere, and god in miniature with supernatural intellect and powers. In this way, such entertainments support the status quo and celebrate the extant social hierarchy. According to Limon, the masque "affirms the political, theological, and cosmological order, it actualizes ritualization periodically and does not distinguish between audience and performers." Similar customs prevailed at Spanish court spectacles. Whether the entertainment bore the label of masque, pageant, or play, members of the Hapsburg court at times donned a disguise and served as actors in the dramatic representation, which is not a surprising practice, given that by convention no clear barrier existed between spectators and performance, and royals habitually found themselves actively engaged in the spectacle at hand. As in England, the king's chair had the perfect position from which to view the stage's focal point, that is, opposite the nexus where the set's orthogonals met and one could fully appreciate the clever portrayal of perspective. Yet, everything about the staging contrived as well to ensure that the audience never lost sight of the king's intimate connection, dramatic and symbolic with the performance under way. While the sovereign watched the spectacle and might have engaged actively in the performance, the rest of the viewers watched him watching the spectacle, even though they might have participated in the entertainment, too.[46]

The aesthetic and interpretive dynamics at play here should by now seem old hat to readers of the *Soledades*, and to readers of this book, for in the theater of the audience's mind the pilgrim gazes at the pastoral world and on occasion involves himself in that fictional cosmos, while readers watch the protagonist viewing the performance through their own reading performance of a beautiful but persistently arcane and recalcitrant text. This perplexing, meticulously wrought spectacle of words, sights, and sounds is never less than exquisite in concept, design, and execution, and gracefully strives to move the reader to wonderment and a higher order of understanding, the objective of the court masque.[47] Yet, what of the king, who does not appear in Góngora's internalized, poetic production of court entertainment? The ever innovative author has staged a quiet revolution in miniature in the *Soledades*, displacing the monarch and replacing him with an ideal audience of superior readers and spectators. In the pact between the author and the solitary performer of the text, the reader is the viewer, actor, and interpreter par excellence, the other alchemist who must complete the transmutation of words into golden truths, who must decipher the emblems and conceits to unmask the ideas hidden within their elaborate linguistic disguises. However, Góngora has reserved for himself the role of authorial divine: the poet, musician, choreographer, and scenographer who has mounted a permanent production in the *Soledades*, an enduring masque of the imagination to inspire *admiratio* for the ages.

Conclusion

As the writing of this book progressed, the court masque gradually emerged as the overarching conceptual model for reading and interpreting Góngora's *Soledades*. A literary hybrid, a complex amalgamation of lyric and narrative, of drama with song and dance, of *emblemata*-based vignettes focusing on themes of identity and metamorphosis, frequently mounted in a garden or with pastoral scenery, or both, and targeted at an aristocratic audience caught up in a wonder-inducing spectacle of shifting perspectives and fields of reference that may demand a sudden switch from active intellectual engagement as a reflective spectator to active performance as a player onstage, the masque serves as a sort of hermeneutic *griphos* for capturing the beauty, variety, vitality, and wonderment of Góngora's masterpiece. The court masque encompasses all of the aesthetic and intellectual threads woven together in the previous pages: the debate over the poetic canon; techniques of meditation and memory theater; the relationship between poetry and its sister arts; the poetics of *admiratio*, alchemy, and transformation; and the refinement of poetic discourse into an instrument of discovery and revelation of recondite, universal truths and the cultivation of poetic language as a lovely, wondrous theatrical performer and pansophical medium in its own right. Although the court culture that gave rise to the enigmatic *Soledades* and the elite who enjoyed closer kinship to the poetics of their gifted, privileged creator have long since disappeared, this book will, I hope, encourage new generations of readers to heed the call of the *Soledades*' pilgrim-poet, and inspire them to enter the aristocratic pastoral landscape of these poems through any or all of the hermeneutic pathways traced by *The* Soledades, *Góngora's Masque of the Imagination*.

Notes

Preface

1. Federico García Lorca, "La imagen poética de Don Luis de Góngora," 120. The translation is my own.
2. Marsha S. Collins, "Reshaping the Canon: The Strange Case of Góngora." The major critical work that takes a Marxist approach to the *Soledades* is John Beverley, *Aspects of Góngora's "Soledades."* For more recent *Soledades* criticism with a political slant, see Heinrich Merkl, "Góngoras *Soledades*—ein politisches Gedicht?"; Elias L. Rivers, "Góngora y el nuevo mundo"; and Betty Sasaki, "Góngora's Sea of Signs: The Manipulation of History in the *Soledades*." For deconstructionist readings of the poems, see Paul Julian Smith, "Barthes, Góngora, and Non-Sense" and *Writing in the Margin: Spanish Literature of the Golden Age,* 64–72; and Lorna Close, "The Play of Difference: A Reading of Góngora's *Soledades.*" On Góngora and the *neobarroco,* see José Lezama Lima, "Sierpe de Don Luis de Góngora"; and Severo Sarduy, "El barroco y el neobarroco." The gender-based approach to the poems of Paul Julian Smith, *The Body Hispanic: Gender and Sexuality in Spanish and Spanish American Literature,* 51–60; and Elizabeth Amann, "Orientalism and Transvestism: Góngora's 'Discurso contra las navegaciones' *(Soledad Primera)*"; along with the close textual analyses of R. John McCaw, *The Transforming Text: A Study of Luis de Góngora's "Soledades";* and Michael J. Woods, *Gracián Meets Góngora: The Theory and Practice of Wit,* provide a sense of the more recent trends in *Soledades* scholarship. Robert Jammes's *Études sur l'oeuvre poétique de Don Luis de Góngora y Argote* is the most comprehensive study of Góngora's life and works.

1. A Journey to the Heart of a Polemic

1. Unless otherwise noted, all quotations from the *Soledades* refer to Robert Jammes's edition of the poems, and all English translations of the poems refer to E[dward] M[eryon] Wilson's translation, *"The Solitudes" of Don Luis de Góngora.* Quotations from the *Soledades* will be cited parenthetically in the text. Roman numerals designate poem number (I, II), and Arabic numbers designate lines of the poems. Due to the complexity of translating Gongorine discourse, numeration of the lines in the Spanish and English versions does not always match. Additional translations in the text, unless otherwise indicated, are my own.

2. For more on the tendency toward dynamism, metamorphosis, and change in the time of Góngora, see José Antonio Maravall, *La cultura del barroco: Análisis de una estructura histórica*, 356–83. Heinrich Wölfflin recognizes dynamism as an essential element of baroque art, as "painterly style" (*Principles of Art History: The Problem of the Development of Style in Later Art*, 18–72). In "Góngora's *Polifemo* and *Soledades* in Relation to Baroque Art," Eunice Joiner Gates applies Wölfflin's principles to Góngora's poetry (61–77). See also Frank Warnke, "Metaphysical Poetry and the European Context," 260–76. On movement and metamorphosis as fundamental themes and elements of style in Góngora's poetry, see William Ferguson, "Visión y movimiento en las *Soledades* de Góngora," 15–18; Pamela Waley, "Some Uses of Classical Mythology in the *Soledades* of Góngora," 201–6; and Leo Spitzer, "On Góngora's *Soledades*," 96–100. For more on Góngora's blending of genres, see Marsha S. Collins, "Crucible of Love in Góngora's *Las firmezas de Isabela*," 197–213; M. S. Collins, "Antiquity and Modernity in Góngora's *El doctor Carlino*," 19–29; and María Cristina Quintero, "Góngora and the *Comedia*," chaps. 4 and 5 in *Poetry as Play: "Gongorismo" and the "Comedia,"* 81–148. "Angélica and Medoro" and "On an Ill Traveler . . ." are poems no. 48 and no. 258, respectively, in Juan Millé y Giménez and Isabel Millé y Giménez, eds., *Obras completas, Luis de Góngora y Argote*, 142–45, 462. For information on the *pastourelle* tradition, consult Peter Dronke, *The Medieval Lyric*, 167–68, 200–206; and William D. Paden, ed. and trans., *The Medieval Pastourelle*, ix–xxxvii.

3. For more on the origin, evolution, and nature of the terms *cultismo* and *conceptismo*, consult Andrée Collard, *Nueva poesía: Conceptismo, culteranismo en la crítica española*, 1–51; and Maurice Molho, "Apuntes para una teoría del cultismo," 471–84. R. O. Jones discusses the author's "poetic pyrotechnics" ("The Poetic Unity of the *Soledades* of Góngora," 190).

4. On Mannerism, see James V. Mirollo, "Mannerism as Term, Concept, and Controversy," chap. 1 in *Mannerism and Renaissance Poetry: Concept, Mode, Inner Design*, 1–71; Helmut Hatzfeld, "Literary Mannerism and Baroque in Spain and France," 423–24; and John Shearman, "The Historical Reality," chap. 1 in *Mannerism*, 15–48. Stephen Gilman, "An Introduction to the Ideology of the Baroque in Spain," 82–107; Leo Spitzer, "The Spanish Baroque," 129–39; Ernst Robert Curtius, *European Literature and the Latin Middle Ages*, 293–301; and Alexander A. Parker, introduction to *Polyphemus and Galatea*, by Luis de Góngora, 8–50, discuss the relationship among *conceptismo*, *culteranismo*, and the values and ideology of the Spanish baroque. René Wellek, "The Concept of Baroque in Literary Scholarship," 69–127; Frank Warnke, introduction to *European Metaphysical Poetry*, 1–83; and Warnke, *Versions of Baroque: European Literature in the Seventeenth Century*, 1–20, subsume *poesía culta* into their respective concepts of baroque style.

5. Dámaso Alonso, *Estudios y ensayos gongorinos*, 71–73.

6. Ibid., 87.

7. Hans Robert Jauss, *Toward an Aesthetic of Reception*, 20–45; Michel Foucault, *The Order of Things: An Archaeology of the Human Sciences*, 29. Frank E. Manuel and Fritzie P. Manuel, *Utopian Thought in the Western World*, 205–21; and R. J. W. Evans, *Rudolf II and His World: A Study in Intellectual History, 1576–1612*, 243–74, discuss pansophy and European court society.

8. Charles Trinkaus, *The Scope of Renaissance Humanism*, 29–30. Of the vast bibliography that addresses the issues of the privileged position of poetry among the *studia humanitatis* and the relationship between Platonic philosophy and humanism, I mention only the following: Trinkaus, "Renaissance Humanism, Its Formation and Development," 3–31; Baxter Hathaway, "Humanism and Poetry: The Quattrocento Poetics of Bartolommeo della Fonte," 88–139; "The Revival of Classical Ideas," chap. 21; "Platonism, Love, Beauty,

and Florence," chap. 25; and "Platonists and Aristotelians," chap. 30, all in *The Age of Criticism: The Late Renaissance in Italy*, 303–9, 341–48, 399–413, respectively; and Bernard Weinberg, "The Classification of Poetics among the Sciences," chap. 1; and "Platonism: 1. The Defence of Poetry," chap. 7, both in *A History of Literary Criticism in the Italian Renaissance*, 1:1–37, 250–96, respectively. Hathaway states that "[p]oetry rather than logic or natural science was the pinnacle of the humanistic philosophic systems" (*Age*, 304).

9. Augustine, *Confessions*, 322–23. For more on the Augustinian view of Nature as text, see Etienne Gilson, *The Christian Philosophy of Saint Augustine*, 20–21; and Joseph Anthony Mazzeo, "St. Augustine's Rhetoric of Silence: Truth vs. Eloquence and Things vs. Signs," 25. Curtius traces the development of the topic of the book of Nature from the Middle Ages to German romanticism (*European*, 319–26). Manuel describes the important relationship between "the Book of Nature and the Book of Scripture, both viewed as equivalent sources of Christian knowledge, both leading to truth but remaining separate, with distinct languages, modes of expression, institutional arrangements and areas of specialization" (*Utopian*, 206).

10. Consult Gilson, *Christian*, 87, 214; and Mazzeo, "St. Augustine's," 23–24, 27, for more on Augustinian hermeneutics.

11. Pedro Salinas, "La exaltación de la realidad (Luis de Góngora)," 268. Kathryn J. Gutzwiller similarly characterizes the pastoral "as a stystem of analogies to analogies. This phrase can refer to the congruence between analogies in form and in content, to the relationship between these more formal analogies and the reader's understanding from them of theme, characterization, and plot, and, finally to the correspondence between the entire internal message of the poetry and external analogies formulated by the reader" (*Theocritus' Pastoral Analogies: The Formation of a Genre*, 17–18). For a fine example of what Gutzwiller describes as a critical interpretation that "balances" mimetic and analogical readings of the pastoral (18), see Howard Wescott for analysis of Garcilaso's bucolic masterpieces, which Góngora undoubtedly knew well ("Nemoroso's Odyssey: Garcilaso's Eclogues Revisited," 474–82).

12. Góngora later altered these lines (probably in response to criticism by his friend the humanist scholar Pedro de Valencia), shortening the passage, eliminating the metaphorical metamorphosis of the river into a complex sentence, and replacing it with the analogy between the river valley and a cornucopia.

13. Spitzer interprets the dedication as the space in which poet and poetry gain mastery and control over a world of disorder, confusion, and restless activity ("On Góngora's," 91–95). In effect, the poet-persona asserts for himself a heroic, superior role in a landscape of solitary poetry. See also Curtius on the enduring Greek tradition of poet as sage and magus, decipherer of cryptic language, and reader and interpreter of nature's and literature's allegories (*European*, 203–7). In Plato's *Symposium*, Socrates recalls Diotima's description of poets as a privileged group of procreators and purveyors of virtue and wisdom, the beauty of the mind, and the essence of the soul (163–68).

On sleep and solitude as liberating states, Paul O. Kristeller recounts the Florentine Neoplatonist's synthesis of Plotinus and Augustine in viewing the soul as perpetually restless and ill at ease in this world. Solitude and sleep free and purify the soul, enabling it to move inwardly and vertically toward a higher realm of understanding, and ever closer to Ideas and God. Through death, of course, the soul attains ultimate repose and freedom, and can return to God (*The Philosophy of Marsilio Ficino*, 211–18). According to Mazzeo, Augustinian thought advances a rhetoric and hermeneutic of silence and solitude as the medium and state of reception that enable the mind and soul to pierce superficial sights and sounds, "read" into and through allegorical texts that represent God's world symbolically, and draw closer to God ("St. Augustine's," 11–22).

14. Spitzer views the duke as a man of action "conquered" by the poet, who demands attention and commands honor and respect from his social superior ("On Góngora's," 94). For an interesting point of comparison, see Robert M. Durling on Ariosto's praise of and commentary on the House of Este in the epic *Orlando furioso* (*The Figure of the Poet in Renaissance Epic*, 112–13, 138–46).

15. Warnke, *Versions*, 90–129; Quintero, *Poetry*, ix–xvi; Jones, "Poetic Unity," 190. In chap. 2, Quintero stresses theatricality and an emphasis on performance and spectacle as fundamental, pervasive aspects of Góngora's poetic style (19–46). Johan Huizinga characterizes poetry as a form of play that unites philosophy and religion, and has both a social and a liturgical purpose: "In touching on the origins of Greek philosophy and its connection with the sacred contest in knowledge and wisdom, we inevitably touch the shadowy borderline between the religious or philosophical mode of expression and the poetic" (*Homo Ludens: A Study of the Play-Element in Culture*, 119). Curtius stresses the close ties between poetry and philosophy (*European*, 207–8).

16. Huizinga, *Homo Ludens*, 119.

17. Gilbert F. Cunningham's translation strengthens the image of love as combat: "The daughter of the foam has wisely found / Feathers are Love's most fitting battle-ground" (1:1090–91).

18. Jean de La Bruyère, *Les caractères de Théophraste traduits du grec avec les caractères ou les moeurs de ce siècle*, 217. For an interesting interpretation of the chess metaphor in relation to narrative contemporary to Góngora, see Karl-Ludwig Selig, "*Don Quixote* and the Game of Chess," 203–11.

19. Baldassar Castiglione, *Il Cortigiano*, 145; George Bull, trans., *The Book of the Courtier*, 119. Huizinga discusses play and the "game of living" as an identifying element of Renaissance and baroque European culture (*Homo Ludens*, 180–86). On etiquette, ceremony, and patterns of human conduct at court, see Norbert Elias, *The Court Society*, 78–116. Elias emphasizes the agonistic nature of relations among aristocrats, stating that court society "draws the individuals forming it into an especially intense and specialized competition for the power associated with status and prestige" and also describes court life as a calculated performance art: "The intensive elaboration of etiquette, ceremony, taste, dress, manners and even conversation had the same function [control and calculation in the pursuit]" (93, 111). Emilio Orozco Díaz, *El teatro y la teatralidad del Barroco (ensayo de introducción al tema)*, 87–118; and Jean Rousset, "Circé ou la métamorphose (Le ballet de Cour)," chap. 1 in *La littérature de l'âge baroque en France: Circé et le Paon*, 13–31, analyze the theatricality and the theatricalization of life at court during the age of the baroque. Maravall also stresses the gamelike quality of baroque culture and the importance of tactics and strategy in human conduct (*Cultura*, 307–51). The introduction of Stephen Greenblatt's classic *Renaissance Self-Fashioning: From More to Shakespeare* focuses as well on literary works as artifacts revealing the author's "self" and his or her relationship to the social structures of power, considering language as a key element of role-playing and self-fashioning (1–9).

20. See Miguel Artigas, *Don Luis de Góngora y Argote: Biografía y estudio crítico*, 128–30, 228–31, for more on Góngora's consultation of Valencia. In "Crucible," I discuss Valencia's possible influence on the poet (208–10). Emilio Orozco Díaz analyzes Fernández de Córdoba's criticism and defense of Góngora (*En torno a las «Soledades» de Góngora: Ensayos, estudios y edición de textos críticos de la época referentes al poema*, 51–145). Later he discusses the difficulty of determining the date of Fernández de Córdoba's original written reply

to Góngora (160–62). José Luis Abellán provides background information on Valencia and Fernández de Córdoba (*La Edad de Oro,* 237–41, 135–36). Marcial Solana offers additional information on Valencia (*Historia de la filosofía española: Epoca del Renacimiento (Siglo XVI),* 1:357–76). Quotations by Valencia and Fernández de Córdoba are from Ana Martínez Arancón, *La batalla en torno a Góngora,* 4, 28. Consult C. Colin Smith, "On the Use of Spanish Theoretical Works in the Debate on Gongorism," 165–76, for more background on the great Góngora war.

21. Artigas, *Don Luis,* 130–36; Orozco Díaz, *En torno,* 147–204, 167–68; Martínez Arancón, *La batalla,* 31–39. For a detailed study of the confrontation between Lope and Góngora over the *Soledades,* see Emilio Orozco Díaz, *Lope y Góngora frente a frente,* 168–88; and Joaquín Roses Lozano, *Una poética de la oscuridad: La recepción crítica de las "Soledades" en el siglo XVII,* 22–27.

22. As Orozco Díaz notes, Lope more than likely had an opportunity to meet Góngora on account of his growing fame and popularity as a playwright. Yet, Lope's fame irked Góngora and inspired jealousy, spiteful condemnation, and wickedly amusing satiric poems on the part of the older, more aristocratic poet. Lope's appeal to and success with the masses never ceased to be a bone of contention between the two literary giants (*Lope,* 103–17). Artigas discusses Góngora's later years (*Don Luis,* 189, 205–14).

23. Castiglione, *Cortigiano,* 38; Bull, *Courtier,* 44.

24. Edgar Wind, *Pagan Mysteries in the Renaissance,* 1–25.

25. Rosalie Colie, *"Paradoxia Epidemica": The Renaissance Tradition of Paradox,* 33–34. Mario Praz, "Emblem, Device, Epigram, Conceit," chap. 1 in *Studies in Seventeenth-Century Imagery,* 11–54; and E. H. Gombrich, *"Icones Symbolicae:* Philosophies of Symbolism and Their Bearing on Art," in *Symbolic Images: Studies in the Art of the Renaissance,* 123–95, offer more detailed accounts of the aesthetics of enigma, allegory, emblem books, and visual imagery. Elias, *Court;* Jonathan Brown and J. H. Elliott, *A Palace for a King: The "Buen Retiro" and the Court of Philip IV;* and R. J. W. Evans, *Rudolf II,* present portraits of court architecture, design, and life as cultural realms laden with cryptic symbolic significance. As Rousset, "Formes Baroques (Du Baroque dans les beaux-arts)," chap. 7 in *Littérature,* 161–80; and Claudia Lazzaro, "Nature and Culture in the Garden," chap. 1; "Ornaments of Art, Mostly about Nature," chap. 6, both in *The Italian Renaissance Garden: From the Conventions of Painting, Design, and Ornament to the Grand Gardens of Sixteenth-Century Central Italy,* 8–19, 131–66, respectively, attest, even court gardens were imbued with their own arcane, intricate systems of imagery and symbolism.

26. All observations on and examples of court entertainment are from N. D. Shergold, "Court Plays and Pageantry to 1621," chap. 9 in *A History of the Spanish Stage: From Medieval Times until the End of the Seventeenth Century,* 236–63. For a discussion of *El premio de la hermosura,* see ibid., 252–55. See Brown and Elliott, *Palace;* Hugo Albert Rennert, *The Spanish Stage in the Time of Lope de Vega,* 229–51; and Shergold, "The Court Theatre of Philip IV, 1622–1640," chap. 10; "The Court Theatre of Philip IV, 1640–1665," chap. 11, both in *History,* 264–97, 298–330, respectively, on the zenith of the court spectacle during the reign of Philip IV.

27. For more on public spectacles in Hapsburg Spain, consult Maravall, *La Cultura,* 203–21; and Orozco Díaz, *El teatro,* 137–41.

28. Artigas, *Don Luis,* 143–45.

29. J. H. Elliott discusses eloquently the tragic waning years of the Spanish empire (*Imperial Spain, 1469–1716,* 281–345).

30. J. H. Elliott, "Mannerism," 88. Evans discusses the philosophical significance of

collections (*Rudolf II*, 176–82). Paula Findlen points out that the museums that emerged from these collections served as mediators of public and private space (*Possessing Nature: Museums, Collecting, and Scientific Culture in Early Modern Italy*, 102).

31. Shearman, *Mannerism*, 112.
32. Martínez Arancón, *La batalla*, 40–41.
33. For a more complete complement of documents and commentary on Lope's battle against *cultismo*, consult Martínez Arancón, *La batalla*, 110–26; Agustín Porqueras Mayo, *La teoría poética en el Manierismo y Barroco españoles*, 71–79, 102–6, 120–21; Orozco Díaz, *Lope*, 312–54; and Roses Lozano, *Una poética*, 22–27.
34. Martínez Arancón, *La batalla*, 203.
35. As Alonso has pointed out, despite the dates of publication, it is uncertain who preceded whom in actually writing a commentary on the *Polifemo*, although Pellicer clearly preceded Salcedo Coronel in commentary on the *Soledades* (*Estudios*, 463–64). On the rivalry between these two commentators, see 462–87; between Pellicer and Lope, see 488–509. For more on the *Soledades*' commentators, consult Roses Lozano, *Una poética*, 54–60.
36. Alonso analyzes the evolution in critical reception of the poet, refuting (among other popular viewpoints) the Mallarmé-Góngora parallel (*Estudios*, 540–88).
37. Martínez Arancón, *La batalla*, 4–5, 17.
38. Ibid., 191–92, 208.
39. Ibid., 17–18, 24, 120–21, 208. For more on the charge of obscurantism in the great Góngora debate, see Roses Lozano, "La oscuridad de las *Soledades*: Impugnaciones y apologías," chap. 3 in *Una poética*, 81–101.
40. Martínez Arancón, *La batalla*, 5, 20, 23.
41. Ibid., 123, 205.
42. Ibid., 27.
43. Ibid., 158, 189. On Jáuregui's view that *gongorismo* is an attack on representational epistemology, see Ted E. McVay Jr., "The Epistemological Basis for Juan de Jáuregui's Attacks on Góngora's *Soledades*," 301–7.
44. Martínez Arancón, *La batalla*, 21. Gutzwiller stresses that pastoral was considered a serious form of discourse in classical antiquity, a fact perhaps known to Góngora (*Theocritus' Pastoral Analogues*, 66–104). Richard Jenkyns, in "Pastoral," examines the pastoral's loss of prestige over time. Wescott looks at Garcilaso's use of the pastoral for instructive purposes in Spain ("Nemoroso's Odyssey," 479–81).
45. Although the *Discursos apologéticos* were published in 1624, Eunice Joiner Gates has argued for a date of composition closer to that of Jáuregui's 1614 *Antídoto* in her discussion of the Jáuregui–Díaz de Rivas debate (*Documentos gongorinos*, 9–30).
46. Salinas, "La exaltación," 262.
47. Martínez Arancón, *La batalla*, 130–31.
48. Ibid., 138, 144.
49. Ibid., 139.
50. Ibid., 141. As Weinberg has pointed out, in Tasso's case the adjective *magnifico* implies rhetorical embellishment, linguistic ornamentation that inspires wonderment (*History*, 1:572). I suggest that Díaz de Rivas uses *magnifico* in the same sense in regard to the *Soledades*.
51. Martínez Arancón, *La batalla*, 138, 141. Weinberg addresses Tasso's notion of variety in the epic and of the relationship between epic and romance (*History*, 2:651–52). Tasso's countrymen Camillo Pellegrino (in 1585) and Lorenzo Giacomini (in 1596) tendered strikingly similar praise for his *Jerusalem Delivered* (1581) (quoted in Weinberg, *History*,

2:1020, 1059). Pellegrino emphasizes Tasso's ability to delight and amaze readers, whereas Giacomini lauds the poet's beauty and variety of expression, his appropriate use of obscure and arcane language, and the rich ornamentation of his verse. Although by 1624 there was certainly widespread appreciation for art that could generate wonderment, given Díaz de Rivas's familiarity with Tasso's theory of the epic, it is reasonable to assume that he was familiar with praise and criticism of *Jerusalem Delivered,* or the critical rhetoric it created, and drew on this body of material and discourse to launch a counteroffensive in support of Góngora.

52. Wind, *Pagan,* 222, 236–37.

53. Frances A. Yates, *The French Academies of the Sixteenth Century,* 1–6.

54. Ibid., 6–10.

55. Castiglione, *Cortigiano,* 44, 52; Bull, *Courtier,* 48, 53.

56. Castiglione, *Cortigiano,* 77–91, 99–101; Bull, *Courtier,* 71–80, 86–87.

57. My sources of information on the nature and organization of sixteenth- and seventeenth-century Spanish academies are José Sánchez, *Academias literarias del Siglo de Oro español,* 10–25; and Willard King, *Prosa novelística y academias literarias en el siglo XVII,* 7–10, 95–103.

58. Quintero, *Play,* 26. Quintero discusses the public and performative nature of poetry during the Renaissance and baroque periods (20–28). As she points out, the battle between advocates of plain and cultivated style played out in the dramatic space of the academies and poetic jousts (27). King captures the festive, combative, and sometimes explosive atmosphere of the academies and *certámenes* (*Prosa,* 85–103).

59. Sánchez, *Academias,* 36–112; and King, *Prosa,* 42–54. The quotation of Lope's letter is from Agustín González de Amezúa y Mayo, *Epistolario de Lope de Vega Carpio,* 95. The statement that Góngora presented the *culto* poems at the Academia Selvaje is made by Luis Fernández-Fuerra y Orbe, *Don Juan Ruiz de Alarcón y Mendoza,* 390–91.

60. Weinberg, *History,* 2:797; Hathaway, *Age,* 5. Weinberg summarizes the attempt to reconcile widely divergent positions in literary criticism in the sixteenth century (*History,* 1:57–60). In chap. 13, "The Tradition of Aristotle's *Poetics:* V. Theory of the Genres," he addresses the growth and impact of literary quarrels, the formulation of theories of genre, and the debate over hybrid genres (2:635–714).

61. Hathaway, "True Wit Is Nature to Advantage Dress'd," chap. 34 in *Age,* 437–59; and Weinberg, "Conclusions on Poetic Theory," chap. 15 in *History,* 2:797–813, provide information on the quarrel between the ancients and the moderns. See also José Antonio Maravall, *Antiguos y modernos: Visión de la historia e idea de progreso hasta el Renacimiento,* 294–98; and Thomas M. Greene, *The Light in Troy: Imitation and Discovery in Renaissance Poetry,* 1–27, on creative dialogue with classical antiquity as a fundamental aspect of the Renaissance concept of modernity.

62. Maravall, *Antiguos,* 33. Greene analyzes the combination of change and continuity in Renaissance aesthetics (*Light,* 40–47, 265). Parker, *Polyphemus,* 54–81; and West, "The Ovidian Source," 153–57, discuss Góngora's engagement with the Ovidian source of the *Polifemo.* Antonio Vilanova's introduction to *Las fuentes y los temas del "Polifemo" de Góngora* offers greater detail on additional sources for Góngora's *Polifemo* (1:13–51).

63. Alonso, *Estudios,* 71–72.

64. For more on Herrera's role as both codifier and shifter of the Spanish poetic canon, see William Ferguson, "Introducción," in *La versificación imitativa en Fernando de Herrera,* 9–14; and, more recently, P. J. Smith, *Writing,* 57–63; and Ignacio Navarrete, "Decentering Garcilaso: Herrera's Attack on the Canon," 21–33 (both of whom stress the subversive

nature of Herrera's *Anotaciones*). Navarrete comments: "The notes attempt to direct the reader's intertextual location of Garcilaso's poetry, while the profusion of source citations undermines the poet's image as a courtier whose poems were acts of *sprezzatura*. Herrera appropriates Garcilaso instead as a predecessor of the learned kind of poetry that he himself writes" (21). Oreste Macrí, in *Fernando de Herrera*, offers a detailed analysis of the formal elements of Herrera's poetic style, including meter and orthography. Also consult Ignacio Navarrete, *Orphans of Petrarch: Poetry and Theory in the Spanish Renaissance*, 191–205, for analysis of Góngora's subversion of the canons of Petrarchism.

65. Bonifacio is cited from Félix G. Olmedo, *Juan Bonifacio (1538–1606) y la cultura literaria del Siglo de Oro*, 198–99. On flowery rhetoric at the time and audience response, see Otis H. Green, "*Se acicalaron los auditorios:* An Aspect of the Spanish Literary Baroque," 413–22. Quintero examines the development of highly theatrical poetry in Spain (*Poetry*, 4–18).

66. Orozco Díaz discusses Lope's authorship of the "anonymous" letter addressed to Góngora (*Lope*, 172–77). For other interpretations of Góngora's *Carta en respuesta*, see Orozco Díaz, *Lope*, 178–88; R. O. Jones, "Neoplatonism and the *Soledades*," 1–2, 12–16; Beverley, "Góngora's 'Carta en respuesta,'" chap. 1 in *Aspects*, 11–25; and Antonio Carreira, "La controversia en torno a las *Soledades:* Un parecer desconocido, y edición crítica de las primeras cartas," 1:151–71.

67. Martínez Arancón, *La batalla*, 42–43.

68. Ibid., 41, 43. Consult Kristeller, *Philosophy*, 308; and Plato, *Phaedrus and the Seventh and Eighth Letters*, 46, on the Platonic notion of inspiration as divine furor.

69. Martínez Arancón, *La batalla*, 43.

70. Jones takes "mysteriousness" to mean a "general theme lying behind the profusion of incident and image in the poem" ("Neoplatonism," 1). Robin McAllister goes one step further with Jones's interpretation, transforming the *Soledades* into a quasi-allegorical, Neoplatonic poem about the soul's return to divine origins ("The Reader as Pilgrim and Poet in Góngora's *Soledades*," 3–5). Beverley comments on Jones's observation: "[W]hat Jones saw as a hidden *content* in the poem is also a feature of its *form*, of its texture of language and meter" (*Aspects*, 15).

71. Martínez Arancón, *La batalla*, 43.

72. Ibid., 44. See Wind, *Pagan*, 190, on the paradoxical nature of Platonic pedagogy. Consult Gilson, *Christian*, 20–21, 214; Joseph Anthony Mazzeo, "Rhetoric," 3, 24–25; and Mazzeo, "Metaphysical Poetry and the Poetic of Correspondence," 53–55, on the concept of correspondences.

73. See Mazzeo, "St. Augustine's Rhetoric," 24, on enigmas and transcendence. Kristeller, *Philosophy*, 209–11, 237, provides insight into Ficino's approach to epistemology. Consult Plato, *Phaedo*, 214–25; and Gilson, *Christian*, 75, on anamnesis.

74. Kristeller, *Philosophy*, 50, looks at Ficino's notion of truth. Wind, *Pagan*, 97.

75. On the Augustinian model of the pursuit of Truth, see Gilson, *Christian*, 19–21, 87; on Ficino's model, see Wind, *Pagan*, 36–41; and Kristeller, *Philosophy*, 304–9.

76. Martínez Arancón, *La batalla*, 44.

77. Ibid.

78. Góngora clearly prized many of the qualities that Shearman has identified with Mannerist art: variety over unity, abundance over brevity, taste for beauty and the monstrous, obscurity over clarity, form over content, and style over decorum ("A 'More Cultured Age' and Its Ideals," chap. 4 in *Mannerism*, 135–70). A glance at the *Soledades* reveals that the poems embody each and every one of these Mannerist aesthetic ideals. Not surprisingly,

much of the criticism leveled at Góngora's *culto* style echoes that directed at the style of poets such as Tasso and Guarini (91–96, 158–62).

2. A Passage to the Contemplative Life

1. Renato Poggioli, *The Oaten Flute: Essays on Pastoral Poetry and the Pastoral Ideal*, 193. Consult chap. 1, "Pastoral and *Soledad*," 182–93, for a more detailed discussion of this trend in Renaissance pastoral. A. Bartlett Giamatti notes that Petrarch transformed the garden into a metaphor of interiority (*The Earthly Paradise and the Renaissance Epic*, 124–28). R. O. Jones regards the notion of a general movement toward withdrawal in the *Soledades*, however, as an unconscious analogy with Gracián's *Criticón*, which in his view begins in a somewhat similar fashion ("Neoplatonism," 4).

2. Umberto Eco, *Six Walks in the Fictional Woods*, 85–88; Eco, *The Limits of Interpretation*, 64–67. Thomas G. Pavel analyzes the transformation of generic conventions over time (*Fictional Worlds*, 131). On Renaissance notions of genre, see Rosalie Colie, *The Resources of Kind: Genre-Theory in the Renaissance*, 113, 119, 123.

3. Díaz de Rivas and Pellicer, quoted by Robert Jammes in his edition of the *Soledades*, 46. Jones analyzes the opening scene of *Soledad* I as an allegorical representation of a moral transition from error to truth initiated by the pilgrim's separation from court followed by his solitary journey into a new, superior moral order ("Poetic Unity," 191–93). Harry Berger Jr. observes that return to the world of everyday experience forms part of the traditional structure of pastoral (*Second World and Green World: Studies in Renaissance Fiction-Making*, 8).

4. Leo Spitzer, "Selections from Góngora's First *Soledad:* Critical Explanatory Notes on Dámaso Alonso's New Edition," 120; Gilman, "Introduction," 107; Karl Vossler, *La poesía de la soledad en España*, 148–49, 154.

5. Antonio Quilis provides a general description of the *silva* form (*Métrica española*, 167–69). For more on the origin, nature, and development of the *silva*, its connection with solitude and the *Soledades*, see Vossler, *La poesía*, 99–104; Maurice Molho, *Semántica y poética (Góngora, Quevedo)*, 42–55; Nadine Ly, "Las *Soledades*: « . . . Esta poesía inútil . . . »," 7–42; Elias L. Rivers, "La problemática silva española," 249–60; Aurora Egido, "La poética del silencio en el Siglo de Oro: Su pervivencia," 93–120; and Egido, "La silva en la poesía andaluza del Barrroco con un excurso sobre Estacio y *Las Obrecillas* de Fray Luis," 5–39. For additional information on Quevedo and the *silva*, consult Eugenio Asensio, "Un Quevedo incógnito: *Las Silvas*," 13–48; and James O. Crosby and Lía Schwartz Lerner, "La silva 'El sueño' de Quevedo: Génesis y revisiones," 111–26.

6. I have synthesized here for the sake of argument the far richer, more complex analysis of the pastoral of Wolfgang Iser, "Renaissance Pastoralism as a Paradigm of Literary Fictionality," chap. 2 in *The Fictive and the Imaginary: Charting Literary Anthropology*, 22–86. See esp. 24, 41–43, 56, 86, 250–56. Although Colie and Iser at first appear to disagree with one another in regard to pastoral's dominant tone (agonic and receptive, respectively), in actuality the difference is more rhetorical than substantive.

7. Maravall, *La cultura*, 165–73, 348–49. For a more detailed study of the Counter Reformation's mobilization of art for purposes of ideological redirection, see Maravall, "Una cultura dirigida," chap. 2 in ibid., 131–73. Poggioli discusses sociohistorical conditions related to the emergence of the pastoral of solitude (*Oaten*, 182–87), as does Vossler (*La poesía*, 94–104).

8. E. M. Wilson, "Spanish and English Religious Poetry of the Seventeenth Century," 234–40, addresses the efforts "to turn the worldly muse into the handmaid of religion" (237). See also Spitzer on the mixture of sensuality and religious faith in the Golden Age ("Spanish Baroque," 123–39), and Maravall on the mobilization of culture for sociopolitical purposes (*La cultura*, 131–223).

9. Fernando R. de la Flor, *Teatro de la memoria: Siete ensayos sobre mnemotecnia española de los siglos XVII y XVIII*, 73. See Wilson, "Spanish," 234–49; and Louis L. Martz, *The Poetry of Meditation: A Study in English Religious Literature*, 1–22. On elements of meditational praxis that make their way into the poetry of the time, consult Warnke, "Metaphysical," 262–63, 272–76.

10. On text play, see Iser, *Fictive*, 250–56; on aleatory rules, see ibid., 274–75. Martz describes the meditational process (*Poetry*, 1). What Martz analyzes as the way in which meditational exercises function is analogous to what Iser characterizes as the way in which the fictive activates and mobilizes the imaginary, making the unconscious conscious, in turn enabling readers to conjure potential, as-if worlds, consequently empowering readers to think and act in accordance with those new possibilities, and thus encouraging self- or social transformation or both ("The Imaginary," chap. 4 in ibid., 171–246). Iser views the pastoral, with its staged interaction of mutually exclusive worlds, as a paradigm of the interplay between the fictive and the imaginary. He concludes, "Pastoralism may be taken as metatext for literary fictionality" (225).

11. Martz presents general information on meditational literature and techniques and explores how self-analysis in meditation generates the self divided between dramatic and critical subjectivities one sometimes finds in sixteenth- and seventeenth-century literature (*Poetry*, 1–40).

12. Donald McGrady, "Lope, Camões y Petrarca y los primeros versos de las *Soledades* de Góngora," 287–96; Crystal Chemris, "Self-Reference in Góngora's *Soledades*, 7–15; and Mary Gaylord, "Góngora and the Footprints of the Voice," 230–53, provide informative studies on the allusive and self-referential nature of the *Soledades*' opening lines. See Mary Gaylord's "Reading the Pastoral Palimpsest: *La Galatea* in Góngora's *Soledad Primera*," 71–91.

13. Gaylord, "Góngora," 232–33; H. Berger, *Second*, 275–76, 278.

14. On Ignatian meditational techniques, see Martz, *Poetry*, 28–30; and Wilson, "Spanish," 244. Ignatius of Loyola, *Obras completas*, 221. Anthony Mottola, trans., *The Spiritual Exercises of St. Ignatius*, 54; for the Fifth Exercise, see 59.

15. See Curtius, *European*, 195–200; Giammati, "Gardens and Paradises," chap. 1; "The First Renaissance Earthly Paradises," chap. 3, both in *Earthly*, 11–93, 123–69, respectively; and Thomas G. Rosenmeyer, "The Pleasance," chap. 9 in *The Green Cabinet: Theocritus and European Pastoral Lyric*, 179–205, for more on the traditional "furnishings" of the *locus amoenus*.

Note the following description of the spot on the banks of Ilissus where Socrates and Phaedrus discuss love: "It is indeed a lovely spot for a rest. This plane is very tall and spreading, and the agnus-castus splendidly high and shady, in full bloom too, filling the neighbourhood with the finest possible fragrance. And the spring which runs under the plane; how beautifully cool its water is to the feet.... But the most exquisite thing of all is the way the grass slopes gently upward to provide perfect comfort for the head as one lies at length" (Plato, *Phaedrus*, 25–26).

16. H. Berger, *Second*, 196–97.

17. On the Augustinian thought process, consult Gilson, *Christian*, 87–93; and Mazzeo, "St. Augustine's Rhetoric," 24–28. Louis L. Martz discusses the searching aspect of Augustinian meditation (*The Paradise Within: Studies in Vaughan, Traherne, and Milton*, 23–30). Teresa Scott Soufas comments: "This intellectual process is effectively recreated in allegorical terms in the *Soledad* I. The reader, like the shipwrecked youth, is submerged in darkness at the beginning. It is only by the effort of meeting the challenge of that darkness—the sea of the difficult language which parallels it—that one finds a light" (*Melancholy and the Secular Mind in Spanish Golden Age Literature*, 157). Soufas observes that the *peregrino* eventually merges with the melancholic landscape of the *Soledades*, leading uncertainly to the continuation of the contemplative state (157–58). For a more sustained allegorical reading of the pilgrim as poet and reader in the context of Augustinian Neoplatonism, see McAllister, "Reader," 3–9.

18. Iser discusses pastoral's treatment of contrasting worlds (*Fictive*, 70–71). Kristeller analyzes Ficino's dynamics of the contemplative mind (*Philosophy*, 221–26), whereas Martz describes a similar dynamics in Augustinian meditation (*Paradise*, 25–27).

19. María Rosa Lida de Malkiel lists specific similarities between the two works ("El hilo narrativo de las *Soledades*," 4–6). Jones draws parallels between the opening scene of the *Soledades* and Pedro de Espinosa's *Soledad de Pedro de Jesús* (1613) ("Poetic Unity," 191–92). Of course, the shipwreck motif is a staple of the Byzantine romance that can be traced all the way back to the archetype, Heliodorus's *Ethiopica*. Góngora's works displays several motifs associated with Petrarchan literature as well, such as nature as a place of solitude and even the natural surroundings intimately identified with poetic and philosophical meditation: forests, fields, rivers, and so on. See Rosenmeyer for this connection (*Green*, 185, 198). Egido also notes the influence of several classical and contemporary poetic texts ("La silva," 24–25). The *Soledades* are a compendium of so many different literary types, genres, and motifs that it is nearly impossible to accept the findings of any study naming a particular source for the poems as conclusive.

20. The criticism of Crystal Chemris, "Self-Reference in Góngora's *Soledades*," 7–15; Chemris, "Time, Space, and Apocalypse in Góngora's *Soledades*," 147–57; and John Beverley, *Aspects*, gives some idea of the wide spectrum of theoretical approaches and interpretations that the *Soledades* appear to sustain. Chemris states: "Góngora chose nihilism, the projection of fear of self-dissolution into a destructive impulse. Góngora's response to the new space is to compete with it, and failing to attain the absolute, to destroy it. His experiments with temporal and spatial boundaries are dazzling and solipsistic, as well as empty; and this emptiness culminates in the end of all time and space" ("Time," 155). Beverley, on the other hand, argues that Góngora has an ideological agenda: "The partisan ambition of the *Soledades* is to be a subjective 'mirror of princes' in the form of a prelude to a new sense of value and social harmony. The dilation of the parenthesis of pastoral exile represents the creation of a time of discourse necessary for the reformation of consciousness in which the spectacle of history can be reviewed at leisure and evaluated" (*Aspects*, 102). Where Chemris envisions apocalypse, Beverley sees apotheosis in an almost allegorical reading of the poems as the embodiment of Ovid's Ages of Metal with Marxian values (92). Contrast these arguments with those of Ferguson, who completely rejects the existence of narrative in the *Soledades*, objecting especially strongly to Lida de Malkiel's findings and asserting that Góngora strives to destroy historical time to create "un mundo ideal y estático" (an ideal and static world) ("Visión," 18). Antonio Vilanova discusses the episodic organization of the poems ("El peregrino de amor en las *Soledades* de Góngora," 3:434–35). Such

widely divergent views on structural, temporal, and spatial organization give some idea of how difficult it is to achieve some sort of consensus regarding the most basic aspects of the poems.

21. See Quintero, *Poetry;* M. S. Collins, "Antiquity," 19–29; and M. S. Collins, "Crucible," 197–213, on Góngora's plays for more on their curious, hybrid nature. In typically paradoxical fashion, *Las firmezas de Isabela,* set in Toledo, and *El doctor Carlino,* set in an unnamed city of Andalucía, are more challenging to visualize and imagine spatially than the *Soledades.* Góngora also seems to have maximized in the poems the inherently inclusive quality of the Spanish *comedia,* with the mix of tragic and comic elements, emphasis on plot and lyricism, incorporation of singing and dancing, and evolution toward more complex stagecraft and spectacle.

22. I am greatly indebted to Frances A. Yates's *Art of Memory* in this chapter in general and in this section in particular. Her book provides the basis for my analysis of the function of "memory" in the *Soledades.* For more on the origins of the art of memory and the conflation of memory and imagination, see "The Three Latin Sources for the Classical Art of Memory," chap. 1, 1–26; and "The Art of Memory in Greece: Memory and the Soul," chap. 2, 27–49. Consult "The Art of Memory in the Middle Ages," chap. 3, 50–81; and "Mediaeval Memory and the Formation of Imagery," chap. 4, 82–104, for more on the Thomist precepts of memory and the impact of the art on meditational and devotional practices. On the art of memory, Hermetic philosophy, and Camillo's theater, see "Renaissance Memory: The Memory Theatre of Giulio Camillo," chap. 6, 129–59; "Camillo's Theatre and the Venetian Renaissance," chap. 7, 160–72; and "Giordano Bruno: The Secret of Shadows," chap. 9, 199–230.

De la Flor, "La compañía de Jesús: Imágenes y memoria," chap. 3 in *Teatro,* 103–13, discusses the incorporation of the art of memory into the *Spiritual Exercises* and the devotional practices of numerous religious orders. Following Yates, de la Flor mentions Saint Thomas Aquinas and Saint Augustine as the principal authoritative sources that inspired and justified the praxis of composition of place, noting as well the tendency to merge the faculties of memory and imagination beneath the rubric "memory." Thus, memory signified both remembrance of the past and the art of conjuring mental images relevant to past, present, and future, which in turn parallels the exercise of memory (past), understanding (present), and will (future) (106).

My heartfelt thanks to the fellows of UNC's Institute for the Arts and Humanities of spring 1991 for encouraging me to pursue this subject, especially to John Headley and Gerald Strauss, who suggested this line of inquiry.

23. Beverley notes the molding of natural energy to serve human needs and wants fruitfully (*Aspects,* 34–35). I think Hermetic philosophy is present as well. Góngora suggests that there is a magical, spiritual link among the inhabitants of the bucolic world, their labor, and products. Their ties to the divine order seem purer, more direct, almost as if divine power passes from the upper world, through their souls, and into their work, harvest, and artifacts—animating the universe in Hermetic fashion.

24. Saint Thomas Aquinas, *De Memoria et Reminiscentia,* 200.

25. Martz, *Paradise,* 23–24, 47–48; and Jones, "Neoplatonism," 2. C. Colin Smith challenges Jones's characterization of nature in the *Soledades* as Platonic ("An Approach to Góngora's *Polifemo,*" 235–38). Jones replies in "Góngora and Neoplatonism Again" (117–20).

26. Water imagery, metaphors, and analogies remain one of the most beautiful and important, but virtually unstudied, aspects of this work. See Philippe Berger, "L'eau dans *Les*

Solitudes," 11–21. Jones describes the *Soledades* as "the course of a sort of river of abundant life in which all living things are swept along" ("Neoplatonism," 14).

27. This appears to be a particular preoccupation of Góngora's, as it supplies much of the dramatic tension, such as it is, in *Las firmezas de Isabela* (see M. S. Collins, "Crucible"). However, the topic also marks the poet as simply a man of his time, given that the conflict between rational and affective faculties was a major subject of debate throughout the seventeenth century, which laid the foundation for modern science.

28. Yates, *Art of Memory,* 229. H. Berger captures the project of those who embraced the Platonic philosophy of the occult (*Second,* 203).

29. Alonso's essay "La simetría bilateral," in *Estudios,* focuses on this aspect of Gongorine style (117–73).

30. Robert Jammes notes the use of hypallage and then cites Díaz de Rivas, who explains the mix of colors as a poetic representation of *una calabriada,* a blend of red and white wines (*Soledades,* 376).

31. Jones, "Poetic Unity," 197.

32. Vilanova, "El peregrino," 421–60; and Jürgen S. Hahn, *The Origins of the Baroque Concept of "Peregrinatio,"* provide excellent background information on the literary antecedents of Góngora's pilgrim and the concept of pilgrimage itself. Hahn, referring to the many dimensions of *peregrinatio* in the *Soledades,* observes: "As in the *peregrina historia* the concept of *peregrinatio* spans a whole spectrum of meanings: the concepts of the style, of the plot and of life itself are woven into one conceptual whole, testifying thereby to the extent to which the idea of *peregrinatio* permeated the thought process of the writer, and, in fact, of an entire era" (173). More recently, Kenneth Krabbenhoft analyzes Góngora's *Polifemo* and the pilgrim as the poles of a Stoic antithesis in which the *Soledades'* protagonist represents the Stoic wise man ("Góngora's Stoic Pilgrim," 1–12).

33. Bruce W. Wardropper examines the poet's strategies to draw readers into the text ("The Complexity of the Simple in Góngora's *Soledad Primera,*" 43–44). H. Berger identifies the emergence of an interlocutory figure with the creation of a third unfixed space, a middle ground, and a gesture that engages and complicates the relationship between fictional and real worlds, even as it underscores the imaginary nature of that fictional world (*Second,* 23). McAllister outlines the poet-pilgrim-reader complex ("Reader," 2–8).

34. Millé y Giménez, *Obras,* sonnet 258, 462. See Rosenmeyer, *Green;* and Kristeller, *Philosophy,* 298–99, on the Epicurean hero and his presence in the pastoral. Stanley E. Fish addresses the Augustinian notion of self-improvement (*Self-Consuming Artifacts: The Experience of Seventeenth-Century Literature,* 20–23).

35. Note the senses Saint Augustine elects specifically to mention in the *Confessions:* "If I am to reach him, it must be through my soul. . . . By it I not only give life to my body but also give it the power of perceiving things by its senses. God gave me this faculty when he ordered my eyes not to hear but to see and my ears not to see but to hear. And to each of the other senses he assigned its own place and its own function" (213). Shortly afterward in book 10, Augustine asserts, "All these sensations are retained in the great storehouse of the memory" in the form of images (214–15). He also states: "Even when I am in darkness and in silence I can, if I wish, picture colours in my memory" (215). Much of book 10 is, of course, an exposition of the Augustinian art of memory. For more on Saint Augustine's concepts of the function of the senses, the relationship between outer world and inner self, and the epistemological and spiritual quest for knowledge, Truth, and God, consult Brian Stock, *Augustine the Reader: Meditation, Self-Knowledge, and the Ethics of Interpretation,* 1–19, 230–75.

36. Weinberg, *History*, 1:44–45.

37. For more on poetry and painting as sister arts, consult Rensselaer Lee, *Ut Pictura Poesis: The Humanistic Theory of Painting*, 3–9, 13–16; Jean Hagstrum, *The Sister Arts: The Tradition of Literary Pictorialism and English Poetry from Dryden to Gray*, 3–10, 45; and Shearman, *Mannerism*, 30–39.

38. The six paintings that bear the title of *Poesie* share the same poetic source of inspiration, Ovid's *Metamorphoses: Danaë, Venus and Adonis, Perseus and Andromeda, Diana and Actaeon, Diana and Callisto,* and *The Rape of Europa.* Titian started but never completed two other canvases: *Medea and Jason* and *The Death of Actaeon.* The future Philip II apparently embraced the age's enthusiasm for Ovid's masterpiece. See Harold E. Wethey for more on this series of paintings ("The *Poesie* for Philip II," chap. 5 in *The Mythological and Historical Paintings*, 3:71–84), and Marcia L. Welles for a succinct overview of Ovid's presence in Spain of the Golden Age (*Arachne's Tapestry: The Transformation of Myth in Seventeenth-Century Spain*, 3–11).

Jonathan Brown observes that Spanish painting of the Golden Age consists primarily of religious subjects, portraiture, and still lifes. Mythological subjects, genre scenes, and landscapes also appeared in collections, but were usually painted in Italy or Flanders. Spanish painters did not travel as much as their peers from other countries, but they did have access to prints, which kept them abreast of the trends elsewhere in Europe (*The Golden Age of Painting in Spain*, 4).

39. Brown, *Golden*, 130–32.

40. Murray Krieger discusses stopping the flow of time in poetry ("The Ekphrastic Principle and the Still Movement of Poetry; or, *Laokoön* Revisited," 107). Consult Howard Hibbard on the lutenist portraits (*Caravaggio*, 31–39).

41. Jammes, *Soledades*, 65–73, 544, 546.

42. Lee, *Pictura*, 4–5, 58; and Hagstrum, *Sister*, 11–12, discuss parallels between descriptive poetry and the visual arts. E. H. Gombrich analyzes the emergence of still-life painting ("Tradition and Expression in Western Still Life," 101–2).

43. For more on the understudied subject of Spanish still lifes, consult William B. Jordan and Peter Cherry, *Spanish Still Life from Velázquez to Goya.* Chap. 1, "The Still Life in Spain: Origins and Themes," offers an excellent introduction (13–25). Brown discusses Castilian familiarity with Flemish and Italian painting at the start of the Hapsburg rule of Spain (*Golden*, 36–38). Brown also addresses the topic of landscape painting in Spain (206, 210–11, 227–28). See Richard A. Turner for more on the type of Italian landscape painting probably best known in Golden Age Spain ("Venetian Landscapes," chap. 6 in *The Vision of Landscape in Renaissance Italy*, 107–32). Thinking of the ruins of isolated buildings that dot the *Soledades'* countryside, it is interesting to note that such subjects were very much in vogue in Italian landscape painting. See Turner, "In Ruinous Perfection," chap. 8 in ibid., 153–74, for more on this topic.

44. Shearman identifies the obsession with the work of art as "an enduring virtuoso performance" with Mannerism (*Mannerism*, 44). Gates's excellent, seminal article "Góngora's *Polifemo* and *Soledades* in Relation to Baroque Art" applies Wölfflin's principles of the baroque to the poet's masterpieces (61–77). For an approach to ekphrasis that emphasizes the tensions and conflicts between words and images, as opposed to their rapprochement in imitation, read James A. W. Heffernan, *Museum of Words: The Poetics of Ekphrasis from Homer to Ashbery.* Mario Praz's classic *Mnemosyne: The Parallel between Literature and the Visual Arts* still provides an excellent introduction to such comparative studies. Hagstrum

links greater emphasis on light with growing interest in Platonic beauty and illumination (*Sister,* 50). Brown discusses the Carducho brothers and Bernardo Cardinal Sandoval y Rojas (*Golden,* 90–100). I am engaging in a bit of speculation over the cardinal's connection to Góngora's advancement at court, but you will recall from Chapter 1 that Góngora participated in the 1616 Toledo festival in honor of Nuestra Señora del Sagrario and the next year moved to the court.

45. Gates, "Góngora's *Polifemo* and *Soledades,*" 61–62, 64–68, discusses materialization and massification in the *Polifemo* and *Soledades,* commenting on the latter work: "The repeated references to flowers and fruits, bees and birds give to the *Soledades* the ornate, massive quality which recalls baroque façades. At other times 'the fractional' view of fruits and animals reminds one of Caravaggio's interest in picturing still life and of the famous *bodegones* of Spanish baroque painters" (67–68).

46. Gwynne Edwards, "The Theme of Nature in Góngora's *Soledades,* 234–38; and Michael J. Woods, "Man and Nature," chap. 6 in *The Poet and the Natural World in the Age of Góngora,* 146–75, discuss the merging of the human and the natural in the poems.

47. Lee examines the notion of expressive power in the sister arts (*Pictura,* 23, 60). My primary sources for information on Caravaggio, El Greco, and the Counter Reformation redirection of art are Hibbard, *Caravaggio;* and Brown, "El Greco," chap. 3 in *Golden,* 68–88. Caravaggio's *Entombment* and *Madonna di Loreto* were painted as altarpieces and, as such, would have played a central, dramatic role in the mass, illustrating parts of the liturgy and signaling to the worshiper that "this is the spot where you should contemplate the mystery and meaning of Christ's life"—perhaps serving as well as a visual counterpart or aid to the meditational exercises of the day (Hibbard, *Caravaggio,* 174–86). According to Brown, the little boy who points to the funeral in the *Orgaz* masterpiece informs spectators to pay attention to the didactic message depicted (*Golden,* 82–83). Gates likens the poet's use of a first-person speaker to the interlocutory figures in baroque painting (and, I would add, to anything or anyone in the intermediary imaginative space) ("Góngora's *Polifemo* and *Soledades,*" 64). Hibbard discusses Augustinian influence as a possible explanation for Caravaggio's interest in hands, mentioning Saint Augustine's reference to the Holy Spirit as the finger of God and Christ's reference to the finger of God in Luke 11:20 (*Caravaggio,* 100–102). Mary Ann Caws, "Look and Gesture," chap. 4 in *The Eye in the Text: Essays on Perception, Mannerist to Modern,* 49–69; and Mirollo, "Hand and Glove: The *bella mano* and the *caro guanto,*" chap. 4 in *Mannerism,* 125–59, analyze hands and gestures as typical Mannerist motifs. The love of dramatic gesture also contributes to the staged emotionalism one finds in the *Soledades.* For more on *contrapposto* as a Mannerist characteristic that adds not only emotional tension but also dynamism to the work of art, see Shearman, *Mannerism,* 83; and Hibbard, *Caravaggio,* 67, 78, who note that the concept was extended in the High Renaissance to include the juxtaposition of various types of extremes: ages, manner, and light and dark. Many Gongorine contrasts would fit this expanded notion of *contrapposto:* the pilgrim and his elderly guide (*Soledad* I) and host (*Soledad* II) (age); the pilgrim and wedding guests and the bitter *serrano* (manner); the tenebrist march inland (light and dark), and so on.

48. Gates analyzes depth and dynamism in the *Soledades,* focusing on the poet's rendering of recessional space and his treatment of movement and metamorphosis ("Góngora's *Polifemo* and *Soledades,*" 68–71). On the serpentine shape, tension, dynamism, and decoration, see Shearman, *Mannerism,* 81–91; and Caws, "Reflections in a Rococo Eye: Arabesques and Serpentines," chap. 5 in *Eye,* 70–86.

49. On the shared ancient origin of music and poetry, and their subsequent divergence, consult John Hollander, "The Poem in the Ear," chap. 1 in *Vision and the Resonance: Two Senses of Poetic Form*, 3–43; and James Anderson Winn, "The Poet as Singer: The Ancient World," chap. 1 in *Unsuspected Eloquence: A History of the Relations between Poetry and Music*, 1–29. Winn discusses the tie between expressivity and structure (123–27), and the comparative treatises on music and poetry (189–93).

50. Winn, *Unsuspected*, 139.

51. On the revival of interest in music and poetry as sister arts during the Renaissance, and the birth of the madrigal, see Shearman, *Mannerism*, 92–93, 99–104; Winn, "The Rhetorical Renaissace," chap. 4 in *Unsuspected*, 122–93; and Alfred Einstein, "Origins of the Madrigal," chap. 2 in *The Italian Madrigal*, 1:116–245.

52. Winn, *Unsuspected*, 140–49.

53. The pilgrim's hiding in a hollow oak is an image reminiscent of the wild man in European literature. See Edward Dudley, "The Wild Man Goes Baroque," 115–39.

54. Einstein, *Italian*, 1:190.

55. Winn analyzes the debate over polyphony and the rise of opera (*Unsuspected*, 167–79).

56. Jones, "Neoplatonism," 2–3.

57. Jones (in ibid., 2–14) offers an excellent analysis of *musica mundana* in the *Soledades*, observing that Góngora follows the Neoplatonic tradition of Plotinus in which "[c]onflict and violence and death do not in any way disrupt the over-riding harmony of the universe" (13). On the origin and evolution of the concept of world harmony, see Leo Spitzer, *Classical and Christian Ideas of World Harmony: Prolegomena to an Interpretation of the Word "Stimmung,"* esp. 5–33, 108–38. Note the Augustinian view of God as a sort of *archimusicus* (32). The various types of lutes that are depicted so frequently in Renaissance portraiture (and in the *Soledades*) function as iconographic shorthand for the themes of cosmic harmony and the attuning of the human soul to divine music. C. S. Lewis describes the Platonic musical cosmology alluded to in *Soledad* II (612–25) (Wilson, II:603–16), when the very firmament responds to human melodies ("The Heavens," chap. 5 in *The Discarded Image: An Introduction to Medieval and Renaissance Literature*, 92–121).

58. Jones rightly states regarding death in the *Soledades*: "Compassionate Nature receives all things back into herself, and every death is compensated by a new birth. . . . Nothing, indeed, wholly, dies" ("Neoplatonism," 14). On the long-standing, pervasive presence of death in the pastoral, see Erwin Panofsky, "*Et in Arcadia Ego*: Poussin and the Elegiac Tradition," chap. 7 in *Meaning and the Visual Arts*, 295–320.

59. Iser, *Fictive*, 70, 83–84.

60. George Steiner, *Language and Silence: Essays on Language, Literature, and the Inhuman*, 37, 39. See Mazzeo on the "rhetoric of silence" ("St. Augustine's Rhetoric," 11, 15–16, 24–25).

61. Stock discusses the Augustinian reading model (*Augustine*, 1–2, 14–18). Egido discusses the poetics of silence ("La poética," 104). For more on the river as manifold symbol for logos, time, eloquence, and so on, consult David Quint, *Origin and Originality in Renaissance Literature: Versions of the Source*, 134–39; and John Hollander, "Spenser's Undersong," chap. 8; "The Footing of His Feet: A Long Line Leads to Another," chap. 9, both in *Melodious Guile: Fictive Pattern in Poetic Language*, 148–63, 164–79, respectively.

3. A Poetics of Alchemy

1. Michael J. Woods, *The Poet and the Natural World in the Age of Góngora*, 176–204; Kitty Scoular, *Natural Magic: Studies in the Presentation of Nature in English Poetry from Spenser to Marvell*, 10–11. On Aristotle, Longinus, and *admiratio*, consult Edward C. Riley, "Aspectos del concepto de *admiratio* en la teoría literaria del Siglo de Oro," 173–75; and Weinberg, *History*, 1:188–90.

2. On the commentaries on Horace, Robortello's interpretation of Aristotle, and Minturno's *De poeta*, see Weinberg, *History*, 1:150–55, 397, 2:737–43. Riley addresses El Pinciano and Cascales ("Aspectos," 175).

3. B. W. Ife, *Reading and Fiction in Golden-Age Spain: A Platonist Critique and Some Picaresque Replies*, 88.

4. Ibid., 87.

5. Ibid.

6. Scoular, *Natural*, 27–29; Woods, *Poet*, 165–75.

7. This much discussed passage originated with Virgil. See the Jammes edition for more on the various interpretations of these lines (226–29, 592–93). I remain convinced that Alcimedon's "invention" refers to the spoon, despite the apparent illogic of the statement.

This quotation offers a small detail of the poetic equivalent of still-life painting, which Colie compares to paradox: "From one perspective, the specific genres of still life and paradox can be seen to be very like, since both, in spite of their concern for precision and exactness in both delineation and expression, rise from such specific details into larger figures of thought, to preach lessons which provoke speculation and contemplation" (*Paradoxia*, 274–75).

8. Jones, "Neoplatonism," 2.

9. This passage has also generated considerable debate. See the Jammes edition regarding interpretation of these lines (212–15).

10. Richard Cody, *The Landscape of the Mind*, 8. For more on the classical origins of this debate, see Edward William Tayler, "Classical Backgrounds," chap. 2 in *Nature and Art in Renaissance Literature*, 38–71, esp. 69 on the triumph of nature over art.

11. Colie, *Resources*, 112–13; Cody, *Landscape*, 12. On the Renaissance discussion of art and nature, see Tayler, "Renaissance Uses of Art and Nature," chap. 1 in *Nature*, 11–37, esp. 29, 36. Praz comments on the Western tradition that likens artistic virtuosity to the rarities of nature: "[A]nother standard prevailed in the appreciation of works of art: the skill of execution, which related a work of art to the other rarities and curiosities of nature. (We must bear in mind that in the early museums, the *Wunderkammern*, natural wonders such as ostrich eggs, coconuts, fossils, and bezoar stones were exhibited side by side with gold and silver artifacts and paintings and sculptures.)" (*Mnemosyne*, 64). Góngora's works indicate his affinity for just such an aesthetic of the exceptional and unusual, whether wrought by nature or the human hand.

12. Elias L. Rivers, "The Pastoral Paradox of Natural Art," 140–44; Jones, "Poetic Unity," 190, 194. At first glance, the examples Jones provides seem to support his case, but he omits all evidence that opposes his thesis, including the obvious "La admiración que al arte se le debe" (Jammes, II:706) (The admiration that is due to art [Wilson, II:691]), which I quoted earlier in this chapter. A Gongorine blanket condemnation of art is not supported by the text, but a qualified one based on certain moral judgments most definitely

is. Jones's overstatement is easily understandable considering that his 1954 article counters the prevailing viewpoint of the time predicated on Dámaso Alonso's description of the *Soledades* as "pure poetry" with no reference to the external world and no transcendent meaning. With deconstructionist readings of the poems such as those of Lorna Close, Paul Julian Smith, and others, twentieth-century criticism of the *Soledades* seems to have come full circle just as the twenty-first century begins.

13. Wardropper, "Complexity," 41, 43, 48–49; Edwards, "Theme," 231–43; Woods, *Poet,* 157–58, 171; Beverley, *Aspects,* 100. I do not share Edwards's view of the hawking scene as sinister and as a climactic condemnation of the court: "For the birds of prey, natural predators, are trained now by men to kill at their bidding and, moreover, for their entertainment: The violence which exists in Nature is exploited by humans, not through necessity but for their own selfish ends. In this final picture of 'civilized' man Góngora imputes to him the charge not only of ravaging Nature but of causing Nature to ravage itself further" (242). Góngora wrote with the sensibility of a seventeenth-century aristocrat, presenting the hawking scene as a magnificent pageant and a spectacle of colors and light and of varied textures, sights, and sounds—a feast for the senses of the mind.

Beverley brings a different ideological perspective to the debate, placing the art-nature dynamic at the service of social change and using biographical data to ascribe a reform-minded political agenda to Góngora.

14. Longinus, *On Sublimity,* 8, 42.
15. Ibid., 8, 27, 33–34.
16. Ibid., 29.
17. Jones, "Poetic Unity," 196–98; Mary Gaylord, "Metaphor and Fable in Góngora's *Soledad primera,* 97–112.
18. Longinus, *On Sublimity,* 43. On the *griphos,* see Rosenmeyer, *Green,* 177–78. Beverley comments on the net conceit: "His tropes, the *silva* itself, are, like the nets of fishermen in the *Soledad segunda,* a 'fábrica escrupulosa, y aunque incierta / siempre murada, pero siempre abierta'" (*Aspects,* 122 n. 9). Norbert Von Prellwitz, "Góngora: El vuelo audaz del poeta," 28, similarly views the net as a metaphor for Gongorine poetics, which he likens to a dialectic between artifice and nature traceable in the poet's rich, varying treatments of the myths of Icarus and Phaëthon: "La batalla ideológica que se combate alrededor del vuelo poético de Góngora, implica una dialéctica entre naturaleza y artificio, entre norma e inovación entre imitación y emulación. . . . En el fondo se trata del mismo conflicto que se puede observar en la evolución de la poesía de Góngora, y que se manifiesta también en la visión ambivalente de las fábulas de Faetón y de Icaro" (32). (The ideological battle that is fought over the poetic flight of Góngora implies a dialectic between nature and artifice, between convention and innovation, between imitation and emulation . . . . At the core it is about the same conflict that is also manifested in the ambivalent vision of the fables of Phaëthon and Icarus.) On paradigms of opposition generating wonderment, see Scoular, *Natural,* 32; and Colie, *Paradoxia,* 10, 22.
19. Longinus, *On Sublimity,* 20, 38.
20. I realize some may disagree both with my translation of the title of Gracián's work and my use of "conceit," "metaphor," and "Gongorine metaphor" almost interchangeably. However, in exploring the rich implications of the parallels between emblem literature and the Gongorine metaphor, the very nature of the comparison between the verbal and the visual defies definitional restrictions, involving other types of rhetorical tropes in critical analysis. I have yet to see an entirely satisfactory translation of these words and certainly do not claim to meet that need.

Consult Joseph Anthony Mazzeo, "A Seventeenth-Century Theory of Metaphysical Poetry," 29–43; Mazzeo, "Metaphysical Poetry," 44–59; and Woods, "Understanding Gracián," chap. 1; "The Rival Theorists," chap. 2, both in *Gracián*, 3–17, 18–32, respectively. Woods has commendably increased appreciation of Góngora's mastery of a variety of rhetorical devices besides metaphor, stressing the poet's fondness for exploring the sometimes playfully fine line between the literal and the figurative. Woods's discussion of the terms *concepto* and *agudeza* illustrates the difficulties of defining and translating them (7–11). He defines "conceit" as "any manifestation of wit," noting "the lack of any suitable alternative term to 'conceit' in English for referring to an *agudeza* which is not based on complex metaphor" (7).

21. García Lorca, "La imagen," 97, 98, 100.

22. Ibid., 102.

23. Ibid., 120, 122.

24. Alonso, *Estudios*, 87, 577; Woods, *Gracián*, 115–16. Woods discusses the issue of "pictorialist" versus rhetorical approaches to metaphor in "Poetry and the Senses," chap. 2; and "The Uses of Description," chap. 3, both in *Poet*, 22–40, 41–82, respectively.

25. Nicolae Babuts, "Text: Origins and Reference," 71, 73–74.

26. Sebastián de Covarrubias Orozco, *Tesoro de la lengua castellana o española*, 460. On the seventeenth-century connection of emblems with set designs and the decorative arts, see Peter M. Daly, *Literature in the Light of the Emblem: Structural Parallel between Emblem and Literature in the Sixteenth and Seventeenth Centuries*, 134, 150–66.

27. Emblems also figure in John McCaw's analysis of the *Soledades* (*Transforming*, 17–29, 166). Héctor Ciocchini, *Góngora y la tradición de los emblemas*; and Antonio Pérez Lasheras, "Imágenes emblemáticas gongorinas: La *Fábula de Píramo y Tisbe*," 3:927–38, also focus on the emblem tradition in works by Góngora.

28. Covarrubias, *Tesoro*, 460–61; Praz, *Studies*, 23–25; Aquilino Sánchez Pérez, *La literatura emblemática española (Siglos XVI y XVII)*, 14–15, 21–22.

29. Covarrubias, *Tesoro*, 461.

30. Praz, *Studies*, 138; Peter M. Daly, *Emblem Theory: Recent German Contributions to the Characterization of the Emblem Genre*, 40.

31. Sánchez Pérez, *Literatura*, 26.

32. Karl-Ludwig Selig, "Gracián and Alciato's *Emblemata*, 5–10. My primary sources of information on Alciati and his influence on the Iberian peninsula are Konrad Hoffmann, "Alciato and the Historical Situation of Emblematics," 1–45; Pedro F. Campa, "Diego López's *Declaración magistrale de las emblemas de Alciato*: A Seventeenth-Century Spanish Humanist's View," 223–48; Sánchez Pérez, *Literatura*, 11–88; and Daly, *Emblem Theory*, 59–67, 80–92.

33. On the Neoplatonic concept of the function of the image, see Gombrich, *Symbolic Images*, 172–75; and Daly, *Literature*, 74, 84–94, 113–15.

34. On emblems, conceits, and the idea of metaphorical system, see Denis L. Drysdall, "The Emblem according to the Italian *Impresa* Theorists," 22–32; Tania C. Tribe, "Word and Image in Emblematic Painting," 247–71; and Daly, *Literature*, 66–102. Daly notes the strong ties between emblems and meditational literature, as does Mario Praz in his *Studies*.

35. David N. Taylor, "Góngora's Sonnet 'Acredita la esperanza con historias sagradas,'" 36.

36. Roland Barthes, "Rhetoric of the Image," 25–40. On the components of the emblem, consult Daly, *Literature*, 6–8; and Praz, *Studies*, 170–71.

37. Andrés Alciato, *Emblemas*, 127.

38. T. H. White, *The Bestiary, a Book of Beasts, Being a Translation from a Latin Bestiary of the Twelfth Century*, 125–29.

39. Ibid., 170–73.

40. The sources of the popular sayings are Juana G. Campos and Ana Barella, *Diccionario de refranes*, 152, 300; and Luis Junceda, *Diccionario de refranes*, xxx. For the Alciati emblem, see Alciato, *Emblemas*, 152–53.

41. In her fascinating article on bird imagery in the *Soledades*, Nadine Ly discusses the poems' identification of the phoenix and the vulture with the cycle of memory ("La république ailée dans les *Solitudes*," 174–77).

42. See Woods for a more general analysis of Gongorine literalization of the figurative ("Between the Literal and the Figurative," chap. 5 in *Gracián*, 58–73). Rosalie Colie notes that the rhypographer provides a double image of landscape and the human portraying the human form as a natural world (*Paradoxia*, 63). She also observes that still-life painting was identified with rhopography, the depiction of trivial things, and comments on the paradoxical aspect of still-life painting, which immortalizes the mutable (276–77). Finally, Colie asserts that certain forms of epistemology tend to be expressed as ocular experience (284). This is certainly true of Augustinian Neoplatonism and clearly characterizes the world of the *Soledades*.

Beverley, *Aspects*, 2–3, 91–93, emphasizes the economic implications of such passages: "The places [the pilgrim] encounters in the *Soledades* confront him with images of *natural* economies and societies where men and women live in close intimacy with manual labor and with the variety of nature, where production is for use rather than personal profit, where equality and generosity still reign" (3).

43. Wilson's translation of *dulce vena* as "gentle vein" is predicated on Dámaso Alonso's interpretation of the passage. I concur with Jammes's edition (420–23), which sees *dulce* as a qualifier of *agua* (water), which thus is to be read *vena [de agua] dulce* (vein of fresh water).

44. For more on Arcimboldo's poetic qualities, consult Roland Barthes, "Arcimboldo, or Magician and Rhétoriqueur," 129–48, who states: "[L]ike a baroque poet, Arcimboldo exploits the 'curiosities' of language, plays on synonymy and homonymy. His painting has a linguistic basis, his imagination is, strictly speaking, poetic: it does not create signs, it combines them, permutes them, deflects them—precisely what the practitioner of language does" (131). Barthes also comments that "[w]ithout resorting to a single letter, Arcimboldo nonetheless constantly verges on the graphic experience. His friend and admirer Canon Comanini saw the composite heads as an emblematic writing . . . ; between the two levels of the Arcimboldesque language (that of the face and that of the signifying features which compose it) there is the same relation of *friction*, a grating relation, which we find in Leonardo da Vinci between the order of signs and the order of images" (135).

The quotation about Arcimboldo is from Thomas DaCosta Kaufmann, "Arcimboldo's Serious Jokes: 'Mysterious but Long Meaning,'" 72. On Arcimboldo in general, see Evans, *Rudolf II*, 165–66, 173–74; Thomas DaCosta Kaufmann, "Arcimboldo's Serious Jokes," 59–86; Kaufmann, *The School of Prague: Painting at the Court of Rudolf II*, 29–30, 66–70, 164–72; Kaufmann, *The Mastery of Nature: Aspects of Art, Science, and Humanism in the Renaissance*, 100–135; and the collection *The Arcimboldo Effect: Transformations of the Human Face from the Sixteenth to the Twentieth Century*, which contains essays representing varied approaches to the artist's work and a comprehensive Arcimboldo bibliography.

45. On the *Cook,* see Barthes, "Arcimboldo," 131–33. Soufas identifies the rhypographic rendition of the Cyclops with the melancholia that sometimes affects artists and can lead to dehumanizing outbursts of violence (*Melancholy,* 4–8, 139–42).

46. Giancarlo Maiorino, *The Portrait of Eccentricity: Arcimboldo and the Mannerist Grotesque,* 68.

47. On the poems about the portraits, and these witty, imperial artworks, consult Kaufmann, "Arcimboldo's Serious Jokes," 60–61; Kaufmann, *Mastery,* 100–135; and Kaufmann, *School,* 66–70.

48. Kaufmann, *Mastery,* 129–35, discusses Ovid's tales of Vertumnus. Welles, *Arachne's,* 39–61, analyzes Ovid's influence on Góngora, as does David Garrison, *Góngora and the "Pyramus and Thisbe" Myth from Ovid to Shakespeare,* 17–50. Waley focuses on mythology in the *Soledades* ("Some Uses," 193–209); the Waley quotation is from 197–98. Elias Rivers discusses the *Soledades'* revitalization of conventions ("Nature, Art, and Science in Spanish Poetry of the Renaissance," 260–61).

49. Waley, "Some Uses," 201. Sara Mack observes the tendency to label Ovid "merely a clever stylist, a first-rate manipulator of words," who possesses superficial brilliance (*Ovid,* 166). Góngora resembles Ovid in the forging of language that self-consciously draws attention to itself, becoming a sort of linguistic performer. One could easily substitute the Spanish poet's name for that of Ovid in Mack's statement: "In every context, whether Ovid is being playful or serious, his language is designed to draw attention to itself in a way that Vergil's never does. Hyperbole, paradox, oxymoron, zeugma, antithesis, parenthesis, irrelevant or unnecessary comments, changes of direction, incongruities between subject and style—these are hallmarks of Ovid's style; all focus our attention on *how* what is said is said, and thus on the language itself" (153). Note, too, that Kaufmann refers to Arcimboldo's royal, composite protraits as imperial metamorphoses that, according to Fonteo, one of the painter's contemporaries, have their roots in Ovid's *Metamorphoses* (*Mastery,* 114–15). Consult Rudolph Schevill, *Ovid and the Renascence in Spain,* 66, 92, 147–48, on Ovid and Golden Age Spain; and Jean Seznec, *The Survival of the Pagan Gods: The Mythological Tradition and Its Place in Renaissance Humanism and Art,* 276–77.

50. Beryl Rowland, *Birds with Human Souls: A Guide to Bird Symbolism,* 170.

51. The 1925 quotation refers to José Ortega y Gasset, *La deshumanización del arte,* 36–37; the 1914 quote refers to his "Ensayo de estética a manera de prólogo," 170. The phrase "emblematic world view" is from William B. Ashworth Jr., "Natural History and the Emblematic World View," 312.

52. Citation on the definition of natural magic is from Lynn Thorndike, *A History of Magic and Experimental Science,* 7:272. See also Brian B. Copenhaver on the ambiguity and vagueness surrounding the term *natural magic* ("Natural Magic, Hermetism, and Occultism in Early Modern Science," 261–301). Woods, the expert on wonder in Góngora's poetry, analyzes the poet's emphasis on variety ("Nature's Plenty," chap. 4 in *Poet,* 83–105). He explores the parallels between Góngora's ability to inspire *admiratio,* seventeenth-century theories of wit (Tesauro, Gracián), and natural magic ("An Age of Wonderment," chap. 7 in *Poet,* 176–204). See also Mazzeo on Tesauro's interpretation of poetic wit and metaphor ("A Seventeenth-Century Theory," 29–43; and "Metaphyscial Poetry," 44–59). Scoular discusses a "habit of wonder" typical of the contemplative attitude characteristic of English readers of the sixteenth and seventeenth centuries, keeping in mind the popularity of emblem books and devotional literature at the time (*Natural Magic,* 10–11). She also notes that the qualities of variety, mystery, and flux are linked to the apprehension of wonder in

the arts and the natural world (4–5). Observe that the *Soledades* express variety, enigma, and flux, and display a preference for topics and imagery pertaining to metamorphoses and the design and style of emblems and enigmas, combining in one work the tendencies of long and short poems.

Note also the pivotal role of Ficino in generating great interest in magic during the Renaissance. Copenhaver summarizes the theoretical, empirical, and doxographic sources confirming Ficino's belief in natural magic ("Natural Magic," 270–81). See, too, Wayne Shumaker on Ficino's influence (*Natural Magic and Modern Science: Four Treatises, 1590–1657*, 4–11, 18–22), and, most important, D. P. Walker, who analyzes Ficino's music-spirit theory and what he characterizes as the tradition of Neoplatonic magic as exemplified by Ficino (*Spiritual and Demonic Magic from Ficino to Campanella*, 3–84).

53. Consult the following on the origins of alchemy, its revival, and expansion in the second half of the sixteenth century: Thorndike, *History*, 5:532–49, 617–51; Jacques Van Lennep, *Art et alchimie: Étude de l'iconographie hermétique et de ses influences*, 13–31; and Gareth Roberts, *The Mirror of Alchemy: Alchemical Ideas and Images in Manuscripts and Books from Antiquity to the Seventeenth Century*, 12–43. See Roberts for more on the elaborately metaphorical language of alchemy, which freely appropriates and amalgamates other forms of discourse, and shows fondness for obscurity, enigma, and paradox (66–91). He concludes: "[A]lchemists inhabited a world where things were not only signified by their likes, but also by their opposites. It was a world where nothing was really unlike anything else" (91). Van Lennep and Roberts provide excellent information on the rich iconographic legacy of alchemy.

54. Torreblanca quoted in Thorndike, *History*, 7:326. On Golden Age Spain, natural magic, and alchemy, consult Thorndike, *History*, 6:409–10, 413, 428–29, 7:323–37; and David C. Goodman, *Power and Penury: Government, Technology, and Science in Philip II's Spain*, 1–19. On Rudolf II and occultism, see Evans, "Rudolf and the Occult Arts," chap. 6 in *Rudolf II*, 196–242. Edward Dudley has reminded me that Góngora must have studied in the old library at the University of Salamanca, which featured a Fernando Gallego ceiling filled with astrological signs.

55. On the basic goals and practices of alchemy, see Harry J. Sheppard, "European Alchemy in the Context of a Universal Definition, 13–17; Van Lennep, *Art*, 15–20; and Roberts, *Mirror*, 44–63. Quotation is from Sheppard, "European," 16–17.

56. Rowland, *Birds*, 79.

57. The Ascalaphus myth appears two other times in *Soledad* II: Jammes, 791–98; Wilson, 778–85; and Jammes, 891–92; Wilson, 877–78. The contexts emphasize different aspects of the rich emblem lore associated with the owl, lore analyzed by Rowland (*Birds*, 115–20). In the first instance, the owl is described as a large, dark, clumsy bird, bringing up the rear in the graceful, elegant procession of hawks, casting an unexpected, dark pall over the brilliant display. In the second case, the golden eyes attract greedy birds and lure them to their deaths, thus strengthening the association between this nocturnal fowl and mortality.

4. The Masque of the Imagination

1. Colie, *Resources*, 13. On art and nature working in tandem in the Italian Renaissance gardens, see Claudia Lazzaro, *Italian*, 131; and John Dixon Hunt, *Gardens and the*

Picturesque: Studies in the History of Landscape Architecture, 3–4. Krabbenhoft has recently stressed the Stoic presence in the *Soledades* ("Góngora's Stoic Pilgrim," 1–2). Along similar lines, Mark Morford, "The Stoic Garden," 151–75, notes that in terms of garden aesthetics, Renaissance Neostoics espoused Seneca's viewpoint that "[o]ne must indulge the mind and from time to time give it relaxation to strengthen and nourish it. One must walk in paths in the open, so that the mind can enlarge and raise itself breathing the fresh air under the open sky" (159). Yet, Morford also notes slippage in the Renaissance tendency to meld Epicurean pleasure and Stoic virtue in garden aesthetics (160–61). Eugenio Battisti, *"Natura Artificiosa* to *Natura Artificialis,"* 1–36, describes Renaissance Italian gardens as a reconciliation of the Epicurean celebration of natural beauty with the Stoic perfection of an artfully crafted landscape: "The Humanists attempted to resolve this contrast and succeeded in giving not only geometrical order but a truly architectural quality to the wonders of Italian nature" (35–36). Consult Anthony Close for the classical sources of the concept of a third nature, which explains in large part the mixture of Stoic and Epicurean ideals in the Renaissance approach to gardens, as well as the cultivation of a hybrid space of artful nature and natural art ("Commonplace Theories of Art and Nature in Classical Antiquity and in the Renaissance," 163–84, 467–86).

2. Lazzaro, *Italian*, 47; John Dixon Hunt, "'Loose Nature' and the 'Garden Square': The Gardenist Background for Marvell's Poetry," 334. Interestingly, the Este family was descended from the Spanish royal family.

3. Hunt notes: "We have just surveyed what might be called the writing of a site, the inscription of meaning—sometimes with actual words, but just as often by a dumb visual language—onto some segment of terrain. If such a description of the cultural making of gardens is allowed, then it follows that what has been written may also be read, at least if we take the trouble to learn the language" (*Gardens*, 13).

On the powerful connection between garden iconography and various literary traditions, see Elisabeth B. MacDougall, *"Ars Hortulorum:* Sixteenth-Century Garden Iconography and Literary Theory in Italy," 47–59; MacDougall, "Imitation and Invention: Language and Decoration in Roman Renaissance Gardens," 119–34; Lazzaro, *Italian*, 2–3; Hunt, "'Loose,'" 338–45; and Roy Strong, *The Renaissance Garden in England*. Evelyne Martín-Hernández's "Les *Solitudes* comme un jardin . . ." is a pioneering article comparing the *Soledades* to a formal Renaissance garden.

4. Battisti stresses that Renaissance gardens constitute a complex conceptual system with multiple meanings and levels of signification (*"Natura,"* 4–6). Richard Patterson discusses the identification of the garden with the rebirth of the academy, noting that Sir Francis Bacon considered the garden a substitute for the university as the place in which to acquire knowledge ("The 'Hortus Palatinus' at Heidelberg and the Reformation of the World," part 2, "Culture as Science," 182–86). For more on the garden of the Medici Villa at Careggi and its association with humanist learning, see Georgina Masson, *Italian Gardens*, 7, 56–58.

5. On Vasari and Montaigne's respective reactions to the Medici gardens, see Masson, *Italian*, 78–79, 137. Elisabeth B. MacDougall and Naomi Miller, *Fons Sapientiae: Garden Fountains in Illustrated Books, Sixteenth–Eighteenth Centuries*, xi–xii; Hunt, "'Loose,'" 333–34; and J. B. Bury, "Some Early Literary References to Italian Gardens," 17–24, discuss the dissemination of information about the formal Italian gardens to England and throughout Europe. Lazzaro, *Italian*, 3–4, 90; and Battisti, *"Natura,"* 10–11, examine the influence of Islamic Spain on Italy's water architecture, whereas Yasser Tabbaa describes the origin and symbolism of water in Islamic gardens ("Towards an Interpretation of the Use of Water in

Islamic Courtyards and Courtyard Gardens," 197–220). None of these analyses, of course, diminishes the impact of Hadrian's Villa on Italian garden aesthetics.

6. Henry Kamen, *Philip of Spain*, 184. Kamen uses the king's own words to indicate how much the monarch esteemed Aranjuez as a place of rest and relaxation (159, 161), constituting just one locale in an extensive system of new and renovated royal palaces and properties, described on 182–86. José Javier Rivera Blanco credits Juan Bautista de Toledo with bringing the Mannerist garden to Spain at Aranjuez, citing Naples's gardens of the Castelnuovo as the architect's source of inspiration (*Juan Bautista de Toledo y Felipe II: La implantación del clasicismo en España*, 123–83). Masson describes the design of even early-fourteenth-century Neapolitan gardens as far ahead of those of counterparts elsewhere in Italy (*Italian*, 52–53). Francisco Iñiguez Almech (140–54) offers a description of some of the Aranjuez garden's furnishings, including the surprise water jets that a disdainful, sophisticated Cosme de Medici found pedestrian and tiresome (151). Aranjuez's current website (http://www.arannet.com/aranjuez) provides an excellent historical and pictorial overview of the evolution of the palace and grounds, from its origins to the present.

7. Hunt, "'Loose,'" 336. For more on the arrangement of space in formal Renaissance gardens, consult MacDougall, *"Ars Hortulorum,"* 46; and Lazzaro, *Italian*, 70–71, 81.

8. Battisti addresses the integration of art and nature in landscape design (*"Natura,"* 14, 28–29). Lazzaro describes garden design's use of the lay of the land to best advantage (*Italian*, 70–72).

9. Hunt, "'Loose,'" 337.

10. MacDougall, "Imitation," 120; Lazzaro, *Italian*, 78–81.

11. MacDougall, "Imitation," 120; Hunt, "'Loose,'" 337.

12. Lazzaro, *Italian*, 13. On garden aviaries, see Patterson, "'Hortus,'" part 1, "The Iconography of the Garden," 97.

13. Lazzaro, *Italian*, 2–3, 48.

14. Ibid., 78–79.

15. William L. MacDonald and John A. Pinto, *Hadrian's Villa and Its Legacy*, 81–89.

16. Battisti credits Sannazaro's influence with the enthusiasm for ruins in the garden landscape (*"Natura,"* 29–30). Lazzaro, *Italian*, 118–30, puts forward a variety of interpretations of the Sacro Bosco, at one point emphasizing the witty, literary quality of the woods: "One of the ways in which this wood is unlike any other is that each of its elements, while related to the whole both visually and conceptually, also contains a conceit, a set of ideas conveyed through subtle plays and puns on both images and words, with specific reference to their context in contemporary usage. These conceits are the creation of an intelligent, witty, well-read, thoughtful, and passionate aristocrat, undoubtedly with the assistance of his learned friends, and they cannot be interpreted independent of the context of a sixteenth-century bosco with its associated ideas and traditional adornments" (124). One cannot help but notice the parallels between this particular aesthetic bias and the one apparent in the *Soledades*. See Waley on the parallels between Góngora's masterpiece and Sannazaro's *Arcadia* ("Some Uses," 193–95).

17. Masson, *Italian*, 137; Lazzaro, *Italian*, 142; Hunt, "'Loose,'" 342.

18. Lazzaro, *Italian*, 16–18, 133.

19. Tracy L. Ehrlich's study, "The Waterworks of Hadrian's Villa," offers an overview of water's aural and visual architecture at Hadrian's Villa, whereas Marcello Fagiolo, "Il significatio dell'acqua e la dialettica del giardino Pirro Ligorio e la «filosofia» della villa cinquecentesca," provides insight into the aquatic symbolism employed by Pirro Ligorio. David R. Coffin analyzes the elaborate symbolic system incorporated into the Este estate's

design by Ligorio (*The Villa D'Este at Tivoli*, 78–97). MacDonald and Pinto examine the waterworks and landscape architecture at Hadrian's Villa (*Hadrian's Villa*, 170–82); quotation is on 177–78. The authors later observe that Charles V's architect Pedro Machuca made considerable use of ideas from Hadrian's Villa in his Spanish designs, perhaps learning of them from Raphael's studies (272). For more on water as a unifying concept in Italian Renaissance landscape architecture, see Lazzaro, *Italian*, 86–90, 130–33. Masson, *Italian*, 137; and Coffin, *Villa*, 22–23, 94–95, describe the history and popularity of the Owl Fountain. In his edition of *Las firmezas de Isabela*, Robert Jammes notes that the curious device of Janelo is mentioned at least three times in the play. He includes an account of the machine by an awestruck contemporary, Ambrosio de Morales (283–85).

20. Lazzaro, *Italian*, 62, 162–65; MacDougall, "*Ars Hortulorum*," 56; Malgorzata Szafranska, "Philosophy of Nature and the Grotto in the Renaissance Garden," 76–85; and Marcello Fagiolo, "Il teatro dell'arte e della natura," 141, provide insight into the complex symbolism of aquatic landscaping, stressing the classical connection with poetic inspiration.

21. Lazzaro, *Italian*, 124–25, 131; Hunt, *Gardens*, 53–54, 117; Hunt, "'Loose,'" 333, 343–44; Shearman, *Mannerism*, 125; and MacDougall, "*Ars Hortulorum*," 46, describe the interactive engagement between visitor and third nature in formal gardens and the programming of itineraries into the gardenist experience. Coffin analyzes the symbolic journey at the Tivoli gardens that is based on the myth of Hercules (*Villa*, 78–85).

22. Martín-Hernández points out the theatrical configuration of space in the poems: "La configuration théâtrale de l'espace que l'on peut observer dans le répertoire monumental, 'coliseo, palestra, teatro,' employé à propos des jeux qui accompagnent les noces, peut être mise en parallèle avec celle de l'architecture des jardins" ("*Solitudes*," 185–86). (The theatrical configuration one can observe in the monumental repertoire, *coliseo* [coliseum], *palestra* [arena], *teatro* [theater], used in regard to the games accompanying the wedding, can be paralleled with that of garden architecture.)

23. Germain Bazin, *The Baroque: Principles, Styles, Modes, Themes*, 306; Lazzaro, *Italian*, 111; Hunt, "'Loose,'" 343; Hunt, *Gardens*, 54–55.

24. On the development of theaters in gardens, consult Battisti, "*Natura*," 14; and Hunt, *Gardens*, 53. Masson describes Villa Aldobrandini's nympheum and Villa Mondragone's water theater (*Italian*, 150–53). Brown and Elliott describe the Buen Retiro's theater (*Palace*, 207).

25. Ellen J. Esrock notes the connection between reading as visualization and Aristotle's notion of images (*The Reader's Eye: Visual Imaging as Reader Response*, 88). Esrock decries the emphasis in most contemporary literary theory on "the textual configuration of words" and condemns "the absence of talk about readerly imagery" as well as "the outright rejection of a role for visualization in reading" (78). She examines the logocentric bias of twentieth-century literary theory in "The Linguistic Turnabout," in *Reader's Eye*, 1–17. Christopher Collins discusses the notion of an inner stage of the mind in "Literacy and the Opening of the Inner Eye," chap. 1 in *Reading the Written Image: Verbal Play, Interpretation, and the Roots of Iconophobia*, 1–21.

26. The first quotation is from Rudolf Arnheim, "A Structure on Time and Space," 80; the second is from Arnheim, "A Plea for Visual Thinking," 147.

27. Arnheim speaks of the imagistic power of poetry ("Plea," 148), and compares poetry reading to painting analysis ("Language, Image, and Concrete Poetry," 94).

28. C. Collins defines peripheral and focal awareness (*Reading*, 106–7). He views reading as "*poiesis*," an act of making, or as a "performance of enactive interpretation" that "corre-

lates both author and reader," with the author using "the evolving text as a web (a *textum*) in which to catch and hold the sensations, memories, emotions, ideas, and options for action that constitute that unresolved complexity we call a 'mood,'" which the reader subsequently uses as "a means of discovering that complexity in oneself" (117, 118). Note the parallel between the notion of text as web and Góngora's metaphorical representation of the poetic text as a fishing net.

29. C. Collins discusses the reader's mind as a *theatron* (viewing place) (*Reading,* 171). See Hunt on the use of the masque idiom to describe gardenist experiences ("Loose," 343). Wotton is quoted by John Dixon Hunt and Peter Ellis, eds., *The Genius of the Place: The English Landscape Garden, 1620–1820,* 48.

30. Northrop Frye, "Romance as Masque," 156.

31. David Lindley, ed., *The Court Masque,* 1; Alastair Fowler, *Kinds of Literature: An Introduction to the Theory of Genres and Modes,* 60–61; Stephen Orgel, *The Illusion of Power: Political Theater in the English Renaissance,* 38; Jerzy Limon, *The Masque of Stuart Culture,* 7. For more on the hybrid nature of masque, consult Limon, *Masque,* 43–44, 50; Hagstrum, *Sister,* 88–95; and Seznec, *Survival,* 315–16. On Jonsonian masque and its cultural context, see Stephen Orgel, *The Jonsonian Masque;* Graham Parry, *The Golden Age Restor'd: The Culture of the Stuart Court, 1603–42;* Roy Strong, *Art and Power: Renaissance Festivals, 1450–1650;* Dolora Cunningham, "The Jonsonian Masque as a Literary Form," 108–24; and the classic studies of Enid Welsford, *The Court Masque: A Study in the Relationship between Poetry and the Revels;* and Allardyce Nicoll, *Stuart Masques and the Renaissance Stage.*

32. Welsford, *Court,* 97–98; Shearman, *Mannerism,* 104–12; and Strong, *Art,* 126–52, discuss the Italian origin of the masque. James M. Saslow, *The Medici Wedding of 1589: Florentine Festival as "Theatrum Mundi,"* provides a fascinating analysis of the Medici wedding as "the creation of material culture" (3).

33. For more on the development of the masque outside of Italy, see Welsford, *Court,* 151–66; and Strong, *Art,* 3–62, 98–125, 153–73. Frye presents the core of his comparison between romance and masque ("Romance," 156–67).

34. Strong, *Art,* 98–125, analyzes the emergence of the *ballet de cour;* as does Margaret McGowan, *L'Art du ballet de cour en France, 1581–1643,* 11–67, describing the elaborate staging and symbolism of *Le Ballet Comique de la Reine* (42–47).

35. Rennert, *Spanish,* 62–76; Shergold, *History,* 122–42; Shergold, "Court Plays and Pageantry to 1621," chap. 9 in ibid., 236–63; and Melveena McKendrick, *Theatre in Spain, 1490–1700,* 209–11, provide the basis for my synopsis of the history of the Spanish masque. Harry Sieber provides insight into Philip III's role as patron of the arts ("The Magnificent Fountain: Literary Patronage in the Court of Philip III," 85–116).

36. Compare Shergold, "The Court Theatre of Philip IV, 1622–1640," chap. 10 in *History,* 264–97; and Stephen Rupp, "Articulate Illusions: Art and Authority in Jonson's Masques and Some *Autos sacramentales* of Calderón de la Barca," 1–26, on the fate of the Spanish masque. McKendrick, "Theatre at Court," chap. 8; and "Theatre in the Street: The *Auto Sacramental,*" chap. 9, both in *Theatre,* 238–60, offers excellent background material for exploring the similarities between the conventions of the masque and those of the post-1611 court plays and *autos,* especially the works composed by Calderón. Brown and Elliott eloquently capture the spectacles at the Palace of the Buen Retiro (*Palace,* 199–213).

37. Limon, *Masque,* 31, 198, 199–200.

38. Ibid., 32. Critics have, of course, recognized for a long time the influence of the masque on more traditional forms. See Welsford for an early case in point ("The Influence of the Masque on Poetry," chap. 11 in *Court,* 302–23).

39. Jammes discusses the duke of Béjar, Alonso Diego López de Zúñiga y Sotomayor (1577–1619), on pp. 73–84 of his edition of the *Soledades*. Sieber looks at the duke of Béjar in the context of royal patronage, analyzing his failed quest to be named *cazador mayor* ("Magnificent," 85–91). L. J. Woodward examines imagery of hunting and walls in the poems ("Two Images in the *Soledades* of Góngora," 773–85).

40. Limon describes the events in a masque cycle (*Masque*, 107–8). Welsford identifies pastoral settings with the masque (*Court*, 318); quotation of affinity between pastoral and masque is from Walter M. Greg, *Pastoral Poetry and Pastoral Drama: A Literary Inquiry, with Special Reference to the Pre-Restoration Stage in England*, 370.

41. Hagstrum, *Sister*, 31–33, 88–89; Rosemond Tuve, "Image, Form, and Theme in a Mask," 115, 123–24.

42. Welsford, *Court*, 313; Tuve, "Image," 143.

43. Welsford, *Court*, 313.

44. Esrock, *Reader's Eye*, 196. Christopher Collins characterizes the "poet of perceptual imagery" and explains the dynamics of saccadic movement (*The Poetics of the Mind's Eye: Literature and the Psychology of Imagination*, 96, 97–98).

45. Ben Jonson, *The Complete Masques*, 75–76. A worthwhile endeavor that lies beyond the scope of this study is a stylistic comparison of Milton's *Comus* (1634) with the *Soledades*.

46. Limon, *Masque*, 64. For more on the king's relationship to court spectacles in England and Spain, see Limon, *Masque*, 58–77; and J. E. Varey, "The Audience and the Play at Court Spectacles: The Role of the King," 399–406.

47. Nicoll, *Stuart*, 155; D. Cunningham, "Jonsonian," 117.

Bibliography

Abellán, José Luis. *La Edad de Oro.* Vol. 2, *Historia crítica del pensamiento español.* Madrid: Espasa-Calpe, 1979.
Alciato, Andrés. *Emblemas.* Ed. Manuel Montero Vallejo. Madrid: Editora Nacional, 1975.
Alonso, Dámaso. *Estudios y ensayos gongorinos.* 2d ed. Madrid: Gredos, 1960.
——, ed. *Las soledades.* 1927. Madrid: Alianza, 1982. Introduction by Alexander A. Parker. Austin: University of Texas Press, 1977.
Amann, Elizabeth. "Orientalism and Transvestism: Góngora's 'Discurso contra las navegaciones' *(Soledad Primera).*" *Calíope* 3:1 (1997): 18–34.
Amezúa y Mayo, Agustín González de, ed. *Epistolario de Lope de Vega Carpio.* Vol. 3, *Lope de Vega en sus cartas.* Madrid: Real Academia Española, 1941.
Aquinas, [Saint] Thomas. *De Memoria et Reminiscentia.* In *Opera Omnia,* 20:197–212. New York: Musurgia, 1949.
The Arcimboldo Effect: Transformations of the Human Face from the Sixteenth to the Twentieth Century. New York: Abbeville Press, 1987.
Arnheim, Rudolf. "Language, Image, and Concrete Poetry." In *New Essays on the Psychology of Art,* 90–101. Berkeley and Los Angeles: University of California Press, 1986.
——. "A Plea for Visual Thinking." In *New Essays on the Psychology of Art,* 135–52. Berkeley and Los Angeles: University of California Press, 1986.
——. "A Stricture on Space and Time." In *New Essays on the Psychology of Art,* 78–89. Berkeley and Los Angeles: University of California Press, 1986.
Artigas, Miguel. *Don Luis de Góngora y Argote: Biografía y estudio crítico.* Madrid: Real Academia Española, 1925.

Asensio, Eugenio. "Un Quevedo incógnito: Las *Silvas*." *Edad de Oro* 2 (1983): 13–48.
Ashworth, William B., Jr. "Natural History and the Emblematic World View." In *Reappraisals of the Scientific Revolution*, ed. David C. Lindberg and Robert S. Westman, 303–32. Cambridge: Cambridge University Press, 1990.
Augustine, [Saint]. *Confessions*. Trans. R. S. Pine-Coffin. New York: Penguin, 1961.
Babuts, Nicolae. "Text: Origins and Reference." *PMLA* 107 (1992): 65–77.
Barthes, Roland. "Arcimboldo, or Magician and Rhétoriqueur." In *The Responsibility of Forms: Critical Essays on Music, Art, and Representation*, trans. Richard Howard, 129–48. New York: Hill and Wang, 1985.
———. "Rhetoric of the Image." In *The Responsibility of Forms: Critical Essays on Music, Art, and Representation*, trans. Richard Howard, 21–40. New York: Hill and Wang, 1985.
Battisti, Eugenio. *"Natura Artificiosa to Natura Artificialis."* In *The Italian Garden*, ed. David R. Coffin, 1–36. Washington, D.C.: Dumbarton Oaks, 1972.
Bazin, Germain. *The Baroque: Principles, Styles, Modes, Themes*. New York: W. W. Norton, 1978.
Berger, Harry, Jr. *Second World and Green World: Studies in Renaissance Fiction-Making*. Berkeley and Los Angeles: University of California Press, 1988.
Berger, Philippe. "L'Eau dans *Les Solitudes*." In *Crepúsculos pisando: Once estudios sobre las "Soledades" de Luis de Góngora*, ed. Jacques Issorel, 11–21. Perpignan, France: Centre de Recherches Ibériques et Latino-Américaines, Presses Universitaires de Perpignan, 1995.
Beverley, John. *Aspects of Góngora's "Soledades."* Purdue University Monographs in Romance Languages 1. Amsterdam: John Benjamins, 1980.
Brown, Jonathan. *The Golden Age of Painting in Spain*. New Haven: Yale University Press, 1991.
Brown, Jonathan, and J. H. Elliott. *A Palace for a King: The "Buen Retiro" and the Court of Philip IV*. New Haven: Yale University Press, 1980.
Bull, George, trans. *The Book of the Courtier*, by Baldesar Castiglione. New York: Penguin, 1976.
Bury, J. B. "Some Early Literary References to Italian Gardens." *Journal of Garden History* 2 (1982): 17–24.
Campa, Pedro F. "Diego López's *Declaración magistrale de las emblemas de Alciato:* A Seventeenth-Century Spanish Humanist's View." In *Andrea Alciato and the Emblem Tradition: Essays in Honor of Virginia Woods Callahan*, ed. Peter M. Daly, 223–48. New York: AMS Press, 1989.

Campos, Juana G., and Ana Barella. *Diccionario de refranes.* Madrid: Espasa Calpe, 1993.
Carreira, Antonio. "La controversia en torno a las *Soledades:* Un parecer desconocido, y edición crítica de las primeras cartas." In *Hommage à Robert Jammes,* ed. Francis Cerdan, 1:151–71. Toulouse: Presses Universitaires du Mirail, 1994.
Castiglione, Baldassar. *Il Cortigiano.* Trans. Carmen Covito and Aldo Busi. Milan: Rizzoli, 1993.
Caws, Mary Ann. *The Eye in the Text: Essays on Perception, Mannerist to Modern.* Princeton: Princeton University Press, 1981.
Chemris, Crystal. "Self-Reference in Góngora's *Soledades.*" *Hispanic Journal* 12:1 (1991): 7–15.
———. "Time, Space, and Apocalypse in Góngora's *Soledades.*" *Symposium* 43 (1989–1990): 147–57.
Ciocchini, Héctor. *Góngora y la tradición de los emblemas.* Bahía Blanca, Argentina: Cuadernos del Sur, 1960.
Close, Anthony J. "Commonplace Theories of Art and Nature in Classical Antiquity and in the Renaissance." Parts 1 and 2. *Journal of the History of Ideas* 30 (1969): 467–86; 32 (1971): 163–84.
Close, Lorna. "The Play of Difference: A Reading of Góngora's *Soledades.*" In *Conflicts of Discourse: Spanish Literature in the Golden Age,* ed. Peter W. Evans, 184–98. Manchester: Manchester University Press, 1990.
Cody, Richard. *The Landscape of the Mind.* Oxford: Clarendon, 1969.
Coffin, David R. *The Villa D'Este at Tivoli.* Princeton: Princeton University Press, 1960.
Colie, Rosalie. *"Paradoxia Epidemica": The Renaissance Tradition of Paradox.* Princeton: Princeton University Press, 1966.
———. *The Resources of Kind: Genre-Theory in the Renaissance.* Ed. Barbara K. Lewalski. Berkeley and Los Angeles: University of California Press, 1973.
Collard, Andrée. *Nueva poesía: Conceptismo, culteranismo en la crítica expañola.* Madrid: Castalia, 1967.
Collins, Christopher. *The Poetics of the Mind's Eye: Literature and the Psychology of Imagination.* Philadelphia: University of Pennsylvania Press, 1991.
———. *Reading the Written Image: Verbal Play, Interpretation, and the Roots of Iconophobia.* University Park: Pennsylvania State University Park, 1991.
Collins, Marsha S. "Antiquity and Modernity in Góngora's *El doctor Carlino.*" *Revista Canadiense de Estudios Hispánicos* 17:1 (1993): 19–29.

———. "The Crucible of Love in Góngora's *Las firmezas de Isabela*." *Bulletin of the Comediantes* 43 (1991): 197–213.

———. "Reshaping the Canon: The Strange Case of Góngora." In *Proceedings of the Seventeenth Louisiana Conference on Hispanic Languages and Literatures*, ed. Jesús Torrecilla et al., 104–11. Baton Rouge: Louisiana State University, 1996.

Copenhaver, Brian P. "Natural Magic, Hermetism, and Occultism in Early Modern Science." In *Reappraisals of the Scientific Revolution*, ed. David C. Lindberg and Robert S. Westman, 261–301. Cambridge: Cambridge University Press, 1990.

Covarrubias Orozco, Sebastián de. *Tesoro de la lengua castellana o española*. Ed. Felipe C. R. Maldonado, rev. by Manuel Camarero. 1611. Reprint, Madrid: Castalia, 1994.

Crosby, James O., and Lía Schwartz Lerner. "La silva 'El sueño' de Quevedo: Génesis y revisiones." *Bulletin of Hispanic Studies* 63 (1986): 111–26.

Cunningham, Dolora. "The Jonsonian Masque as a Literary Form." *Journal of English Literary History* 22 (1955): 108–24.

Cunningham, Gilbert F., trans. *"The Solitudes" of Luis de Góngora*. Baltimore: Johns Hopkins University Press, 1968.

Curtius, Ernst Robert. *European Literature and the Latin Middle Ages*. Trans. Willard R. Trask. Princeton: Princeton University Press, 1973.

Daly, Peter M. *Emblem Theory: Recent German Contributions to the Characterization of the Emblem Genre*. Nendeln, Liechtenstein: KTO Press, 1979.

———. *Literature in the Light of the Emblem: Structural Parallels between the Emblem and Literature in the Sixteenth and Seventeenth Centuries*. Toronto: University of Toronto Press, 1979.

De la Flor, Fernando R. *Teatro de la memoria: Siete ensayos sobre mnemotecnia española de los siglos XVII y XVIII*. Salamanca: Junta de Castilla y León, 1988.

Dronke, Peter. *The Medieval Lyric*. 2d ed. London: Hutchinson, 1978.

Drysdall, Denis L. "The Emblem according to the Italian *Impresa* Theorists." In *The Emblem in Renaissance and Baroque Europe: Tradition and Variety, Selected Papers of the Glasgow International Emblem Conference, 13–17 August 1990*, ed. Alison Adams and Anthony J. Harper, 22–32. Leiden, Holland: E. J. Brill, 1992.

Dudley, Edward. "The Wild Man Goes Baroque." In *The Wild Man Within: An Image in Western Thought from the Renaissance to Romanticism*, ed. Edward Dudley and Maximillian E. Novak, 115–39. Pittsburgh: University of Pittsburgh Press, 1973.

Durling, Robert M. *The Figure of the Poet in Renaissance Epic*. Cambridge: Harvard University Press, 1965.

Eco, Umberto. *The Limits of Interpretation*. Bloomington: Indiana University Press, 1990.

———. *Six Walks in the Fictional Woods*. Cambridge: Harvard University Press, 1994.

Edwards, Gwynne. "The Theme of Nature in Góngora's *Soledades*." *Bulletin of Hispanic Studies* 55 (1978): 231–43.

Egido, Aurora. "La poética del silencio en el Siglo de Oro. Su pervivencia." *Bulletin Hispanique* 88:1–2 (1986): 93–120.

———. "La silva en la poesía andaluza del Barroco (con un excurso sobre Estacio y *Las Obrecillas* de Fray Luis)." *Criticón* 46 (1989): 5–39.

Ehrlich, Tracy L. "The Waterworks of Hadrian's Villa." *Journal of Garden History* 9 (1989): 161–76.

Einstein, Alfred. *The Italian Madrigal*. Trans. Alexander H. Krappe, Roger H. Sessions, and Oliver Strunk. 3 vols. Princeton: Princeton University Press, 1949.

Elias, Norbert. *The Court Society*. Trans. Edmund Jephcott. New York: Pantheon, 1983.

Elliott, J. H. *Imperial Spain, 1469–1716*. New York: NAL, 1966.

———. "Mannerism." *Horizon* 15:3 (1973): 84–94.

Esrock, Ellen J. *The Reader's Eye: Visual Imaging as Reader Response*. Baltimore: Johns Hopkins University Press, 1994.

Evans, R. J. W. *Rudolf II and His World: A Study in Intellectual History, 1576–1612*. Oxford: Oxford University Press, 1984.

Fagiolo, Marcello. "Il significato dell' acqua e la dialettica del giardino Pirro Ligorio e la «filosofia» della villa cinquecentesca." In *Natura e artificio: L'ordine rustico, le fontane, gli automi nella cultura del Manierismo europeo*, ed. Marcello Fagiolo, 176–89. Rome: Officina, 1979.

———. "Il teatro dell' arte e della natura." In *Natura e artificio: L'ordine rustico, le fontane, gli automi nella cultura del Manierismo europeo*, ed. Marcello Fagiolo, 137–43. Rome: Officina, 1979.

Ferguson, William. *La versificación imitativa en Fernando de Herrera*. London: Tamesis, 1981.

———. "Visión y movimiento en las *Soledades* de Góngora." *Hispanófila* 29 (1986): 15–18.

Fernández-Guerra y Orbe, Luis. *Don Juan Ruiz de Alarcón y Mendoza*. Madrid: Real Academia Española, 1871.

Findlen, Paula. *Possessing Nature: Museums, Collecting, and Scientific Culture in Early Modern Italy*. Berkeley and Los Angeles: University of California Press, 1994.

Fish, Stanley E. *Self-Consuming Artifacts: The Experience of Seventeenth-Century Literature.* Berkeley and Los Angeles: University of California Press, 1972.

Foucault, Michel. *The Order of Things: An Archaeology of the Human Sciences.* 1971. Reprint, New York: Vintage, 1973.

Fowler, Alastair. *Kinds of Literature: An Introduction to the Theory of Genres and Modes.* Cambridge: Harvard University Press, 1982.

Frye, Northrop. "Romance as Masque." In *Spiritus Mundi: Essays on Literature, Myth, and Society,* 148–78. Bloomington: Indiana University Press, 1976.

García Lorca, Federico. "La imagen poética de Don Luis de Góngora." In *Conferencias I,* ed. Christopher Maurer, 85–125. Madrid: Alianza, 1984.

Garrison, David. *Góngora and the "Pyramus and Thisbe" Myth from Ovid to Shakespeare.* Newark, Del.: Juan de la Cuesta, 1994.

Gates, Eunice Joiner. *Documentos gongorinos.* Mexico City: Colegio de México, 1960.

———. "Góngora's *Polifemo* and *Soledades* in Relation to Baroque Art." *Texas Studies in Literature and Language* 2 (1960–1961): 61–77.

Gaylord [Randel], Mary. "Góngora and the Footprints of the Voice." *MLN* 108 (1993): 230–53.

———. "Metaphor and Fable in Góngora's *Soledad primera.*" *Revista Hispánica Moderna* 40 (1978–1979): 97–112.

———. "Reading the Pastoral Palimpsest: *La Galatea* in Góngora's *Soledad Primera.*" *Symposium* 36 (1982): 71–91.

Giamatti, A. Bartlett. *The Earthly Paradise and the Renaissance Epic.* Princeton: Princeton University Press, 1969.

Gilman, Stephen. "An Introduction to the Ideology of the Baroque in Spain." *Symposium* 1 (1946): 82–107.

Gilson, Etienne. *The Christian Philosophy of Saint Augustine.* Trans. L. E. M. Lynch. 1960. Reprint, New York: Octagon, 1983.

Gombrich, E. H. *Symbolic Images: Studies in the Art of the Renaissance.* 3d ed. Chicago: University of Chicago Press, 1985.

———. "Tradition and Expression in Western Still Life." In *Meditations on a Hobby Horse and Other Essays on the Theory of Art,* 95–105. 4th ed. Chicago: University of Chicago Press, 1985.

Goodman, David C. *Power and Penury: Government, Technology, and Science in Philip II's Spain.* Cambridge: Cambridge University Press, 1988.

Green, Otis H. "*Se acicalaron los auditorios:* An Aspect of the Spanish Literary Baroque." *Hispanic Review* 27 (1959): 413–22.

Greenblatt, Stephen. *Renaissance Self-Fashioning: From More to Shakespeare.* Chicago: University of Chicago Press, 1980.
Greene, Thomas M. *The Light in Troy: Imitation and Discovery in Renaissance Poetry.* New Haven: Yale University Press, 1982.
Greg, Walter M. *Pastoral Poetry and Pastoral Drama: A Literary Inquiry, with Special Reference to the Pre-Restoration Stage in England.* New York: Russell and Russell, 1959.
Gutzwiller, Kathryn J. *Theocritus' Pastoral Analogues: The Formation of a Genre.* Madison: University of Wisconsin Press, 1991.
Hagstrum, Jean. *The Sister Arts: The Tradition of Literary Pictorialism and English Poetry from Dryden to Gray.* Chicago: University of Chicago Press, 1958.
Hahn, Jürgen S. *The Origins of the Baroque Concept of "Peregrinatio."* Studies in the Romance Languages and Literatures 131. Chapel Hill: University of North Carolina Press, 1973.
Hathaway, Baxter. *The Age of Criticism: The Late Renaissance in Italy.* Ithaca: Cornell University Press, 1962.
Hatzfeld, Helmut. "Literary Mannerism and Baroque in Spain and France." *Comparative Literature Studies* 7 (1970): 419–36.
Heffernan, James A. W. *Museum of Words: The Poetics of Ekphrasis from Homer to Ashbery.* Chicago: University of Chicago Press, 1993.
Hibbard, Howard. *Caravaggio.* New York: Harper and Row, 1983.
Hoffmann, Konrad. "Alciato and the Historical Situation of Emblematics." In *Andrea Alciato and the Emblem Tradition: Essays in Honor of Virginia Woods Callahan,* ed. Peter M. Daly, 1–45. New York: AMS Press, 1989.
Hollander, John. *Melodious Guile: Fictive Pattern in Poetic Language.* New Haven: Yale University Press, 1988.
———. *Vision and the Resonance: Two Senses of Poetic Form.* 2d ed. New Haven: Yale University Press, 1985.
Huizinga, Johan. *Homo Ludens: A Study of the Play-Element in Culture.* Boston: Beacon, 1955.
Hunt, John Dixon. *Gardens and the Picturesque: Studies in the History of Landscape Architecture.* Cambridge: MIT Press, 1992.
———. "'Loose Nature' and the 'Garden Square': The Gardenist Background for Marvell's Poetry." In *Approaches to Marvell: The York Tercentenary Lectures,* 331–51. London: Routledge and Kegan Paul, 1978.
Hunt, John Dixon, and Peter Willis, eds. *The Genius of the Place: The English Landscape Garden, 1620–1820.* London: Paul Elek, 1975.

Ife, B. W. *Reading and Fiction in Golden-Age Spain: A Platonist Critique and Some Picaresque Replies.* Cambridge: Cambridge University Press, 1985.
Iñiguez Almech, Francisco. *Casas reales y jardines de Felipe II.* Madrid: CSIC, 1952.
Iser, Wolfgang. *The Fictive and the Imaginary: Charting Literary Anthropology.* Baltimore: Johns Hopkins University Press, 1993.
Issorel, Jacques, ed. *Crepúsculos pisando: Once estudios sobre las "Soledades" de Luis de Góngora.* Perpignan, France: Centre de Recherches Ibériques et Latino-Américaines, Presses Universitaires de Perpignan, 1995.
Iversen, Erik. *The Myth of Egypt and Its Hieroglyphs in European Tradition.* Copenhagen: GECGAD, 1961.
Jammes, Robert C. *Études sur l'oeuvre poétique de Don Luis de Góngora y Argote.* Bordeaux: Institut d'Études Ibériques et Ibéro-Américaines de l'Université de Bordeaux, 1967.
——, ed. *Las firmezas de Isabela.* Madrid: Castalia, 1984.
——. *Soledades,* by Luis de Góngora. Madrid: Castalia, 1994.
Jauss, Hans Robert. *Toward an Aesthetic of Reception.* Trans. Timothy Bahti. Minneapolis: University of Minnesota Press, 1982.
Jenkyns, Richard. "Pastoral." In *The Legacy of Rome: A New Appraisal,* ed. Richard Jenkyns, 151–75. Oxford: Oxford University Press, 1992.
Jones, R. O. "Góngora and Neoplatonism Again." *Bulletin of Hispanic Studies* 43 (1966): 117–20.
——. "Neoplatonism and the *Soledades.*" *Bulletin of Hispanic Studies* 40 (1963): 1–18.
——. "The Poetic Unity of the *Soledades* of Góngora." *Bulletin of Hispanic Studies* 31 (1954): 189–204.
Jonson, Ben. *The Complete Masques.* Ed. Stephen Orgel. New Haven: Yale University Press, 1969.
Jordan, William B., and Peter Cherry. *Spanish Still Life from Velázquez to Goya.* London: National Gallery, 1995.
Junceda, Luis. *Diccionario de refranes.* Madrid: Espasa Calpe, 1996.
Kamen, Henry. *Philip of Spain.* New Haven: Yale University Press, 1997.
Kaufmann, Thomas DaCosta. "Arcimboldo's Serious Jokes: 'Mysterious but Long Meaning.'" In *The Verbal and the Visual: Essays in Honor of William Sebastian Heckscher,* ed. Karl-Ludwig Selig and Elizabeth Sears, 59–86. New York: Italica, 1990.
——. *The Mastery of Nature: Aspects of Art, Science, and Humanism in the Renaissance.* Princeton: Princeton University Press, 1993.

———. *The School of Prague: Painting at the Court of Rudolf II.* Chicago: University of Chicago Press, 1988.
King, Willard F. *Prosa novelística y academias literarias en el siglo XVII.* Madrid: Real Academia Española, 1963.
Krabbenhoft, Kenneth. "Góngora's Stoic Pilgrim." *Bulletin of Hispanic Studies* 73 (1996): 1–12.
Krieger, Murray. "The Ekphrastic Principle and the Still Movement of Poetry; or, *Laokoön* Revisited." In *The Play and Place of Criticism,* 105–28. Baltimore: Johns Hopkins University Press, 1967.
Kristeller, Paul O. *The Philosophy of Marsilio Ficino.* Trans. Virginia Conant. 1943. Reprint, Gloucester, Mass.: Peter Smith, 1964.
La Bruyère, Jean de. *Les caractères de Théophraste traduits du grec avec les caractères ou les moeurs de ce siècle.* Paris: Garnier-Flammarion, 1965.
Lazzaro, Claudia. *The Italian Renaissance Garden: From the Conventions of Painting, Design, and Ornament to the Grand Gardens of Sixteenth-Century Central Italy.* New Haven: Yale University Press, 1990.
Lee, Rensselaer. *Ut Pictura Poesis: The Humanistic Theory of Painting.* New York: W. W. Norton, 1967.
Lewis, C. S. *The Discarded Image: An Introduction to Medieval and Renaissance Literature.* 1964. Reprint, Cambridge: Cambridge University Press, 1974.
Lezama Lima, José. "Sierpe de Don Luis de Góngora." In *El reino de la imagen,* ed. Julio Ortega, 238–57. Caracas: Ayacucho, 1981.
Lida [de Malkiel], María Rosa. "El hilo narrativo de las *Soledades.*" *Boletín de la Academia Argentina de Letras* 29 (1964): 3–13.
Limon, Jerzy. *The Masque of Stuart Culture.* Newark: University of Delaware Press, 1990.
Lindley, David, ed. *The Court Masque.* Manchester: Manchester University Press, 1984.
Longinus. *On Sublimity.* Trans. D. A. Russell. Oxford: Clarendon, 1965.
Loyola, [Saint] Ignatius of. *Obras completas.* Ed. Ignacio Iparraguirre and Cándido de Dalmases. 3d ed. Madrid: Biblioteca de Autores Cristianos, 1977.
Ly, Nadine. "La république ailée dans les *Solitudes.*" In *Crepúsculos pisando: Once estudios sobre las "Soledades" de Luis de Góngora,* ed. Jacques Issorel, 141–77. Perpignan, France: Centre de Recherches Ibériques et Latino-Américaines, Presses Universitaires de Perpignan, 1995.
———. "Las *Soledades:* «... Esta poesía inútil ...»." *Criticón* 30 (1985): 7–42.
MacDonald, William L., and John A. Pinto. *Hadrian's Villa and Its Legacy.* New Haven: Yale University Press, 1995.

MacDougall, Elisabeth B. "*Ars Hortulorum:* Sixteenth-Century Garden Iconography and Literary Theory in Italy." In *The Italian Garden,* ed. David R. Coffin, 37–59. Washington, D.C.: Dumbarton Oaks, 1972.

———. "Imitation and Invention: Language and Decoration in Roman Renaissance Gardens." *Journal of Garden History* 5 (1985): 119–34.

MacDougall, Elisabeth B., and Naomi Miller. *Fons Sapientiae: Garden Fountains in Illustrated Books, Sixteenth–Eighteenth Centuries.* Washington, D.C.: Dumbarton Oaks, 1977.

Mack, Sara. *Ovid.* New Haven: Yale University Press, 1988.

Macrí, Oreste. *Fernando de Herrera.* 2d ed. Madrid: Gredos, 1972.

Maiorino, Giancarlo. *The Portrait of Eccentricity: Arcimboldo and the Mannerist Grotesque.* University Park: Pennsylvania State University Press, 1991.

Manuel, Frank E., and Fritzie P. Manuel. *Utopian Thought in the Western World.* Cambridge: Harvard University Press, Belknap Press, 1979.

Maravall, José Antonio. *Antiguos y modernos: Visión de la historia e idea de progreso hasta el Renacimiento.* 1966. Reprint, Madrid: Alianza, 1986.

———. *La cultura del barroco: Análisis de una estructura histórica.* Barcelona: Ariel, 1975.

Martínez Arancón, Ana. *La batalla en torno a Góngora.* Barcelona: Antoni Bosch, 1978.

Martín-Hernández, Evelyne. "Les *Solitudes* comme un jardin. . . ." In *Crepúsculos pisando: Once estudios sobre las "Soledades" de Luis de Góngora,* ed. Jacques Issorel, 179–90. Perpignan, France: Centre de Recherches Ibériques et Latino-Américaines, Presses Universitaires de Perpignan, 1995.

Martz, Louis L. *The Paradise Within: Studies in Vaughan, Traherne, and Milton.* New Haven: Yale University Press, 1964.

———. *The Poetry of Meditation: A Study in English Religious Literature.* New Haven: Yale University Press, 1962.

Masson, Georgina. *Italian Gardens.* New York: Harry N. Abrams, 1961.

Mazzeo, Joseph Anthony. "Metaphysical Poetry and the Poetic of Correspondence." In *Renaissance and Seventeenth-Century Studies,* 44–59. New York: Columbia University Press, 1964.

———. "A Seventeenth-Century Theory of Metaphysical Poetry." In *Renaissance and Seventeenth-Century Studies,* 29–43. New York: Columbia University Press, 1964.

———. "St. Augustine's Rhetoric of Silence: Truth vs. Eloquence and Things vs. Signs." In *Renaissance and Seventeenth-Century Studies,* 1–28. New York: Columbia University Press, 1964.

McAllister, Robin. "The Reader as Pilgrim and Poet in Góngora's *Soledades*." Ph.D. diss., Princeton University, 1975.
McCaw, R. John. *The Transforming Text: A Study of Luis de Góngora's "Soledades."* Potomac, Md.: Scripta Humanistica, 2000.
McGowan, Margaret M. *L'Art du ballet de cour en France, 1581–1643*. Paris: Centre National de la Recherche Scientifique, 1963.
McGrady, Donald. "Lope, Camões y Petrarca y los primeros versos de las *Soledades* de Góngora." *Hispanic Review* 54 (1986): 287–96.
McKendrick, Melveena. *Theatre in Spain, 1490–1700*. Cambridge: Cambridge University Press, 1989.
McVay, Ted E., Jr. "The Epistemological Basis for Juan de Jáuregui's Attacks on Góngora's *Soledades*." *Hispanic Journal* 13 (1992): 301–7.
Merkl, Heinrich. "Góngoras *Soledades*—ein politisches Gedicht?" *Romanistisches Jahrbuch* 40 (1989): 308–25.
Millé y Giménez, Juan, and Isabel Millé y Giménez, eds. *Obras completas, Luis de Góngora y Argote*. Madrid: Aguilar, 1967.
Mirollo, James V. *Mannerism and Renaissance Poetry: Concept, Mode, Inner Design*. New Haven: Yale University Press, 1984.
Molho, Maurice. "Apuntes para una teoría del cultismo." *Bulletin Hispanique* 87:3–4 (1985): 471–84.
———. *Semántica y poética (Góngora, Quevedo)*. Barcelona: Crítica, 1977.
Morford, Mark. "The Stoic Garden." *Journal of Garden History* 7 (1987): 151–75.
Mottola, Anthony, trans. *The Spiritual Exercises of St. Ignatius*. Garden City, N.Y.: Doubleday, 1964.
Navarrete, Ignacio. "Decentering Garcilaso: Herrera's Attack on the Canon." *PMLA* 106 (1991): 21–33.
———. *Orphans of Petrarch: Poetry and Theory in the Spanish Renaissance*. Berkeley and Los Angeles: University of California Press, 1994.
Nicoll, Allardyce. *Stuart Masques and the Renaissance Stage*. 1938. Reprint, New York: Benjamin Blom, 1963.
Olmedo, Felix G., ed. *Juan Bonifacio (1538–1606) y la cultura literaria del Siglo de Oro*. 2d ed. Madrid: Sociedad de Menéndez Pelayo, 1939.
Orgel, Stephen. *The Illusion of Power: Political Theater in the English Renaissance*. Berkeley and Los Angeles: University of California Press, 1975.
———. *The Jonsonian Masque*. Cambridge: Harvard University Press, 1965.
Orozco Díaz, Emilio. *En torno a las «Soledades» de Góngora: Ensayos, estudios y edición de textos críticos de la época referentes al poema*. Granada: University of Granada, 1969.

———. *Lope y Góngora frente a frente*. Madrid: Gredos, 1973.

———. *El teatro y la teatralidad del Barroco (ensayo de introducción al tema)*. Barcelona: Planeta, 1969.

Ortega y Gasset, José. "La deshumanización del arte." In *La deshumanización del arte y otros ensayos de estética*, ed. Paulino Garagorri, 11–54. 1983. Reprint, Madrid: Revista de Occidente en Alianza, 1994.

———. "Ensayo de estética a manera de prólogo." In *La deshumanización del arte y otros ensayos de estética*, ed. Paulino Garagorri, 152–74. 1983. Reprint, Madrid: Revista de Occidente en Alianza, 1994.

Paden, William D., ed. and trans. *The Medieval Pastourelle*. 2 vols. New York: Garland, 1987.

Panofsky, Erwin. *Meaning and the Visual Arts*. Garden City, N.Y.: Doubleday, 1955.

Parker, Alexander A. Introduction to *Polyphemus and Galatea*, by Luis de Góngora. Trans. Gilbert F. Cunningham, 7–106. Austin: University of Texas Press, 1977.

Parry, Graham. *The Golden Age Restor'd: The Culture of the Stuart Court, 1603–42*. New York: St. Martin's, 1981.

Patterson, Richard. "The 'Hortus Palatinus' at Heidelberg and the Reformation of the World." *Journal of Garden History* 1 (1981): 67–104, 179–202.

Pavel, Thomas G. *Fictional Worlds*. Cambridge: Harvard University Press, 1986.

Pérez Lasheras, Antonio. "Imágenes emblemáticas gongorinas: La *Fábula de Píramo y Tisbe*." In *Hommage à Robert Jammes*, ed. Francis Cerdan, 3:927–38. Toulouse: Presses Universitaires du Mirail, 1994.

Plato. *Phaedrus and the Seventh and Eighth Letters*. Trans. Walter Hamilton. New York: Penguin, 1973.

———. *The Portable Plato: Protagoras, Symposium, Phaedo, and the Republic*. Trans. Benjamin Jowett. Ed. Scott Buchanan. New York: Penguin, 1977.

Poggioli, Renato. *The Oaten Flute: Essays on Pastoral Poetry and the Pastoral Ideal*. Cambridge: Harvard University Press, 1975.

Porqueras Mayo, Agustín. *La teoría poética en el Manierismo y Barroco españoles*. Barcelona: Puvill, 1989.

Praz, Mario. *Mnemosyne: The Parallel between Literature and the Visual Arts*. Princeton: Princeton University Press, 1967.

———. *Studies in Seventeenth-Century Imagery*. 2d ed. Rome: Storia e Letteratura, 1964.

Quilis, Antonio. *Métrica española*. Barcelona: Ariel, 1996.

Quint, David. *Origin and Originality in Renaissance Literature: Versions of the Source.* New Haven: Yale University Press, 1983.
Quintero, María Cristina. *Poetry as Play: "Gongorismo" and the "Comedia."* Purdue University Monographs in Romance Languages 38. Amsterdam: John Benjamins, 1991.
Rennert, Hugo Albert. *The Spanish Stage in the Time of Lope de Vega.* New York: Hispanic Society of America, 1909.
Riley, Edward C. "Aspectos del concepto de *admiratio* en la teoría literaria del Siglo de Oro." In *Studia Philologica: Homenaje ofrecido a Dámaso Alonso por sus amigos y discípulos con ocasión de su 60.° aniversario,* 3:173–83. Madrid: Gredos, 1963.
Rivera Blanco, José Javier. *Juan Bautista de Toledo y Felipe II: La implantación del clasicismo en España.* Valladolid, Spain: Universidad de Valladolid, 1984.
Rivers, Elias L. "Góngora y el nuevo mundo." *Hispania* 75 (1992): 856–61.
———. "Nature, Art, and Science in Spanish Poetry of the Renaissance." *Bulletin of Hispanic Studies* 44 (1967): 255–66.
———. "The Pastoral Paradox of Natural Art." *Modern Language Notes* 77 (1962): 130–44.
———. "La problemática silva española." *Nueva Revista de Filología Hispánica* 36 (1988): 249–60.
Roberts, Gareth. *The Mirror of Alchemy: Alchemical Ideas and Images in Manuscripts and Books from Antiquity to the Seventeenth Century.* Toronto: University of Toronto Press, 1994.
Rosenmeyer, Thomas G. *The Green Cabinet: Theocritus and the European Pastoral Lyric.* Berkeley and Los Angeles: University of California Press, 1969.
Roses Lozano, Joaquín. *Una poética de la oscuridad: La recepción crítica de las "Soledades" en el siglo XVII.* Madrid: Tamesis, 1994.
Rousset, Jean. *La littérature de l'âge baroque en France: Circé et le Paon.* Paris: José Corti, 1953.
Rowland, Beryl. *Birds with Human Souls: A Guide to Bird Symbolism.* Knoxville: University of Tennessee Press, 1978.
Rupp, Stephen. "Articulate Illusions: Art and Authority in Jonson's Masques and Some *Autos sacramentales* of Calderón de la Barca." Ph.D. diss., Princeton University, 1984.
Salinas, Pedro. "La exaltación de la realidad (Luis de Góngora)." In *Ensayos completos,* ed. Solita Salinas de Marichal, 1:260–69. Madrid: Taurus, 1983.
Sánchez, José. *Academias literarias del Siglo de Oro español.* Madrid: Gredos, 1961.

Sánchez Pérez, Aquilino. *La literatura emblemática española (siglos XVI y XVII)*. Madrid: Sociedad General Española de Librería, 1977.
Sarduy, Severo. "El barroco y el neobarroco." In *América Latina en su literatura*, ed. César Fernández Moreno, 167–84. Mexico City: Siglo XXI, 1972.
Sasaki, Betty. "Góngora's Sea of Signs: The Manipulation of History in the *Soledades*." *Calíope* 1:1–2 (1995): 150–68.
Saslow, James M. *The Medici Wedding of 1589: Florentine Festival as "Theatrum Mundi."* New Haven: Yale University Press, 1996.
Schevill, Rudolph. *Ovid and the Renascence in Spain*. University of California Publications in Modern Philology 4. Berkeley and Los Angeles: University of California Press, 1913.
Scoular, Kitty W. *Natural Magic: Studies in the Presentation of Nature in English Poetry from Spenser to Marvell*. Oxford: Clarendon, 1965.
Selig, Karl-Ludwig. "*Don Quixote* and the Game of Chess." In *The Verbal and the Visual: Essays in Honor of William Sebastian Heckscher*, ed. Karl-Ludwig Selig and Elizabeth Sears, 203–11. New York: Italica, 1990.
———. "Gracián and Alciato's *Emblemata*." *Comparative Literature* 8 (1956): 1–11.
Seznec, Jean. *The Survival of the Pagan Gods: The Mythological Tradition and Its Place in Renaissance Humanism and Art*. Trans. Barbara F. Sessions. 1972. Reprint, Princeton: Princeton University Press, 1995.
Shearman, John. *Mannerism*. London: Penguin, 1967.
Sheppard, Harry J. "European Alchemy in the Context of a Universal Definition." In *Die Alchemie in der europäischen Kultur—und Wissenschaftgeschichte*, ed. Christoph Meinel, 13–17. Wiesbaden, Germany: Herzog August Bibliothek Wolfenbüttel, 1986.
Shergold, N. D. *A History of the Spanish Stage: From Medieval Times until the End of the Seventeenth Century*. Oxford: Clarendon, 1967.
Shumaker, Wayne. *Natural Magic and Modern Science: Four Treatises, 1590–1657*. Medieval and Renaissance Texts and Studies 63. Binghamton: Center for Medieval and Early Renaissance Studies, SUNY at Binghamton, 1989.
Sieber, Harry. "The Magnificent Fountain: Literary Patronage in the Court of Philip III." *Cervantes* 18 (1998): 85–116.
Smith, C. Colin. "An Approach to Góngora's *Polifemo*." *Bulletin of Hispanic Studies* 42 (1965): 217–38.
———. "On the Use of Spanish Theoretical Works in the Debate on Gongorism." *Bulletin of Hispanic Studies* 39 (1962): 165–76.
Smith, Paul Julian. "Barthes, Góngora, and Non-Sense." *PMLA* 101 (1986): 82–94.

———. *The Body Hispanic: Gender and Sexuality in Spanish and Spanish American Literature.* Oxford: Clarendon, 1989.

———. *Writing in the Margin: Spanish Literature of the Golden Age.* Oxford: Clarendon, 1988.

Solana, Marcial. *Historia de la filosofía española: Epoca del Renacimiento (siglo XVI).* 3 vols. Madrid: Asociación Española para el Progreso de las Ciencias, 1941.

Soufas, Teresa Scott. *Melancholy and the Secular Mind in Spanish Golden Age Literature.* Columbia: University of Missouri Press, 1990.

Spitzer, Leo. *Classical and Christian Ideas of World Harmony: Prolegomena to an Interpretation of the Word "Stimmung."* Ed. Anna Granville Hatcher. Baltimore: Johns Hopkins University Press, 1963.

———. "On Góngora's *Soledades.*" In *Leo Spitzer: Representative Essays,* ed. Alban K. Forcione, Herbert Lindenberger, and Madeline Sutherland, 87–103. Stanford: Stanford University Press, 1988.

———. "Selections from Góngora's First *Soledad:* Critical and Explanatory Notes on Dámaso Alonso's New Edition." In *Leo Spitzer: Representative Essays,* ed. Alban K. Forcione, Herbert Lindenberger, and Madeline Sutherland, 104–21. Stanford: Stanford University Press, 1988.

———. "The Spanish Baroque." In *Leo Spitzer: Representative Essays,* ed. Alban K. Forcione, Herbert Lindenberger, and Madeline Sutherland, 123–39. Stanford: Stanford University Press, 1988.

Steiner, George. *Language and Silence: Essays on Language, Literature, and the Inhuman.* New York: Atheneum, 1967.

Stock, Brian. *Augustine the Reader: Meditation, Self-Knowledge, and the Ethics of Interpretation.* Cambridge: Harvard University Press, Belknap Press, 1996.

Strong, Roy. *Art and Power: Renaissance Festivals, 1450–1650.* 1974. Reprint, Berkeley and Los Angeles: University of California Press, 1984.

———. *The Renaissance Garden in England.* London: Thames and Hudson, 1979.

Szafranska, Malgorzata. "Philosophy of Nature and the Grotto in the Renaissance Garden." *Journal of Garden History* 9 (1989): 76–85.

Tabbaa, Yasser. "Towards an Interpretation of the Use of Water in Islamic Courtyards and Courtyard Gardens." *Journal of Garden History* 7 (1987): 197–220.

Tayler, Edward William. *Nature and Art in Renaissance Literature.* New York: Columbia University Press, 1964.

Taylor, David N. "Góngora's Sonnet 'Acredita la esperanza con historias sagradas': An Emblemorphic Reading." *Calíope* 3:1 (1997): 35–50.

Thorndike, Lynn. *A History of Magic and Experimental Science.* 8 vols. New York: Columbia University Press, 1923–1958.

Tribe, Tania C. "Word and Image in Emblematic Painting." In *The Emblem in Renaissance and Baroque Europe: Tradition and Variety, Selected Papers of the Glasgow International Emblem Conference, 13–17 August 1990,* 247–71. Leiden, Holland: E. J. Brill, 1992.

Trinkaus, Charles. *The Scope of Renaissance Humanism.* Ann Arbor: University of Michigan Press, 1983.

Turner, A. Richard. *The Vision of Landscape in Renaissance Italy.* Princeton: Princeton University Press, 1966.

Tuve, Rosemond. "Image, Form, and Theme in a Mask." In *Images and Themes in Five Poems by Milton,* 112–61. Cambridge: Harvard University Press, 1962.

Van Lennep, Jacques. *Art et alchimie: Étude de l'iconographie hermétique et de ses influences.* Brussels: Meddens, 1966.

Varey, J. E. "The Audience and the Play at Court Spectacles: The Role of the King." *Bulletin of Hispanic Studies* 6 (1984): 399–406.

Vilanova, Antonio. *Las fuentes y los temas del "Polifemo" de Góngora.* 2 vols. Madrid: CSIC, 1957.

———. "El peregrino de amor en las *Soledades* de Góngora." In *Estudios dedicados a Menéndez Pidal,* 3:421–60. Madrid: CSIC, 1952.

Von Prellwitz, Norbert. "Góngora: El vuelo audaz del poeta." *Bulletin of Hispanic Studies* 74 (1997): 19–35.

Vossler, Karl. *La poesía de la soledad en España.* Buenos Aires: Losada, 1946.

Waley, Pamela. "Some Uses of Classical Mythology in the *Soledades* of Góngora." *Bulletin of Hispanic Studies* 36 (1959): 193–209.

Walker, D. P. *Spiritual and Demonic Magic from Ficino to Campanella.* London: Warburg Institute, 1958.

Wardropper, Bruce W. "The Complexity of the Simple in Góngora's *Soledad Primera.*" *Journal of Medieval and Renaissance Studies* 7 (1977): 35–51.

Warnke, Frank. "Metaphysical Poetry and the European Context." In *Metaphysical Poetry,* ed. Malcolm Bradbury and David Palmer, 260–76. New York: St. Martin's, 1970.

———. *Versions of Baroque: European Literature in the Seventeenth Century.* New Haven: Yale University Press, 1972.

———, ed. and trans. *European Metaphysical Poetry.* New Haven: Yale University Press, 1961.

Weinberg, Bernard. *A History of Literary Criticism in the Italian Renaissance.* 2 vols. Chicago: University of Chicago Press, 1961.

Wellek, René. "The Concept of Baroque in Literary Scholarship." In *Concepts of Criticism*, ed. Stephen G. Nichols Jr., 69–127. New Haven: Yale University Press, 1963.

Welles, Marcia L. *Arachne's Tapestry: The Transformation of Myth in Seventeenth-Century Spain*. San Antonio: Trinity University Press, 1986.

Welsford, Enid. *The Court Masque: A Study in the Relationship between Poetry and the Revels*. Cambridge: Cambridge University Press, 1927.

Wescott, Howard B. "Nemoroso's Odyssey: Garcilaso's Eclogues Revisited." *Hispania* 78 (1995): 474–82.

West, David. "The Ovidian Source." In *Polyphemus and Galatea*, by Luis de Góngora, 153–57. Ed. Dámaso Alonso. Trans. Gilbert F. Cunningham. Introduction by Alexander A. Parker. Austin: University of Texas Press, 1977.

Wethey, Harold E. *The Mythological and Historical Paintings*. Vol. 3, *The Paintings of Titian*. London: Phaidon, 1975.

White, T. H. *The Bestiary, a Book of Beasts, Being a Translation from a Latin Bestiary of the Twelfth Century*. New York: G. P. Putnam's Sons, 1954.

Wilson, E[dward] M[eryon]. "Spanish and English Religious Poetry of the Seventeenth Century." In *Spanish and English Literature of the Seventeenth Century*, ed. D. W. Cruickshank, 234–49. Cambridge: Cambridge University Press, 1980.

———, trans. *"The Solitudes" of Don Luis de Góngora*. Cambridge: Cambridge University Press, 1965.

Wind, Edgar. *Pagan Mysteries in the Renaissance*. 1967. Reprint, London: Faber and Faber, 1968.

Winn, James Anderson. *Unsuspected Eloquence: A History of the Relations between Poetry and Music*. New Haven: Yale University Press, 1981.

Wölfflin, Heinrich. *Principles of Art History: The Problem of the Development of Style in Later Art*. Trans. M. D. Hottinger. New York: Dover, 1950.

Woods, Michael J. *Gracián Meets Góngora: The Theory and Practice of Wit*. Warminster, England: Aris and Phillips, 1995.

———. *The Poet and the Natural World in the Age of Góngora*. Oxford: Oxford University Press, 1978.

Woodward, L. J. "Two Images in the *Soledades* of Góngora." *Modern Language Notes* 76 (1961): 773–85.

Yates, Frances A. *The Art of Memory*. Chicago: University of Chicago Press, 1966.

———. *The French Academies of the Sixteenth Century*. Studies of the Warburg Institute 15. London: University of London, 1947.

Index

Academies: origin and development of, 31–34; development in Spain, 34–37
Actaeon, 7, 158
Admiratio, 83, 112–35, 137, 138, 147, 151, 159, 164, 167, 177–88 *passim,* 199, 204, 219, 237*n1*, 238*n18*
Adonis, 158
Aeneas, 82
Alarcón y Mendoza, Juan Ruiz, 37
Alchemy, 5, 112, 164, 165–67, 170, 173, 191, 242*nn53,55*. *See also* Philosophers' stone
Alciati, Andrea, 140, 141, 142, 144–45, 149, 239*n32*. *See also* Covarrubias, Sebastián de; Emblems
Alcimedon, 119, 120
Almansa y Mendoza, Andrés de, 14, 21
Alonso, Dámaso, 3–4, 41, 54, 77, 137, 146
Amaltheia, 176
Ancients and moderns: quarrel between, 38–41, 42, 227*nn61–62*
Apollo, 121, 158, 161, 162–63
Aquarius, 188
Aquinas, Saint Thomas, 74, 75, 196
Arcas, 87
Arcimboldo, Giuseppe, 154–57, 240*n44*
Aretino, Pietro, 33
Arion, 64, 87
Ariosto, Lodovico, 2
Aristotle, 22, 23, 115, 116, 196
Ascalaphus, 7, 158, 168–69, 187
Augustine, Saint, 5, 22, 47, 82, 83, 99, 107; and hermeneutics, 6–7, 47–50, 71, 85–86, 110–11, 149; and meditation, 57, 66, 69, 71, 74–75, 146–47

Bacchus, 76, 77, 78
Bacon, Francis, 171
Bassano, Jacopo, 93
Béjar, duke of, 1, 8–9, 59, 69, 147, 185–86, 205–6
Bembo, Pietro Cardinal, 3, 82, 101; *Bembismo,* 3, 101
Boccaccio, Giovanni, 34
Boiardo, Matteo Maria, 172
Bonifacio, Juan de, 42–43
Botticelli, Sandro, 87, 88
Brocense, El, 141, 142
Brueghel, Pieter and Pieter the Younger, 93
Bruno, Giordano, 74
Burmeister, Joachim, 101
Bustamante, Jorge de, 157

Cabinet of curiosities. *See Wunderkammer*
Calderón de la Barca, Pedro, 36, 204
Callisto, 87, 121
Camillo, Giulio, 81
Camões, 59
Canossa, Count Lodovico da, 33, 34
Caravaggio, Michelangelo Merisi da, 90, 94, 97, 98
Carducho, Bartolomé and Vicente, 93
Cascales, Francisco, 24, 25–26, 116
Castiglione, Baldassar, 12–13, 14–16, 32–34, 122, 135
Castor and Pollux, 87
Castro, Guillén de, 36

267

Ceres, 168–69
Certamen, 35, 36, 37. *See also* Academies
Cervantes, Miguel de, 1, 26, 36, 38, 171
Charles V, 19, 90, 174
Chrysostom, Dio, 70
Cicero, 72, 115, 116, 122; Ciceronianism, 3
Clotho, 213
Clytie, 158, 161
Collecting and collections: private, 18–20, 87, 88, 92, 173, 179–80
Colonna, Francesco, 172
Comanini, Gregorio, 156
Correggio, Antonio Allegri da, 95
Cortés, Gerónimo, 166
Covarrubias, Sebastián de, 139–40, 141, 143. *See also* Alciati, Andrea; Emblems
Crashaw, Richard, 55
Culteranismo. See Cultismo
Cultismo, 2–4, 13, 17, 123–24, 125, 128, 133–34, 135–36, 138, 142–43, 222n3; battle over, 20–51
Cupid, 88, 125, 158, 190, 212

Daedalus, 132, 133
Danae, 158
Dante Alighieri, 34, 82
Daphne, 158, 162–63, 186
David, king of Israel, 38
Da Vinci, Leonardo, 91, 95
Diana, 213
Díaz de Rivas, Pedro, 22, 27–31, 39–40, 54, 145, 205

Echo, 158, 161–62
Emblems, 5, 15, 17, 33, 46, 139–56, 158, 169, 172–73, 213, 217, 239nn26–27,34,36. *See also* Alciati, Andrea; Covarrubias, Sebastián de
Enigma: aesthetics of, 15, 16–17, 46, 47–48, 133–34, 154, 225n25
Epic: and romance, 2; vs. lyric poetry, 8–9; vs. pastoral and romance, 27, 30–31
Erasmus, Desiderius, 23, 135
Este, Ippolito Cardinal d', 187
Estilo culto. See Cultismo
Europa, 87, 158
Euterpe, 8, 9, 62

Fernández de Córdoba, Francisco, 13–14, 20, 23, 24, 25, 26, 27, 28
Ficino, Marsilio, 5, 6, 31, 32, 45, 48–50, 69, 74, 76, 107
Flora, 87, 147, 148, 151, 155–56
Fonteo, Giovanni, 156

Ganymede, 63, 64, 82, 87, 158
García Lorca, Federico, 136–37
Gardens and garden design: aesthetics of, 171–92, 194–95, 242–43n1, 243nn3–4
Gentileschi, Orazio, 90
Glaucus, 168
Góngora, Luis de: move to court, 13–16; recent critical approaches to, 221n2, 231–32n20
—Works: "Angélica y Medoro," 2; *Fábula de Polifemo y Galatea,* 2, 13, 14, 20, 22, 26, 27–31, 37, 38, 39–40, 41, 54, 155, 157, 180, 205; *Las firmezas de Isabela,* 2, 71, 188; "De un caminante enfermo," 2, 83; *El doctor Carlino,* 12, 71; *Carta en respuesta,* 43–51, 53, 55, 69, 123–24, 149, 157, 165, 217, 218; "La ciudad de Babilonia," 157
Gongorismo. See Cultismo
Gonzaga, Elisabetta. *See* Urbino, duchess of
Gracián, Baltasar, 36, 57, 135, 142–43
Granvelle, Cardinal de, 19
Greco, El, 97, 98

Hadrian's Villa, 172, 173, 183, 187, 190
Heliodorus, 31
Heraclitus, 107
Herbert, George, 55
Hercules, 191–92
Hermes Trismegistus, 165
Hernández de Villaumbrales, Pedro, 57
Hero of Alexandria, 187, 188
Herrera, Fernando de, 41, 227–28n64
Herrera, Juan de, 174
Holbein, Hans, 95
Homer, 28, 38
Horace, 7, 23, 28, 38, 86, 115–16
Horapollo, 160–61
Horozco y Covarrubias, Juan de, 140
Hymen, 163, 209, 210

Icarus, 7, 84, 89, 133, 147, 158
Ignatius of Loyola, Saint, 57, 60–61, 62, 63, 71, 79
Isabel la Católica, Queen, 202
Isaiah, 38

Jáuregui, Juan de, 21, 26, 27, 39, 42, 93
Jeremiah, 38
Jones, Inigo, 143, 202
Jonson, Ben, 143, 200, 202, 204–5, 217–18
Juno, 121
Jupiter, 63, 64, 129, 130, 158, 169

Kunstkammer. See Wunderkammer
Kunstschrank. See Wunderkammer

La Bruyère, Jean, 11, 12
Lachesis, 213
Leda, 87, 158
Ledesma, Alonso, 141
Lerma, duke of, 17, 18, 36, 90, 94, 165, 206
Ligorio, Pirro, 187, 188
Llull, Ramón, 4, 165
Lomazzo, Giovanni, 97
Longinus, 115, 124–35, 146, 196
López, Diego, 141, 142
Ludic principle: and poetry, 9–11; and court life, 11–16, 177; of *serio ludere,* 31, 32–33, 34, 35, 37, 46, 47–48, 50, 57, 141, 154

Machiavelli, Niccolò, 14
Madrigal, 55, 101, 106
Mannerism, 3, 19–20, 51, 55, 135, 154, 175, 177, 189, 222*n*4, 228–29*n*78
Margaret of Austria, Queen, 202–3, 205
Mars, 68, 113, 211
Marvell, Andrew, 52, 53, 60, 145
Masque, 5, 16, 17, 198–220, 246*nn31–33,35–36*
Maximilian II, 154
McLuhan, Marshall, 106
Medici, Cosimo de, 31
Meditational literature, 56–69, 71, 79, 85, 109, 111, 191
Medrano, Sebastián Francisco de, 36

Memory: art of, 72–76, 81–82, 86, 110, 172–73, 232*n*22; in Scholastic tradition, 74, 75; in Platonic tradition, 74–76
Mercury, 212–13
Minturno, Antonio, 23, 116
Montaigne, Michel, 173–74
Montemayor, Jorge de, 56, 69
Monteverdi, Claudio, 104
Music: and the *Soledades,* 100–109, 110; and poetry, 236*nn49,51,57*

Narcissus, 186
Natural magic, 164–66, 173, 241–42*n52*
Natural philosophy, 5
Neptune, 154
Nereus, 211–12
Niebla, count of, 90

Opera, 5, 104, 106
Ortega y Gasset, José, 164
Ovid, 2, 22, 40, 45, 157–58, 165, 186, 214

Painting: *ut pictura poesis,* 86, 91, 138–39; and the *Soledades,* 87–100, 110, 113; and poetry, 234*nn37,38,42,* 234–35*n44,* 235*nn47,48*
Pales, 87, 167, 168, 209
Pallas, 209
Pan, 68, 113, 211
Pansophy, 4–6, 32
Paracelsus, 165
Parmigianino, 95
Pastoral: and the *Soledades,* 52–69, 109–10, 132; and debate over art vs. nature, 122–23, 130; and Renaissance gardens, 173, 181
Pellicer, José de, 22, 36, 54, 205
Pérez de Montalbán, Juan, 36
Petrarch, Francesco, 5, 23, 34, 42, 52, 59, 70, 82, 101, 103
Phaethon, 126, 127, 131, 158
Philip II, 19, 87, 166, 174–75
Philip III, 2, 13, 16, 17, 20, 93, 174, 175, 202–3, 205–6
Philip IV, 16, 17, 20, 36, 195, 203
Philosophers' stone, 17, 166–67, 170, 191. *See also* Alchemy

Pico della Mirandola, Count Giovanni, 31–32, 74; and poetic theology, 16–17, 29–30
Pinciano, El, 116
Pindar, 13, 28, 29, 38
Plato: influence on Renaissance thought, 4, 5, 6, 10, 32, 45, 62, 63, 69, 74–76, 86, 87, 96, 116, 172; cave analogy, 29; Plato's Academy, 31, 173; exile of poets from the Republic, 44; on poetic inspiration, 45; and silent speech, 48; cycle of love, 49–50; Neoplatonism, 49–50, 56, 58, 65, 69, 105, 138–39, 217; on art vs. nature, 122; influence on Renaissance notions of images and emblems, 143, 144, 196, 217
Plotinus, 6
Pluto, 168–69
Poliziano, Angelo, 55
Pomona, 184
Propertius, 157
Proserpine, 168–69, 187
Psyche, 158

Quevedo, Francisco de, 1, 14, 21, 36, 55
Quintilian, 23, 72, 116

Robortello, Francesco, 116
Rubens, Peter Paul, 90
Rudolf II, 19, 154–55, 156, 157, 166

Salcedo Coronel, García, 22, 205
Saldaña, count of, 36
Salinas, Francisco, 104, 105
Salinas, Pedro, 7, 28, 112
Sánchez de Viana, Pedro, 157
Sandoval y Rojas, Bernardo Cardinal, 18, 94
Sannazaro, Jacopo, 23, 157, 172, 181, 184–85
San Pedro, Jerónimo, 57
Scaliger, Julius Caesar, 23
Seneca, 23
Silva, 37, 54–55, 70, 101, 125–26, 133, 229*n*5
Silva, Francisco de, 36–37
Snayers, Peter, 93
Sophocles, 38
Soto de Rojas, Pedro, 36–37

Spectacles: in Hapsburg Spain, 15, 16, 17–18, 225*nn26–27*
Statius, 55
Syrinx, 158, 186

Tasso, Bernardo, 23
Tasso, Torquato, 30–31, 55, 82
Tesauro, Emanuele, 57, 118, 135, 143
Tethys, 152, 154, 213
Theocritus, 122, 149
Tintoretto, 93
Tirso de Molina, 36
Titian, 87, 90, 93, 95
Toledo, Juan Bautista de, 174, 175
Torreblanca, Francisco, 165
Turriano, Janelo, 188

Ulysses, 82
Urbino, duchess of, 33

Valencia, Pedro de, 13–14, 20, 23, 24, 25, 38, 115
Vasari, Giorgio, 173
Vega, Garcilaso de, 23, 56, 122–23
Vega, Lope de, 14, 17, 21, 24, 25, 35, 36, 38, 39, 41, 43–44, 50, 57, 59, 93, 203
Vejamen, 35, 37. *See also* Academies; *Certamen*
Velázquez, Diego, 89
Vélez de Guevara, Luis, 36
Veneto, 90
Venus, 88, 125, 126, 127, 158
Vermeer, Jan, 95
Veronese, Paolo, 93
Vertumnus, 159, 160
Villa d'Este, 171–72, 173, 174, 175, 177, 180, 186, 187–88, 191–92
Villar, Francisco del, 21
Virgil, 22, 23, 26, 28, 29, 38, 122
Visualization: and reading, 196–98, 216–17, 245*n25*, 245–46*n28*
Vos, Paul de, 93
Vulcan, 87

Wotton, Henry, 198–99, 203
Wunderkammer, 19, 46, 86, 115, 118, 180

Zosimos of Panoplis, 165

OHIO UNIVERSITY LIBRARY
Please return this book as soon as you have finished with it. In order to ~id a fine it must be returned by the late ~tamped below. All books ~ ' after two weeks or im~ ~e~ve.